Spanish Roots of America

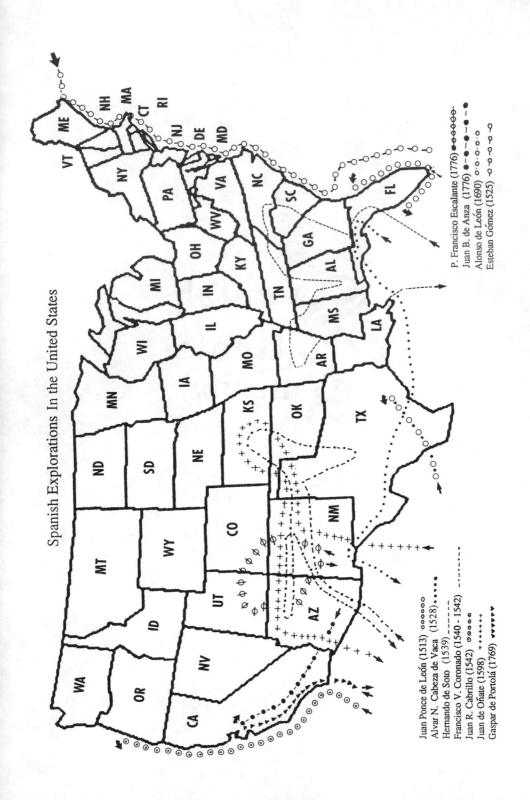

Spanish Explorations In the United States

Juan Ponce de León (1513) ooooooo
Alvar N. Cabeza de Vaca (1528) •••••
Hernando de Soto (1539) ——————
Francisco V. Coronado (1540 - 1542) ——·——·——
Juan R. Cabrillo (1542) ⊘⊘⊘⊘⊘
Juan de Oñate (1598) +++++++
Gaspar de Portolá (1769) ▼▼▼▼▼

P. Francisco Escalante (1776) ⊘-⊘-⊘-⊘-⊘
Juan B. de Anza (1776) ●-●-●-●-●
Alonso de León (1690) ○-○-○-○
Esteban Gómez (1525) -○--○--○--○

Spanish of Roots America

Bishop David Arias

Our Sunday Visitor Publishing Division
Our Sunday Visitor, Inc.
Huntington, Indiana 46750

Our Sunday Visitor Publishing Division
Our Sunday Visitor, Inc.
200 Noll Plaza
Huntington, Indiana 46750

International Standard Book Number: 0-87973-476-0
Library of Congress Catalog Card Number: 91-66665

PRINTED IN THE UNITED STATES OF AMERICA

Cover design by Monica Watts

476

DEDICATED

—To my parents, Atanasio and Magdalena, who brought me to life and taught me its most important values.

—To León, my native land, and to its noble and industrious people.

—To Spain and the United States, bonded by a common heritage.

ACKNOWLEDGMENTS

It has been said that the writing of a book somehow resembles the bringing of a child into the world, and that makes a lot of sense. As one goes forth into deeper research, into analysis and synthesis of data, then into arrangement, drafting, revision, and editing, one realizes that it is a real gestation process, requiring the cooperation of many people to bring it to a successful delivery.

This is what has happened to me. Dealing with a work that entails so many names, dates, and historical data has required a long gestation and continual assistance. I am deeply indebted to many persons and institutions who have supported me with their time, resources, and experience.

In the first place, I wish to acknowledge the valuable service provided by Seton Hall University, which, through its splendid library, has served as a base of operations and as a means to put me in touch with many libraries across the country. To Sister Concetta Russo, M.P.F., Msgr. William Field, and Msgr. James Turro, many thanks. The service provided by other libraries " the Hispanic Society of America, City University of New York, New York Public Library, New Jersey Historical Society, Rutgers University, and Academy of American Franciscan History " deserve my appreciation. I sincerely thank the Archdiocese of Newark for its support through its Deparments of Research and Planning, Communications, and Business Administration. Many persons have generously given of their time for matters related to translation and editing. Among them I would like to mention Sisters Henrietta Aprile, M.P.F., Ann Marie Sullivan, S.S.J., and Bettyanne Schultz, O.P.; Fathers Joseph Girone, Robert Becerra, Joseph Plunkett, John Murphy, Joseph C. Doyle, Frederick Eid, John Quill, and Sean Cunneen.

Historians such as Emilio González López of City University of New York, Joseph F. Mahoney and Father Bob Wister of Seton Hall University, Odon Betanzos of the North American Academy of the Spanish Language, and Daniel Juday of the Office of Publications of the National Conference of Catholic Bishops deserve my sincere gratitude. In a special way I wish to acknowledge the Cultural Office of the Embassy of Spain in Washington, D.C., for the assistance and cooperation provided toward this work.

I wish to express my special thanks to my administrative secretary, Cristina Pardo, so busy with my handwriting, for her patience and dedication in typing everything and putting it into the computer. She has been helped in this taxing but necessary task by María de Paula, Anne Marie Freda, Elizabeth Melillo, Janet Gordon, Maribel Román, Maria Meléndez, Janice Keels, and José Pardo. Debbie Quintana has placed a touch of her art in the graphics and maps. To all these marvelous persons, my appreciation and gratitude.

Finally, I am indebted to my brothers, sisters, and relatives for their encouragement and moral support in bringing this work to completion.

TABLE OF CONTENTS

FOREWORD

As the observance of the Columbus Quincentennial begins, the publication of Bishop Arias's *Spanish Roots of America* proves most timely. But this work does not merely recall the exploits of the Genoese sailor whose voyages began the European exploration of the New World. Were that the case, it would be but one of a number of commemorative volumes which would be casually scanned and soon forgotten. Bishop Arias has set himself a different and more difficult task.

To counter the prevailing American unawareness of the centuries-long Spanish presence within the boundaries of what is now the United States, he has gathered the many strands of that complex tale into one volume. Part One of the work provides a context for understanding the efforts of Spain and Hispanics to colonize the New World and to bring the benefits of European civilization — especially Christianity — to the native inhabitants. Its seven brief chapters limn the large outlines of Hispanic exploration and settlement, of Indian resistance and Indian conversion throughout the southern half of the lower forty-eight states, from Atlantic to Pacific, and brings the story up to current developments. Part Two is a chronology of Hispanic activity, detailing year-by-year the interaction of the Spanish with the land, the native inhabitants, and other European groups similarly involved in expansion. It is an immense task, ably completed.

A work of such scope is bound to stir controversy, particularly now that a vigorous reevaluation of the results of Columbus's voyages is taking place. Bishop Arias does not address that argument, but his work provides a background for understanding precisely what the Spanish sought to accomplish, the reasons they chose the means they did, and the extent of the efforts they put forth in pursuit of their goals. Perhaps more importantly, as the American educational system and the American people increasingly appreciate the need to understand the many different cultural strands which compose the warp and woof of American society, this work presents an overview of one of the most significant, if often overlooked, threads in that pattern.

Spanish Roots of America is a work of many potential uses. Part One can provide the reader with a basic understanding of Spanish colonial development, of the first European efforts in what is now the Southern half of the United States, and of the history of Hispanics in the United States. The story will prove an eye-opener to many, whose traditional

11

perspective on American development has been an East-Coast, English-oriented one. The book is also a valuable research tool, its encyclopedic coverage of the Hispanic presence within the borders of the United States making it an invaluable aid to those who are teaching or studying our history or researching particular aspects thereof.

Spanish Roots of America is not the last word when it comes to integrating an understanding of the Hispanic influence on American development into our national consciousness. It is, rather, one of the first efforts to make widely available the knowledge upon which a broader national awareness must be based. It is therefore a work to be welcomed heartily and perused carefully, in the confident expectation that the knowledge gained from it will expand our understanding of our past and will facilitate a more civil and sophisticated grappling with our present and future.

> Joseph F. Mahoney, Chairman of the History Department
> Seton Hall University
> October 27, 1991

INTRODUCTION

The presence of Spain and of Spanish-speaking countries in territories that now are part of the United States was both protracted and profound. That presence has left impressed on the nation's geography and history a footprint that belongs to its national identity. Talking, however, with fairly well-educated persons, one gets the feeling that very little is known about this participation; that the Hispanic contribution to the human and spiritual reservoir of this country has long been considered something fortuitous, superficial, and fleeting.

It is not known that three-fourths of the land was under the sovereignty of Spain for more than two hundred years; that the Spanish flag waved over this country longer than any other, including the stars and stripes; and that the Spanish borders in 1800 stretched from Cape Horn in Argentina to the banks of the Mississippi River. It is really sad that the abundant evidence documented in American libraries and archives has never been passed on to the people, either through the school system or through the communications media.

This incomprehensible omission of events, persons, and achievements from our history deprives the American people of knowing a heritage that plays an integral part in the history of many states, and therefore of the country as a whole. At the same time, this deficiency calls into question the authenticity of what is being taught.

Thomas Jefferson once said, "The oldest history of the United States is written in Spanish." Aware of the "information gap," John F. Kennedy said: "I have always felt that one of the great inadequacies among Americans of this country in their knowledge of the past has been the knowledge of the whole Spanish influence and exploration and development in the sixteenth century in the southwest of the United States, which is a tremendous story. Unfortunately, too, Americans think that America was discovered in 1620 when the Pilgrims came to my own state, and they forget the tremendous adventure of the sixteenth and seventeenth centuries in the southern and southwestern United States."

Inspired by this adventure, historian Charles Lummis exclaimed:

"The honor of giving America to the world belongs to Spain, the credit not only of discovery but of centuries of such pioneering as no other nation ever paralleled in any land. . . . One nation practically had the glory of discovering and exploring America, of changing the whole world's ideas of geography and making over knowledge and business to herself for a century and a half. And that nation was Spain ... it yet remains for someone to make as popular the truths of American history as the fables have been."

The purpose of this book, then, is to highlight the contribution of Spain and of the Spanish-speaking countries to the forming of the United States of America, and to show year by year a presence that has been unbroken since the dawn of Spanish discovery of America in 1492. This brief historical summary gives events in the present territories of this country that involved Spain or the Hispanic countries. From among the many events that might have occurred in a given year, only a few have been taken. The facts are given in a brief and concise form because the purpose is to point out the deeds, not abundant details, which would lead to a more voluminous work. What is intended here is to state clearly that the Hispanic presence in this land has been continuous over the past five hundred years. The fact that the events are portrayed briefly should not be taken to mean those events were sporadic or fortuitous. Almost always those events or projects were the result of long thought and planning that involved the participation of many people, years of silent tasks, sizable investments, and very often the cost of many lives. Examples of this are the founding of a city, the construction of a fort, or preparation for a maritime exploration. Of these, only the year of the event and the salient features are mentioned.

We could say that the present United States is something like a great forest where many different trees are growing; similar are the diverse ethnic groups that have arrived in this land. The tree of "Hispanidad" is not just breaking ground now. It struck roots in this land just a few years after Columbus landed in America. It has been growing ever since on many sites in this great forest, at times filled with prosperity and vitality, at times facing the rigors of tempests and plagues, and at times afflicted with weakness and menaced by extinction. The "Hispanidad" tree begins now to manifest visibility and in the near future will begin to impart the flowers and fruits of its own particular identity. The best of the "Hispanidad" tree is yet to come.

In order to obtain the information gathered here, the works of hundreds of distinguished historians have been consulted and many important libraries visited. The task of synthesizing and organizing the information has run through five years of research and labor. At the end of the book a bibliography is listed, serving to identify the main sources of information. Throughout the book no author in particular is mentioned, because very often the data are a summary of what several of them relate.

The book has two parts: in the first, some aspects that have characterized the Hispanic presence in the United States are given in broad lines and serve as basis for understanding of what later is presented in a concise manner; the second gives a year-by-year account of events that took place within the current territories of the United States. If the present work succeeds in bringing a more complete knowledge to the people of this country it will have achieved its purpose; the invested effort will have brought the satisfaction of having contributed to filling a vacuum and making richer the American heritage.

The Author

PART I

*Spanish Roots of America —
Significant Aspects*

*Queen Isabella I (Isabel the Catholic), after a painting
by Luis Madrozo in the National Library at Madrid, Spain*

I

The Policy of Spain in America

By the end of the fifteenth century, Spain had brought to a conclusion the reconquest of her territories, expelled the Arabs from her land, and achieved national unity. This enterprise had lasted seven centuries, and people from all her regions had taken part in it. At the end of this long crusade to bring about national unity, many of the officers and soldiers, after years of military service, did not find it attractive to go back to their villages and farms to till the land. They were eager, though, to continue the adventure, see new places, and conquer new lands for Spain and God. The discovery of America happened in the midst of this situation, and this event paved the way for many of these soldiers, mariners, and merchants, presenting a golden opportunity to pursue their aspirations and to put their experience to the test.

The Catholic king and queen had authorized and sponsored the voyage of Columbus led by two driving motives: the possibility of finding a shorter way to the Orient while discovering new lands, and bringing the Catholic faith to the people in those lands.[1] Those two motivations would be constant concerns in all the decisions of the Spanish crown for many years to come. These factors would inspire her policy and legislation, her royal charters of exploration and colonization, her government and economy. As we look through history, we cannot say that one concern was superior to the other or that one was at the service of the other. To put it plainly, both were important — the conquest helped the evangelization, and the evangelization helped the colonization. This is clear to the objective reader of history. From the human point of view, the conquest of these immense territories of America with just a handful of men would not have been possible without the support and motivation of faith. At the same time, evangelization would not have achieved such excellent results without the support and the protection of the institutions of the crown.

The conquest and colonization of America did not occur as something unplanned; it was the result of a policy that was seriously thought out, discussed at the highest levels, and executed afterward by means of decisions and institutions. Just a few years after the discovery, the Council of the Indies was created. This council was a body of learned and expert people whose function was to counsel the crown and supervise all activities related to America, such as legislation, government, exploration, colonization, trade, and the establishment of missions. Through a concession of the Pope, the royal patronage was also extended to America. It was through this concession that the king and queen of Spain had the power to appoint bishops and other ecclesiastical dignitaries, and at the same time assumed certain responsibilities such as building churches, monasteries, missions, and paying a subsidy to the missionaries.[2] It is true that this institution created conflicts between religious and civil authorities, but it is also true that it helped to facilitate and move forward the activity of the Church. This concern and involvement of Spain in her colonies, both those that now are part of the United States and those in the rest of the Americas, are reflected in three aspects that have characterized her policy toward America: first, the vision of her sovereignty over the territories; second, a centralized power; and third, a concern for the native, who was considered a subject.

1. By the Bull *Inter Coetera*, Pope Alexander VI granted Spain sovereignty over lands west of a north-south line a hundred leagues west of the Azores Islands. The concession of this sovereignty was attached to the subsequent evangelization of natives and was the continuation of a practice, commonly accepted in Europe for centuries, through which the Pope justified conquest and granted sovereignty. To understand this practice, one has to understand the mentality of the fifteenth century, when all Europe was Catholic. Though pacts were signed among sovereigns, there was not, strictly speaking, an international law as we know it now. But all sovereigns acknowledged the Pope as the only worldwide figure enjoying moral authority, at least in the religious aspect. Hence, his decisions would have legal effects and would sanction disputes among the various countries.[3] The purpose of this decision was to prevent future conflicts between Spain and Portugal that were claiming rights over some newly discovered lands, unknown to other European countries. Spain, therefore, claimed to be sovereign over all America, over its land and its people. The last will of Queen Isabella clearly states: "When the Islands and Lands of the Ocean Sea, discovered or yet to be discovered, were given to us by the Holy See, our main intention was . . . to make an effort to

procure and to draw their people and convert them to our holy Catholic Faith. . . . I request the King, my Lord, not to consent or permit that the Indians . . . be persecuted in their persons and in their properties."[4] This sense of sovereignty impelled the crown to make decisions such as requiring all foreign sailors or explorers, even Amerigo Vespucci,[5] Sam Houston, or Daniel Boone, to become Spanish citizens and take an oath of fidelity to the king of Spain.

When an explorer or navigator arrived at a land not yet explored, the first thing he would do was plant a cross in the ground,[6] raise the flag, lift his sword, and, in the presence of his companions and natives whom he requested to accept the sovereignty of Spain, pronounce words by which he took possession of that land in the name of the king of Spain. This was a ritual always observed; once it was performed, the territories were added to the Spanish empire, a map of the place was drawn, and it was registered under the Spanish crown. This was done by Ponce de León upon his arrival in Florida in 1513, Juan de Oñate in New Mexico, Bodega y Quadra in Alaska, and so on. This was the official way of taking possession of land.

Many of the explorations and subsequent colonizations had as their main goal to keep Spanish sovereignty before other European nations that wanted to occupy those lands. Thus we see Menéndez de Avilés organizing his expedition to expel the French from Florida, or Commander Bodega y Quadra going to the northern Pacific to prevent Russia from settling California.

Both the Atlantic and the Pacific Coasts were often surveyed by Spanish sailors through the first half of the sixteenth century and were considered by Spain as part of her domains, as can be seen in the maps of Juan de la Cosa (1500) or of Diego de Ribeiro (1529). The best proof of this assertion is the fact that no other European nation made a permanent settlement on either coast through the whole sixteenth century; their activities were limited to fishing in Newfoundland, selling slaves brought from Africa, or engaging in piracy.

2. Another characteristic of Spanish policy in America was the centralization of power.[7] Spain was a juridical state, in that the Spanish monarchs themselves governed, not by absolutist decisions, but through approved laws, "The Laws of the Indies." In the same way, government officials were expected to govern according to established law. To verify that this was the case, royal inspectors were sent frequently. It was also policy to hold an investigation (*residencia*) for each royal official at the end of his term of office. Legality was always emphasized in the Spanish colonies to the point that it often thwarted private enterprise;[8] but it also prevented many abuses, such as mistreatment or elimination of the In-

dians. Spanish legislation was often resented by the colonial middle class for being exclusively protective of the Indians; but breaking the law in this regard was always severely punished. The main decisions were always made in Spain, and the Council of the Indies conveyed them to the four viceroys of New Spain (Mexico), New Granada (Colombia), Peru, and La Plata (Argentina). These, in turn, channeled them to the governors of the provinces. Coastal territories now part of the United States were under the authority of the viceroy of Mexico. From the Pacific to the Mississippi River they were under the authority of the governors of New Mexico, Texas, and Louisiana. From the Mississippi to the Atlantic Ocean they were under the governor of Cuba, and later the governor of Florida. Laws were used to regulate the form of government, exploration, and colonization; agriculture, commerce, and the economy; founding of new settlements, missions, and forts; appointment of governors and other civil and religious officers. For example, all those going to America, including missionaries, had to be approved by the Council of the Indies, and they had to have a clean record of behavior. Neither criminals nor prisoners were ever allowed to embark for America, as was the case with other European countries that used to empty their jails by dumping inmates in their faraway territories. Spain's policy was to keep these people under close watch, and naturally they would be under tighter control at home than let loose in faraway America.[9] Emigration control for America was in Seville. Departure was not permitted to criminals, fugitives from the law, and other undesirables; it was thought that they would cause problems and, being far away, would be difficult to control. Authorization was required to organize an expedition, while the commander (*adelantado*) had also to be appointed. This centralized authority had its advantages, such as keeping good control of business, clearly defining responsibilities, and exacting accountability. At the same time, it made the process slow in situations when immediate action was needed. Spain and king were far away, and information on the matter was often incomplete, on account of subjectivity or the interests of those submitting a report. Because of necessarily slow communications, by the time the report reached Spain and was studied for a decision, the answer arrived too late. Also, some individuals, in order to obtain a quick response from the authority, resorted to exaggerations, false reports, or ingenious schemes: for example, Father Marcos de Niza's exaggerations (see below, chapter II, #3) in order to expedite the conquest of New Mexico; or the move of another friar who wrote a letter designed to be intercepted, thereby inviting a French military garrison to occupy the eastern section of Texas and forcing Spanish authorities to establish military posts and missions precisely in that area to protect it against a French invasion (ibid., Alonso de León). The policy of France and England in this respect was much more decentralized: persons to whom a charter was given had absolute freedom to operate in regard to people and land, as long as they paid taxes.

3. A feature that pervades the whole Spanish policy in America is that it was centered in the person. The true historian knows well that the main concern of the Spanish crown, the laws of the Indies, the sending of missionaries, civilization, and evangelization revolved around a fundamental concern for the person of the native American. At no time or place in her colonization were slavery, destruction, eviction, or placement of Indians on reservations a part of Spain's policy. On the contrary, by any means, with great difficulty, and at high cost, Spain always tried to change their nomadic life and to settle them into missions or pueblos with the intent of civilizing and evangelizing them;[10] that is the case with the Güale Indians of Georgia and the Comanche in Texas. The expeditionaries and missionaries understood that as long as the Indians remained nomads their own efforts would be useless.

For anyone asking why, the answer is simple. First, from the very beginning the native was considered subject to the crown, and therefore entitled to human advancement and salvation through evangelization. Second, the territories were huge, and Spain did not have enough people to settle and develop conquered land, raise crops or cattle, and work the mines. She was lacking in manpower. In the mid-sixteenth century, Spain scarcely had eight million people and they were needed in Europe to protect her domains, promote her own internal life, and defend her borders against incursions from other European nations. That is why Spain needed native Americans, and also a powerful reason why her policy was centered on the preservation of the native as a means to reach material prosperity. This is so true that when it was not possible to settle them in a mission or pueblo, or when the Indians returned to their nomadic life, the Spanish would abandon the place, as it happened with the Jesuits in Georgia. We can see that Spain always looked to the advancement of the native in her tireless effort in settling them in pueblos where they were taught European notions of self-government, work, dress, nourishment, family life, agriculture, cattle raising, manual skills, and handcrafts. We see that in the missions there was always a concern for their religious instruction, moral formation, and basic culture.

4. There are often charges of banishment or extinction of the native, as if Spain had started a campaign of elimination. The truth is that the

dwindling number of Indians was due mainly to illnesses or epidemics such as smallpox, measles, whooping cough, scurvy, and influenza that were difficult to prevent, given the state of the medicine at that time. It was also due to illnesses that came as a result of the mingling (*mestizaje*) of the two races, and in this case, both natives and Spaniards were the victims.[11] To illustrate this we can take the case of Hernando de Soto, who landed in Florida in 1538 with more than a thousand men. After four years of exploration, more than three fourths had died, among them De Soto, for the most part in epidemics. The same thing can be said of the settlement established by Vázquez de Ayllón in 1526 in South Carolina. Now, it is true that there were abuses, as in the case of the "*encomiendas*," where many of the landowners took advantage of the native and, breaking the stipulated laws, subjected them to excessive work, neglecting their material welfare and religious instruction as provided by the law.[12] It was precisely because of these abuses that in a matter of a few years the system of "*encomiendas*" was abolished. Another bias in the minds of some people is that the Spanish conquest was full of cruelty. Unfortunately, all conquest in the history of mankind has been done through the shedding of blood; it was true yesterday and it continues to be true today. One thing that can be said is that the Spanish conquest of America was much more humane than conquests undertaken by some native Americans in their land. The example of the Aztec wars in Mexico or the Comanche raids on their neighboring tribes can be mentioned. The victimized tribes helped the Spanish in their conquest and asked them for protection. One of the positive effects of the coming of the Spanish to North America was their contribution to establishing peace among tribes that were in a permanent state of war with other tribes and threatened with destruction. All this has been thoroughly proved.

The right of Spain to the conquest of America was a theme of ample debate in the University of Salamanca by the mid-sixteenth century. Salamanca became famous for the teachings of Fathers Francisco de Vitoria and Francisco Suárez, who are considered the founders of modern International Law. At the same time, the University of Valladolid held several discussions which were very illuminating on this matter. As an effect of these discussions (which gave birth to the enactment of human rights provisions in International Law by such prominent theologians as Vitoria and Suárez), a new policy was formulated to guide the conquest and colonization of America. The words of American historian Herbert Bolton are enlightening in this respect: "We must admit that the accomplishments of Spain remain a force which made for the preservation of the Indians as opposed to their destruction so characteristic of the

24

Anglo-American frontier."[13] Upon the arrival of an expedition to a place, the principle was not to attack the natives and destroy them, but to offer them peace, to ask their obedience to the king of Spain, and to respect their property. The term "pacification" used at that time conveys this policy quite well. Only in the case of being attacked were Spaniards to respond. It is true that there were cases of cruelty, but these were the exception, and they came from both sides. As a general rule, instances of bloodshed in history were due to the reaction of the Spanish soldiers to surprise attacks of the natives, to rebellions, or to aggressions against the missions or missionaries. Examples of these include the Battle of Acoma in New Mexico or the reprisal imposed by Menéndez de Avilés against those responsible for the slaying of five Jesuits in 1570 in Virginia. Not only were the Indians not attacked, but also the strategy was a peaceful conquest, "pacification," which was based in setting up "pueblos of Indians already converted to the Faith in places not yet pacified or civilized"; this process is what has been called "The Indian conquest of America."

Since the main concern of the crown and of the Church revolved around the protection of the native,[14] voices were raised in the University of Salamanca or by missionaries like Antonio Montesinos or Bartolomé de las Casas denouncing the abuses that were taking place. Father Las Casas, in his great love for the natives, preached, wrote, and traveled to eradicate the bad treatment. In order to achieve his goal, he enormously exaggerated the situation by inflating the numbers, generalizing the cases, and heightening the facts. Unfortunately, his writings, motivated by a sincere intention, have maliciously been used from the sixteenth century by rival nations to cast a black shadow on the civilizing and evangelizing work of Spain in America. This, along with exaggerated accounts of the Spanish Inquisition, is what has been called the "Black Legend," originating in Holland and England, that spread to the northern European nations and later to the United States. Philip W. Powell's book *The Tree of Hate* gives a good presentation of this matter. The truth is that Americans are unaware of the monumental task of civilization and evangelization that Spain performed through three hundred years in the three fourths of the territories now part of the United States. The American people have the right to know the history of this nation in its integrity. Charles Webber has this to say: "It had been handed down to generations of Americans, a thoroughly exaggerated view of Spain's failings in regard to the natives. Abuses there certainly were, but the objective student of history recognizes these as relatively insignificant, alongside the more positive aspects of Spain's colonial policies."[15]

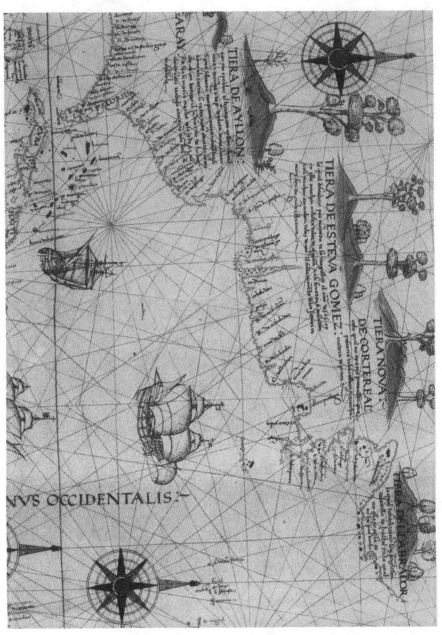

Perpendicular: Diego Ribeiro's map of the world in 1529 shows the extent of Spanish activity in the New World by the early sixteenth century, including Vázquez de Ayllón's colony on the Atlantic Coast. (Reproduction courtesy of the Carter Brown Library, Brown University, Providence, Rhode Island)

II

Explorations in
the United States

The seventy-five years that followed the discovery of America were characterized by restlessness and intense searching activity among the men of Spain. It was the period of the great explorations and conquests. It was natural that the new and unknown world would goad their curiosity, their interest, and their dreams; therefore, exploration was the first step, followed by conquest, colonization, and evangelization. It is important to note, though, that all explorations had to be authorized,[1] and if somebody dared to undertake one without the permission of the Council of the Indies, viceroy, or the local governor, he would risk being arrested or jailed, as is the case in 1590 of Castaño de Sosa in Texas.[2] Throughout those years, most of the lands of this country from the Pacific to the Atlantic, from the Rio Grande in Texas to Nebraska, were already explored by great men like Juan Ponce de León, Esteban Gómez, Lucas Vázquez de Ayllón, Hernando de Soto, Alvar Núñez Cabeza de Vaca, Francisco Vázquez de Coronado, Tristán de Luna, Juan Rodríguez Cabrillo, Pedro Menéndez de Avilés, and others in truly daring epics. These men faced daily uncertainty and risks in exhausting journeys on land, crossing forests, rivers, swamps, ridges, and canyons; or in perilous trips by sea, defying tempests and hurricanes. Of these men Charles Lummis says: "They were Spaniards who had carved their way into the far interior of our own land, as well as that area to the South, and founded their cities a thousand miles inland long before the first Anglo-Saxon came to the Atlantic seaboard. That early Spanish spirit of 'finding-out' was fairly superhuman. Why a poor Spanish lieutenant with twenty soldiers pierced an unspeakable desert and looked down upon the greatest natural wonder of America or of the world — the Grand Canyon of the Colorado — three full centuries before any 'American' eyes saw it, we will never know! And so it was, from Colorado to Cape Horn. Heroic, impetuous, imprudent Balboa had walked that awful walk across the Isthmus and found the Pacific Ocean. He built on its shores the first ships that were ever made in the Americas and sailed that unknown sea. Balboa had been dead more than half a century before Drake and Hawkins saw it."[3]

1. In the explorations, the will and interest of the Spanish authorities intervened on the one part, and on the other the desire and availability of the explorer. Both sides would sign the agreed conditions, a royal charter was extended, a title was given, and the petitioner or responsible party would then begin preparing and organizing the expedition. Normally it was formed by a number of soldiers, who sometimes volunteered their services, arms, and horses with the hope of sharing later in the fruits of the enterprise. At other times they were paid by the crown, by the recipient of the charter, or by both.[4] Depending on the nature of the expedition, on some occasions, there were also settlers and their families if the purpose of the expedition was to start a settlement there.[5] Even some of the soldiers would take their families with them. What was never missing in any exploration was a retinue, at times large, of already Christian natives who served as guides, interpreters, helpers, intermediaries, and the first settlers of the new indigenous village to be established in these North American lands. Therefore, there were not only persons from Spain who came in the expeditions; many were Creole-born in Cuba, Puerto Rico, Santo Domingo, Mexico, Peru, and even Africa, as is the case of Esteban Azamor, companion of Cabeza de Vaca in the adventures across Texas. The same role was also played by the various natives of this land. The Spanish presence in the United States territories from the very beginning gave origin to an ethnic pluralism that has always been the hallmark of this country. Morales Padrón is accurate when he says that the indigenous "was fundamental in the conquest, as he was also in the colonization because he was a factor of great importance who quickly assimilated the Spanish culture and together with his own gave rise to the new and different culture that we all know."[6] We can say, therefore, that the exploration and colonization of this country was begun by Spain jointly with all Latin America.

2. The explorers chosen to carry out the expeditions were given the title of "*adelantado*," captain general, sometimes governor, and there were two or three requisites: good preparation or experience, good reputation, and often a good fortune.

Good preparation and experience were important because these expeditions, composed of many people and pieces of equipment, required vision, organizational skills, and discipline. Also they were very expensive, and naturally the crown did not wish to risk the investment by placing the project in the hands of callow or inexperienced leaders. Hernn Cortés, Francisco Vázquez de Coronado, Hernando de Soto, and Juan de Oñate were university-educated persons,[7] while Juan Ponce de León, Pedro Menéndez de Avilés, and Pánfilo Narváez were individuals with great military experience either in Europe or America. The boat pilots were expert people who received a theoretical and practical preparation in the sailing school of Seville under the guidance of the major pilot, and they had to be certified.

Good reputation was another quality sought in the commander of an exploration. Thus, we see that Juan de Oñate was the son of Count Oñate, Governor of New Galicia; Tristán de Luna was a highly respected person in Mexico City with profound religious convictions; Bernardo de Gálvez was the son of the Viceroy of Mexico and nephew of the president of the Council of the Indies.

Economic resources were also a fact to which attention was paid. The explorations, though approved and sponsored by the crown, were a type of enterprise where the responsible explorer invested much money in the hopes of getting a good return once it was accomplished, which, in fact, often did not happen. Witness the case of Menéndez de Avilés who invested about two hundred thousand ducats in his expedition to Florida; somewhat similar were the cases of De Soto, Ponce, and Oñate.

The commander was a person with expert qualities. This was advantageous because in many land or sea explorations there were university people, cartographers, physicians, reporters, merchants, artists, controllers, and all sorts of craftsmen such as carpenters, masons, tanners, and blacksmiths. There were also experts in firearms and gunpowder manufacturing. Of course, we cannot forget the missionaries who, in addition to their ministry, would know a little of everything else.[8]

3. There were many reasons why the explorations were organized, but as has been said before, all of them can be summed up into two: to discover new lands for Spain, and to convert the people to the Catholic faith. Octavio Paz, the Mexican winner of the Nobel Prize of Literature, rightly says: "Evangelization is what distinguishes Spanish conquest from that of other European nations." Another North American writer is also correct when he states that the Spanish "Conquistadors" were motivated by three G's: God, Gold, and Glory.[9] It is undeniable that these three elements had much to do with the Spanish conquests, and for some of them one of the G's had a higher emphasis than the others. At the same time, we can point out that the Spanish explorations in the United States pursued four objectives: conquest of the Seven Cities of Cíbola and the Gran

Quivira, finding the Strait of Anian,[10] looking for mines and fertile lands, and maintaining Spanish sovereignty along the Atlantic and Pacific Coasts.

Franciscan friar Father Marcos de Niza, entranced by the adventure tales of Cabeza de Vaca, asked for authorization and, in 1540, traveled northward with the black man Estebanico and a few Indians. He reached New Mexico and, upon his return, said he had seen the fabulous cities of Cíbola, as large as Mexico City, whose houses had golden roofs. Though his eyes never saw such a thing, his imagination made him believe it so. The good Franciscan was exaggerating in order to have an expedition authorized, and thus to evangelize the Indians of the region. It was a pious trick, but it netted the intended results. Within a few months, the Viceroy of Mexico appointed Francisco Vázquez de Coronado to organize a great expedition for conquest of the region of Cíbola, which turned out to be just humble Indian villages. However, it led to the exploration of New Mexico, the discovery of the Grand Canyon of Colorado, and to the exploration of the Gran Quivira (Kansas), where, in 1542, the first martyr of the United States, Father Juan Padilla, met his death.

After Vasco Núñez de Balboa found out in Panama in 1513 that there was another ocean, which he called the South Sea, the Spanish navigator and the explorers searched restlessly for a strait connecting the Atlantic and the Pacific — the hypothetical Strait of Anian.[11] Spain was greatly interested in finding such a channel to establish a shorter western route for her galleons linking Spain, America, and the Philippines. Esteban Gómez, in 1525, combed the Atlantic from Newfoundland to Florida seeking the strait. Menéndez de Avilés, in 1566, went from Florida to Virginia with the same idea in mind. Cabrillo in 1542, Fuca in 1560, Vizcaíno in 1603, Héceta in 1775, and others searched the Pacific north coast with the same purpose. They did not find the strait, but the truth is that this objective spurred the discovery of new lands, bays, rivers, and sea routes of great importance.

Mines of precious stones and metals were always a primary goal of all Spanish explorations;[12] to find a mine meant to make a fortune almost instantaneously. It was a much faster process to become rich than engaging in farming or cattle raising, which many of the great explorers and military officers did not find very attractive. De Soto found some crystal mines in southeast Appalachia; Oñate and Espejo discovered several gold, silver, and potassic salt mines in Arizona. These discoveries, and others of lesser importance, were below their expectations and did not equal the ones found in Mexico. Fertile lands were also sought near areas of rivers, and many of them were discovered and developed by the mis-

30

sions. As a result of this exploratory activity, fertile lands began to be farmed in California, Arizona, all along the Rio Grande in New Mexico and Texas, in Florida, and South Carolina. Though the search for gold was one of the main objectives of the great explorers, there were also others who looked to invest their gold on behalf of the natives. A typical case was Don Alonso Zorita, a judge in Mexico, who wrote to the king of Spain in 1560 telling him: "This servant of yours does not want or seek lands, nor ranches, nor earthly things for himself or related to him, because he does not have children to whom he may pass it on, though he has been married for twenty years. He only seeks to serve God and Your Majesty on this journey, and to spend in it his life and the salary that Your Majesty, may wish to give him without saving anything."[13]

Another very important motivation for the explorations was to defend the sovereignty of Spain over the lands of North America. Many areas, lightly explored or even unexplored, were considered part of her sovereignty by the simple fact that a title protecting them was given by the Pope.[14] The awareness of her sovereignty was much more explicit when a citizen of hers had planted the cross in a certain place, had taken possession in the name of the king, and had the place registered and entered onto a map. Even though the region was not yet explored or colonized, when the former particulars had taken place, the presence of another European power was considered an intrusion, and it gave way to a military expedition. Thus is the case of Menéndez de Avilés in Florida, Georgia, South Carolina, and Virginia; that of Diego Peñalosa in Nebraska in 1682, and of Alonso de León in East Texas in 1689, against possible French settlements. The same can be said of the expeditions of Juan de Anza in California in 1776, and of Bruno de Heceta and Juan Bodega y Quadra in Alaska to prevent the establishment of Russian and British settlements on the Pacific Coast. During the decade of the 1770s, Heceta, Bodega, and other Spanish seamen explored and took possession of the Strait of Fuca, Nutka Bay, Vancouver, Port Trinidad, Martyrs' Sound, Port Remedios, St. Elias Cape, Valdes Bay, Regla Islands, Kodiak and Unalaska Islands, Bucarelli Bay, and Prince of Wales Island.[15] It was at this time that Count Lacy, the Spanish Ambassador in Moscow, informed Charles III that Catherine II of Russia was preparing boats, settlers, and traders to establish a post for the trade of furs on the Pacific North coast, and that there were some posts already established. The king, alarmed at the news, immediately ordered the Viceroy of Mexico to take the necessary measures and verify if the information given by the ambassador concerning the Russian presence in North America had any value. If it were confirmed, action had to be taken to expel the subjects of Catherine II by

force if need be.[16] To implement the king's order, the above-named expeditions were dispatched. Expeditions to the various regions of North
America always originated from one of three places: Mexico, Cuba, or
Spain. The ones originating in Mexico followed a threefold route from
South to North: one along the West Coast to California and Alaska; a
second, through the center to Arizona, New Mexico, and Texas; and a
third, along the East Coast from Veracruz to the lands on the Gulf of
Mexico. The expeditions departing from Cuba normally went to Florida,
which in the sixteenth century stretched from southern Florida to New-
foundland. Those originating in Spain, as a general rule, made a stop in
Cuba to get the final provisions and went to the Atlantic Coast also.

4. The results obtained by the numerous Spanish explorations to
North America were extraordinary. Although their importance and effects were not immediately seen, they contributed to the formation and
organization of the country. When in the nineteenth century, the
southeastern, southern, and western territories entered to form part of
the United States, they were not unknown or desolated areas, but lands
well explored, traveled, and settled.[17] They had legislation, mining,
agriculture, cattle raising, trade, and the industries of the times well established. To realize the importance, it may suffice to say that three
fourths of the actual size of this country was under Spanish
sovereignty. In 1800, Spain's frontiers in the New World stretched
from Cape Horn in Argentina to the banks of the Mississippi and Missouri Rivers in North America. Her sons had discovered and/or sailed
through such rivers as the Potomac, Hudson, St. John, Apalachicola,
Arkansas, Rio Grande, Colorado, Columbia, and many others. They
had crossed the Great Plains of the buffalo, the valleys of California,
Texas, and Louisiana. They had climbed ridges like the Appalachians,
the Rocky Mountains, and the Sierra Nevada. They had discovered the
Grand Canyon of Colorado,[18] established a fluvial trade along many
rivers and opened maritime routes from the Philippines to Monterey
and San Diego, from Spain to Florida, from Alaska to the southern tip
of Chile on the Pacific, and from St. Augustine to the Strait of Magellan in Argentina on the Atlantic. Those great explorers, from the time
when Menéndez de Avilés built the first highway of the United States
between St. Augustine and Jacksonville, Florida, in 1566, engaged in
building a net of roads to traverse this land from East to West and
North to South.[19] Thus we have the Old Spanish Trail connecting St.
Augustine, Tallahassee, New Orleans, San Antonio, Santa Fe, and San
Diego; the Santa Fe Trail extending from Santa Fe to St. Louis, Mis-

souri; the King's Trail from St. Louis to New Orleans; and the *Camino Real (King's Highway) from San Diego to San Francisco.*

More than one person has asked himself the question: "How is it possible that a handful of Spaniards could conquer those immense territories?" It is not easy to give an answer. On occasion, the natives believed that they had come from heaven, and it is true that the Spaniards took advantage of such a belief. This fable, which might have helped the conquest in some places, had a fleeting effect on others, as in Añasco, Puerto Rico, where it is said that some Taino Indians, in crossing a river, took a Spanish soldier and submerged him in water to see if he would die.[20] Seeing that he drowned, they discovered that the Spaniards were not gods but men like them. What is certainly true is that the conquest would never have been possible without the participation of native people who always joined the Spaniards in substantial numbers.

5. The explorers sought fame and adventure; they were sons of those times full of romanticism, when literature abounded in describing imaginary kingdoms and legendary knights.[21] Adventure and romance played a part in the exploration of three quarters of the United States as important as greed for gold; the motivations of Ponce de León and De Soto are a clear example of this. They dreamed of great conquests and fabulous treasures; but while some clothed themselves with glory, most died in oblivion, and all endured countless hardships and suffering. It was not an easy challenge to face, tramping untamed nature in its power and wildness, sailing seas enraged by tempest in a feeble boat, and the hostility and fierceness of the Indians along the way. Almost all explorations exacted a good number of victims to hunger, epidemics, and natural elements.[22] In spite of the fact that expeditions would start with abundant provisions, frequently they spoiled, were lost in a shipwreck, or simply got depleted. And then the famines were terrifying, forcing men to eat roots, wild plants, or their own cavalry animals, as happened to De Soto. Malaria, typhus, scurvy, and other sicknesses peculiar to semitropical or swampy places brought havoc to the daring pioneers. What Hernando del Valle said about Coronado could very well be said about most of the explorers: "He endured calamities such as hunger, cold, and hot weather, loss of blood from the many wounds inflicted upon him by the natives that took him to the borders of death, and many a time he risked and endangered his life for the sake of serving His Majesty." In the expedition of Gaspar de Portolá to colonize San Diego, three boats departed with 219 men; one of them got lost with all on board; of the other two, only 100 men arrived, while the rest died en route from scurvy and other such

calamities.[23] From all the endured resistances that accompanied every expedition, two should be mentioned concretely: the sea storms and hurricanes in the Gulf of Mexico and the bellicosity of the natives.

The Gulf of Mexico is that sea held by two arms of land called Yucatn and Florida, stretching into the Atlantic Ocean as if they wanted to tame its fierceness. Great currents of water and wind running through its sources not only make its surface violent but also shake its depths. It is a tough and difficult sea that throughout history has provided the stage setting for great epics and great tragedies during the exploration and colonization of the United States. The caravels, brigantines, and galleons that plowed its waters, endured the power of stormy waves, hurricane winds, and impetuous streams with the strength of a "thousand rivers of water," as Ponce has put it. Its victims included the twenty ships with a thousand aboard traveling from Mexico to Cuba in 1553; the expedition of Tristán de Luna in 1559; and the fleet of Glvez near New Orleans in 1781. But perhaps the most tragic of all, vividly described by one of the survivors, was that one headed by Pánfilo de Narváez in 1528. He sailed from Cuba with five hundred men. After exploring western Florida and going through many vicissitudes, they were battered by a horrible hurricane. Only four survived to walk from Houston to El Paso to Mexico City after eight years of hardship and risk.[24] We can say that this sea is the largest marine tomb on the planet. It would be interesting for a historian to tally the total of shipwrecks and people resting in its depths.

The other challenge that the explorers had to deal with was the hostility of the natives. According to recorded documents, they encountered much greater hostility on the northern side of the Rio Grande than they had experienced in Mexico or South America. The Calus and Timucua from Florida, the Güale from Georgia and Carolinas, the Comanche and Apache from the Great Plains always posed a fierce resistance to the Spanish presence. They battled with them whether opposing them from the moment of their arrival, luring them with promises of wealth into the interior and falling on them by surprise, or pretending to be friends and treacherously attacking them later.[25] This hostility made both the colonization and the evangelization difficult. Among the groups of natives who posed a greater hostility and aggressiveness to the explorers were the Apache in the area of New Mexico and West Texas. The Comanche on the Great Plains of Texas, whose trade with the French of Louisiana from the beginning of the eighteenth century added horses and firearms to their bow-and-arrow arsenal.[26] Noteworthy were the great battle of Acoma in 1599, and the rebellion of the Pueblo Indians in 1680, with many dead and wounded on both sides. The period of the great

Spanish explorations and conquests in America filled the sixteenth century. What happened afterward was the emphasis placed on the colonization and minor explorations to extend the already known lands, to defend them, or to search them in greater detail. In fact, the period of the Spanish conquest was more or less ended in 1573.[27] The great explorations and conquests were not peaceful adventures, like Father Garcés' crossing the Grand Canyon for the first time and exploring Lake Utah in 1776, but rather were accompanied by difficulty, suffering, and often death. The success of Spanish explorations and conquests was the result of a combination of wisdom, diplomacy, courage, and shrewdness of those men who, though few, knew how to conquer enormous territories.[28] The courage, physical qualities, and strong motivations of these explorers and conquistadors will furnish an endless theme for writers of all times. As Bolton says, "The conquistadors who threaded the unknown way through the American wilderness were armored knights upon armored horses; proud, stern, hardy, and courageous; men of punctilious honor, loyal to the king and to Mother Church, humble only before the symbols of their Faith." Those pioneers of America deserve to shine more prominently in the pages of this country's history books and to lend their names to the streets and parks of its cities.

*Adelantado and Armada Commander Pedro Menéndez de Avilés
fought off Indians, pirates, and French colonizers while
establishing Spanish rule in Florida. He founded the
settlement of St. Augustine, oldest permanent city in the
United States, of which many vestiges can still be seen*

III

Colonization
in the United States

At the news of discovering new land, or sometimes at a mere rumor, the first step taken was the organization of an exploration looking to its colonization and the evangelization of the natives. Though we use the word *colonization*, it should not be understood in the strict sense of its meaning, because Spain never established colonies to be exploited, but kingdoms that were an extension of herself. Therefore, they were called viceroyalties, such as New Spain (Mexico), New Castile (Peru), New Granada (Colombia), and Rio de la Plata (Argentina). Even the regions were given the names of the Spanish provinces or regions: New Andalucía, New León, New Galicia, New Vizcaya, and so on. We can truly say that Spain in her enterprise intended her extension, her prolongation in America. Therefore when we say colonization we want to indicate that the policy of Spain was one of conveying to America the substance of her cultural wealth. Colonization was always a primary objective in Spanish thought; that is why we find this sort of colonization in every place of this country where Spain was. Colonization consisted of introducing human, cultural, religious, and material values from Spain into her territories. As a result, the values carried by her people, joined to human and material values found in the newly discovered lands, created a new people of the indigenous colonization that we may now call Hispanic. The Spanish did not come here to exploit resources by taking advantage of the natives, and they returned to Spain without bringing back anything.[1] History is a witness to this. We can say with certainty, they came to America to be "Americanized," to remain here, to be part of this land, to produce wealth and promote progress with the development of all aspects of life: religious, cultural, and human.[2] True, perhaps five percent of those who came to America returned to Spain, especially high government officers, and the crown had a tax, as governments today have; but what was produced by all, Spanish as well as natives, was their private property, and it remained here.

37

If we compare Spanish colonization with that of other European peoples, such as the British, Dutch, or French, many differences will be observed. The Spanish mixed with natives everywhere to a notable degree. They did not isolate themselves to live in exclusive regions; they never expelled natives from their natural territories, nor put them in reservations. They would live with the natives and mingle with them. They always imparted their faith, their language, their culture, and the human developments that existed at that time.[3]

Perhaps what deserves to be emphasized is cross-breeding or *mestizaje*.[4] The majority of people participating in an expedition were young single males. Those who were married and brought their wives with them were relatively few; for example, women counted for less than five percent in De Soto's expedition to Florida, Oñate's to New Mexico, or Portola's to California. Most of the expeditions took more than five hundred men. As a general rule, both soldiers and colonists took native women to form a family.[5] It is recorded that the soldier Juan Ribas married Luisa, a beautiful native of North Carolina, during an expedition. The Spanish merchant Manuel Lisa had as his wife a young princess of the Omaha tribe in Nebraska. We know that the wife of Juan de Oñate was a granddaughter of Hernán Cortés and great-granddaughter of the Aztec Emperor Montezuma. Records say that Clemente Bernal married the Timucuan chief lady Doña Maria in Florida. At times the half-breed marriages were a compromise, as in the case of Menéndez de Avilés. Cumberland Island's Indian chief made the gift of two of his sisters as wives, and Menéndez had to take them both to avoid a serious problem. This was also the case for De Soto, to whom the chief of the Chickasaw offered two beautiful young women of "*pechos abundosos*" (abundant breasts), as he himself says. This aspect of *mestizaje* occurred everywhere Spaniards went. This was a reality that gave origin to a new people in the history of mankind, a people which, while retaining great diversity, is linked by blood, by faith, by language, and by culture to Spain.[6]

It might be that this half-breed aspect of Spanish colonization caused it to be slower and more costly, but it made it more human by putting aside genocide or racism in the process. To be sure, the Spanish colonization of America was a costly affair, because it was not a mere exploitation taking away gold and silver in galleons, as it has been portrayed. What is not often said is that those galleons came to America loaded with goods from Spain: trained people, faith, culture, art, agriculture, animals, and industrial products. All of this had to be bought, transported to America, invested, made productive, and developed. This operation was very expensive. It is true that the crown used to take one fifth of the gold and silver,[7] as is done today by most governments, but the other four-fifths remained in the place of origin, in the hands of the owners, employees, and institutions related to mining. The Spanish colonization entailed a beneficial interchange of persons, values, and commodities that benefited both Spain and the colonies. It would be good to mention some concrete aspects of the Spanish colonization of North America.

1. One of the marks that clearly reveals the influence of Spain in America is the formation and government of *pueblos* (towns) and cities. Through the sixteenth and seventeenth centuries, many of the towns or cities of North America were born within the mission. Here there was always a section built for the dwellings of natives who were already Christians or preparing to be baptized. When their numbers grew, construction of more dwellings started around the mission, giving rise to a town.

On other occasions a new town was started with the arrival of a large expedition of soldiers and settlers together with a number of Indians. Coronado, for example, brought eight hundred native Christians along. They would begin by drawing the plan of the town by square blocks having the main square in the center of the town and reserving its four sides for institutional buildings like the church, the city hall, the hospital, the school, or others of this type.[8] Away from the main square, streets were marked by rope in straight lines and crossed by others; houses were built on both sides of the street. In New Mexico and Texas the houses were made of stone and adobe (sun-dried clay blocks), in Florida or the Atlantic Coast, of wood and often stone. Sometimes, by their own decision, natives formed pueblos made up only of Indians, while the Spanish formed their own nearby; this was the case with San Antonio de Valero in Texas or San Gabriel in New Mexico. Gradually over time the towns would come together with normal integration. The value of the main square in every Spanish town is to be emphasized, because it was the heart of religious, social, economic, and commercial life of the town; this was the place where the residents convened and converged, working strongly toward integration.[9]

When a mission grew and a town was formed around it, the missionary tried to establish a type of autonomous government under his supervision. The Indians elected the mayor, the council members, and the sheriff; they were taught about their role and the rules of government in regard to public order, socializing, work, and justice.[10] It was not an easy job to replace the tribal form of government with a new civic formula. The *presidio* or military post was a little away from the town. Naturally, the towns that were established with a number of Spanish settlers and

Christian Indians who came with them began to function under the authority of a local governor, with town meeting, municipal officers, and Spanish legislation; that is how Santa Fe, New Mexico, St. Augustine, Florida, and San Francisco, California, began.

The settling of Indian tribes, especially those of nomadic culture, was one of the main obstacles to the formation of towns. Here the missionaries played a very important role, using several methods for this purpose. One of them was to give natives little gifts that were bright and colorful, or useful objects much appreciated by the Indians. The missionaries used to bring along a good supply of these gifts. Another method was to use natives who were already Christian to form the nucleus of the town, gradually inviting others to join them. A strategy used by the Jesuits in Georgia was to employ agriculture as a means to attach hunting tribes to the land; sowing, cultivation, and harvest required a certain permanency in a place.[11]

Many towns faced difficult moments at their beginning.[12] The adaptation of the persons, plants, and animals to the new lands often delayed the harvest or production more than was expected, and they were subjected to scarcity and hunger. That is what happened in Pensacola, Florida, and St. Helena, South Carolina. Some of the towns were supported by the *situado*, something like a subsidy provided by the government mainly to cities on the coast; these places did not make a living from agriculture or cattle raising, but from activities related to ships stopping for trade, repairs, storage, or for their strategic location, as was the case of St. Augustine in Florida, or San Juan in Puerto Rico.[13] The raids of other Indian tribes on the incipient towns, like San Diego in California, Yuma in Arizona, or Tequesta (Miami) in Florida, made their progress very difficult at the beginning. In addition to this, the attacks of French and English pirates, above all in the Atlantic, left the cities desolate, causing the loss of many lives and thwarting material progress. That was the case in Drake's raid on St. Augustine in 1586 and Clifford's on San Juan, Puerto Rico, in 1598. The formation of pueblos and cities had a difficult history, glorious at times, but always costly.

2. Another aspect of Spanish colonization in North America was the spreading of culture. From the first moment of contact with native Indians, efforts were made in this respect. One of the components of every mission was a small school where the Indians, mainly the children and the young, were taught reading, writing, mathematics, and religion.[14] Their training and formation in regard to work habits, the use of clothing, and monogamy in marriage was an important cultural process that required

dedication, patience, and skills that deserve to be mentioned. Particularly the introduction of monogamy in marriage was a sensitive and difficult task that in some cases brought death to missionaries, like the five Franciscans killed in 1597 in Georgia.[15] One of the difficulties experienced in the transmission of culture was the multiplicity of languages, since almost every tribe spoke a separate tongue.[16] There were more than three thousand tribes in the New World, differing from one another in race, government, degree of culture, language, religion, and customs. The name "Indians" does not express a characteristic common to all; it is really a later term given by the Europeans to designate the inhabitants of the newly discovered continent. The Güale Indians of Georgia had nothing in common with the Iroquois of the North or with the Apache of the South, much less with the Aztec of Mexico or the Inca of Peru. The Indians of the New World did not know that they were Indians. They were grouped under that name by the Europeans.[17] Their diversity of languages was a serious obstacle for communication and human advancement. To solve this problem some of the explorers used to take a number of young men with them to Cuba, Mexico, or Spain to be educated in the colleges operated by missionaries. After some months or years, these youths returned to their lands and served as guides, interpreters, and catechists for the explorers and missionaries.[18] Among the well-documented facts, we can mention the joint project of Pedro Menéndez de Avilés and the Jesuits in 1567 to establish a school in Havana to educate one hundred youths of Florida in the Spanish language, religion, sciences, and arts so that they might return to their tribes and share what they had learned. One of the greatest contributions Spain might have made to the natives and to America is her language.[19] With more than three thousand tribes in the New World, most of them speaking different languages, they obviously had no unity of language or understanding. The fact that Spain gave her language to the whole continent ought to be viewed as a contribution of great importance for all natives and for America, because they were given an important element of unity and a common vehicle of expression. This made it possible for Paraguayan Guarani, Peruvian Incas, Mexican Aztecs, and North American Navajo to understand one another. That is fantastic. That is what English would mean later for all natives and immigrants of many nations who would come to this country. Without a common language, a great confusion would have followed, with natural hindrance of progress. The problem of communication prompted the missionaries to learn indigenous languages. Before beginning their work, they would study the indigenous tongues in Havana, St.Augustine, or Santa Fe, learning and practicing with natives residing there. Once in their mission field, with a better command of the language, they began to write grammars, dictionaries, and catechisms in a bilingual edition. A sample of this is the grammar in Spanish and Güale, a language spoken by the Indians of Georgia, written in 1569 by the Jesuit Brother Agustín Báez and preserved in the archives of Spain.[20]

From the beginning the Indians were taught music to sing in civic and religious activities and also to play various musical instruments. The visit of the governor or the bishop to a town was a special occasion to show their musical achievements in artistic concerts or processions. This was also an occasion to enjoy the grand parades, where soldiers marching to military bands, government officers, Indian chieftains, and other native leaders wearing colorful bands and insignia participated. In such special occasions there were also poetic recitals and theater pieces typical of Spanish culture.[21] We see this happening at the arrival to New Mexico, when Captain Marcos Farfán wrote a play portraying Franciscan evangelization near El Paso, Texas. This was the first theatrical piece ever written and presented in United States territories. Many others would follow and become a tradition, not only among the Spanish but among the mestizos and the Indians as well. The same thing can be said of painting;[22] this was taught in the mission to both men and women. To a great extent, paintings, murals, and ornamentations found in churches were done by mestizo and Indian people. This is also true of Latin America, because once again we wish to recall that the Spanish border, up until the nineteenth century, was not the Rio Grande, but the Mississippi.

3. Spanish colonization, during the three hundred years that Spain remained in North America, did not neglect agriculture. When Juan Ponce de León landed in Puerto Rico in 1508, he began farming in the lands given to him by the Taino chief Agueybana.[23] In most sixteenth-century expeditions, the explorers used to take seeds, plants, and tools along, always ready to use their farming knowledge and experience.[24] What was brought by the Spanish, together with what they found in the rich lands of America, gave rise to a well-organized agriculture for those times. The missions were always established on rich lands with plenty of acreage, because it was expected that they would be self sufficient and would help in the establishment of other missions. Gradually fertile lands like those of Santa Fe, New Mexico, and southeast Texas were opened to farming, as well as areas of California, Florida, Georgia, and South Carolina. Valleys were also open to farming on the plains of rivers like the Colorado and Río Grande; on other rivers in Texas like the San Antonio, Trinidad, Neches, and Sabinas; on the rivers of Florida such as the

St. John and Apalachicola, or Altamaha in Georgia and the Wateree in South Carolina.

New plants, unknown in this hemisphere, were introduced, such as wheat, rye, barley, oats, sugar cane, coffee, peas, onions, watermelon, melon, dates; also, orange trees, lemons, bananas, almonds, hazelnuts, apples, pears, plums, peaches, figs, olives, grapes, and many other plants.[25] As a small example of the concern and difficulty experienced in bringing new plants, it is well to mention the anecdote of a Spanish sailor who was bringing a little geranium plant on the boat with him to plant it in America. In the middle of the trip there was such a scarcity of drinking water that it was rationed. He shared his small ration of water with that little plant, and finally he managed to bring it alive. This was the first geranium to arrive in the New World, thanks to the sacrifice of an immigrant. There are extensive reports of the agricultural products of the missions and towns. About ninety percent of what was consumed in the missions was produced right there; there was, therefore, little needed to be imported. The Spanish increased agricultural production enormously by means of canalization of water and irrigation, such as in San Juan, New Mexico.[26] This was one thing they knew quite well; they would also run a ditch of water along the main street in Indian towns to provide for the needs of the residents. Another means that helped to increase production was the import of farm equipment such as plows and the animals used to pull them. Surprising but true is the fact that the wheel was not known here, and its introduction advanced cultivation, gathering, and transportation of agricultural products. Agriculture developed adequately for that time and satisfied the normal nutritional needs of both Spanish and Indians. One of the things that persuaded Indians to settle in a mission pueblo was precisely the desire to share in the beautiful crops they saw grown by the mission.

4. It would be good to recall something about the development of cattle raising in North America. In every exploration, the participants used to bring animals, either for food and help in the exploration or for reproduction when the purpose of the expedition was to settle a certain area. It is documented that Vicente Yáñez Pinzón, the famous pilot who came with Columbus on the first trip and commanded the caravel called the *Niña*, was named governor of Puerto Rico in 1505. In one of the several trips that he made to America, he set loose some goats and hogs in Puerto Rico so that they might multiply. Ponce de León arrived in Florida in 1513 accompanied by his faithful "*Becerrillo*," the first dog to arrive in the United States. Among all the animals that were imported, the cow and the

horse deserve to be singled out, both for the great numbers arriving here and for the usefulness they provided.[27]

In his expedition to Florida in 1521, Ponce de León brought 50 horses; Narváez in 1528 arrived with 40; de Soto in 1538 disembarked 200; Tristán de Luna in 1559 came with 240, Coronado arrived at New Mexico in 1540 with 552, and so on. There were horses in every mission and town, and all the Spanish settlers used to breed them. The animal was used for conquest, defense, transportation, and work. Father Eusebio Kino, S.J., because of his frequent traveling on horseback along with other missionaries, was called the "Padre on Horseback," which an author took as a title for a book.[28] In the seventeenth and eighteenth centuries the number of horses multiplied enormously; San Fernando Mission in California in 1806 had some 2,400, and the *potrero* (ranch) of Espíritu Santo near Brownsville, Texas, had several thousand. The horse was a prize sought by the Comanche, who frequently organized attacks to stampede and steal them. Of those horses brought by De Soto and other explorers on their way across Arkansas and Texas, many became wild and took the name of "*mesteño*" (mustang) or *cimarrón*.[29]

Cattle were first brought to this country at the beginning of the sixteenth century. Most of the expeditions that arrived to settle a place also brought cattle, as Coronado brought a good number of cows from Mexico to New Mexico. Normally, the cattle arriving in Florida came from Spain, or at any rate from the Caribbean; to bring them from Spain was problematic and costly.[30] The cattle had multiplied vastly in the Caribbean Islands; for example, it is estimated that in Santo Domingo in 1574, only the *cimarrón* (wild) cattle numbered about a million head.[31] Those arriving in New Mexico, California, and Texas always came from Mexico. This was the origin of many of those Texas cattle ranches that later in the eighteenth century became well known, such as "King Ranch" and "Carricitos"[32] — these were the farms where the Mexican longhorns multiplied and became very famous. In 1754 the Rosario Mission in Texas had some thirty thousand head of cattle.

Already in the sixteenth century we find mules. These were the animals used for freight to transport the expeditionaries, to carry the provisions and supplies, to move the commercial goods from one place to another in wagon trains of forty to fifty units. We know that Coronado brought six hundred mules. Sheep and goats arrived also in great numbers. They did not adapt well to the tropical weather of Florida, but they prospered in Arizona, New Mexico, and California. De Soto brought a good number of hogs in 1538, and they walked alongside the explorers through Florida, Georgia, Alabama, and Tennessee. They crossed many

44

rivers (the Mississippi among them) and arrived in Arkansas.[33] After De Soto died there, his men decided to return to Mexico by way of the Mississippi, abandoning a number of hogs which became wild, the ancestors of the famous "razorback hogs" of Arkansas. Spanish imports included dogs, cats, donkeys, chickens, ducks, and even the swallows that return every year from Argentina to the San Juan Capistrano Mission on March 19, the feast of St. Joseph.

5. Architecture has always been the hallmark of Spanish civilization. Spain constructed great buildings, not only in the metropolis but also throughout her territories in America. Already in the sixteenth century we see the most beautiful expressions of baroque, gothic, or renaissance architecture in cathedrals, palaces, monasteries, monuments, statues, aqueducts, squares, markets, etc.[34] This was taking place in Puerto Rico, Santo Domingo, Cuba, Mexico, Colombia, Peru, and Argentina, just to name a few places. Cities like Taxco and Guanajuato in Mexico, Antigua in Guatemala, Cuzco in Peru, Quito in Ecuador are themselves beautiful monuments. All of them are witness still today that Spain did not come to America only for the purpose of enrichment, as she has been maliciously portrayed, but also to make a greater Spain in America, to stretch herself in the New World and pour into her lands all her rich spiritual, cultural, and artistic heritage. But this did not happen only from the Rio Grande to South America; it also happened to the North, where her men left engraved the imprint of their genius, their art, and their gusto. Cities like St. Augustine in Florida, San Antonio in Texas, Santa Fe in New Mexico, or San Diego in California still show us today their ample squares, ancestral mansions with balconies and ironwork; all of them still speak today of a legacy " the oldest inherited by this country.

In the field of architecture, it is important to recall that churches are the places where it finds its best expression. In every town, perhaps before any other building, the church was built, and generally it was the most artistic of them all, because according to the way of thinking of that time, the best must always be for God. It was built through the commitment of the rich and the poor, the Spanish and the Indian; one would lend his money, the other his work. Experienced artists used to come for the construction of these churches and monasteries, but these were places also where creole, mestizo, and native artists were forged with great achievement. The architectural aspect was considerable. Through the years that Spain was present in North America, more than two hundred five missions were built. It would be good to remember here some that are still standing today: San Miguel in Santa Fe, New Mexico; San Javier del Bac in Tucson, Arizona; San Antonio (El Alamo), Texas; Santuario of Chimayo in New Mexico, and the cathedral, presbytery, and cabildo in New Orleans, which were built by the Spanish architect Andrés Almonester when Louisiana was under the sovereignty of Spain.[35]

We should also mention the forts, since they were so connected to the process of colonization and at times were true pieces of engineering. They were built to maintain sovereignty over the territories and to defend the people, both missionaries and settlers; some twenty to one hundred fifty soldiers were assigned to each of them. For their lodging, barracks were built which were called the *presidio*;[36] when the structure was larger and stronger, it was called fort or castle (*alcázar*). Spain built in North America some seventy-one forts and presidios. Each of them was used to protect the missions and towns of a region. Among them, the best-known we recall is San Marcos in the city of St. Augustine, built in 1565 by Menéndez de Avilés, burnt by the natives and razed by the pirates on several occasions, but always rebuilt. Even today, it shows its mastery facing the sea and the land. Among others are San Bernardo in Pensacola, San Fernando de Béjar and La Bahía in Texas, St. Augustine in Arizona, and San Diego in California.

6. Another aspect of colonization was the trade activity in these northern territories. It seems that trade is innate to humans. From the first moment that Columbus arrived in America, the exchange began, the swap, the projects, and the plans, the interchange of products between Spain and America. On his return to Spain, Columbus took birds, plants, and gold that he got from Indians in exchange for some trifles. On his second trip, the Catholic king and queen sent him with seventeen boats loaded with seeds, plants, and animals.[37] By 1503 the trade activity was of such a magnitude that the Casa de la Contratación (Trade Board) was established in Seville. This was an agency of the government to supervise all commercial activity and to gather information about everything related to products, prices, taxes, transportation . . . a complete board of trade. The Spanish colonies were not allowed to trade with other European nations, nor were these nations permitted to trade in the colonies, although smuggling was always present. Between Spain and her colonies, however, and the latter among themselves, there was always an intense trade. All were connected by sea and land routes for a regular flow of commercial traffic, like the galleon line that traveled regularly between areas of the Philippines, Monterey, and Acapulco. The fleet of Spain arrived in Cuba, and from here it would sail to Florida, Puerto Rico, Cartagena, or Rio de la Plata in Argentina. The fleet sailed to Monterey, Acapulco,

Lima, and Santiago in Chile. Internal routes would cross the lands from north to south, like the one between Santa Fe and Mexico City every two years, or from east to west as was the case between St. Augustine and Tallahassee. It was sort of a common market,[38] since the products of one place used to pass freely to another using the same money, tariffs, and regulations. Naturally, the northern territories were included in this trading activity. It should be mentioned, though, that the trade intensity here was not as high as in the other territories farther south, with the exception of Louisiana during the Spanish presence there. This was due to the distance from power centers, the lack of personnel to develop them, and the fact that important mines were not discovered there as in other places. Wherever there was a strong mining activity, there was the driving force to develop other industries, trade, and even cattle ranching.[39] Even though this was the case, we will mention something about this mining activity.

In his exploration through South Carolina in 1566, Juan Pardo discovered some crystal mines and silver not far from Altamaha River in Georgia, and also some of minerals with which the Indians used to paint their bodies and which later would be exploited to a greater extent. Through the sixteenth, seventeenth, and eighteenth centuries and in several places of Arizona, mines were discovered containing gold, silver, copper, and potassic salts, and they began to be exploited. At the end of the eighteenth century Julián Dubuque, who, though Canadian in origin, was a Spanish citizen, began to exploit silver in the Spanish mines in Iowa and thus began considerable commerce.[40]

Another item of great commercial activity was animal fur.[41] From the times when Cabeza de Vaca had seen buffalo in 1534 on the plains of Texas, a restlessness developed to commercialize the furs. Thus in the sixteenth century we find some explorers trading with the Navajo and Comanche Indians, returning to Mexico loaded with hundreds and even thousands of buffalo hides. The hides were tanned in the missions[42] and they were among the main articles that wagon trains carried from New Mexico to Mexico. With the later development of cattle farming, the hides of cattle were also objects of intense trade. This was happening in the southern territories, but in the north there was another important center for fur trading, and this was St. Louis, Missouri.[43] Initiated by France, it was developed by the Spaniards in the second half of the eighteenth century. The trading companies of Manuel de Lisa and José Vigo used boats with 18 or 20 men to search the banks of the Mississippi River. Their activity was especially centered along the Missouri River and its tributaries all the way up to the Yellowstone in Montana. Along these extensive routes they had several important posts, such as Fort Lisa in

Nebraska. Their purpose was to hunt for the fur of beaver, deer, and other animals whose hides had a high value and trade demand. The trade developed by the Missouri Fur Company, founded by Lisa, was considerable; its volume of trade was $600,000, and there were about 100 people employed. It was the largest fur company south of Canada at that time.

Other articles that were part of trade, above all in the Gulf of Mexico and California, were pearls. A search for them had been initiated by Hernán Cortés, followed by others and pursued until our day.[44] The missions were important centers of production or manufacture of products that were exported, as well as distribution of incoming goods to the area. It is important to bring this information to light in order to eradicate the idea that the only thing Spain did was to plunder natural resources. The Archives of the Indies in Seville or Mexico are open to anyone to check on the shipment of goods. Year after year Spanish fleets from Spain to America shipped plants, animals, tools, minerals, building materials, equipment for the missions, fabrics, food products, printing presses, books, various metals, ceramics, firearms, wood, wines, and furniture. Those are only typical of hundreds of items the ships would bring. These, together with great numbers of well-educated persons who arrived in the colonies, show clearly that Spain sent to America as much as or even more than what she imported.[45] What happened was that goods arriving in Spain came from the whole American hemisphere and, by the fact that they were gathered at one point, became more visible. Meanwhile, those products that came from Spain were scattered over dozens of ports in America and became less visible. Commodities that came to these northern territories, for example, were generally cattle, iron tools, furniture, fabrics, equipment for different skills, and church provisions. From here they took hides, blankets, dry fruits, textiles mainly produced by natives of New Mexico's missions, and some mining products.

An obstacle to the sea trade, both between Spain and her colonies and among the colonies themselves, was the activity of pirates. From the end of the sixteenth century on, they organized fleets of fifty to a hundred craft whose task was to assault the commercial ships of Spain or the seashore cities. Those pirates were largely English, French, or Dutch, and often they counted on the approval or even the support of their governments.[46] Spain, then, had to organize *armadas* (armed fleets) to escort her merchant navy on voyages across the Atlantic Ocean twice a year.

The Spanish colonization of America has not been adequately valued in the agricultural, cattle raising, cultural, commercial, industrial, and religious aspects. This constituted an investment of initiative, effort, talent, and organization that cannot be measured by money. It would be wonderful if someone, some day, could undertake the task of showing the great spiritual and human contribution of Spain to the New World.

Perpendicular: Typical pages from a pictorial catechism for the Indies developed by Father Pedro de Gante, painted in bright colors and expecially designed for evangelization of Native Americans by missionary priests in the field

IV

Evangelization
in the United States

It is evident that Spain had a genuine interest in the evangelization of the natives of America. It was clearly expressed by the Catholic king and queen to Columbus before authorizing the first voyage. It was demonstrated by policies followed thereafter through royal charters, legislation, and ordinances. Naturally, Spain also entertained economic and political interests, but evangelization was always a primary goal of her policy in the New World. She undertook the propagation of the faith as a natural task to be exercised as a response of her religious identity.[1] Papal bulls reminded the king and queen that evangelization was something inherent to their sovereignty over those lands. Spain, therefore, wanted to bring the faith to the natives, but how was it to be done? This was the big question. After long and careful thinking about the matter, she tried to carry it out through the *encomienda* (trust) system. Abuses occurred, voices were raised to denounce them, and this experience was terminated within a few years. She then tried military conquest, and though, militarily speaking, it was successful, this method was also abandoned because it did not achieve the expected results.

Since the above methods were considered inadequate, and given that the colonization and the evangelization were to continue, the learned people in Spain thought and discussed at length on the methods to be employed. The question was reflected upon by royal counselors, bishops, religious congregations, and university doctors. After serious deliberation, a way was found to continue and the mission system was adopted. We may say that the mission is an institution that combines the participation of both Church and State to continue and extend the work of colonizing and bringing the natives to the faith at one and the same time. It would be run by religious personnel provided by the Church while the State would provide the finances and the protection needed to make the project succeed. As a matter of fact, religious congregations accepted the challenge of evangelizing America with great generosity and commitment. Tens of thousands of religious missionaries departed from Spain and gave of themselves to plant the faith in America from the dawn of the discovery.[2] The State added its share in the project, which indeed was very costly.[3] The royal treasury covered the expenses of transportation for each missionary and a yearly subsidy for his sustenance, which in 1758 was $450 a year. The State also took over the payment for the building of the mission and its equipment, while it had to pay also for the construction of the presidio (barracks) and the salaries of the soldiers assigned to protect the mission. If we take into consideration that over a period of 300 years there were some 200 Spanish missions established in the area of what is now part of the United States, with two missionaries in each of them, and that these missions were protected by 71 regional forts with an average of 50 soldiers in each of them, we may get an idea of the heavy expenditure on the part of the government to support the work of evangelization. The construction of the first missions in California were particularly expensive; all building materials and provisions had to be brought by sea, since a passage connecting the interior and California by land had not yet been discovered.[4] The Dominican Congregation relates in its chronicles that the crown covered the traveling expenses for each missionary from Spain to Mexico. This was done in the following manner: seven reales daily from the day they left the monastery until they arrived in Cádiz, the port of departure; two daily during their stay there; 907 by way of provisions such as books, clothing, and various items; 539 for the boat fare from Cádiz to Mexico; 110 for transportation from Mexico to the various destination places such as New Mexico or Florida. At times, in addition to the subsidies provided by the royal treasury, private persons made contributions, such as Pedro de Terreros, who gave $150,000 to establish some missions in Texas for the conversion of the Apache Indians or the pious fund established in Lower California by the Jesuits with private donations to support the missions. It was expected, nevertheless, that each mission would be self-sufficient in the not-too-distant future.

The mission was a frontier institution established to advance the borders. Once the bases for colonization and evangelization of the natives were laid down in a territory, another mission was established at the new frontier, and thus the process went on.[5] In this way, the mission achieved peaceful conquest, colonization, and evangelization at the same time. It was envisioned from the beginning that its existence as such should have a provisional character. It was expected that once the bases of colonization and evangelization were established in a given territory, the native Christians would begin the formation of a pueblo (town) with its own land, services, and institutions, in other words, to start a municipality. Though it was thought to be this way, often it took longer than expected. The mission was born and developed with a tight collaboration of Church and State, and without denying difficulties that resulted from this joint association, we can state that the problems were truly superficial when compared to the excellent results that occurred everywhere. The close partnership of Church and State in the mission was a weak starting point for evangelization in some aspects; but it must be also said that it was, at the same time, its greatest strength.[6]

1. We could say the mission was the embryo of a town. Its physical structure was formed by a complex of buildings where the life of a community developed.[7] As a general rule, it was a square of about three hundred feet on each side. One side was destined to be the convent where the missionaries lived, and this was generally square, with an arched inner patio where flowers and various trees were planted and a freshwater well was located in the middle.[8] Near the convent were the offices, the infirmary, and the classrooms; on the same side there was the mission church with a tower and bell. Another side was used for the living quarters of the native Christians, which were very simple. On another side were the shops for the various crafts: carpentry, blacksmithing, pottery, tannery, olive press, and flour mill. Finally, the last side was reserved for warehousing crops, mainly cereals, and for animal stables. In the middle of the mission there was always a big courtyard with a well to supply needed water. Some missions were surrounded by a wall and had only one entrance gate protected by turrets, like the one in San Antonio, Texas, as a defense against the attacks of the wild Indians. Surrounding the mission were the fields where the missionary and the soldiers taught the natives how to farm and raise various products such as cereals, vegetables, and fruits that the mission needed for its sustenance and for trading. There also were grazing fields for the animals, where the natives learned the basics of raising cattle.

The life of the mission was directed by the missionaries, who were mostly Franciscans, Jesuits, and Dominicans in the U.S. area. Though each of these congregations had its own characteristics, shown in the way they ran the missions, all of them had elements in common such as religious formation, teaching of humanities, and communal work.[9] All rose at sunrise, and the first order of the day was prayer.[10] Children and teenagers would attend Mass, learned to recite prayers and Creed in a loud voice, and were given religious instruction all day. At sunset the rosary was recited by all in the mission, together with some prayers and singing of the *Salve* or *Alabado* (praise). Sunday was, naturally, the day when everyone attended the main Mass, where there was music with instruments they had learned to play. At some festivities they would hold processions, singing the rosary, and during Lent all attended daily Mass. On Sunday, a missionary said, "They are required to wear their clothing, poor but clean, and all well washed and combed."

Daily in the mission there was a time devoted to teaching principally the children and the young.[11] The teaching consisted of reading and writing in Spanish, of learning the four basic arithmetic operations, poetry, music, and chant. This teaching was given by the missionary himself, along with some other person who had come with him or whom he had trained to help him in this task. In addition to this work that we could call academic, other teaching was also imparted at the mission, vocational training in the various skills necessary or useful for the well-being of the mission, such as carpentry, smithery, or tanning. Women were taught to spin, knit, paint, cook, sew.[12] Most of this training was given by other Indians who had come from Cuba, Mexico, Santo Domingo, or Puerto Rico, or by natives of the area who had already been trained. Education was given not only in the mission but also outside. The missionaries established the practice of sending youths to be educated in schools of Mexico, Cuba, or Spain, spending one or several years there.

In the mission, together with religious formation and academics, natives were educated in the habits of work.[13] This was an element of particular importance; in addition to introducing an element of organization and stability in the native's daily life, he acquired new skills and produced what he and the mission needed for sustenance. There were two main periods of work every day; one in the morning from sunrise until noon, when it was time for dinner and rest; another in the afternoon until some time before sunset.[14] During these times, everyone in the mission was busy at the assigned work, whether in the fields, attending cattle, in the shops, or at some other labor. Everything in the mission was organized in a lifestyle where discipline had a special importance.[15] The tower bell was the voice of the mission; it not only called the people to prayer, but it really regulated the life in the community with its daily tolling in the morning, mid-day, and evening. The bell also called the people for special occasions: festivities, wakes, guest visits, farewells. This life in the mission was only possible when the natives agreed to settle down. Missionaries unanimously agreed that making converts outside the mission system was an almost hopeless task.[16] We have a clear example of this truth in the missions of northeast Texas; progress in evangelizing there was very slow because of the nomadic condition of the people.

In order to maintain good discipline and for the protection of the people, every mission had a group of soldiers who lived nearby and sometimes served also as instructors in farm work or vocational skills. The presence of soldiers in the mission has frequently been portrayed as negative for the conversion of the natives because of abuses committed, but this is an exaggeration. Often forgotten or silenced is the positive role soldiers played, both as a help to the mission and as a guarantee of protection for its dwellers. This is so true that the existence of the mission, and therefore colonization and evangelization, would have been impossible without their presence. What the missionaries complained about is the improper conduct of some soldiers and interference at times in matters not their business, but they never questioned their need.

The mission was a definite success for the preservation of the Indian, his introduction to the faith, and his human progress. In reference to the last aspect, John F. Bannon says, " The civilizing function of the typical Spanish mission, where the missionaries had charge of the temporalities as well as of the spiritualities, was evident from the very nature of the mission plant. While the church was ever the center of the establishment, and the particular object of the minister's pride and care, it was by no means the larger part. Each fully developed mission was a great industrial school of which the largest, as in California, sometimes managed more than two thousand Indians. There were weaving rooms, blacksmith shops, tannery, wine press and warehouses; also there were irrigating ditches, vegetable gardens, and grain fields; and on the ranges roamed thousands of horses, cattle, sheep and goats."[17]

We have to say, then, that the mission was a center of evangelization where the Indian was inducted and developed in Christian doctrine. It was a center of civilization where he learned the civic way of living with others, was educated for forming skills in art and the professions, trained in industries of making wine, oil, and sugar. The mission was a center of government where the head of the family played his role in the election of officers, making of rules, administration of justice, and appointment of supervisors. It was certainly one way of autonomous government under the supervision of the missionary.[18]

2. The evangelization work in the territories now part of the United States was carried out, as we said before, by three religious congregations: Franciscans, Jesuits, and Dominicans. The Franciscans, though they had taken part in some expeditions before, began their work on a permanent basis after the arrival of Menéndez de Avilés in 1565. A few years later, when the Jesuits withdrew from Florida in 1572, Franciscans

replaced them along the Atlantic Coast; they grew in such a way that they established a formation house in St. Augustine, Florida, and in 1612 the new province of Santa Elena was founded.[19] Their work was even more intense in New Mexico, Texas, and California, where they were practically the only ones carrying out missionary work. There were extraordinary men like Juan de Padilla, the first martyr in the United States, Alonso de Benavides, and Junípero Serra. The Jesuits arrived in Florida with Menéndez de Avilés in 1566;[20] they spread to Georgia and Virginia, but stayed a short time because St. Francis Borgia, their general, decided to send them to Mexico. At the end of the seventeenth century they went up from Mexico to Arizona, where they labored very intensely. Well-known persons among them were Father Eusebio Kino and Father Juan Salvatierra. The Dominicans were sporadically in Florida, where Father Luis Cáncer died a martyr in 1549. Later, at the end of the nineteenth century, they went to California.[21]

Most of these missionaries had been born in Spain. When they were young they had gone to the various parts of America to work for several years, but it must be mentioned that some of them had already been born in America. As many indigenous people from different lands came with the Spanish explorers, so it was with the missionaries; some had been born in Mexico, Cuba, Puerto Rico, or Santo Domingo. Generally speaking, Franciscans would come from the Colegio de la Santa Cruz in Querétaro or San Fernando College in Mexico City; Jesuits arrived from Spain, Cuba, and Mexico; Dominicans came from Santo Domingo, Puerto Rico, and Mexico. The Franciscans sent 30 expeditions to Florida with some 461 friars almost all through the seventeenth century.

Missionaries sent from Spain to America were supposed to have certain qualifications. According to the norms of the Council of the Indies, they had to have good reputations and credibility. Religious congregations, in addition, looked among their members for individuals known for virtue and apostolic zeal. In most cases, as among the Franciscans, only those who volunteered themselves were sent.[22] But permission was not given to those on whom was imposed a penance due to a more or less serious infringement of the law. The self-giving of Spanish missionaries to the native Americans was absolute and total, not only regarding evangelization but also their human progress and well-being. Clear to any serious historian is the courage they showed before all kinds of obstacles as well as their sacrifice in giving up family, profession, and homeland to commit their lives for the salvation of others' souls, many times by shedding their own blood. It can truly be said that the Catholic faith in America is watered with the blood of martyrs.

The trip from Spain to America was not easy four or five centuries ago. Getting from various parts of Spain to the embarkation place, usually Seville or Cádiz, required many days of traveling afoot, fatigue, hunger, and uncomfortable sleeping. There were frequent delays of days, weeks, or even months before departure, caused by bad seas, late arrival of the ship, the threat of piracy, or political hostilities with other nations. On the day of departure the missionaries would march in procession from a convent to the harbor behind a religious banner, reciting or singing litanies of Mary. Once in the port, a selected missionary would preach a farewell sermon "till eternity" before the assembled crowd. Once aboard the ship, volunteers had to be ready to spend forty days at sea, enduring the inherent challenges of seasickness, heat, narrow sleeping space, pirate attacks, sea storms, and boredom. It does not seem strange that once in a while some missionaries would jump ship at the first port of call.

Pedro Borges, in his book, *El Envío de Misioneros a America durante la Época Española* (*The Sending of Missionaries to America during the Spanish Era*), says that 10,465 ships left Spain for America between 1506 and 1650; about 171 of them were sunk by pirates, storms, or other causes. The missionaries on board all perished. Many of the missionaries had extensive academic preparation as well as experience in teaching in various schools or colleges.[23] Among them let us mention the famous Dominican Antonio de Montesinos in South Carolina, the Jesuit Juan Bautista Segura, a martyr in Virginia, and the Franciscan Alonso de Benavides in New Mexico. Many of them wrote grammars, dictionaries, catechisms, interesting reports on geography of these lands, explorations, and indigenous customs. It is to be mentioned that among them there were cartographers, astronomers, and artists. The chronicles of the Dominicans report that the 1510 expedition to Santo Domingo was like the *"primitiae"*[24] (the cream) of the order, to give God in the new lands "the best of the order for the furthering of our faith." Most of them were persons of deep faith and generous commitment, not only to the salvation of natives (the main objective) but also to their human development. They left family, homeland, and positions to devote themselves to the work of evangelization in the lands of America, never to return home in most cases. Curiously enough, whenever the opening of a new mission in a territory was announced and a brother had died as a martyr, it was then that more applications were received in order to fill his place.[25] It was an indication of the high missionary spirit and the readiness to give one's life for others that prevailed at that time, especially in the sixteenth and seventeenth centuries. As a matter of fact, here in the United States we have the extraordinary example of many who shed their blood for the sake of their faith, such as Father Pedro Martínez in 1566 in Florida, Father Pedro Corpa and confreres in 1597 in Georgia,[26] and eighty more whose names are given in this book. The list is numerous, but now we give only a few names to represent those who planted the faith in these lands and watered it with their blood. Anyone who would like to read the lives and deeds of these great men would be greatly impressed. Besides being missionaries, these men were also explorers who opened new routes to civilization,[27] as in the case of Father Silvestre Vélez de Escalante, who crossed the mountains of Colorado and Utah to find a passage to California. They were also *pacificadores* (pacifiers), who entered new lands offering peace to the natives and settling among them. They were reporters who documented the activities and events so useful for the future, as did the *Memorial* of Father Alonso de Benavides. Historian Pedro Borges points out that the number of missionaries Spain sent to America up to 1822 was 16,000, more or less, who were members of various religious orders. This number does not include diocesan priests or lay people who went to do evangelization work, nor priests or religious already born in America.

3. There were some points related to the evangelization of the Indians that, in the first half of the sixteenth century, were already generally observed. One was the obligation felt by all civil authorities, from the king to the least officer of the crown, to promote the conversion of natives to the Catholic faith. This seems very clear in agreements made with the expeditionaries, in letters of appointment of officers, and in the norms coming from the Council of the Indies. Another was the freedom of natives to accept the Catholic faith or not.[28] No method was to be used to force the Indians to embrace the faith, but they should be "attracted" without use of force and with much sweetness and softness. Another conclusion drawn early was that the conversion of the Indians could not be effected unless they remained settled in a place. That is the reason for the establishment of "reductions" to settle the nomadic or semi-nomadic people in missions or pueblos. Reduction and mission are similar institutions, though there may be some variations between them, as there are also differences between mission and mission. The term reduction has been applied preferably to the Jesuit missions of Paraguay.

The various methods used to pursue evangelization in the sixteenth century can be reduced to four: the *encomienda* system, conquest followed by evangelization, peaceful evangelization, and peaceful evangelization with protection.[29] The *encomienda* (royal grant) system was abandoned after a few years. Then it was thought that the best and fastest way to achieve the conversion of the natives was through armed conquest of the territory. Once victory was achieved, the natives would accept the religion of the victors. This method was used in some parts of Latin America, and thus we see the conquests of Hernán Cortés in Mexico and Francisco Pizarro in Peru. Once victory was achieved, however, there remained the most important task: the settling of the Indians, making them subjects of the crown, and the passing of culture and faith. All this was not so easy to achieve, because of the opposition and resentment that always remained in the ones defeated, and also the violence that all armed conflict carries in itself. Seen from all angles, it was clear that this method did not accomplish the goals that Spain intended in colonizing America, and a few years after the mid-sixteenth century the method was suspended. In the territories now part of the United States this method was never applied, since a good part of the Spanish presence before 1550 had an exploratory nature. In some cases there were attempts to colonize that never materialized, such as the expedition of Ponce de León in 1521, of Ayllón in 1526, or of Coronado in 1540. In the conquered territories, however, Spain had to continue the work of colonization and evangelization. Though the method was discontinued, it favored the quick conversion of the Indians because the missionaries were able to move about freely. They could also neutralize the influence of idolatry and sorcerers, which would not have been possible if conquest had not preceded their work. This method had unacceptable elements, but it must be admitted that it also offered advantages for both colonization and evangelization.

The third was what may be called the "peaceful method." This was based on the idea that the missionaries were emissaries of peace and bearers of faith, and therefore they should go to the natives without any military protection. It was expected from this method that the Indians would settle in towns, peacefully accepting the sovereignty of Spain, civilization, and faith. The method was tested in different places and at different times. It was a method filled with a great ideal, but its outcome was sterile. It was obvious that the results were few and the martyrs many. Father Juan Padilla in 1542 in Kansas, Father Luis Cáncer in 1549 in Florida, the five Jesuits in 1570 in Virginia, and many others were convincing proof that this method was not viable, even though some of the missionaries wanted to continue that way.

The fourth was the "protected method."[30] It was envisioned through this method that the missionary would assume responsibility for advancing the frontier while working on civilizing and evangelizing the natives, but under the protection of an escort of soldiers. In this case, the arms came not before but after; they were used not to attack but to defend, and they were employed to defend not the Gospel but the missionaries. In reality, the mission was the result of adopting this method, which shared something of the two previous types. It was a method through which peace and friendship were offered to the Indians, and it was expected that a conquest, now peaceful, would follow through culture and faith. The military presidio (fort) was at a distance from the mission and was designed to protect the missions of the region. From this fort two to five soldiers were assigned to each mission, and they were stationed nearby to protect against surprise attacks of not-yet-christianized Indians. In a report of Father Cartagena, O.F.M., to his superior, he said: "What makes these missions permanent are the Catholic arms. Without them the pueblos are often abandoned and the ministers are killed by the savages. Every moment we see that in the missions where there are no soldiers, there is no progress either. . . . The soldiers are needed to protect the Indians against their tribal enemies and to win over the Indians of the mission, either to encourage them or to notify the closest presidio in case of a problem. Two soldiers are needed for both the spiritual and the material progress of the missions because total confidence cannot be placed solely on the Indians, especially when they are just recent converts." Frequently these soldiers helped teach agriculture or various skills to the natives, but at times they were also obstacles to evangelization work because of their not always ideal conduct.[31] This evangelization method was almost the only one used in all the territories now part of the United States from the sixteenth to the nineteenth century. On occasion changes were introduced, as in the case of Yuma, Arizona, in 1781 where a group of settlers worked their own fields near the mission lands. Problems arose between the two groups which caused a rebellion of the natives; they killed Captain Rivera, Father Garcés, Father Díaz, and some one hundred white persons.[32] The mission, in general, was a great success for both civilization and evangelization of the Indians. They felt comfortable and protected, and when a native would leave the mission to visit a relative or a friend, it seems he or she always returned bringing a new candidate. John G. Shea says: "Many learned Spanish thoroughly, and all acquired a knowledge of the Christian religion, which they faithfully practiced. Thus, they gained two great benefits, peace and comfort in this life, and means of attaining happiness in the next."

Regarding the kind of relationship that existed between the missionary and the people of the mission, John D. Forbes, quoted by Shea, says: "The best and most unequivocal proof of the good conduct of the Franciscan Fathers is to be found in the unbounded affection and devotion invariably shown toward them by their Indian subjects. They venerate them, not only as friends and fathers, but with a degree of devotion approaching adoration. On the occasion of removals which have taken place in recent years from political causes, the distress of the Indians in parting with their pastors has been extreme. They have begged to be allowed to follow them in their exile, with tears and laments, and with all demonstrations of true sorrow and unbounded affection."[33]

Within the mission the missionaries employed several strategies to succeed in converting the natives. I will mention three that I consider of greater importance.

The first was the use of other natives already Christian. Most of these came from Mexico, although there were some from the Caribbean and Central or South America.[34] They were a part, sometimes considerable, of every expedition. With Coronado, eight hundred natives came to New Mexico; some one hundred Tlaxcaltecan families were sent to Pensacola; another group was sent to San Sabas, Texas, to facilitate the conversion of the Apache Indians. Also from Sonora, the Optata Indians were brought up to Arizona as teachers of the Pima Indians. The role of these natives was to serve as helpers, guides, interpreters, and public relations persons with the Indians near the mission. They would invite them to become part of it, teach them farming, cattle raising, and various skills. They served also as catechists, organizers, and pacifiers and were an element without which the mission could not easily evolve and grow. It was the case of the Indian helping the Indian. Another point to be kept in mind is that the Indians living in a mission were not all of the same tribe or tongue, but they belonged to several and were often foes among each other. However, faith, Spanish language, culture, and the presence of Indians already Christian helped as a unifying element.

The second strategy consisted in using native children as interpreters and catechists.[35] Soon the missionaries and expeditionaries realized that such a multiplicity of Indian languages was a serious problem in their work. Therefore, from the first moment they would teach Spanish to some children and youth so that they would help them as interpreters. It was also a practice to select youngsters from various tribes and send them to Cuba, Spain, and Mexico to receive an education. Afterwards they were returned to their original tribes to help in the mission as interpreters and catechists.[36] The Franciscans and Dominicans had established, even before 1520, two schools in Santo Domingo and Puerto Rico to educate native children, above all those of Indian leaders and chiefs. Once these youths, normally ten to fourteen years of age, returned to their native land speaking Spanish, the missionary would give further instruction on Christian Doctrine, and then these youths instructed others in their native language. Captain Gaspar Pérez de Villagrá from the expedition of Oñate in 1598 states that after the battle of Acoma Rock in New Mexico the Spanish took sixty native girls of the Pueblo tribe to the viceroy of Mexico so that they might be educated in the convents of the nuns.[37] The participation of these children was tremendously important in the process of evangelization, since it resulted in a better understanding and acceptance coming from a person of the same origin than coming from a foreigner.

The missionaries also employed another strategy for transmitting the faith. They concentrated on converting the chief of the Indian tribe.[38] They knew quite well that once this was achieved, the evangelizing task would be easier and faster. Examples of this technique were the invitations of Menéndez de Avilés to the Indian chief of Tocobaga to go to Havana; the conversion of the woman chief María near St. Augustine; the conversion of the chief of St. Catherine Island, Georgia, on the proposal of some soldiers that it would rain if he became a Christian, which actually happened; the conversion of Don Domingo, chief of St. Simon Island in Georgia, and many others. The attention of Spanish officials and missionaries centered not only on the Indian chief, but they also chose as priority the conversion and education of other persons of the tribe with leadership qualities or their relatives. To this end the Franciscans established in 1524 in Mexico a kind of seminary to form a native clergy with the children of native leadership of New Spain.[39] This school would later be followed by the foundation of the Colegio Santa Cruz (Holy Cross College) of Tlaltelolco. Sons, brothers, or cousins of the leadership class were also taken and trained in Cuba and Spain.

Unfortunately, not all cases brought the expected results because some of these youths betrayed the faith and confidence that the missionaries had placed in them. Once returned to their native lands, they became heads of rebellion and foes of their benefactors. This is the case of Magdalena, who went back to Florida with Ponce de León in 1521; that of Don Luis, brother of the chief of Axacan (Virginia) in 1570; that of Juanillo, son of the chief of Tolomato, Georgia, in 1597;[40] that of Luis Saric, chief of the Pima Indians in Arizona in 1751. All these methods and procedures reveal a genuine concern of the missionaries on behalf of the natives. They tried various approaches and methods of education, psychological resources for cooperation, and means for improvement. The driving force behind all these endeavors is to be found only in their deep faith, generous commitment, and heroic sanctity.

4. Opening a way for faith, starting to build a Christian community has been, from the first days of Christianity, a hard task, undertaken with

difficulty by persons of weak spirit. These were the hardships that the missionaries had to face when they arrived at these lands of North America. Only highly motivated persons, not expecting human gratification, would be able to overcome them. These difficulties were many.

There were those that we could call geographical.[41] Attention is drawn to the fact that through the sixteenth and seventeenth centuries there were immense territories not yet explored, and naturally there were no roads. The Spanish advanced by breaking paths. In Florida they found a tropical climate with marshes, swampy lands, clouds of mosquitoes that caused diseases, bushy land that made the march difficult, exhausting heat, or bitter cold like the weather that decimated Ayllón's expedition in 1526 in Carolina.[42] In New Mexico and Arizona they had to face the howling desert and rugged mountains. There also persisted a lack of adequate medicines, primitive means of transportation, extensive territories as in Texas or California that made access to supplies and protection in case of need very difficult.

In addition to the above, there were obstacles posed by nature, and others of an anthropological nature related to evangelization. The nomadic life was one of those problems that had to be solved by the missionaries. A good many of the tribes of Florida and Georgia had a nomadic way of life. They fed on vegetables and wild fruits and moved from place to place according to the season or harvest time. The Jesuits Rogel and Villarreal resorted to different methods to settle some Güale tribes. They used gifts, endeavored to teach them farming so that the natives could have food all year round, and even built houses for them.[43] All these efforts produced meager results and left the missionaries discouraged. Texas was a region where most of the tribes were nomadic, living from hunting. Best known among them were the Apache and the Comanche Indians. Some time later, above all in the eighteenth century, these tribes of northeast Texas established contact with the French settlers of Louisiana, who sold them firearms. Their use of firearms, together with the horses they had learned to ride, not only made the missionary work slower, but also more difficult and dangerous.[44] With the aid of the already Christian Indians, agriculture, and the fort's soldiers, the missionaries were able to overcome this problem.

The hostility and generally bellicose attitude of the Indians of North America posed great hardships and frustrated a number of colonizing attempts. Since these lands were never conquered militarily, the natives were therefore never disarmed as was in the case in Latin America. Indians generally adopted a strong hostility to the Spanish presence in these lands.[45] It is well known that throughout Florida most of the settlements were attacked in their initial stages. This happened, for example to Ponce de León in 1521 in Charlotte Harbor, to Menéndez de Avilés in 1566 in Tocobaga (Tampa), in Caloos (Charlotte Harbor), and in Tequesta (Miami); to all settlements of New Mexico in 1680; to Portola in 1769 in San Diego, and so on. This bellicose attitude was characteristic of the tribes of these territories. Existing documentation speaks of the constant battles among tribes[46] and of the cruelty inflicted upon the defeated; it could be said that they lived in a permanent state of war. Similar situations prevailed in other parts of Latin America, but this intertribal bellicosity ended as a result of the Spanish military conquest. Often the hostility toward settlements or missions came from the sorcerers or religious leaders, who encouraged uprisings against the missionaries because they tried to introduce beliefs and practices contrary to their own. The natives, frightened by these religious leaders with terrible misfortunes if they accepted the new faith, gave in at times to the pressures and raided the towns or missions. On occasion they attacked the missionaries directly, as in the case of Father Francisco Porras, O.F.M., who was poisoned in 1633 by sorcerers of the Hopi Indians in Arizona.[47] The Indian hostility that slowed the progress of settlements and missions was aroused in part by other Europeans who, spurred by political rivalries in Europe, thirsted for more land through pirate activity. These caused setbacks in the beginning settlements. This situation was typical of Georgia, Florida, the Gulf of Mexico region, and the Caribbean; the raids of James Moore in 1704 and of James Oglethorpe afterwards are typical examples.

The multiplicity of dialects was also a great obstacle that hindered the work of evangelization. An author states that in the area of the Rio Grande alone there were more than two hundred languages; Father Ortíz, quoted by Bolton, says: "The ministers who have learned some languages of the Indians of these missions assert that it is impossible to compose a catechism in their idiom because of the lack of terms in which to explain matters of faith. The best-informed interpreters say the same. There are as many languages as there are tribes, which in these missions aggregate more than two hundred." Although they mixed with one another and somehow manage to communicate, there were about twenty languages more commonly used by the majority of tribes.[48] But even among these, the words of one are very different from another; for example, the word "earth" is expressed in Tehna as "naha"; in Queres, "hah-ats"; in Zuñi, "on-lok-nan-nay."[49] Learning them, writing the catechisms in these languages, or teaching Spanish to children and youth in order to reach the adults through them was a slow and difficult process which required a dedication and patience beyond the norm.

However, the hardest obstacle that missionaries had to overcome was the uprooting of beliefs and practices that were incompatible with Christian faith.[50] Idolatry was one of them. In addition to various objects, some tribes worshiped the evil spirit and offered him human sacrifices so that their warriors would stay stronger than the enemies. John G. Shea says that Father Juan Rogel, a Jesuit, after eight months of instruction at the Santa Elena Mission, South Carolina, at the moment of asking renunciation of the devil before Baptism, met with a firm opposition from the council of Indian chiefs.[51] Polygamy was another practice common to many tribes, and it was a problem that required much work, patience, and even blood to be replaced by monogamy; this was the reason for the death of five Franciscan martyrs in Georgia in 1597.[52] Historian John A. Caruso, in his book *The Southern Frontier*, mentions a list of bloody practices related to baby girls, wives, and defeated enemies that were part of the ritual, and more that needed to be eliminated.[53] This was a silent and hard work that engaged missionaries for centuries to elevate the native and to introduce him to a higher level in life. These missionaries who over three hundred years labored steadfastly in these lands are truly unsung heroes that are not yet known by the American people.

The progress of faith among natives was not as fast as it could have been because of the bad example of some persons who came to plant the Gospel. There were civil authorities who, in violation of the laws, abused their power and committed acts of cruelty; this was always an occasion for serious conflict with the missionaries. There were times when even the governor was removed, as in the case of Pedro de Peralta in New Mexico.[54] On other occasions, it was the settlers who wanted to take advantage of the services or the cheap labor of Indians on their farms or ranches. The improper or even indecent conduct of some soldiers was a common headache for the missionaries and a bad example for the newly converted Indians. The military protection, however, was a necessary element for the survival of the mission. The missionaries had to resort to ways so that the soldiers were not an obstacle to their work; therefore in most places the soldiers did not live in the mission but relatively close.

Missionaries had to face all these obstacles. That tells us that only men of great virtue could devote their entire lives to this thankless task. The words of Herbert Bolton sum up this evangelization toil well: "The Missions were agencies of the State as well as of the Church. They served not only to christianize the frontier, but also to aid in extending, holding, and civilizing it. Since Christianity was the basic element of European civilization, and since it was the acknowledged duty of the State to extend the faith, the first task of the missionary from the standpoint of both State and Church, was to convert the heathen. But neither the State nor the Church nor the missionary himself in Spanish dominions considered the work of the mission as ending here. If the Indian were to become a worthy Christian or a desirable subject, he must be disciplined in the rudiments of civilized life. The task of giving the discipline was likewise turned over to the missionary. Hence, the missions were designed to be not only Christian seminaries, but in addition were outposts for the control and training schools for the civilizing of the frontier."[55] Maynard Geiger adds: "The Spanish mission system was doubtless one of the greatest humanitarian efforts that the world has ever seen for the amelioration and spiritual development of backward and non-Christian people."[56]

*Bernardo de Gálvez, appointed governor of Louisiana, won
military and naval victories over the British in the Florida
and Louisiana territories, contributing mightily to the
defeat of British occupational forces and the independence
of the fledgling United States in the American Revolution*

V

Spain and the Independence
of the United States

The participation of Spain in the independence of the Thirteen Colonies is a fact unknown to most of the American people. Recognition is given to France and Poland, but for some mysterious reason the decisive role Spain played is not shown in the textbooks of our schools or in history books available to the general public. It is neither presented through the communications media nor shown in the lists of names given to streets, parks, or public institutions; the Spanish heroes in this land are not placed alongside others who played a sizable role in the formation of this country. What are the reasons for such an omission when all the facts are well documented? One cannot help but think that it might be a result of the Black Legend that was spread through this country to minimize or obscure the image of Spain in this nation whom she helped bring to birth. So that the American people may have at least an idea of the Spanish contribution to the War of Independence, I wish to offer an informational summary.

1. From the geographical point of view, in 1763 the domains of England in North America stretched from Yukon Bay in the North to the Gulf of Mexico in the South, from the Atlantic Ocean in the East to the Mississippi River in the West. Spain was sovereign on the rest of the Western Hemisphere, from the Mississippi River in the North to the Antarctic Sea in the South, including the main islands in the Caribbean Sea.[1] In 1763, when Louisiana was given to Spain by France, the latter had lost nearly all other territories in North America. This geographical picture is to be kept in mind because of the strategic and commercial implications for the Thirteen Colonies. These were surrounded on the north and south by English land and on the east by the Atlantic Ocean, with the British navy in control of all major seaports. The western side of the Mississippi River and a small piece of the South was Spanish territory. This space was vital for the supply of provisions and munitions to the revolutionary colonists.

2. Politically, we have to recall the climate prevailing in Europe. In 1763, the Seven Years War had ended with England overcoming France and Spain. This gave Florida to England, and France gave up almost all her territories in America, including Louisiana, which was secretly ceded to Spain. This situation had resulted in a hostile attitude toward England on the part of France and Spain, who looked for an occasion to compensate for the loss. Thus France and Spain had a common interest, and at the same time both kings belonged to the Bourbon dynasty and were closely related by blood; Louis XVI of France was a nephew of Charles III of Spain. When the Thirteen Colonies rose against England in 1775, the political opportunity arrived to get revenge. Very soon after the uprising, the colonists realized that independence was very difficult to achieve without the support of foreign powers. In June of 1776, they decided to send Benjamin Franklin and Thomas Jefferson to Paris to obtain the aid of France and Spain; both countries showed great sympathy for the American cause.[2]

3. From the economic point of view, the Seven Years War had been very expensive for England, and her debt at that time reached some 130 million pounds.[3] As a means to offset the debt, she decided to apply high taxes to the colonies; among the items taxed were tea, sugar, and other products. This measure was met with a violent reaction by the Thirteen Colonies, who declared: "No taxation without representation." Through several years, events related to taxes took place that pitted the colonists against the mother country. The death of some colonials in Boston came in April of 1775, and it was the spark that ignited a fire of rage among the colonists, who decided to declare their independence on July 4 of the following year. This declaration faced a critical situation: the colonies did not have an army of their own, or sufficient money, weapons, munitions, or materials. All these were in the hands of England.[4] The colonies could not export or import anything because the Atlantic seaports were blocked by the British fleet, and the left bank of the Mississippi River as well; the North and the South were also cut off by the British army. Soon, the colonists realized that their situation was desperate. This is the reason they decided to seek help from France and Spain.

4. Pressed by the development of those events, they began to use diplomatic activity. In 1776 Silas Deane, and later that year Benjamin Franklin and Arthur Lee, arrived in Paris seeking economic and military aid.[5] By helping the cause of the colonists, France pursued at the same time the weakening of British military power, to increase her trade and to

70

get back part of her lost territories in America. To do that, France was ready to sign an agreement with the colonies, but "counting on Spain to whom everything should be made known . . . since they are inseparable by reason of blood relationship and friendship."[6] Spain was also ready to help, but she had to provide this aid very discreetly, because of possible consequences for her own colonies in America. In her negotiations with the American delegates, she always maintained this philosophy: provide as much military and economic aid as possible, as long as it was kept secret. At the beginning of the struggle, Spain worried over the possibility that the Thirteen Colonies, aware of the difficulty of victory, might arrive at a peace treaty with England.[7] Were this to happen, the consequences for the Spanish territories in America would be devastating. It was with this reasoning that Spain supported the American cause, but she did not want an open confrontation with England. This explains the fact that Spain helped the Colonies secretly for three years, until — finally convinced of the strong determination of the revolutionaries to gain independence — she openly declared war on England. All diplomatic activity between Spain and America was conducted by the prime minister, the Count of Floridablanca, and the ambassador of Spain in Paris, the Count of Aranda.

In January of 1777, Franklin requested a meeting with the Spanish ambassador and presented him with a series of petitions from the Continental Congress for King Charles III.[8] Within a few days the king convened a meeting of all his counselors in which they amply discussed the situation of the Thirteen Colonies. The decision was the same: avoid direct confrontation with England and secretly help the Thirteen Colonies as much as possible.[9] At Franklin's request, Arthur Lee journeyed to Madrid to speak directly with the court about the promised Spanish aid. This action was considered imprudent because the English ambassador in Madrid was tuned into everything that took place in the Spanish court. The Spanish prime minister left Madrid and met with Lee in Burgos, explaining to him that aid would be sent to the colonists from both Spain and several points in America.[10] He also briefed him on the negotiations between Bernardo Gálvez, the governor of Louisiana, and Charles Lee, the representative of the colonies; he also, curiously, offered to send them several Irish officials who were working for Spain in the Spanish army. With this information, Lee returned to Paris satisfied with his efforts.[11] In September 1777, Franklin asked for considerable supplies of munitions and arms, and a loan of two million sterling pounds. He also requested permission to go to Madrid. The court did not consider such a dangerous voyage necessary. While representatives of the Thirteen Colonies were holding negotiations with Spanish officials in Europe, Spain had personnel in Philadelphia and New York. Among them were Juan de Miralles, Diego de Gardoqui, and Francisco Rendón, who reported on the status of the revolution and, at the same time, acted as liaisons for aid from Spain for the revolutionaries. Although all this diplomatic activity was carried out with utmost discretion and reservation, England was suspicious and, on several occasions, offered claims to Spain protesting this diplomatic activity, also complaining about the presence of American ships in its colonial ports.[12] Spain replied that they were English ships engaged in legitimate commercial activity and she saw no reason to deny them entry. The question of whether or not they were revolutionary was an area in which Spain would not interfere. This was the tenor of diplomatic activity until April of 1779.

5. At the same time that this significant diplomatic activity was going on, considerable economic aid was being granted. It was done in three ways: a) loans; b) material gifts, ammunition, clothes, medicine, etc.; and c) protection of the revolutionaries' ships while being refueled and stocked. This aid left Spain through her ambassador in Paris, also coming from Cuba and New Orleans. On June 9, 1776, the King of Spain had opened an account of a million

Turin pounds (some $5 million) to help the Thirteen Colonies.[13] This money bought 216 cannons, 209 gun cartridges, 27 mortars, 12,826 bomb shells, 51,134 bullets, 300,000 pounds of gunpowder, 30,000 rifles with bayonets, 30,000 army uniforms, 4,000 camp tents, and a large quantity of lead for the bullets.[14] This extraordinary cargo arrived in the Thirteen Colonies, and their representatives in Paris acknowledged receipt. General Charles Lee, through his messenger George Gibson, made an appeal from Virginia to the Governor of Louisiana on two occasions to maintain Fort Pitt. Their ammunition was almost depleted, and because of the English blockade, they were unable to receive supplies.[15] Lee promised that if they were victorious they would return Pensacola to Spain. Gálvez consulted with Spain, and the Spanish government promised to send aid via Havana; the government instructed Gálvez to provide all necessary aid, but with great caution. Gálvez sent Lee by way of the Mississippi River $74,000, 100 kegs of gunpowder, 300 rifles with bayonets, 108 bales of cotton, eight cases of medicine, and six cases of quinine.[16] In this emergency operation Gálvez worked in close collaboration with the famous patriot and businessman Oliver Pollock,[17] who together with Robert Morris is considered the leading financier of American independence. In 1778, Gálvez permitted James Willing to sell a cargo of varied products in New Orleans; the profits were channeled by Pollock to the desperate patriots. In the same year, Gálvez sent another shipment of arms, munitions, and medicine worth $100,000; this cargo arrived from Spain via Mexico and was transported on the steamer *Morris*. Gálvez also helped and gave his cooperation to General George Rogers Clark, sending him provisions and ammunition for the conquest of Vincennes, Kaskaskia, and Kohokia west of the Mississippi River. Don Diego Gardoqui was entrusted with $103,000 for the American cause, and an additional 34,000 blankets were involved in this donation. The National Historical Archives in Madrid has on file an invoice for: eight warships, copper and tin for cannons, 300,000 military uniforms, 1,000 rifles and cannons, 60,000 pairs of shoes, ten tons of gunpowder, 80,000 blankets, 80,000 shirts, 3,000 saddles . . . the amount of the invoice totals $7,730,000.[18]

6. Of equal importance to this aid was the protection afforded by Spain to the ships belonging to the Thirteen Colonies, because the ports of the Atlantic Coast were blockaded by the British fleet. American ships had free entry to the ports of Havana and New Orleans. There ships were repaired and cargoes of ammunition were loaded or unloaded to supply the colonies. Normally they would sail from Havana to New Orleans. Many of these ships bore the Spanish flag, and on some occasions these ships were "seized" on the high seas by the Spanish Navy and taken captive to New Orleans, in full view of the British. Once in New Orleans, they were set free to do their business. Gálvez used this strategy on many occasions.[19] It is important to mention that England controlled the left bank of the Mississippi River and that a large part of the supplies for the Thirteen Colonies arrived on the west side of the river. From the Ohio River in boats bearing the Spanish flag, other supplies arrived from territories beyond both of these rivers until they reached West Virginia and Pennsylvania. This was a vital supply line.

This scenario was played out from 1776 until 1779. Toward the middle of 1779, the war was at a decisive stage, and Spain was now convinced of the determination of the Thirteen Colonies to win their independence. Spain also realized that it was no longer possible to establish peace between the two sides. So she sent a communiqué) to England demanding a cease-fire and asking for recognition of American independence. England rejected the petition and warned Spain not to interfere. She made her own offer to Spain: In exchange for Spain's neutrality, England would return Gibraltar and Florida, and she would also grant fishing rights off Newfoundland.[20] Spain did not accept, and Charles III declared opened hostility by royal decree on June 22, 1779,[21] alleging as reason the harassment and seizure of Spanish ships by England.[22] Spain now began a multiple-level military operation. Her strategy was to keep the English forces occupied in many places so that they could not concentrate their pressure on the freedom fighters. In Europe, Spain put her fleet out to the Atlantic; General Antonio Barceló blocked Gibraltar. Tactics such as these prevented the British from sailing to America risking attack by the Spanish in Europe. In America, the Spanish attacked the Bahamas, while Admiral José Solano with twelve ships protected the coastline of the Thirteen Colonies. Captain General Luis Córdoba seized the English ships near the Azores and rerouted several others in the Cape of Espartel. José Gálvez, the uncle of Bernardo, attacked the British forces in Central America, and General Miguel Cajígal captured the Bahamas.[23]

In New Orleans, Bernardo Gálvez called all his military officers to a war council. Present were the following captains: Francisco Cruzat of St. Louis; Juan d'Elevillebeauvre from the South of Louisiana; Alejandro Caussot from Arkansas; Pedro Favrot, Hilario Esténoz, Joaquín Blanca, Manuel Nava and Martín Monzún. Also present were Colonels Manuel González, Esteban Miró, and Pedro Piernás, as well as Commander Jacinto Panis. Gálvez announced the state of war, explaining that Spain had united herself to the struggle for independence on the part of the Thirteen Colonies. The unanimous reaction was: "We offer you our lives and our fortunes if any remain. Gálvez organized his troops, marched against the English fort of Manchac in September and, after an arduous battle, captured it. Two weeks later, with an intense volley of cannon fire, he conquered the Fort of Baton Rouge, defended by general Alexander Dickson and five hundred English soldiers. In order to avoid more deaths, General Dickson surrendered the Fort of Pan Muré in Natchez.[24] With these victories, Gálvez totally controlled all navigation on the Mississippi River. In the upper part of Louisiana, Lieutenant Governor Leyba repelled an attack by the English General Sinclair. Shortly afterwards, a Spanish battalion under the command of Captain Eugenio Purré approached Lake Michigan and took the English fort of St. Joseph by surprise. Now Gálvez preferred to attack Mobile with eight hundred of his own men in twelve ships, plus a reinforcement of four ships sent from Havana; Gálvez entered the Bay of Mobile, defended by General Elias Durnford with twelve hundred soldiers. After twenty days of intense struggle on land and sea, Durnford surrendered Fort Charlotte and the city on February 12, 1780.

Pensacola was the main defense of the English army in the South. The city and its bay were defended by the imposing Fort Barrancas

Coloradas and Fort George with a combined army of ten thousand soldiers and several thousand Indian warriors, all under the command of General John Campbell. The valiant Gálvez began the siege of Pensacola. Under his command he had seven thousand men and forty-nine ships; four thousand men came from Cuba, two thousand from Mexico, and the other thousand from Puerto Rico, Santo Domingo, Venezuela, New Orleans, and Mobile, an army that was truly Hispanic. All eyes were on this young Spanish general. Gálvez launched a surprise attack on March 9, 1781, by invading the Bay of Pensacola. Despite the cannon fire from the two forts, his men were able to land during the night, dig trenches, and set up their own cannons. Now Gálvez was able to attack both by land and sea. He was seriously wounded by a piece of shrapnel but was able to take control and exhort his troops. In the midst of the cannon fire, a Spanish cannon hit its mark in the gunpowder storeroom of Fort Barrancas; an extraordinary explosion killed many English soldiers. Gálvez now launched an all-out land attack. With bayonets fixed, his army assaulted the fort and bombarded the English forces. General John Campbell, after a two-and-a-half-month resistance, surrendered the square, the city, and the bay to the Spanish general.[25] This was a decisive victory for the cause of the Thirteen Colonies because it put fourteen thousand soldiers of the English southern army out of action and into prison. The colonies now had this flank covered and were able to concentrate their attention on the central area.

Here, however, the revolutionary forces were going through a crucial situation because of their defeats suffered during the first six months of 1781. During 1780, monetary resources of the Thirteen Colonies had been depleted by the necessity of paying war debts. Without advising Spain, the Continental Congress drew on Minister John Jay's account the sum of one hundred thousand sterling pounds, to be paid by the Spanish government. Spain didn't like it but accepted the fact, asking however for two years to pay it. Again, at the beginning of 1781, Jay went to Madrid looking for more help. Payments totaling $100,000 were sent to Philadelphia through Diego Gardoqui's company. But this still wasn't enough because the army of General Rochambeau, by spring, did not have the resources to continue the war, so the General sent three vessels to Havana seeking urgent aid. The governor of Cuba, Miguel Cajigal, took up a collection and obtained one million two hundred thousand Turin pounds plus arms, clothes, and munitions; all of this was loaded on twelve ships and sent to Rochambeau. This aid financed the Battle of Yorktown on October 17, 1781, putting an end to the War for Independence. Even Father Junípero Serra asked all the Spanish of California to help with at least two dollars, and he begged each Indian to donate one dollar for the cause. All the monies collected by him were sent to Washington, thus contributing to the triumph of the Thirteen Colonies.[26]

7. All of this information is well documented in the archives of both the United States and Spain. The detailed information that we have presented shows not only the active collaboration of Spain in the struggle for independence by the American Colonies, but also that this collaboration was substantial and vital. If I may, I would like to add that included under the banner of Spain were her American colonies, because many of the people who were active in the struggle were born in Latin America. Many of the resources given to the Thirteen Colonies were brought from these countries through taxes and hard work. It was offered in the name of Spain, but certainly Spain offered it also in the name of all those lands that call her their "Mother Country." George Washington understood the tremendous contributions of Spain when he wrote to a friend on September 3, 1779: "I'm happy to tell you that Spain has finally taken decisive action . . . let's hope that this union with the House of Bourbon will soon allow the establishment of independence in America."[27] And he was right.

It is important now that the American people be aware of this contribution.

Perhaps there is no better way to close this chapter than to quote a few words of the famous Archbishop Fulton J. Sheen:

"Spain was a friend of ours from the very beginning. Even before the Declaration of Independence was signed, Spain admitted all our ships into her ports. Great Britain protested, said they were rebel ships. Portugal was not allowing our ships to enter into her harbors. Spain said that our ships would be given free admittance. Then the King of Spain gave us five million dollars to aid in the cause of our freedom. And the five million dollars was a lot of money in those days. . . . Spain told General Charles Lee that she would give him a blank check and he could draw on it for all expenses necessary for the Revolutionary War. . . . Then, in 1778, more money was given, still more munitions, and in 1779, Spain asked Great Britain to cease hostilities and to recognize the independence of the American colonies. Great Britain refused. . . . On June 22, 1779, Spain broke diplomatic relations with Great Britain for the sake of America. And then, in 1780, Spain began sending over soldiers who took Pensacola — thus getting back Florida — and captured Mobile. Then in the following year, as our soldiers were very much occupied in the North and there was danger of a defeat in the South, twelve ships came over from Cuba. Finally came the Battle of Yorktown, and Spain had made its contribution to the freedom of the United States. This is an unwritten bit, unknown bit for the most part, of our American history, and it is fitting that on this day, as Americans, when we think of our heritage and those that have been compounded into our greatness, that we acknowledge Spain."[28]

Perpendicular: Christopher Columbus's first landing in the New World on October 12, 1492, as it was envisioned by Currier and Ives (courtesy of the Library of Congress)

VI

'Hispanidad' in the United States

The events which followed the invasion of Spain by Napoleon in 1808 had tremendous repercussions in her territories of the Americas. In the fifteen years that followed, Spain lost sovereignty over an entire continent that had taken more than three hundred years to conquer and colonize. In 1803 Spain returned Louisiana to France. In turn, France sold it to the United States in the same year. In 1819 Spain ceded Florida to the United States.[1] Two years later, after Mexico gained its independence, it inherited from Spain the territories of Texas, New Mexico, Arizona, California, parts of Oklahoma, Colorado, Utah, and Nevada. But Mexico was just beginning its existence as an independent nation and naturally was neither consolidated nor organized. The tendencies and divisions which had prevailed during the struggle for independence perpetuated a condition of internal and political instability. This situation brought about the inability to adequately organize and control the territories north of the Rio Grande. When Mexico tried to maintain the abolition of slavery, Texas declared itself independent in 1836. In the following decade, Mexico lost all of its other territories. In 1848, the United States and Mexico signed the Treaty of Guadalupe-Hidalgo, by which Mexico ceded the entire territory in exchange for a nominal sum of money and the meeting of three conditions: that the United States respect the land rights of the inhabitants of the region, their language, and their Catholic religion.[2]

1. The situation for inhabitants of the annexed territories now made a complete turn. A wave of persons of European descent came from the East, hungry for land. Also, with the arrival of the migrations in the first half of the nineteenth century and prior to the opening of the frontier to new lands, a veritable avalanche of new settlers descended.[3] More than eight thousand Anglos had arrived in California by 1848, goaded by "Gold Fever." In little more than two decades, they had taken possession of practically all the properties of that enormous region. This occupation

simultaneously brought the organization of political life, elections, and appointment of legal authorities. The legislative structures implemented were those of the Thirteen Colonies, and the educational, economic, and social institutions established were those most familiar to them. In less than thirty years they had totally changed the physiognomy of the region. The three conditions — to preserve property, language, and religion — were completely ignored. The original inhabitants of these regions of the South and the West faced drastic changes. They found themselves strangers in their own land, without property, under authorities of a different culture with a strange language and a faith not their own.[4]

2. The new political situation in the former territories of Spain had serious repercussions for the settlers of the region. During the time these territories were governed by Mexico, certain governors and colonists arrived who primarily sought personal enrichment. These men granted themselves great estates of land. All state aid to the missions was halted, and they were subjected to secularization.[5] By virtue of this process, missions were to cease their existence. Their inhabitants were to form a town or municipality, and the missionaries were to change the structure of the mission into a regular parish, and at times even relinquish it to secular clergy. As a consequence of these measures, many abuses occurred: influential people appropriated sizable portions of mission lands or sold them; they sought to exploit the Christianized Indians, and these, governed now by civil authorities, were subjected to taxes. Many missionaries were replaced by secular priests with consequent protests from the Indians. Between 1821 and 1848, a good portion of the missions disappeared. Many of the natives returned to their tribes. Fields that had once flourished with crops and cattle remained semi-abandoned because of a lack of manpower. Many of the mission buildings, now lacking state funds, suffered extensive deterioration while equipment and supplies disappeared. These were the effects of secularization, and this was the situation at the time when the whole region passed over to the United States.[6]

3. With the change in sovereignty over the territories, there was also a change in the philosophy of its colonization. During the presence of Spain in North America, a particular political policy was followed that centered on the person of the native American. All human and religious activity revolved around him: to place him in settlements near the mission; to advance him in culture and customs, evangelizing him to make him part of the Church; to make use of his work in exploiting natural riches, and counting on him to maintain Spanish sovereignty in territories which

other European powers sought to settle. Centering on the native was difficult and costly. At the same time, it constituted a slow and prolonged process to achieve the objective of colonization and evangelization.[7] It is clear, then, that the philosophy of Spain since the time of the Catholic king and queen had native Americans as its primary objective, primarily because that was the Spanish conviction and secondarily because Spain needed them. It must be taken into account that Spain had a relatively small number of inhabitants at the time, yet needed to maintain sovereignty in Europe and vast dominions beyond the sea. Spain had to drain herself in order to press forward with the conquest and colonization of America, even though, comparatively speaking, few Spaniards took part in that colossal task in America. Extraordinarily small numbers participated in the North American territories, simply because Spain had few people to send to these lands. On the other hand, Spain did not permit the immigration of other European people to its colonies. Therefore, Spain needed the natives in order to achieve her ends, consequently never espousing the philosophy of ignoring them or eliminating them. This does not mean that there were no abuses or excesses.

The colonists that arrived in the southern and western territories from the Thirteen States after 1848 had a very different philosophy. Their principal idea centered on the possession and exploitation of land. For them, the natives were mostly an obstacle, or at best merely something secondary. The policy they followed was to evict the Indians from the land or concentrate them on reservations. Because of the thousands of immigrants from Europe to the Atlantic Coast, skilled in agriculture and ranching or expert in commerce and other trades, they soon seized, organized, and developed the region. On the other hand, they were motivated by a more individualistic view of life, less controlled by intervention of the state in the acquisition and management of properties.[8]

4. Results of these political and demographic changes were several. One of them was that the majority of the previous political and civil leaders fled to Mexico.[9] At Spain's, and later Mexico's, exit from the region, many religious leaders also departed, leaving few to attend to the Hispanic Christians who remained. Part of the civil population, afraid over the prospect of war and the uncertainties of the future, also opted to flee south of the Rio Grande. A portion of the Christian Indians returned to their original tribes and later were sent to reservations. Those that remained found themselves without any leadership, at the mercy of the new colonists who now controlled the life of the region. Their situation was one of almost complete submission, submerged in a culture totally

different from their own. It was only within their own families that they continued living the values of their faith, their language, and their traditions. Part of the Hispanic culture, however, has survived. As Bolton says: "In legal matters, the principles related to mines, water rights over streams, and property rights of women, just to mention a few, have been retained from the Spanish regime of the Southwest."[10] Among other things that the colonists adopted were foods like tamales and tortillas, the "sombrero," and Hispanic women. Many of the colonists took Hispanic women as wives. The Anglo colonists preferred them because, as W. Beck mentions: "They are much prettier than those of their own class in America."[11]

The second half of the nineteenth century was a period of adjustment to the new situation by the Hispanics remaining in those territories of the United States. In spite of the fact that the Rio Grande now served as a political boundary between Mexico and the United States, communication and the movement of people back and forth remained open. The population on both sides of the river had people and interests on each side that united them down the entire length of the Rio Grande. That is why, at the beginning of the present century when the Mexican revolution broke out, Mexicans naturally began to flow north looking for greater security.[12] This flow continued in the following decades of political instability and religious persecution created by Mexican President Plutarco Elías Calles. In the third decade, almost half a million Mexicans crossed the border. These migrations were like injections reviving the Hispanic community north of the Rio Grande. Among the new immigrants were many highly skilled people trained in various professions.[13]

5. Another factor with a great impact on the life of the Hispanic community was the participation of many of its young men in World War I. At the end of this conflict, these young men returned to their homes with a new mentality and a new restlessness. Taking advantage of veterans' benefits of this war, many acquired skills, found new employment, or began higher-level studies. It was then that community organizations began demanding the rights and defending the values of the Hispanic community. However, a deplorable act occurred at the end of the 1930s. It was due to the effects of the Great Depression that many Hispanics with legal residence were expelled from the country. It is believed that about two hundred thousand went south of the border. But during these first decades, as a consequence of the Spanish-American War, small groups of Puerto Ricans and Cubans settled principally in New York City. Immigrants from Spain also arrived and established themselves

mostly in New York and Newark, New Jersey. These were able to count on two churches in each city for their religious needs.[14]

World War II also had a singular impact on the Hispanic community. In the South and West, many young men enlisted in the army. Consequently, there was a great shortage of labor in the fields and factories. Once again a flow across the border began, leading to the farm-labor movement.[15] It had been thought that this would be a temporary situation and that after the war young people would return to their old jobs. This, however, did not happen; many preferred other types of work. Keeping this in perspective and motivated by the cheap labor they provided, employers continued to depend upon Hispanics. Something similar happened in Puerto Rico. A great number of young men who had been in the army decided to transfer to the mainland at the end of the war. Thus began a new current: before 1945, there were 60,000 Puerto Ricans residing in New York City;[16] by 1950 that number had gone up 350,000, and today the total reaches some 2,500,000 residents on the mainland.[17]

The Cuban exodus began in 1960 with the establishment of a Marxist regime on the island under Fidel Castro. In the following years, approximately 1,000,000 Cubans abandoned the island, with a majority finding refuge in the United States, primarily in Florida and New Jersey.[18] In 1980, another 150,000 left Cuba by the port at Mariel and arrived in Miami. Another great flow of Hispanic immigrants occurred during the 1970s with the arrival of refugees from the Dominican Republic. It is calculated that today there are more than 500,000 in the New York-New Jersey metropolitan area. Also in that same decade a good number of Hispanics arrived from South America, principally from Colombia, Ecuador, and Peru. The turbulent political situation in Central America caused the arrival of numerous people from El Salvador, Nicaragua, Honduras, and Guatemala. All these immigration movements added to an accelerated growth pattern, due to a high birthrate index as compared to the rest of the population. This made the Hispanic community in the United States visible and increasingly important.

6. Relationships between the United States and Latin American countries during the second half of the nineteenth century and part of the present one were influenced by the attitude of "Manifest Destiny" prevalent in this country. This was considered by many to mean a new chosen people fated to Americanize the entire continent. The Monroe Doctrine seemed an expression of this movement: "America for the Americans," with the exclusion of any interference by European countries in the affairs of the New World. This was its thesis. Various Pan-

American conferences condemned that ideology, and frequent military interventions confirmed its existence.[19] An element that provided great opposition and resistance to American annexation tendencies was Catholicism. Rightly, Theodore Roosevelt said after visiting Argentina: "While these countries remain Catholic we will not be able to dominate them." These relationships had their negative side but also had positive aspects, such as mediating peace on the occasion of conflicts between different countries, or the building of the Panama Canal. The Spanish-American War of 1898 began a change in the situation of Cuba, which was able to gain its independence a few years later. It also changed Puerto Rico into a country tied to the United States and maintaining a limited sovereignty, with its own definitive political situation left pending.

7. In the second half of the nineteenth century, the religious situation of Hispanics in the southern United States was truly lamentable. Various factors contributed to this. Among them were the disappearance of the missions and of a large number of the missionaries, the presence of new political and religious structures that ignored or paid little attention to Hispanics, and the lack of services in their language. During this time, the Catholic Church established various dioceses in Texas, New Mexico, and California. The clergy that arrived in the region did not speak Spanish and dedicated themselves to caring for the ten percent or so of the Catholic population that did not speak Spanish. Meanwhile, the remaining ninety percent of Catholics who were Hispanic were served by an insignificant number of priests. It is said that in 1850 only two Spanish-speaking priests served the Hispanic community in the entire state of Texas. Similar things occurred in the other southern states. In the midst of their poverty and abandonment, Hispanics maintained their Catholicism within strong family structures.[20] With the beginning of this century, and with greater consolidation of the Church in southern states, the situation greatly improved; with the new waves of immigrants came a good number of priests. Everywhere the number of churches or chapels that serviced Hispanics grew. Religious congregations of men and women arrived to serve the people; civic and religious organizations were formed, and some Spanish-language newspapers and magazines began to appear. For example, there were eighty-three thousand Catholics in the diocese of Corpus Christi; seventy thousand of which were Hispanics. The Diocese of El Paso found itself in a similar situation a little later. By 1930, the Church in California had reached an extraordinary development. By then, the Dioceses of Sacramento, San Francisco, Monterey, Fresno, and Los Angeles had been established. San Diego followed a little later. All of

these had large numbers of parishes, schools, and charitable agencies.[21] The presence of Hispanic clergy was very limited, and even though the Hispanic Catholic presence was considerable, it had little representation and influence in ecclesiastical affairs.

We have already mentioned the arrival of a great number of people from Puerto Rico, Cuba, the Dominican Republic, and Central and South America in the eastern half of the United States. It would be worthwhile to add that the Church has been responding to them and has been of service. It has invited Religious congregations of both men and women, has trained non-Hispanic priests in Spanish language and culture, and has provided social services. It is true that this care has not been the same in all of the dioceses and has been insufficient in all of them, considering the greater number of Hispanic Catholics in some areas. From 1970 to the present, twenty-one bishops of Hispanic origin have been named. A National Commission of Bishops for Hispanic Affairs has been created and headquartered in Washington.[22] Five Hispanic regional enters now exist to coordinate activities and train leaders, and 125 dioceses have established special offices for the pastoral care of Hispanic Catholics.[23] In the past eighteen years, three Encuentros Hispanos on the national level have taken place in Washington, D.C., preceded by extensive consultations to discuss problems, decide on priorities, and formulate a pastoral plan of action to better attend to the needs of the Hispanic community.[24] Serious problems remain that will have to be resolved in the immediate future by the Church if she is to keep the Hispanic Catholic community within the faith. Among the problems are: the lack of sensitivity on the part of many priests in the parish to welcome and serve Hispanics according to their language and culture; aggressive proselytizing by diverse sects; the shortage of Hispanic and Spanish-speaking priests, and the invasion of materialism.

8. A description of the Hispanic community in broad strokes at present would be as follows: From a demographic point of view, according to the latest data from the Office of the Census obtained in 1989, Hispanics number about twenty-three million people.[25] This is a conservative estimate which does not include those not tabulated in the census, undocumented persons, or the inhabitants of Puerto Rico. It would not be an exaggeration to say that the real number is probably closer to twenty-five million or, in other words, ten percent of the population of this country. It is a young community whose median age is twenty-five years and which has grown over the past ten years by thirty-nine percent.[26] This information indicates that it is a large community, quite young, which

grows rapidly because of high birthrates and steady immigration.[27]

As far as their economic situation is concerned, the latest data show that the median income of Hispanic families is $21,800, substantially lower than non-Hispanic families at $31,200.[28] However, because of its formidable size, the net buying power of the Hispanic community is estimated at around $173 billion, which if well handled gives this community a tremendous economic and social "clout."

Gradually, Hispanic companies of considerable size and net sales volume can be seen springing up in places like New York, Miami, Los Angeles, and Chicago. Enterprises like Goya Foods Company had sales in 1989 well over three hundred million dollars. A middle-class, entrepreneurial, commercial, and financial force can be seen arising slowly but surely. The net volume of sales of the principal five hundred Hispanic businesses is around ten billion dollars. In the Miami area alone, there are twenty thousand small to large Hispanic-owned businesses; the same can be said of Los Angeles, Chicago, New York, northern New Jersey, San Antonio, El Paso, and other cities. Of the total number of Hispanics, thirty-five per cent are professionals or office workers, fifty per cent are commercial or industrial workers, and nine per cent are agricultural laborers. It is also important to note that a high percentage of Hispanics, especially those who arrived in this country in the last twenty-five years, financially assist their families, which still reside in their countries of origin. For many countries, this represents the number-one avenue of foreign exchange.

The academic level which the Hispanic community enjoys in relation to the rest of the country is inferior, although it is improving. In 1988, sixty percent of Hispanic young people completed their high school studies, while ten percent graduated from universities.[29] The proportion of those who dropped out of high school is about thirty-one percent, a figure that is still too high. While there is still a need for improvement in educational aspects, a progressively larger presence of Hispanics can be detected as lawyers, doctors, accountants, professors, movie stars, reporters for major television networks, and other professionals. These are of Puerto Rican, Mexican, Cuban, and Spanish descent, as well as from other countries of Central and South America, and the Caribbean " which is surely a sign of hope.

The Hispanic community in the United States does not as yet have a political representation proportionate to its size. Actually, those of Hispanic origin are ten congressmen, 129 state legislators, 351 county officials, 23 mayors of major cities, and four members of the President's Cabinet. The total number of Hispanic elected officials is 3,660 in the nation. Given its strategic geographical distribution, if the Hispanic community were to be united in presidential or state elections, it could wield the decisive factor in the election of the President of the United States or a state's governor. The highest percentage of Hispanics is found in California (34%), Texas (21%), New York (10%), Florida (8%), Illinois (4%), and New Jersey (3%).[30] The sum total of electoral votes of the seven states adds up to approximately two-thirds of the electoral votes in a presidential election. In each of these states, the voting is often very divided among the dominant parties. If the Hispanic vote could be united, it could be, in certain cases, the decisive factor in the final result. But the Hispanic community has not become aware as yet of the power of its vote. It does not unite itself, and low numbers of Hispanics turn out to vote.

As far as the social situation is concerned, we see that the Hispanic community is one of great diversity, with a lower standard of living when compared with the rest of the country, and with socio-economic problems that still need to be resolved. A good number of the Hispanics who live in the South and Southwest are the descendants of those Spaniards who came to New Spain and mixed with the natives to form a mestizo people. This group settled and have remained there since the time of Oñate (1598) in New Mexico. They are the first settlers of European blood in the United States; the first pioneers of "Hispanidad." Others came with Martín de Alarcón (1718) to Texas, or from Canary Islands settlers who founded New Iberia (1778) in Louisiana. Others came in massive immigrations at the beginning of this century. Some arrived in the last fifty years, and some are still arriving. They come from all the Hispanic countries and in numbers so vast that it can well be said that the United States is the country in which "Hispanidad" has its most evident representation. Also it is the country that is fifth in line in the number of its Spanish-speaking population. A high percentage of Hispanics are concentrated in the large cities. They live in predominantly Hispanic neighborhoods, their livelihood in many cases being less than adequate and their level of unemployment some four points higher than the rest of the population. This forces many to turn to welfare.[31] A relatively high percentage of families are headed by women (twenty-three percent), and their condition in relation with the issue of health is also below the national level.[32] In spite of this somewhat somber situation, which often goes hand in hand with that of recent immigrants, statistics indicate a steady progress in all areas. At the same time we see the emergence of a middle class which is slowly leveling off with that of the rest of the nation.

The Spanish-language media play a very important role in the life of the Hispanic people. The business world has realized that Hispanics constitute a great source of income, since a large number of their customers speak Spanish and have a tremendous buying power. These factors have brought a marshaling of the mass media.[33] At present there are three television networks that broadcast in Spanish and can be seen throughout the country through numerous affiliated stations. There are local stations founded for cultural or religious purposes, and also cable stations that broadcast some programs in Spanish. Radio stations that offer total Spanish-language broadcasting number around 140. Some 450 stations which normally broadcast in English offer programming in Spanish from one to several hours a week: news, music, soap operas, and sports are the major part of their content. Another means of communication in Spanish is the press. Although generally it is said that Hispanics read little and show greater inclination for television and radio, the great proliferation of daily, weekly, and monthly newspapers and magazines indicate that they are well received. There are eleven daily Spanish-language newspapers and 165 weeklies in existence in the nation. There are also numerous biweeklies and monthlies, possibly more than 300. A good part of these are maintained by the advertisements of businesses in the area where the papers are distributed.[34] The market for books depends almost exclusively on publishing houses in Spain, Mexico, and Argentina. These communications media help the Hispanic people to maintain their identity, preserve their own language, and maintain ties to their country of origin.

We have said previously that the number of Hispanics in the United States is close to twenty-five million. Considering that eighty-five percent of them are Catholic, we realize that thirty-eight percent of North American Catholics are of Hispanic origin. This is an important statistic to keep in mind, because the rate of growth due to high birthrates and immigration projections indicate that in the next twenty years half of the Catholic Church in the United States will be comprised of people of Hispanic origin. Faced with this reality, the American Bishops said, in a pastoral letter directed to the nation's Catholics in 1983, that the Hispanic community is a "blessing and an opportunity."[35] A blessing because they hold human and Christian values which enrich society and the Church; and an opportunity because their vast numbers constitute a considerable force and presence for the future. Naturally, obstacles exist that need to be overcome, like the shortage of priestly vocations from the community and the integration of these into the existing institutional structures. There are situations that need to be accelerated, such as an increase in Hispanic representation in positions and institutions, or the naming of more diocesan bishops, pastors, pastoral agents in diocesan offices, and lay leaders in parish councils. According to a recent survey, perhaps five per-cent of Hispanics profess no religion at all, and another ten percent are distributed among a variety of different denominations and fundamen-talist sects. The survey, taken by the Gallup Company, indicates that ninety-five per cent of the Hispanic community are believers, and that for a large number of them religion plays a very important role in their lives.[36]

Francisco Vázquez de Coronado (foreground) explored seven states' territory in search of the "seven cities of Cíbola," discovering wonders like the Grand Canyon of the Colorado instead of riches (painting by Albert Turner Reid)

VII

Great Figures of Hispanic Origin in the United States

A considerable number of prestigious persons of Hispanic origin have made notable contributions to the formation and enrichment of this country, but they are not known by the American people. In a succinct way, we present here just a few of them.

JUAN PONCE DE LEÓN (1460-1521). He was born in Valladolid, Spain. As an officer in the army of the Catholic king and queen, he fought several wars. He embarked with Columbus on his second voyage and landed in Puerto Rico. In 1508, he took an expedition there and was appointed governor. He prepared another expedition and arrived in Florida in 1513 with the title of *Adelantado*. He returned again in 1521 to establish a settlement with two hundred fifty colonists. During his stay, he was seriously wounded by an arrow in a fight with the natives. He died in Cuba and was buried in the Cathedral of San Juan, Puerto Rico.

HERNANDO DE SOTO (1496-1542). His birthplace was Badajoz, Spain. In 1514 he went to Central America and then to Peru; there he took the Inca King Atahualpa prisoner, and eventually they became friends. He returned to Spain, sold all his possessions, and invested the proceeds in preparation for an expedition to Florida, where he arrived in 1539. For four years he explored Florida, Georgia, both Carolinas, Mississippi, Tennessee, and Arkansas, constantly showing great courage and fearlessness. In 1542, he died on the banks of the Mississippi River. His body was laid at the bottom of the river by his soldiers.

FATHER JUAN PADILLA, O.F.M. (1500-1542). He was born in Málaga, Spain, and became a Franciscan. Father Padilla arrived in New Mexico in 1540 with the expedition led by Coronado. He evangelized the Tiguex and Pueblo Indians, continuing his task in Quivira (Kansas), and although the Coronado expedition returned to Mexico, he decided to remain. For several months he labored with the natives of Kansas without protection until one day, because of enmity between two rival tribes, Father Padilla was riddled with arrows while on his knees praying for his would-be executioners. He is the first martyr in North America.

FRANCISCO VAZQUEZ DE CORONADO (1510-1565). Born in Salamanca, Spain, he was appointed governor of New Galicia, Mexico. In 1539 he organized a large expedition and explored New Mexico, Arizona, Colorado, Utah, Kansas, Texas, and Arkansas. Through his four years of exploration he made noteworthy discoveries, among them the Grand Canyon of Colorado. While riding a horse, he suffered a fall. He was returned to Mexico, where he eventually died.

ALVAR NUÑEZ CABEZA DE VACA (1507-1559). Born in Extremadura, Spain, he was appointed recording secretary of Pánfilo de Narváez's expedition to Florida. After enduring a hurricane and a shipwreck, he went by foot across Texas, part of New Mexico, and Mexico, accomplishing an extraordinary odyssey " he became a slave, merchant, physician, magician, teacher, and reporter. After his adventure, he wrote the books *Naufragios* (Shipwrecks) and *Comentarios* (Commentaries). He returned to Spain and was appointed governor of Rio de La Plata (Argentina), and later judge of the High Court.

PEDRO MENÉNDEZ DE AVILÉS (1519-1574). Born in Asturias, Spain, he was a seaman who from his youth fought pirates on the Spanish coasts. Appointed *Adelantado* of Florida by Philip II, he arrived here heading a large expedition funded by his personal fortune. He established St. Augustine, the first city in the United States. He also built forts along Florida's coasts and established missions and settlements in Georgia and Carolina, going as far north as Virginia. He returned to Spain to prepare the Spanish Armada, but he died shortly after the outset.

JUAN DE OÑATE (1549-1624). Born in Mexico, he was the son of New Galicia's governor. He was appointed governor of New Mexico, where he arrived in 1598 at the head of a large expedition of soldiers and settlers. He established several towns, among them San Juan, the first in New Mexico. He subdued several of the Indian tribes, founded missions, and began agriculture and cattle raising in the region. He finally returned to Mexico, where he died.

FATHER EUSEBIO KINO, S.J. (1644-1711). A Jesuit missionary born in Trent, he went to Mexico and later to the lands of Arizona, where he did extraordinary work on behalf of the Indian population in spite of difficult circumstances. He walked great distances, founding towns and missions. It is said that he baptized some forty thousand indigenous people. In 1681 he wrote a book titled *Astronomic Exposition of a Comet*. He died in Mexico.

JOSÉ AZLOR DE VIRTO, MARQUIS OF AGUAYO (1677-1734). Born in Spain, late in life he went to Mexico. After distinguished service in the northern provinces, he was appointed governor of Texas and Coahuila. He was noteworthy for his campaign in Texas, from the Rio Grande to the Mississippi River, where he established settlements, missions, and forts. Among them were Los Adais, Louisiana, and La Bahía, Texas. Once he finished his term as governor in 1722, he returned to Mexico.

JUAN BAUTISTA DE ANZA (1734-1788). A forceful captain and explorer, he was born in Tubac, Arizona. Succeeding his father, he was appointed commander of the Fort of Tubac. He found a land passage to connect Arizona with California, where in 1776 he arrived and established the city of San Francisco with its Mission Dolores. Upon his return he was appointed governor of New Mexico, which at that time formed one province with Arizona and Colorado. There he defeated the army of the Comanche led by Chief Greenhorn, and in 1786 he signed a treaty with them at Santa Fe, New Mexico.

FATHER JUNÍPERO SERRA, O.F.M. (1713-1784). A Franciscan missionary born in Mallorca, Spain, he arrived in San Diego in 1769 and began his work establishing missions along the coast of California. He was a tireless and persevering man in spite of poor health. He gave himself totally to the conversion of the natives. After having established nine missions by himself, he died at Carmel, California. He was beatified in 1989 by Pope John Paul II. His statue is kept in the Rotunda of Illustrious Persons at the Capitol in Washington, D.C.

ALEJANDRO O'REILLY (1725-1794). Born in Ireland, he became a citizen of Spain, where he was educated. He pursued a military career and achieved great success in campaigns of Europe. He was appointed governor of Louisiana in 1769, reorganized the region, and declared Spanish as the official language. He also promoted commerce from New Orleans along the Mississippi and Missouri Rivers, and he brought peace to the area using his great leadership qualities. He returned to Spain and was honored with the title of count.

JUAN DE LA BODEGA Y QUADRA (1743-1794). Explorer and sailor born in Lima, Peru, he was educated in the Navy School of Spain, and headed an important exploration along the North Pacific Coast reaching Alaska. His goal was to find a northern passage from the Pacific to the Atlantic. In 1775 he arrived at Bucarelli Bay on the 55° latitude aboard his schooner *Sonora*. He also headed several other explorations. In 1792, when he arrived in Nutka Bay on what is now Vancouver Island, he gave it his name, "Isla de Quadra." He is now memorialized at Bodega Bay, California.

BERNARDO DE GÁLVEZ (1746-1794). Born in Málaga, Spain, he made here a brilliant military career and, being a colonel, was appointed governor of Louisiana. He actively and decisively participated in the independence of the United States, providing arms and provisions. He defeated the southern flank of the British army in Mississippi, at Mobile, Alabama, and Pensacola, Florida. In recognition of his courage, the king of Spain gave him the title of count, appointing him governor of Cuba and later Viceroy of Mexico, where he died when he was only forty-eight years old. This hero of the American Revolution is memorialized only at Galveston (Gálvez-town), Texas.

DAVID G. FARRAGUT (1801-1870). Born in Tennessee, he was the son of Jorge Farragut, a Spaniard from Menorca, Spain. He made his career in the Navy and during the Civil War he became famous for his victories at New Orleans and Mobile, defeating Confederate forces. Because of his valor he was named admiral, the first in the United States. In command of a fleet, he arrived in 1867 for a visit to Menorca, where he was acclaimed as a hero by his countrymen. He died in Portsmouth, New Hampshire.

FATHER FELIX VARELA (1802-1877). Born in Cuba, he was later ordained a priest, taught philosophy at the University of Havana, and was appointed representative of Cuba at the Parliament in Madrid. He advocated for the independence of Cuba and was exiled to New York. There Father Varela continued his literary career, contributed to several newspapers and magazines, and was appointed Vicar General of the Archdiocese of New York. He died in St. Augustine, Florida.

MARIANO VALLEJO (1808-1890). Born in Monterey, California, he became a member of the territorial legislature and was sent to prison in the "Bear Flag Revolt," which declared California a republic before it was ceded to the U.S. In 1849 he was one of the Californians elected to the state constitutional convention, and soon after that he was elected a state senator. At the end of his life he wrote a book on the history of California.

LUIS MUÑOZ RIVERA (1859-1916). Born in Barranquitas, Puerto Rico, he signed the "Autonomy of the Island" in 1896. He later became a resident of New York City, where he founded the newspaper *Puerto Rico Herald*. After his return to Puerto Rico he formed a political party called "Partido de la Unión de Puerto Rico" (Union Party of Puerto Rico). He was appointed resident commissioner at Washington, D.C., and helped pass the "Jones Act," which gave American citizenship to the Puerto Rican people.

GEORGE SÁNCHEZ (1906-1972). Born in Albuquerque, New Mexico, he graduated from Berkeley University and became one of the finest educators of his time. He promoted bilingual education and was a prolific writer of hundreds of articles in newspapers and magazines. He is the author of the book *The Forgotten People* (1940).

JOSEPH MONTOYA (1915-1978). Born in New Mexico, he was elected to the U.S. House of Representatives, and later to the Senate. He fought for the interests of Hispanic people, at the same time promoting their unity. During his terms of office he initiated and supported programs to help the poor, workers, elderly, native Indians, and Hispanics.

This is just a short list of significant people of Hispanic origin in the United States. An analysis of the life and contribution of these individuals to the history of this nation allows any objective observer to draw the conclusion that they are figures of no lower category than John Smith, Walter Raleigh, Henry Hudson, Daniel Boone, General von Steuben, General Rochambeau, or General Pulaski. They are figures who have made substantive work, worthy to be remembered in the historical annals of this country.

PART TWO

Spanish Roots of America —
Chronicle and Chronology

Perpendicular: Caravels of Columbus's first fleet, Niña, Pinta, and Santa María, sail in replicas built by the Spanish navy (PBS photo)

1492-1500:
Discovery and Encounter

Sent by Ferdinand and Isabella, the Catholic king and queen of Spain, Columbus arrives in America, and the first contacts take place.

1492

1. In this year, Christopher Columbus arrives in America. Columbus, who was probably born in Genoa, thinks that by leaving Spain for the West he can reach the East. His idea is not accepted in France or Portugal, nor at Salamanca University. The Catholic king and queen of Spain, Ferdinand and Isabella, urged by the Franciscans from the Monastery of La Rábida, finally accept Columbus's idea and give him three caravels: the *Santa María*, the *Pinta*, and the *Niña*. They will be commanded by Columbus, Martín Alonso Pinzón, and Vicente Yáñez Pinzón. A crew of 120 men, among them expert sailors and artisans, form the expedition. The king and queen sponsor and absorb the cost of the project. Once everything is ready, the men go to confession, receive Holy Communion, pray, and say good-bye to their families. On August 3, they leave for the Canary Islands, and from there to the unknown. During the trip, they suffer, become discouraged, and pray every day.

Early in the morning of October 12, Rodrigo de Triana shouts, "Land!" All go ashore, and Columbus, his knee on the ground, holding the flag of Castile and León in his left hand and his sword in his right, plants the cross. Before the natives, he takes possession of the place in the name of Spain and gives the name of San Salvador to the island the natives call *Guanahani* (Bahamas). For three months they sail through the Caribbean Islands and visit Hispaniola (Dominican Republic/Haiti), where they find the cacao tree, and Cuba, where they find the tobacco plant. On Christmas Day, the caravel *Santa María* runs aground in the North of Hispaniola, and with its wood they build the "*Navidad*" Fort. Columbus leaves some of his men there, and with the *Pinta* and the *Niña*, taking with him six indigenous people, some birds, and various products of the land, he begins his journey back on January 16. He now takes the northern route toward the Azores Islands. Taking advantage of the winds that blow from the West, he arrives in Spain eight months after his departure.

2. According to a report, there are presently some 80,000 descendants of Columbus and of the sailors who joined him on his First Voyage, there are 3,500 in the United States and 50,000 in Puerto Rico and the Caribbean.

1493

1. Columbus returns to Spain in March and reports the results of his trip to the Catholic king and queen, who receive him in Barcelona with demonstrations of great pomp and joy.

2. Ferdinand and Isabella order a second voyage headed by Columbus, toward which the Duke of Medinasidonia gives five million maravedis. It is composed of three galleons, each one weighing one hundred tons, and fourteen caravels with fifteen hundred men. Among the men is Boabdil, the last Moorish king from Granada, whom they leave on the Coast of Africa by orders of the king and queen of Spain. Twelve missionaries also embark: Father Bernardo Boil (Benedictine); Juan Pérez, Rodrigo Pérez, Juan de la Deule, Juan Tisin, and Father Alonso (Franciscans), Juan Infante and Juan Solórzano (Mercedarians); Father Ramos (Trinitarian), Ramon Pane (Jeromite); Pedro de Armas, Father Jorge, and the Abbot of Lucena. Also transported are animals, plants, seeds, and tools. They arrive at the Virgin Islands, a name given by Columbus in honor of St. Ursula and the Eleven (or Eleven Thousand) Virgins. On September 19, they arrive in Puerto Rico, and Columbus exclaims: "We arrived at a beautiful large island called 'Boriquén.' " They continue toward Hispaniola, where they find that the Navidad Fort has been burned, and they remain there for two months. From here, Columbus sends the sick back on twelve vessels.

3. By the Papal Bull *Inter Coetera*, dated May 4, Pope Alexander VI sanctions an agreement between Spain and Portugal assigning to Spain the West, and to Portugal the East, from a North-South line that goes one hundred leagues west of the Azores Islands, thus trying to prevent skirmishes between the Christian monarchs.

1494

1. Columbus establishes the Village of Isabella in Hispaniola. Various problems and the bellicosity of the natives make him abandon this place, and later on he picks another area to build the city of Santo Domingo. On January 6, Father Bernardo Boil celebrates Mass in Santo Domingo. It is the first recorded Mass in America. In this year, the king and queen of Spain send three additional caravels under the leadership of Bartolomé Colón with provisions for the people in the colonies. Father Boil returns to Spain in one of them.

2. On June 7, Spain and Portugal sign the Treaty of Tordesillas, by which the demarcation line is moved from 100 to 360 leagues to the west of the Islands of Cabo Verde. Under this agreement, Portugal will claim Brazil.

1495

Columbus experiences difficulties and makes serious mistakes in the governance of Hispaniola. He sends five ships full of Indians back to Spain to be sold as slaves in Seville. This angers the Spanish monarchs and causes Isabella to exclaim: "What power does the Lord Admiral have to give my subjects to another?" She affirms their freedom and says that if they work they are to be paid a just wage, "like the free persons they are and not slaves."

1496

1. Leaving his brother Bartolomé in charge of Hispaniola, Columbus returns to Spain, using the first two ships built in the New World, to defend himself against the many accusations leveled against him. He takes thirty natives along with him. He is well received by the monarchs, who bestow on him the title of duke and give him a large portion of land in Hispaniola, as well as a percentage of the profits realized from his three years of exploration.

2. On July 29 in the Monastery of Guadalupe, Spain, two of the natives that Columbus brought with him are baptized, with Commander Varela acting as their godfather; to one is given the name Pedro, to the other Cristóbal.

1497

The Catholic Monarchs order that preparations be made for a third voyage. This time, Columbus has serious disagreements with Bishop Fonseca, who will be in charge of the House of Trade in Seville. Finally, ships are obtained and the search for men and provisions begins.

1498

On May 30, Columbus sets sail from Spain on his third voyage with seven ships and more than two hundred passengers, taking a more southerly route. He arrives at the coast of South America and contemplates the mouth of the Orinoco River. He continues his journey northeast and, on arriving in Santo Domingo, must contend with a violent revolt. The Spanish monarchs appoint a governor and order the two Columbus brothers back to Spain.

1499

1. Vicente Yáñez Pinzón (captain of the *Niña* on Columbus's voyage), Alonso de Ojeda, Amerigo Vespucci, Juan de la Cosa, Alonso Niño, and Cristóbal Guerra are sent by their Catholic majesties in two

ships to explore new territories. They sail along the coast of Brazil, explore the mouth of the Amazon and Marañon Rivers, continue along the Gulf of Mexico and the coast of Florida, go on through the Bahamas, and get as far as Chesapeake Bay. Here they go ashore and spend thirty-seven days repairing damage to their ships. After several months at sea, with a cargo of pearls and a number of natives, they return to Spain. About the same time, having heard many accusations about the administration of Columbus and his two brothers, the Catholic monarchs send judge Francisco de Bobadilla to look into the matter. Upon witnessing executions ordered by them, Bobadilla arrests Columbus and sends him to Spain.

2. Fleets from Spain and other countries labor in the area of Terranova (Newfoundland) in search of codfish.

Heroes: Ponce de León (left) discovered Florida, and Hernán de Soto, conqueror of Peru, explored the entire region of the Southeastern United States before he died on the banks of the Mississippi and was buried beneath it.

1500-1550:
Exploration and Conquest

The lands of this country are explored and shown on maps under the sovereignty of Spain.

1500

1. Juan de la Cosa, owner and captain of the *Santa María* caravel, who traveled with Columbus on his first trip to America, draws the first world map or navigation chart where America's coastline definitely appears. This is published two years later at the Puerto de Santa María and is presented to Queen Isabella. Filed in the House of Trade of Seville and later in the Archives of the Indies, the map is stolen, taken to France, and finally recovered by Spain. It is kept now in the Naval Museum of Madrid.

2. Franciscan missionaries Francisco Ruiz, Juan Robles, Juan Trasierra, and Rodrigo Pérez arrive in Santo Domingo on an expedition from Spain.

3. In Seville, García Rodríguez de Montalvo, prolific writer of adventure novels, publishes a book that enjoys great success, *Las Sergas de Espandian*. In the novel he mentions a great island populated by amazons who use pearls and diamonds to adorn their bodies. The fantasy island has the name California, after the reigning queen, who was Calafia. This name of California would be given, a few years later, to the peninsula and region now bearing it, which at that time was thought to be an island.

1501

The navigator Gaspar Corterreal explores the North American Atlantic coastline, gives his name to the lands of New England, and arrives at the peninsula of Labrador. At the same time, Rodrigo de Bastidas travels from Venezuela to Panama, while Juan de la Cosa conducts another expedition on the Gulf of Mexico, exploring the Gulf of Darien, and the Atrato River, where he finds samples of gold.

1502

The Catholic monarchs of Spain appoint Nicolás de Ovando governor of Hispaniola. Ovando departs in February with 32 ships and 2,500 expeditionaries. Three months later, they send Columbus on his fourth and last trip to America. On May 11, he leaves with 150 men, accompanied by the following Franciscans: Alonso Espinar, Bartolomé Turégano, Antonio Carrión, Francisco de Portugal, Antonio de los Mártires, Mateo Zafra, Pedro Hornachuelos, Juan Escalante, Lucas Sánchez, Pedro Martínez, Juan Baudin. Juan Francés, Pedro Francés, Bartolomé Sevilla, Juan Hinojosa, Alonso Hornachuelos, Juan Martín, plus a cargo of animals, plants, and seeds. He sails by the Island of Martinique and continues to Santo Domingo, where he spends some time. He then continues his trip and explores the Central American coastline looking for a passage to Asia. After a two-year trip and a shipwreck at Jamaica, he finally returns to Spain, his body almost paralyzed by severe arthritis.

2. Florida's coastline, seen long ago by other Spanish navigators, appears on a map drawn by Alberto Cantino.

1503

1. The Spanish crown advises the governor of the Dominican Republic that the Indians ought to have "the same way of life as the people of our kingdom." In other words, each one with his wife and children, having his own land and cattle, and respecting another's properties. This will be Spain's standard policy, throughout the years in all her domains.

2. The "Casa de la Contratación" (House of Trade) is created in Seville to regulate the financial matters related to the New World. It is of great importance during the first twenty-five years, until the founding of the Council of the Indies.

1504

Columbus returns from his fourth voyage without finding the passage to the Orient. That same year, Queen Isabella, protagonist of the discovery of America, dies. Her death leaves Columbus without a protector. She always defended him in his difficulties. Queen Isabella leaves a model of Christian testament which could be called the "Magna Carta of America."

1505

In Toro, Spain, King Ferdinand assembles the navigators Vicente Yáñez Pinzón and Amerigo Vespucci. He names Yáñez Pinzón "Corregidor," governor of the Island of Puerto Rico, and he grants Vespucci Spanish citizenship. Yáñez leaves for the third time for the New World and explores Puerto Rico. He orders his pilot, García Alonso Cansino, to release some pigs and goats to reproduce on the island.

1506

On April 21, after four trips to the New World and convinced that he had arrived at the Indies in the Orient, Columbus dies in Valladolid and is buried there.

1507

Aware that Amerigo (now Americo) Vespucci had gone to the New World, the German writer Martin Waldseemuller says, "The fourth part of the world, after it was discovered by Americo Vespucci, can be called America." This colossal error caused the New World to be called America. Mr. Waldseemuller thought that Vespucci had arrived in 1492 at the head of the expedition.

1508

1. Ferdinand the Catholic convokes a seminar for navigators in Burgos, Spain. He invites Vicente Yáñez Pinzón, Americo Vespucci, Juan de la Cosa, and Juan Díaz Solís. He also invites the bishop of Burgos, Juan Rodríguez Fonseca, head of the House of Trade, and together for a month they discuss everything related to the newly discovered lands and any others that might be discovered in the future. The position of *"Piloto Mayor"* (Royal Pilot) is created, whose function would be to educate and train all navigators intending to set sail for the Americas. It is decided to search for a sea passage to the Orient, and also to establish the posts of Darien and of Veragua on the new continent.

2. Juan Ponce de León arrives in Puerto Rico; he was born of a noble family from the ancient kingdom of León in San Servas del Campo. He is a veteran military man in the army of the Catholic monarchs, and had gone to Santo Domingo on Columbus's second voyage. He had a large plantation in Hispaniola and dedicated himself to the development of agriculture and the raising of cattle; he was a very rich man. Having arrived on an expedition at the southern part of Puerto Rico, with his smart and inseparable dog *"Becerrillo"* and fifty soldiers, he visits the Tahino Chief Agueybana, who receives him cordially. Together they traverse the island until they arrive at the area which today is the capital; here Ponce and his men build a dock, a road, and a stone house, thus giving rise to the town of Caparra. Here he leaves some soldiers and a few natives he has taken with him to cultivate the land. He then departs for Hispaniola.

3. Pope Julius II grants the kings of Spain the privilege to extend the royal patronage to their domains in America, by which the king commits himself to promote and administer the Catholic Church. Accordingly, the

king commits himself to take up the costs of erecting churches, monasteries, and missions, and of supporting the missionaries.

1509

1. On August 14, King Ferdinand names Ponce de León governor of Puerto Rico. His plan is to promote agriculture among the natives, search for gold in the rivers, build houses, and establish a farm along the Toa River for the purpose of agricultural experiments. Through a misunderstanding, Governor Diego Colón of Hispaniola, who claims jurisdiction over Puerto Rico, names Juan Cerón mayor of Puerto Rico. Ponce hands over the command to him, and waits in Hispaniola until the king resolves the problem.

2. The first group of Dominican missionaries leaves from Spain for Hispaniola. They are Domingo de Mendoza, Pedro de Córdoba, Antonio de Montesinos, and Bernardo de Santo Domingo — all of them highly educated persons. A short time later, another group of eleven will also arrive, and some of them will go to Puerto Rico.

1510

Ponce de León is confirmed as governor of Puerto Rico, returns to the Island with one hundred more settlers, and continues the building of Caparra. A gold foundry is set up, and the cultivation of the soil and cattle raising continue to develop. Franciscans who come with the settlers begin the work of evangelization. The instructions of the king are as follows: that the natives be well treated and instructed in the Catholic faith; that a Franciscan monastery be constructed, and that the friars be "persons of solid doctrine and generous in providing solace"; that the church be called St. John the Baptist; that the greatest number of native children possible be gathered up and, once instructed themselves in the language and the faith, be placed in charge of teaching these to the rest. In this same year, Spain occupies the island of Jamaica.

1511

1. Because of mistreatment, the natives of Puerto Rico rebel, and a bloody struggle ensues which finally is quelled. The Franciscans begin building a school in order to teach the natives reading, writing, religion, arts, and crafts.

2. Pope Julius II, in the Bull *Romanus Pontifex*, dated August 8, establishes the Diocese of San Juan, Puerto Rico, and gives permission for the construction of its cathedral. The new diocese is linked to the Archdiocese of Seville, and the doctoral canon of Salamanca, Don Alfon-

so Manso, is named the first bishop of San Juan, Puerto Rico. King Ferdinand grants the settlement the status of a city and confers on it a coat of arms: a green field with a silver Lamb reclining on a red book, the initials of Ferdinand and Isabella (FI), plus castles and lions. The name Caparra is changed to Puerto Rico. In the same papal bull the Dioceses of La Vega and Santo Domingo in Hispaniola are erected, also suffragans of Seville. The House of Trade recognizes the privilege of Diego Colón to name governors, and so the latter once again names Juan Cerón governor of Puerto Rico. With this, Ponce returns to his plantation at Salvaleón in Hispaniola.

1512

1. Don Alfonso Manso is consecrated bishop in Seville and arrives in Puerto Rico on December 25. He is the first bishop to set foot in America. He encourages the grammar school, assigning to it "a teacher, a bachelor of arts, a graduate of the university" with a good salary paid by the Spanish crown. He carries out his duties for twenty-two years, until his death. The children meet twice a day and are taught to read, write, and learn Christian prayers.

2. Ponce de León requests the permission of the king to discover and explore "an island called Bímini" (Florida) by the natives, who say that there is a fountain of youth. On February 23 permission is received and Ponce begins to make preparations, using his own money to get ships, soldiers, and supplies. His motives seem a bit romantic: already more than fifty years old, he has fallen in love with the beautiful Beatriz de Córdoba, who is much younger. Because of the love he has for her, he forgets his wealth, his fame, and his power, risking all on an expedition to find the fountain of youth. But the king's charter reminds him that he is to colonize and christianize the natives in the lands of Bímini north of Puerto Rico.

1513

1. Ponce de León, accompanied by his faithful dog *"Becerrillo,"* leaves San Germán, Puerto Rico, for Aguadilla and from there, on March 3, departs with a galleon, a ship and a brig for points north. On the 27th of the month he reaches the continent near the mouth of St. John's River, goes ashore with his men, plants the cross and, in the presence of the stunned natives, who are dressed in deer skins and adorned with tatoos, Ponce takes possession of Bímini, which the natives call Cantio, in the name of the Spanish crown. He baptizes it with the name Florida, since that week was Easter Week. He continues along the coast towards the

south in the area of Cape Canaveral, which he names Cape of the Streams. He discovers the Gulf Stream, which in the future will be the sea route the Spanish galleons will sail in returning to Spain. But toward the south in the area of Tequetesta (Miami) the natives are belligerent. He takes two of them in order to instruct them and uses them as interpreters. They turn at the point of the Peninsula and go up the western coast to the north, arriving at the Islands of San Carlos, Estero, Captiva, and Sanibel, near Fort Myers. After a while they continue until they reach Charlotte Bay, which they sail across in order to arrive later in Tampa Bay. Here they disembark and explore the area, but are attacked by natives; a fierce struggle ensues in a place called Matanzas. An arrow passes through the throat of one of the soldiers; several die, and Ponce himself is also wounded by an arrow, so they retreat without having found the miraculous fountain. During their three months' expedition they verify that the natives are also cannibals. Ponce decides to return to Puerto Rico and is named "Captain of the Land and Sea of San Juan" and "Governor of Florida and Bímini."

2. The young Spanish Captain Vasco Núñez de Balboa, with some 170 men and his faithful leonese mastiff called "Leoncio," undertakes an expedition to the interior of Darien (Panama). After a difficult trek through rugged terrain, he climbs to the top of a mountain and sees the Pacific Ocean, which he calls the South Sea. On September 29, he wades into its waters and claims possession of it in the name of the Spanish king. During the sixteenth, seventeenth, and eighteenth centuries the Pacific will be, for all practical purposes, a Spanish sea, since only Spanish commercial ships will sail its waters between the Philippines and the Spanish colonies of America. Only a pirate ship from time to time will dare to intrude.

1514

1. Again a royal charter is issued, this time on September 27, in behalf of Ponce de León's colonizing and christianizing of Bímini and Florida. The Spaniards are to proceed peaceably and only if the natives attack them first are they to respond using force.

2. Learning about the discovery of the Pacific Ocean by Vasco Núñez de Balboa, King Ferdinand sends Pedro Arias Dávila to the region of Darien as governor. With him go Diego Almagro, Hernando de Soto, Francisco Vázquez Coronado, Bernal Díaz del Castillo and the historian Fernandez de Oviedo, among others. Construction of a road through the isthmus begins, and Panama City is founded on the Pacific side.

110

1515

1. Ponce de León organizes an armada to defend the population of Puerto Rico from the fierce Caribe Indians. He pursues them all the way to the Island of Guadalupe, but then has to retreat. This action on Ponce's part leads to a diminution of attacks by the Caribes on the more peaceable Taino Indians of Boriquén.

2. There begins the sale of black slaves brought to America from Africa by Portuguese, French, and English merchants. Their increasing numbers in Hispaniola begin to cause worry among the white population.

1516

1. King Ferdinand, the Catholic monarch, dies. He has given great impetus and direction to the Spanish political system in recently discovered America.

2. The navigator Diego Miruelo, having set sail from Cuba with just one ship, heads north and arrives at the coast of Florida. Here he trades with the natives, who give him some gold artifacts. Since there is no map, it is difficult to determine exactly where he was.

1517

1. Francisco Hernández de Córdoba leaves Havana for the Bahamas with three ships and 110 men. After going through a storm they reach Florida, which the first mate, Antón Alaminos, recognizes since he had been there before with Ponce de León. In the bay of Charlotte Harbor, while taking on a supply of water, they are attacked by a band of natives, who wound Alaminos in the throat. They decide to head back to Cuba.

2. Cardinal Cisneros makes four recommendations regarding Puerto Rico: the admission to the island of black people, the importation of Spanish laborers, the cultivation of grain, grape vines, and cotton, and the planting of sugar cane.

1518

1. Juan de Grijalva arrives in the area of Galveston, whose island has successively had the names San Luis, Isla Blanca, and Isla de Aranjuez until it received its present name. At the same time, Diego Velázquez sails from Cuba and explores the area of Santa Elena, now South Carolina.

2. A royal order is issued so that the House of Trade in Seville might take care of organizing the departure of missionaries from Spain to America. The House will adopt norms to this purpose, and permission to embark will be denied to anyone without the written approval of his superior, provincial, or general.

1519

1. The governor of Jamaica, Francisco de Garay, orders Alonso Álvarez de Pineda to explore the region around the Gulf of Mexico, at that time known as "Amichel." Pineda leaves with four ships and four hundred soldiers, exploring the west coast of Florida, and arrives in Mobile Bay, which he names after the Holy Spirit. He stays there some forty days exploring the surrounding region and trading with the natives. He then continues on course to the West and finds himself at the mouth of the Mississippi River. Astonished at the magnitude of this body of water, Pineda christens it the River of the Holy Spirit. He now continues skirting the coast of Texas and arrives at the mouth of the Río Grande, to which he gives the name River of the Palms. They go up the river a few miles, find various Indian villages, and speak to the natives. Having made an almost perfect map of that coast, Pineda returns with his people to Jamaica.

2. The Villa of Caparra, Puerto Rico, founded by Ponce de León, is transferred to the islet where today stands the city of San Juan.

3. Hernán Cortés arrives in Mexico with 250 soldiers. He sinks his ships in order to prevent any of his men from getting the bright idea of returning to Cuba, and so he begins the conquest of the Aztec empire, which he carries out with astonishing bravery, astuteness, and determination. This famous conquest constitutes one of the greatest of all epics in the history of the world.

4. Spain prepares an expedition that is to circumnavigate the earth. At its head is the expert seaman Ferdinand Magellan, who sets sail from San Lucar de Barrameda on September 20 with five ships and 265 men. He arrives in South America, passes through the Strait to which he gives his own name, crosses the Pacific Ocean, and arrives in the Philippines.

1520

1. The attorney Lucas Vázquez de Ayllón, mayor of Santo Domingo and a wealthy plantation owner besides, sends seaman Francisco Gordillo on a ship with several soldiers to explore the Atlantic Coast. Gordillo joins up with another seaman, Pedro Quexos, and both head toward Chícora (Carolina). They reach Cape Fear, plant the cross, and take possession of that land in the name of Spain on June 24. They traverse the area and familiarize themselves with the natives; they trade with them and invite them to come on board their ships. Once on board, they weigh anchor and make off with 150 natives, intending to sell them into slavery in Santo Domingo. When informed of this, Governor Diego Colón becomes furious and orders the natives to be returned to their land. He

severely reprimands their captors; later, Vázquez de Ayllón does the same with Gordillo.

2. Around this time Father Pedro de Córdoba, O.P., writes a famous catechism in Hispaniola, which is used later in the whole of America for the religious instruction of the native peoples. The catechism begins like this: "My dear brothers and sisters, please know that we love you with our whole heart. . . . God has sent us to announce to you that He desires you to be His children and bestows on you His goodness and His blessings."

1521

1. Juan Ponce de León arrives in Charlotte Harbor to begin the work of colonizing Florida. He takes with him several Dominican missionaries, 250 soldiers and colonists, 50 horses, different kinds of cattle, seeds, and farm equipment. They begin building some houses, but the continued hostility of the Indians presents a serious obstacle. In one struggle, Ponce is wounded in the leg by an arrow, so too some of his soldiers. Finally they leave the place and head back to Cuba, where Ponce dies. His remains are transferred to Puerto Rico and placed in the Cathedral of San Juan with a Latin epitaph, which attorney Juan Castellanos translates into Spanish like this: "This narrow place is the tomb of the man who was a lion in name, but much more in deed."

2. Pope Leo X issues the Bull *Super Speculum* erecting the land of Florida as a diocese; the bishops of Palencia and the Canary Islands will fix its boundaries. Its parish church and cathedral is to be called Santiago, and Don Jorge de Priego, prior of San Marcos in León and a doctor of jurisprudence, is chosen as its first bishop.

3. Ferdinand Magellan, on his heroic voyage around the world, visits the Hawaiian Islands and arrives at Guam on March 6, calling the natives there "*chamorros*." In the future, the Spaniards would constantly stop at these islands en route to the Philippines. The Jesuits and the Augustinian Recollects would evangelize here, and several of them would be martyred. These islands will become the territory of the United States in 1898. After Magellan arrives at the Philippines, he dies on April 27.

1522

1. Juan Sebastián Elcano takes charge of the expedition and continues to voyage towards the West, passing through the Cape of Good Hope in Southern Africa and reaching Spain on September 6, 1522, aboard the ship Victoria. This brave Spanish captain, who survives the eventful crossing, is the first man to circumnavigate the globe.

2. Through the efforts of Fathers Antonio Montesinos and Pedro de Córdoba, a Dominican Monastery is founded in San Juan, Puerto Rico. Its first prior is Father Luis Cáncer, who years later will die a martyr in Florida.

1523

1. Attorney Lucas Vázquez de Ayllón receives a royal charter on June 12, authorizing the colonization of Florida and the conversion of the natives to the Catholic faith. He begins to prepare the expedition.

2. The Governor of Jamaica, Francisco de Garay, departs with 16 ships and 750 men and arrives at the mouth of the Río Grande with the intention of founding a city there bearing his name. Not finding this place to his liking, he decides to head further south, and finally ends up in Mexico City, where he dies a short time later.

3. The first sugar mill extracting sugar from cane is set up in Añasco, Puerto Rico.

1524

1. The Council of the Indies is officially established in Spain. It is like a present cabinet ministry. Its sole purpose will be to issue and supervise the policy, government, finances, and personnel appointment in America. Its decisions need the approval of two thirds of its membership. Many of these decisions would be carried out through the *Casa de la Contratación* (House of Trade) of Seville.

2. Spanish navigator Diego Miruelo sails again from Santo Domingo to Florida and explores its western coast.

1525

The seaman Esteban Gómez, in a ship especially built to navigate through the waters of the North Atlantic, leaves La Coruña by order of King Charles I with twenty-nine sailors. His mission is to discover a passage from the Atlantic to the Pacific. He arrives at Newfoundland, goes along the coasts of New Brunswick, Nova Scotia, Cape Cod, which he calls the Cape of St. Mary's, and Nantucket. He goes down along the coast of Long Island, which he calls the Island of the Holy Apostles; he enters New York Bay and sails the Hudson River, which he calls the River of St. Anthony. He calls the lands of New England the Lands of *Corterreal* (Royal Court) and to those of New Jersey, Delaware, and Pennsylvania he gives the name of Lands of Esteban Gómez. Because of damage to his ship, he enters Chesapeake Bay and, near what is now White Haven, Maryland, carefully glides through a fierce storm. He has to repair his ship, and stays there about forty days. Continuing his voyage to Florida, he later arrives in Cuba and finally goes back to Spain in August of the following year. His ship is called the *Anunciada*, weighing fifty tons and carrying supplies for twelve months. Gómez does not find the sea route he was looking for, but he does see and baptize many new lands, which a short time later will appear on maps with their respective names.

1526

1. In this year, King Charles I of Spain in a letter concerning colonization in America says: "The principal reason behind the discovery of these new lands is so that the inhabitants or natives there, who are without the light and knowledge of the faith, may be drawn to knowledge of the truths of our holy Catholic faith, so that they may understand them, become Christians, and be saved. This is the main reason you must keep in mind and hold onto in this enterprise."

2. The attorney Lucas Vázquez de Ayllón, a native of Toledo, sails from Santo Domingo in order to colonize Chícora (the Carolinas); he takes five ships, the Dominicans Father Antonio de Montesinos, Father Antonio Cervantes, and Brother Pedro Estrada, five soldiers, and settlers, including women. A native of that land, Francisco Chícora, goes along as interpreter. Ayllón gets as far as Chesapeake Bay, where Father Montesinos says the first Mass ever in Virginia, near Jamestown. They then turn south and on September 29 reach the mouth of the Cape Fear River, to which they give the name Jordan River, near Cape Fear. At the entrance to the bay, one of the ships runs ashore, and they disembark. Ayllón orders a new ship built to replace the damaged one. This was the first ship built in the United States. They stay here for several days. While exploring the region, they begin to realize that it is not the ideal place in which to settle, since it is very swampy. They continue sailing along the coast toward the south and finally disembark in an area which is now Georgetown, South Carolina, at the entrance to the Pee Dee River, which they call the Guadalupe. Here they begin to construct a town, a chapel, and a fort called St. Michael of Guadalupe, the first of seventy-two forts Spain will build in her territories which now are a part of the United States. Francisco Chícora, who had been educated for four years in Santo Domingo and knew how to speak Spanish very well, disappears, and Ayllón is now left without a guide or interpreter. With the town settled, Ayllón dies on October 18. His death, the epidemics, the winter cold, hunger, and disagreements decimate the group, and finally they decide to go back to Santo Domingo. Just a few people stay behind in St. Michael of Guadalupe, the first European settlement in the United States.

1527

1. Hernán Cortés, having heard of the voyage of Magellan, sends a flotilla from Mexico to the Philippines under the command of Alvaro Saavedra. After a few days at sea, they run into a terrible storm and one of their ships is wrecked near the Hawaiian Islands. Some Spaniards are saved by swimming to the Island of Kauai. They are very well received by the natives. They marry native women, and many Hawaiian families trace their origin to these intermarriages.

2. Luis Ponce de León, the only son of Don Juan Ponce de León, first governor of Puerto Rico and discoverer of Florida, is ordained to the priesthood. He renounces his inheritance in order to enter the Dominican Order and takes up residence in the Convent of San Juan.

1528

Pánfilo de Narváez arrives in Tampa Bay on April 14. He was born in Valladolid and is a veteran military man; he lost an eye in a battle against Hernán Cortés when he was sent to expel the latter from Mexico under orders from governor Velázquez of Cuba. The king has given him a royal decree for the purpose of exploring and colonizing the coast along the Gulf of Mexico from the River of the Palms (the Río Grande), all the way to Florida. On his expedition, Narváez takes along six hundred soldiers and colonists, some with their wives, in five ships. Father Juan Juárez goes along at the head of a group of Franciscans; Alvar Núñez Cabeza de Vaca goes as historian and treasurer, Alonso Enríquez as comptroller, and Alonso Solís as consultant. When they arrive, Narváez takes possession of the land, using the accustomed rite, and then for a few days explores the bay and territory of Tocobaga (Tampa); five hundred people go by land to the north with forty horses and other animals, while the others travel by ship along the coast in hope that the groups will meet each other up north. Those traveling on land have to ford the Withlacoochee, the Suwanee, and other rivers by devising makeshift boats. They proceed very slowly because of the animals they have taken along, and often they fight skirmishes with the Indians. They arrive at a region known as Apalaches (Tallahassee) and once again are set upon by Indians. After exploring the region for various weeks they go down to the coast near what is now St. Mark in the hope of meeting the ships, but this does not happen. So great is the misery, sickness, and hunger they endure after months of exploring that they decide to return to Mexico by sea, thinking it is close by. Using tree trunks and horsehide as sails, they throw together five rafts on which they all climb. They go along the coast, near the Bay of Pensacola, to Mobile, where they stop, and then continue in hope of finding the mouth of the Mississippi. Here a violent storm catches them, separating the rafts from one another; Narváez and the majority of the expedition perish. One raft with its eighty crewmen is thrown by the storm into the Bay of Matagorda; plague and hunger finish off almost all of them in a few weeks. Only four survive: Cabeza de Vaca, Andrés Dorantes, Alonso Castillo, and Esteban Azamor (Estebanico, the Black). Narváez, who had departed with the intention of establishing a settlement in Florida, ended up tragically. Father Juan Juárez, who carried with him his appointment as designated bishop of the new diocese of River of the Palms, never was able to establish it.

1529

1. The four survivors of the shipwreck, Cabeza de Vaca, Dorantes, Castillo and Estebanico, a little while after beginning their trek through Texas, fall captive to the Indians; Cabeza de Vaca, born in Jerez, is a man of great erudition, the son of a noble family who took part in the Battle of Las Navas de Tolosa against the Moors and whose grandfather had taken part in the conquest of the Canary Islands. The four captives now have to adapt themselves to the lifestyle of the Indians, a diet of meager food, and walking about naked like them.

2. Diego Ribeiro, map maker for King Charles I, publishes an extraordinary map in which there appears, perfectly depicted, the Atlantic Coast of the United States, as well as the islands of the Caribbean. On it also appeared all the territories discovered, with the Spanish names the explorers and navigators had given them, such as Lands of Esteban Gómez (New Jersey/Pennsylvania), St. Anthony's River (the Hudson), Lands of Ayllón (Delaware/Maryland/the Carolinas), etc.

1530

1. The Dominican Order establishes the Province of the Holy Cross of the Indies, which includes the houses and personnel of Hispaniola, Cuba, Jamaica, and the Convent of San Juan in Puerto Rico.

2. Some five hundred Caribe Indians in eleven longboats attack near Luquillo, Puerto Rico, killing twenty settlers, torching and destroying property, and carrying away twenty-five people in order to eat them, according to a letter of that time.

3. Pedro Martyr de Angleria publishes his book *Decadas* (Decades) on the activities of the Spaniards in America. This book is an important source for the many details related to the first explorations and discoveries in America. Among other things, he describes the expedition of

Francisco Vázquez de Ayllón to Chícora (North Carolina), of the Jordan River (Cape Fear River), the pearls found there, and of the customs of the "*chicoranos*" (native Indians).

1531

1. According to a tradition, Mary, under the title of Guadalupe, appears December 12 to the Indian Juan Diego on the Tepeyac Hill, Mexico; she leaves her image stamped on the Indian's mantle in the presence of Archbishop Juan de Zumárraga, who then gives permission to build a church there in her honor. The devotion to Our Lady of Guadalupe will spread years later to the territories now part of the United States.

2. Cabeza de Vaca, Dorantes, Castillo and Estebanico, after being held prisoner by the natives, make their escape from the area around the Bay of Matagorda, but they are once again taken prisoner. Cabeza de Vaca performs as doctor, learns the customs and language of the tribes, and becomes respected by them in the area between the Sabine and Trinity Rivers. Here they remain for about eight months, naked, their feet injured, their backs scorched from the sun, and in constant hunger. At this time, Cabeza de Vaca and Estebanico, prisoners of one tribe, meet up with Dorantes and Castillo who are prisoners of another tribe. They conspire to escape, Estebanico doesn't see it as a possibility. Finally, the Indians carry off Dorantes and Castillo to another place.

1532

Taking advantage of an opportunity, Cabeza de Vaca and companions escape from their captivity. They walk toward the West and once again are captured by yet another tribe. Here they are forced to clean animal skins and are taken on a nomadic route up to the Brazos River and then on to the Colorado, where the Indians use powder and antimony to paint their faces and bodies. They flee once again and go across the buffalo plains of Texas, thus becoming the first Europeans to see this particular animal. During these years of captivity and nomadism, Cabeza de Vaca plays the roles of doctor, missionary, and businessman, earning the respect of many of the tribes. One of his problems, however, is that all the tribes want to keep him for themselves. Not wanting to let him go, they come to consider him sent by their gods.

1533

1. Because of piracy in the Atlantic, preying on Spanish ships sailing between America and Spain, Spain decides to mount an armada in order to defend her commerce. Moreover, relations between France and Spain are very tense, and fear exists that war might break out, and consequently an intensification of the attacks at sea.

2. Hernán Cortés sends Gonzalo Jiménez de Quesada to explore the west coast of Mexico, and he discovers Baja (Lower) California.

1534

After months of walking over the central plains of Texas, Cabeza de Vaca and his companions arrive at the area of Marfa and Presidio, where the Río Grande meets the Conchos. Here he finds seeds and edible fruits and observes that certain natives are wearing emerald and turquoise stones. He continues his journey toward the West.

1535

Cabeza de Vaca heads west, though it is uncertain whether it is along the northern or the southern bank of the Río Grande. He and his companions arrive in the vicinity of what will become Fabens and El Paso, enter the southeastern part of New Mexico, cross the Río Grande, enter the Sonora Valley, and finally reach Culiacán, where they are cordially greeted and, for a few weeks, are able to regain their strength before heading down to Mexico. Cabeza de Vaca and companions may be considered precursors of the evangelization of Texas and New Mexico. Considered semi-deities by the tribes they were with for some six months, they could more easily teach them the Christian faith and "made on them the sign of the Cross." In his famous work *Shipwrecks*, written sometime later, Cabeza de Vaca says: "We told them, using signs and gestures by which they understood us, that in the skies there was a man whom we called God who had created the heavens and the earth and that this God we adored and cling to as Lord, and that we did what He commanded us to do, and that from his hand flowed every kind of good thing, and that if they did the same, it would go very well for them; and so great was the eagerness we found in them that if there were a language with which we might have been perfectly understood, we would have made Christians of them all." This book by Cabeza de Vaca and another entitled *Commentaries* are interesting sources of information concerning the customs of the Texas tribes, and his heroic adventures in the lands of the southern United States. They are the oldest books on matters pertaining to this country.

1536

1. On July 24, Cabeza de Vaca and his companions reach Mexico City, and are received by the viceroy, Antonio de Mendoza. He relates his accomplishments and raises great expectations among the inhabitants of the Mexican capital. His achievements give impetus to the later explorations of Father Marcos de Niza and of Coronado throughout the southern portion of the United States. Cabeza de Vaca returns to Spain, and begins to write the books that would be published in Mexico in 1542. He turns down an invitation from the king to return to Florida at the head of another expedition, but he does accept an appointment to be governor of Río de la Plata and Paraguay. His eight-year journey across Florida, Alabama, Mississippi, Louisiana, Texas, and New Mexico, covering some ten thousand miles on foot, his extraordinary adventures, his propensity for learning the native languages, and the books in which he relates his accomplishments make him worthy of being declared the greatest explorer of the United States and its first historian. His name should not be omitted from history books.

2. Juan de Zumárraga, bishop of Mexico City, establishes Santa Cruz de Tlaltelolco School there to educate the children of the *caciques* (chiefs) and other native leaders. Some Indian youths from regions north of the Río Grande — Don Luis de Velasco and others — will be educated here.

1537

1. Pope Paul III issues the bull *Sublimis Deus*, in which he declares there should be no doubt in anyone's mind that the natives of the Indies, as the human beings they are, have dominion over their goods and are free, and "it is not permitted to deliver them up to slavery, but, on the contrary, they are to be led to eternal life through teaching and good example." The Pope threatens with excommunication anyone who does the contrary.

2. Hernando de Soto is authorized by King Charles I to organize an expedition to Florida, given the title of *Adelantado* (Vanguardsman). De Soto, born in Extremadura, is a brave official who has participated in the conquest of Central America with Pedro Arias Dávila and in that of Peru with Francisco Pizarro. After several years in America, and after having amassed a great fortune, he went back to Spain and married Isabel, the daughter of Pedro Arias Dávila. Once in possession of the royal charter, he sells his fortune, valued at about one hundred thousand gold pesos, and with the money begins preparing his expedition to Florida. He stocks up on seeds and farm equipment, buys boats, and gathers soldiers and set-

tlers, many of whom also sell their property and prepare themselves for the expedition, bringing along their horses and firearms.

1538

1. On April 6, De Soto leaves San Lucar de Barrameda with ten ships and about a thousand persons, among them soldiers, sailors and settlers. He reaches Cuba, having been appointed its governor, orders a fort to be built, sends out the cosmographer Juan Añasco to make a map of the coasts of Florida, and puts the final touches on his plans to carry out the expedition.

2. A printing press arrives in Mexico City and begins to function there. The first press will arrive in the territory of the thirteen original colonies of the United States one hundred years later.

1539

1. The first book published in the New World is printed in Spanish. It is a bilingual compendium of religion in both Spanish and Nahuatl and receives the approval of Bishop Juan de Zumárraga of Mexico.

2. On March 7 of this year Father Marcos de Niza, O.F.M., a man well-trained in cosmography and navigation and a missionary with experience in Mexico and Peru, obtains permission from the viceroy to trek north in search of the seven cities of Cíbola. Accompanied by Estebanico, the companion of Cabeza de Vaca, Brother Onorato, and a group of Christian Indians as helpers and interpreters, he reaches the region of New Mexico inhabited by the Zuñi Indians. He builds an altar of stones, celebrates Mass, gives thanks to God and takes possession of the lands of Cíbola in the name of Spain. Father Niza returns to Mexico and relates marvelous things about those lands, replete with so much wealth and such great cities. It seems the good Father has exaggerated quite a bit about the situation in order to encourage the viceroy to organize a big expedition for the purpose of converting the natives. This exaggeration will give rise to the expedition prepared by Coronado.

3. In July of this year the navigator Francisco Ulloa leaves Acapulco in order to explore the coast around the Gulf of California. He goes along the southern point and then up along the West Coast toward the north. He reaches the latitude of San Diego, thus proving that Lower California was a peninsula. However, the idea that it is an island still is accepted; Ulloa invests two years in his expedition.

4. Father Francisco de Vitoria, from the University of Salamanca, proclaims the doctrine: "The Indians recently discovered have rights as well as duties since they are human beings, and this is antecedent to, and

independent of, the state, religion, culture or state of grace or of sin"; by this he shows the Christian concept of man, and with good reason he will be called "the Father of Human Rights."

5. King Charles I makes a donation to Father Luis Cáncer and Father Antonio Dortas of" half a ton of books to each one"; with these they are able to open some schools in Puerto Rico.

6. On May 12, De Soto departs Cuba for Florida with eleven ships and about a thousand people, among them soldiers and colonists, besides an undetermined number of natives from the Caribbean. A total of twelve priests go as well, among them the Dominicans Diego Bañuelos, Francisco Rocha, Federico Gallegos, Francisco Pozo, Juan Torres, Juan Gallegos, and Luis Soto. They take two hundred horses, cattle, dogs, pigs, seeds, and many supplies. On June 1 they reach Tampa Bay, and a contingent of soldiers disembark near the area of present Ruston, reconnoitering the area. They stumble upon Juan Ort1z, a Spaniard from the expedition of Narváez, who has been held captive by the Indians for eleven years. He has married the daughter of the chief, and now with his wife he joins them, serving as their guide and interpreter. De Soto with his expedition heads north and reaches Ocale in spite of great difficulties due to the swampy region, the hostility of the natives, and trouble crossing the rivers. They get to Apalache (around Tallahassee), where Narváez has been eleven years before. Here in the village of Anhaica they spend Christmas and the winter, and from here they send to Cuba for more provisions.

1540

1. In May De Soto's expedition heads north, crosses Georgia, and upon their arrival at the Ocmulgee River near where Macon is today, a baby is baptized in the waters of the river and given the name Pedro. They reach the area around Augusta, enter South Carolina, and head for Silver Bluff near Camden. In Cofitachequi, an Indian princess comes out to greet them. She offers them food and gems and for a few days tries to win De Soto's love. They reach Guatari in North Carolina, then Joara, near Marion. Continuing on to the Blue Ridge Mountains in Cherokee territory, they cross the Tennessee River around the area of Nicholas Ford and pass through Guasali, Chiaha, Tali and Coosa until they reach the Alabama River in the area of Monroe County. In Mabila, near present Montgomery, Alabama, between the Alabama and Tombigbee Rivers, there reigns a giant chief named Tuscaloosa who, in friendly fashion, invites De Soto and his expedition to enter his village. It is a trap, and De Soto has to defend himself with extraordinary courage. For nine hours he

and his men wage a fierce battle against thousands of Indians who try to wipe them out. Finally, Tuscaloosa is defeated. Seventy Spaniards are dead, along with two thousand Indians and Tuscaloosa himself. At this battle all items necessary for Mass are lost. Through the two following years the accompanying priest, vested with a buckskin chasuble, will celebrate a "Dry Mass," or the service of the word without consecrating the bread and the wine, as related by the Inca Garcilaso de la Vega. De Soto continues his exploration following the current of the Tombigbee River, until he arrives in the area of the Chickasaws in what is now the State of Mississippi. Here they are forced to do battle again, this time at night. They lose another forty men and about fifty horses; in spite of hostilities on the part of the natives, they are still able to spend a few days in the region. While there, De Soto is informed that Maldonado has arrived in Mobile Bay with the supplies he had requested. Confronted with the possibility that his people might decide to abandon the expedition and return instead to Havana, De Soto ignores the arrival of the provisions and reinforcements, not knowing that with them came his wife Isabel. She waits for several days in Mobile, plants a few fig trees in memory of her husband, and, seeing that he is not coming, leaves the area on one of the ships. On December 9, the Hidalgo of Elvas (De Soto) makes his way north, hoping to arrive at Columbus and there, in the territories of the Chickasaw Indians, spend Christmas and the winter months.

2. After hearing of the marvels that Father Niza saw in the North, the viceroy of Mexico chooses Francisco Vázquez de Coronado to head up the exploration and conquest. Coronado was born in Salamanca and studied at its university before going to Mexico, where he was named governor of Nueva Galicia. He prepares for his expedition over the period of several months, investing a substantial amount of money in it. Finally, in February, he leaves from Compostela with 336 soldiers and settlers, 100 native Mexican Christians, 552 horses, 600 mules, 5,000 sheep, and 500 cows, goats, and pigs. With him he also takes Franciscan Fathers Marcos Niza, Juan Padilla, Antonio Castilblanco, Juan Escalona, and Luis de Ubeda. They enter through southeastern Arizona and, on July 7, reach the village of Hawikuh, the most prominent of the Zuñi villages and one of the seven cities of Cíbola in what is now New Mexico. Coronado establishes headquarters here and sends García López de Cardenas with a group to explore the Northwest. They go as far as the Colorado river, which they call the River Tizón, and for the first time the eyes of Europeans behold the grandeur of the Grand Canyon. Another group with Father Padilla explores the Northeast, while Coronado himself, in October, reaches the Río Grande near Bernardillo. After a difficult battle

with the Indians, Coronado conquers that side of the river. He establishes his headquarters there, and prepares to spend the winter among the Tiguex Indians. On their expedition, the group with Father Padilla and Hernando de Alvarado reaches as far as northwestern Texas, where for the first time they see buffalo (American bison).

3. Sent by the viceroy of Mexico, Hernando de Alarcón travels up through the Gulf of California, reaches the mouth of the Colorado River, and goes as far as Yuma, Arizona. Earlier, Hernán Cortés has made four expeditions in his attempt to explore those lands to the north, but he did not get much further than the coast around the thirty-ninth parallel, near what is now Ensenada, Lower California.

1541

1. In March there is a dispute between De Soto's soldiers and the Chickasaws, with several soldiers and Indians killed. De Soto continues his march through Mississippi in order to reach the area around Memphis on May 8 and there contemplate "the Father of Rivers," the Mississippi. They prepare to cross, and De Soto orders several rafts built using trees cut down in the area. To the astonishment of the natives, they cross the great river to the other shore: soldiers, travelers, horses, pigs and various other animals. On arriving in Pacaha, Arkansas, they have little trouble conquering it, and De Soto reconciles its chief with the chief of the Casqui tribe. Both chiefs offer him their daughters in marriage. Here on March 26 De Soto raises a large pine-tree cross and gives the first catechesis to the Indians of the place in these words: "This was He who made the sky and the earth and man in His own image. Upon the tree of the cross He suffered to save the human race and rose from the tomb on His third day ... and, having ascended into heaven, is there to receive with open arms all who would be converted to Him." The "Hidalgo de Elvas" journeys on to Hot Springs where, delighted by the thermal waters, he decides to spend the winter. For this stay he decides to build a stockade in the Indian village of Autiamque. At this place Ortíz, De Soto's guide and interpreter, dies.

2. In April Coronado, with a group of soldiers and some missionaries, leaves Albuquerque, New Mexico, and heads northeast, crossing a section of northwest Texas (the Panhandle), and there in Palo Duro Canyon Father Juan Padilla says Mass. A feast follows at which they eat the game they have caught during a hunt and, above all, offer thanks to God for His many blessings. It is May 29, the first Thanksgiving Day celebrated in what is now the United States. They continue on to Oklahoma and into the legendary Gran Quivira (Kansas), crossing the Arkansas River on

June 29, and search for the great cities and mines that the natives and their famous guide, El Turco, has spoken to them about so much. They journey to Wichita, reach Junction City, and for three months explore this region of the Great Plains, but find nothing of what they had been promised; this deception costs El Turco his life. With autumn already well underway, Coronado decides to go back to his camp along the Río Grande.

1542

1. De Soto starts to move again in March; he passes through Arkadelphia and Camden, Arkansas, enters Louisiana and reaches the Mississippi River by a westerly route. He has with him three hundred soldiers and forty horses. Ravaged by the effects of an epidemic and seeing his own end in sight, he appoints Luis Moscoso to be his successor. On June 20 this valiant explorer dies at forty-two years of age near present-day Ferriday. His men lay his body at the bottom of the great river which serves as his final resting place. Moscoso orders the construction of seven boats in which they navigate down the river for some seventeen days until reaching the area around what is New Orleans today. Then they pass through the Gulf to the entrance of the Panuco River, Mexico. With a loss of seven men in the expedition, the survivors travel on to Mexico City, where Viceroy Mendoza warmly receives them.

2. For three long years De Soto has explored various states of what is now the United States; his brilliance, daring, and nobility merit for him a place among the greatest heroes of this country. His explorations and contributions will be valuable assets for the future. It is sufficient to remind ourselves that the "razorback" hogs of Arkansas are the descendants of the pigs De Soto brought from Cuba. The "cimarrón" and "mustang" (mesteño) breeds come from horses which broke loose during his expedition in those lands and subsequently became wild.

3. In the spring, Coronado decides to make his way back to Mexico, where he arrives in July and makes his report to the viceroy concerning his discoveries. The latter punishes him for his failure and having come back without being called, stripping him of his post as governor of Nueva Galicia. During his three years of exploration, although apparently he failed to find great cities and gold mines, Coronado nonetheless accomplished many important things that will help the future settlement and Christianization of the Southwest. Without attempting to do so, De Soto, journeying from Florida toward the West, and Coronado, from New Mexico towards the East, were on the brink of meeting up with each other. If they had, it would have been quite a feat, with the whole South

125

linked together from East to West already in the middle of the sixteenth century. Coronado, stripped of his post, spends the rest of his private life dedicating himself to his own affairs. He is without a doubt one of the greatest men ever to set foot in this country.

4. After Coronado's expedition returns to Mexico, Father Juan Padilla asks to remain in the Gran Quivira (Kansas) for the purpose of evangelizing the Pawnees and the Guias. With him remain, too, Father Luis de Ubeda, two Mexican Indians (Lucas and Sebastián) who were Franciscan postulants, Captain Pedro Castañeda de Najera, the soldier Andrés Ocampo, and a handful of other soldiers. Father Padilla becomes a great friend of the Indians of that locality and works with them for several months, but he wishes to reach other tribes as well. Captain Castañeda de Najera opposes this. Father Padilla, accompanied by Ocampo (on horseback), Lucas and Sebastián, and a hunting dog, travels for several months to distant areas. When they meet the Aciales Indians, enemies of the previous tribe, on November 30, the natives attack Father Padilla, who immediately kneels down and is pierced repeatedly from a barrage of arrows, while Ocampo, Lucas and Sebastián escape on horseback. At the site of his martyrdom, near present Dodge City, Kansas, Father Padilla and companions "had placed a cross, and raising it, he promised to keep it standing there for as long as it was possible for him to do so." These are the words of witnesses who relate the story of the first martyr in the United States. Sometime later his companions return to bury his body. They make a map, and years later his remains will be transferred to the Isleta Mission in New Mexico. Father Padilla was born in Andalucia and was a soldier before entering the Franciscan Order. Meanwhile, Father Luis de Ubeda has gone to evangelize the natives of Pecos, and Father Juan Escalona to those in the area of the Río Grande; both also die as martyrs. The soldier Ocampo, Lucas, Sebastián, and their dog wander for several years through the lands of Kansas, Oklahoma, and Texas until finally they arrive back in Mexico City, where Ocampo will relate all that has happened.

5. Ruy López Villalobos, Juan Gaetano, and Gaspar Rico set sail from Acapulco for the East with six ships; they reach the Hawaiian Islands, which they call the Islands of the King. In the next few years in the Pacific, the Spaniards will also explore the Solomon Islands, the Marshall Islands, the New Hebrides Islands, and northern Australia.

6. The viceroy of Mexico entrusts to the navigator Juan Rodríguez Cabrillo the task of exploring the coasts of the North Pacific. He sets sail with two ships, the *Salvador* and *Victoria*, accompanied by his helmsman Bartolomé Ferrelo. They reach San Diego Bay (Ballast Point) on September 28, discover the Island of Santa Catalina, and pass through the Santa Barbara Canal. While on the island of San Miguel, Cabrillo dies on June

3. He is buried on the island, and Ferrelo continues at the head of the expedition. Passing the thirty-seventh parallel the crew are able to see hills which they call the Hills of San Martín (today San Lucas), but because of dense fog they fail to see Monterey and San Francisco Bays. They continue north to the cape they call Mendocino in honor of Viceroy Mendoza, on to Cape Blanco, and then up to the forty-fourth parallel near what is now Florence, Oregon. Here, Ferrelo begins the journey back down the coast and, having made a map of his spectacular voyage, reaches Mexico after a whole year of exploration, the first along the northern Pacific Coast.

7. Don Rodrigo Bastidas is named Bishop of Puerto Rico. In a short time two more parishes are needed. The population of the island in the middle of this century is small, and is cared for by ten priests.

1543

King Charles I promulgates some laws regarding native Americans: The Indians are to be left free to live in their own communities; they are permitted to elect their own authorities and advisors. No Indians are to be enslaved; no Indian is to live outside of his own village. No Spaniard may live in an Indian village for more than three days, unless he is sick or there on business. The Indians are to be instructed in the Catholic faith.

1544

In Mexico, on the press of Juan Pablos, the work *Christian Doctrine* is printed in both Castilian and the Nahuatl language. Its author is Dominican Father Pedro de Córdoba. This book is a catechism or compendium of the Christian faith that soon will be used extensively in all of America.

1545

1. Lorenzo de Tejada, judge of the royal high court, is informed about Francisco Vázquez, governor of Cíbola, Tiguex, and Quivira. It has been rumored that he is better qualified to govern his own household rather than anything outside of it. Also he is not the same person as before, because of certain problems resulting from a fall from his horse while exploring New Mexico.

2. Don Jerónimo Lebrón finishes his term as governor of Puerto Rico and is replaced by Don Iñigo López Cervantes.

1546

1. Father Luis Cáncer, O.P., requests permission of the viceroy of Mexico to embark on a spiritual conquest unaccompanied by soldiers.

2. Father Alonso de Molina, O.F.M., publishes a catechism that is used extensively by the Franciscans. It becomes very popular in America and is translated into various Indian languages.

1547

1. Already by this year Puerto Rico is beginning to cultivate sugar cane, which the Spaniards brought from the Canary Islands. Juan de Santaolalla is owner of three sugar mills and several stone houses in which many people work, so the bishop grants permission for a priest to be sent there to act as their pastor.

2. Nicolaus Valard de Dieppe publishes a map showing Florida with the Bay of Ponce de León clearly marked out along with six other bays farther north.

1548

In a letter, the bishop of San Juan, Puerto Rico, states to King Charles I the following: "In this city stands a monastery of Dominican Friars; of such great size is this building that it is sufficient for a town of two thousand residents because it was erected during a time of great prosperity on the island." The order by this time has holdings and property that the friars donated to it when they entered religious life.

1549

Father Luis Cáncer, O.P., dies a martyr in Florida on June 26. Father Cáncer, born in Zaragoza, asked to go to the New World spurred on by apostolic zeal; he was a missionary in Santo Domingo, Puerto Rico, Guatemala and Mexico. He was a companion of Friar Bartolomé de las Casas and was convinced of the idea put forth by Friar Pedro de Córdoba of evangelizing the natives without being accompanied by troops for protection. He asks the viceroy of Mexico to allow him to go on a mission of evangelization to Florida. A ship is placed at his disposal, and he sails from Veracruz with his companions Gregorio Beteta, Juan García, Diego de Tolosa and Brother Fuentes; they take along as helmsman Juan Arana, plus a group of Mexican Indians and various helpers. They stop at Havana in order to take on supplies and an interpreter, Magdalena, a native of Florida who had lived in Cuba for some time. On Ascension Day they arrive in the area of Tampa Bay.

Father Tolosa and Brother Fuentes, along with Magdalena, go ashore in order to meet later with those still in the ship. Two weeks later, those in the ship disembark too, and Father Cáncer celebrates Mass. Soto, one of Hernando de Soto's soldiers, who was held captive by the Indians for the past ten years, approaches and informs them that the two missionaries have been killed and that Magdalena has disrobed and returned to her primitive way of life. This news deeply affects Father Cáncer, who is responsible for the mission. From the ship he spies a group of natives approaching. Contrary to the opinion of all, Father wishes to investigate the fate of his companions, jumping off the boat and wading ashore to preach the Gospel. In the sight of his companions on board, the natives surround him, remove his hat, and strike him on the head with a club, killing him. They then unleash a barrage of arrows in the direction of the ship, whose crew have no choice but to speed away and return to Mexico. Once again it is verified that the sending of missionaries to evangelize without the protection of soldiers does not produce good results, only more martyrs. Father Cáncer, distinguished philosopher and author of various works in the Zapoteca and Quechua languages, is the first martyr of Florida and is called "Standard Bearer of the Faith."

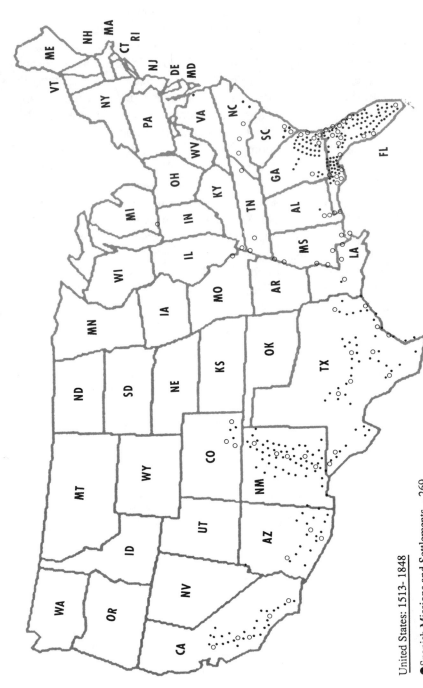

United States: 1513- 1848

● Spanish Missions and Settlements - 269

○ Spanish Forts - 83

1550-1600:
Colonization and Evangelization

The first permanent settlements are established: missionary work begins.

1550

At the end of his term of office as Governor of Puerto Rico, Antonio de la Vega is replaced by Luis Vallejo, who will govern the island for the next four years, promoting agriculture and colonization in general. The work of evangelization is also progressing, carried mainly by the Franciscans, Dominicans, and diocesan clergy.

1551

The authorities of Puerto Rico ask the king to send fifty Castilian soldiers to whom plots, farming land, and people will be given in order to promote agriculture. In return, the soldiers will promise to stay on the island for a minimum of eight years.

1552

1. The French pirate François LeClerc ("Wooden Foot") attacks several villages on the coast of Puerto Rico, steals possessions, and destroys property. Barcia Carballido says that this year, "The Florida seas are infested with pirates."

2. The book of Father Bartolomé de las Casas titled *Brief Relation of the Destruction of the Indies* is published in Seville. The book has as its goal to serve the protection of the Indians, something that is praiseworthy. But its statements are mounted on much overgeneralization, exaggerations, and outright falsehoods. The distortions of the truth found in this book will be soon used, without any critical analysis, by countries and writers, foes of Catholic Spain, particularly Holland and England, to create and spread a negative and despicable image of Spain, Spaniards, and their work. That image has been passed over to this country and has been accepted as veritably part of its cultural tradition and history to the point that it is still taught in the schools. This unfortunate book has been used as historical background to justify political ventures against Spain and to denigrate her formidable religious achievement in America; the *Brief Relation* has been used to engender the so-called "Black Legend" by anti-Catholic writers and anti-Spanish political forces from the sixteenth through the nineteenth centuries when Spain was still a world power. The

nobility of the goal pursued in the book does not justify the use of improper means.

1553

Several boats crossing from Mexico to Cuba and carrying about a thousand people, including five Dominican friars, are dashed by a terrible hurricane on the coast of Corpus Christi, Texas. The Indians take away all the clothes from the three hundred survivors " men, women and children. They are left completely naked. Eventually, many of these survivors will die or be killed, and a few of them will return by land to Mexico. The Dominicans, Diego de la Cruz, Hernando Méndez, Juan Ferrer, and Juan Mena, die as martyrs, according to narration later by Father Marcos Mena.

1554

1. Bartolomé de las Casas becomes interested in the evangelization of Florida and sends some Dominican friars there. This is mentioned by Father Toribio de Benavente (Motolinia) in a letter written to King Charles I.

2. The book *Historia General de las Indias* (General History of the Indies) by Francisco López de Gómara, published two years before, is translated and edited in several languages and is one of the most widely read books of its time. Its information on the lands discovered by Spain in America awakens intense rivalry in several European countries.

3. Because of his experience at sea and his success in the fight with pirates of European seas, Pedro Menéndez de Avilés is appointed captain general of the armada (fleet) of the Indies. He holds this important position until he is named adelantado (governor) of Florida.

1555

The archbishop and viceroy of Mexico and the bishop of Cuba exhort the king to attempt once again the colonization of Florida, and the conversion of its inhabitants to the faith, because "it is a pity that so many thousands of souls be lost by not having anybody to teach them, in spite of the fact that they are so close to Mexico." The king then appoints Don Tristán de Luna, the son of Yucatan's governor, who had previously accompanied Coronado, to conduct an expedition.

1556

1. Because the shortage of women in Cuba (most of the native women having married Spanish men), there are many single men on the

island. Diego Sarmiento, Bishop of Cuba, writes a letter to the king asking him to send women from Florida to Cuba to solve this problem. This is a clear indication of how the Spanish people mixed with the natives of America, thus creating a new race.

2. Havana and other places in the Caribbean are left in a precarious state of affairs by raids of pirate Jacques de Sores throughout the previous year. The defensive system of Spanish colonies here has not yet been thoroughly planned or consolidated. That is why Pedro Menéndez de Avilés, captain general of the fleet to the Indies, writes from Mexico to the House of Trade in Seville expressing his concern for the safety of his convoy. He also mentions some of the precautions he will take against a possible attack of the French pirates.

1557

1. The book about the expedition conducted by Hernando de Soto, titled *Relación Verdadera* ("True Story"), is published this year. All details of the famous expedition to North America are narrated in this book.

2. Dr. Pedro de Santander, an inspector of the crown, writes to Philip II making the proposal to establish a series of settlements and missions stretching from Pensacola, Florida, to Santa Elena (Port Royal), South Carolina. He gives several reasons for such a proposal, among them the defense of Spanish sovereignty on said territory, the protection of Spanish fleets in their passage between America and Spain, the expected profit of the enterprise, and the punishment and conversion of the Indians who had killed many Spaniards throughout the preceding years. Philip II, after assessing the value of the project, gives his approval to carry it out and puts it in the hands of Luis de Velasco, the viceroy of Mexico.

1558

On September 3, Viceroy Luis Velasco of Mexico sends Guido de los Bazares with a group of soldiers and sailors in search of a good bay in Florida to establish a village. He arrives at the Bay of Mobile and names it "Filipina Bay," in honor of Philip II, the new king of Spain. He explores and finds a forest nearby with a variety of trees which he considers to be of importance for the construction of boats and houses. He also finds a large meadow for pasture, and in the houses of the natives he sees corn, beans, and pumpkins. He takes possession of that bay in Alabama and returns to Mexico to report his findings. Once informed, Viceroy Don Luis de Velasco orders the preparation of thirteen armed ships to colonize Florida. The fleet will leave Veracruz at the beginning of the following summer.

1559

Sent by the viceroy of Mexico, Don Tristán de Luna arrives at Pensacola Bay and founds the city of the same name. Luna is one of those robust Castilians of strong faith and impeccable conduct and enjoys an excellent reputation. He left in June from Veracruz with 13 ships, 1,500 volunteer colonists, several natives from Florida who had accompanied previous explorers to Mexico, 240 horses, cattle to reproduce, seeds, farm equipment for agriculture, and abundant provisions. The Dominicans Pedro Feria, Domingo de la Anunciación, Domingo Salazar, Juan Mazuelas, Diego de Santo Domingo and Bartolomé Mateos also went along. During the passage, there was a violent hurricane and one ship was lost. Although their plan was to reach Mobile Bay, explored by Guido de los Bazares, they arrive at Pensacola Bay on August 14 and begin to build a town on a hill overlooking the bay. This will be the first of three towns that Don Tristán has planned to establish in order to convert the natives to the Catholic faith. He advises the colonists that they should start by being role-model neighbors.

1560

1. Don Tristán sends a ship to Mexico to bring provisions. At the same time he organizes three expeditions to explore the region and find fertile lands for agriculture. Mateo del Sauz, Father Domingo de la Anunciación, Father Salazar, one hundred fifty soldiers, and some horses navigate the Choosa River in Alabama up to the Talladega area. There Sauz forms an alliance with the Coosa to fight against the Natchez, their enemies. They follow them to the Mississippi River, where they meet the enemy. At the request of the Spanish, a peace treaty is signed, and no blood is shed. Sauz sends a delegation to notify Luna about the region, but he soon decides to go himself, with all his entourage, to Pensacola. Father Feria, with another group, travels up the Escambia River, and Luna himself also travels into Alabama, where he establishes a settlement and a mission which he calls Santa Cruz de Nanicapan (Claiborne area). But after a couple of months, everyone returns to Pensacola. Then, Luna sends Father Feria with two small ships in search of provisions to Cuba or Mexico; a hurricane has sunk all the other ships. There are not enough provisions, and discontent is growing. Under these conditions, Jorge Cerón incites the colonists to rebel against Luna and to ask him to return to Mexico after having remained for more than a year.

2. Provisions for the Luna expedition are sent on July 1 aboard five ships heading to Pensacola: the *San Juan de Ulúa*, the *San Antón*, the *Trinidad*, the *Santiago*, and the *San Juan*. Father Gregorio Beteta, Luis

Daza, and Captain Diego Viedma with a group of soldiers go along also. They take horses, sheep, goats, chickens, corn seeds, and other provisions.

1561

In March, Angel Villafañe, born in Valencia de Don Juan, León, arrives in Pensacola with two shiploads of provisions, filling the hungry colonists with joy. Together with the provisions, he brings the order to move the group to the Atlantic Coast, leaving only some seventy soldiers in the town of Pensacola. Villafañe, replacing Luna, leaves with the colonists. He makes a stop in Havana, where some remain and others embark, among them the Dominicans Juan Contreras, Gregorio Beteta from León (who had already been in Florida), and Brother Mateo de la Madre de Dios. Villafañe leaves once again, taking along Captain Antonio Velázquez, Alonso González de Arroche, and Juan Torres aboard the caravel *Catalina*, and heads northwest, reaching the coast of Virginia, which he explores. He then turns to the South, heading down the coast of North Carolina to reach the area in South Carolina where they disembark. Here, in Santa Elena (Parris Island), they remain for some time but do not find the place to their liking. Finally, they receive an order to return to Cuba and then Mexico. Villafañe brings along some natives whom he plans to educate in the Christian faith and language. Among them is Paquiquineo, the brother of the cacique of Axacan (Virginia). He is introduced to the viceroy of Mexico, Don Luis de Velasco, who then baptizes him. Soon after, Villafañe brings him to Spain, where he is received by Philip II. During his time in Spain, he is educated in several Spanish and later Mexican schools. A few years later, Father Segura will bring him to evangelize Axacan (Virginia).

1562

1. Jean Ribault suggests the idea of establishing a port in Florida to Elizabeth I of England and Admiral Coligny of France. Both lend their support and aid, and he prepares an expedition with other French Huguenots. They arrive in Florida and establish Port Royal, but the group disappears shortly thereafter.

2. Diego Gutiérrez, navigator for the crown and examiner of navigators, publishes a detailed map of the Americas in which California appears for the first time.

3. Lucas Vázquez de Ayllón, Jr., claims his right to settle Chícora, where his father had died years before. The king grants him permission to take three caravels with 250 soldiers and settlers, eight Dominican mis-

sionaries, cattle, pigs, sheep, and some goats from Puerto Plata. He is also to experiment with plantations of sugar cane, vines, olive trees, and other plants of Castile. Naturally, he is to convert the Indians by peaceful means and establish two towns. He begins to look for ways to finance his expedition and get settlers, soldiers, and ships. He finds it very difficult until, in October of the following year, he finally sails to Hispaniola. There most of the settlers desert him, and the expedition fails. To avoid financial responsibilities, Ayllón escapes to Colombia, where he will die some time later fighting the Tupe Indians.

1563

1. Tomás Terrenot, Sieur de Chantone, ambassador of Spain in France, writes to Philip II informing him that Admiral Gaspard de Coligny and the Queen of England have financed Ribault's expedition to Florida to establish a port. This could be used to attack Spanish fleets sailing through that area on their way from the Americas to Spain.

2. John Hawkins, an English pirate, brings a big load of African persons to America; three ships with three hundred black males arrive in the West Indies to be sold as slaves.

3. General Juan Menéndez, the son of Pedro Menéndez de Avilés, who was commander of a fleet of thirteen ships on their way from Havana to Spain, perishes in a sea storm near the islands of Bermuda in the month of September. His flagship *La Concepción* will never be found.

1564

1. Philip II orders an expedition to establish the commercial route between Mexico and the Philippines. Four ships with four hundred men under the orders of Captain Miguel López de Legazpi and Father Andrés de Urdaneta, with another five Augustinian missionaries, arrive in the Philippines. Legazpi remains there, and Father Urdaneta is sent to find a return route. He finds favorable winds from the west and arrives in California. He travels down the entire coast to reach Acapulco once again. Thus the Pacific commercial route for galleons is plotted; this route will be used during the coming centuries between Mexico and the Orient.

2. A series of pirate attacks from the French port of Florida against Spanish commercial ships convinces Philip II that he should occupy Florida and dislodge the Huguenots brought there by Laudonnière. The king considers the French port an intrusion in the lands discovered, explored, and populated at different times by Spain. He chooses for this undertaking the experienced naval commander Don Pedro Menéndez de Avilés, who has also asked the king to go to those lands with the hope of

finding his only son, Juan, who had disappeared in a shipwreck of the Spanish fleet. Menéndez thinks that his son could be alive and held captive by some tribe. He is also prepared to invest his large fortune into this adventure, which includes the conversion of the Florida natives.

3. On May 14 by an order of Philip II, Diego Mazariegos, governor of Cuba, sends Captain Hernán Manrique aboard the frigate *Our Lady of Conception* to identify the place in Florida where the French have established their post. Manrique searches all inlets and bays north of Cape Canaveral. At Santa Elena Bay (Port Royal), he finally finds Charlesfort, built by the French and recently abandoned. Manrique destroys it and returns to Havana to report on his expedition. The report is immediately sent to Spain. Between 1559 and 1564 Spain spends over two hundred thousand gold pesos in four attempts to colonize Florida.

4. The Armada de las Carreras de las Indias (Armada of the route to the Indies) is established. It consists of the formation and organization of an armed fleet to defend Spanish commercial ships sailing between Spain and the Americas against the attacks of British, French, and Dutch pirate ships. The Armada will escort the ships from Spain to Havana, whence they will leave to bring provisions to the colonies in South, Central, and North America. Once they return from the different places in America with other products or goods to Havana, they will be escorted on their passage to Spain. The fleets will usually make two trips a year, and they sail through the channel between Florida and the Bahamas toward the Azores and Spain. At this time, Spain claims the Atlantic Coast from Florida to Newfoundland as part of its sovereignty. To defend those fleets traveling through the channel, she plans to establish a city near the current Annapolis, South Carolina, while she also continues looking for a strait or channel which will join the Atlantic with the Pacific in that area.

1565

Pedro Menéndez de Avilés arrives in Florida on August 28 and establishes the city of St. Augustine. Menéndez was born in Avilés (Asturias), and since his youth, has shown great intelligence and courage at sea, fighting for 15 years against pirate ships in command of a fleet. It is said that he is generous, honest, friendly, good-natured, and brave. His deeds made him so popular that Philip II brought him along on his fleet to England for his marriage to Mary Tudor. He saved the king's life and was named a knight of the Order of St. James. Philip II chooses him now as chief of the expedition to Florida, designating him captain and governor. Menéndez begins, then, to prepare his trip and spends a fortune, approximately 200,000 ducats; however, a galleon, 200 soldiers, and 95 sailors are financed by the king. Menéndez sets sail from Cádiz on July 28 with 12 ships bearing 2,646 persons, among them soldiers, sailors and colonists; there are also carpenters, blacksmiths, masons, and locksmiths; 20 are married; there are also 12 Franciscan missionaries, eight Jesuits, four diocesan, and one Mercedarian. The 900-ton flagship is that of Don Pelayo, and after a stop in the Canary Islands he arrives at the coast of San Agustín, Florida, on August 28. Its people disembark to begin founding the town, and Menéndez takes possession of the land in the name of the king of Spain on September 8. Without losing any time, he travels by land with five hundred soldiers toward to the inlet of the St. John River, where the French had established their port. After four days of a difficult journey due to the area's marshes, thickets, heat, and mosquitoes, they arrive near Fort Caroline on September 20. Early in the morning they make a surprise attack and take the fort, capturing the entire French garrison. Menéndez changes the name of the fort to San Mateo Fort. He remains there one week, organizing everything. He leaves 300 soldiers to defend it and returns with the rest to St. Augustine, where he is received by a jubilant population singing "*Te Deum*" in thanksgiving. In a few days, when Menéndez learns that another group of Huguenots is further south, he hurries there and eliminates everyone, including Ribault. But he spares the lives of those who confess to be Catholic. Ribault offers Menéndez 300,000 ducats as ransom, which is rejected. The site is called Matanzas. Thus, Menéndez returns Florida to Spanish sovereignty and gives a lesson to French pirates, who ten years earlier had set fire to Havana and sown terror with their pillage and murder. Fathers Francisco López de Mendoza and Gonzalo Solís de Meras, along with other priests, celebrate Mass and begin to build the city. The layout of the San Marcos Fort, the first hospital, the first school, and the first parish, of which Father López de Mendoza will be the first parish priest, are begun. At Cape Canaveral, Menéndez orders the construction of a ship and the country's first road, which will link the city of St. Augustine with San Mateo Fort near Jacksonville, Florida. At the sametime he begins construction of the "Old Spanish Trail" that will connect St. Augustine, Florida, with San Diego, California, and will take two years to complete. From the start, Menéndez also begins the construction of the forts of Santa Elena, South Carolina, San Marcos in St. Augustine, Cape Canaveral, Tequesta (Miami), Calus (Charlotte Harbor), and Tocobaga (Tampa). He encourages the cultivation of the land, tries to establish friendly relations with the natives, and attempts to convert them, in accordance with what Philip II writes to him in a letter: "The main objective which you must always remember and achieve is the conversion of the Indians to the Catholic Faith. Thus, a religious person must accompany you." Therefore, to convert the natives, Menéndez establishes the Name of God Mission near St. Augustine, where Father Francisco Pareja and other missionaries will put forth arduous apostolic efforts years later. Asking for help from the king, Menéndez tells him that Florida, "after all, is a suburb of Spain, as it takes no more than 40 days to sail here and usually the same time to return."

1566

1. Menéndez writes to Spain to make a progress report and asks for more aid. He begs San Francisco de Borja to send some missionaries, and in June the Jesuits Pedro Martínez, Juan Rogel and Brother Francisco Villarreal leave in a Dutch ship. On September 28, they reach Cumberland Island, Georgia, called "Tacatacuru" by the natives. Father Martínez and nine volunteers travel by canoe to search for drinking water and to ask where the city of St. Augustine is located. Natives surround them and strike Father Martínez in the head with a club, killing him; they do the same to the rest. Meanwhile, the ship is propelled along by a storm and ends up in Cuba. Here the missionaries dedicate themselves to learning the native language with 18 Indians from Florida. Among them is the sister of the cacique whom Menéndez had sent to Cuba to be trained as a catechist. Menéndez visits the Orista region (Santa Elena, South Carolina), reconciles this cacique with that of Güale (Georgia) who were at war with each other, and then invites both to a grand banquet. Right after this visit, a garrison of soldiers is established here, and the construction of San Felipe Fort is begun on Parris Island, South Carolina. Santa Elena Mission is also established, headed by Father Rogel. From here Menéndez sends an expedition under Captain Juan Pardo and Sergeant Hernando Boyano with 125 soldiers, who arrive in what is now Columbia. They find very fertile land and quartz mines. The soldier Juan Ribas also finds a beautiful native woman, whom he marries; she takes the name of Luisa. A priest and four soldiers are left here. Then they continue traveling in the lands of North Carolina, and they build a small fort in Polk County named San Juan de Xualla, where they leave Boyano with 13 soldiers. Pardo continues East, and in Guatari, two friendly women caciques receive them and say they want to become Christians. Father Sebastián Montero remains there with four soldiers while Pardo and the others return to Santa Elena. In the area of Anderson County, North Carolina, Father Montero remains with the Indians for six years and has a great success among them. He teaches the natives catechism, Sunday observance, abstinence on Fridays, the Ten Commandments, the Spanish language, writing, and reading. According to a witness soldier, many of

them learn Spanish, especially the chieftains, to whom the priest gives more time. After six years Father Montero becomes sick and retires from the place.

2. Menéndez also reaches the Tampa area this year, where he leaves a garrison of soldiers, near Safety Harbor.

3. Menéndez writes to Philip II. He suggests the possibility of taking products from the interior of Florida by raft on the rivers flowing from St. Augustine to Tampa and sending them later to Veracruz or Cuba on his galleons.

1567

Menéndez leaves Havana with a new expedition made up of fourteen ships, fifteen hundred men, several Jesuits and indigenous catechists who were in Cuba. He also takes along seed, a wide variety of animals, and abundant provisions. He reinforces the garrisons that he had previously established in Tampa, and orders a house to be built for Antonia, the sister of Cacique Carlos. But once she returns, Antonia escapes with her tribe. The regions explored by Menéndez are Calus (Charlotte Harbor area), Tocobaga (Tampa), and Tequesta (Miami). The Jesuits Rogel and Villarreal work for a time there to eradicate idolatrous beliefs, stop polygamy, and pacify the chiefs of enemy tribes. Christian morality is very hard for the natives to observe. Rogel tries to convert the cacique so that the entire tribe of Calus may follow his example. He travels to Havana to look for provisions. While there, he teaches catechism and baptizes a native woman from Florida whom Menéndez had brought. He orders that they care for her and recommends that she marry a Spaniard so that when she returns to Florida she can help convert the natives. Sometime later, Rogel returns with three ships loaded with supplies for Tampa. Members of a group of soldiers go on land and learn that the Spanish garrison has been wiped out by the natives. Then, they make their way toward Charlotte Harbor Bay. In Tequesta (Miami), Menéndez has established a garrison with thirty soldiers, who built twenty-eight houses and a small church inside a stockade. There Brother Villarreal, with several indigenous catechists, teaches Christian doctrine daily and venerates a large cross erected in the town. The natives resist Christian beliefs, and a quarrel takes place between a soldier and a prominent native which causes several deaths. Then the captain orders the garrison and missionary to withdraw to Calus (Charlotte Harbor). Menéndez returns to Spain in search of reinforcements and brings the cacique's brother and another six prominent Indians, offered by the cacique to accompany him to Spain. There he tries to convince the Jesuits to send more personnel to

Florida. He suggests the idea of founding a school in Havana for a hundred Indian children brought from Florida and some twenty from Spain, so that the former learn Spanish and then return to Florida as interpreters and catechists. Once the natives who had come with Menéndez are instructed, they are baptized in Seville's cathedral by the bishop of Chile. Present are Menéndez, Sevillian authorities, officers from the House of Trade who serve as godfathers, and the future Jesuit missionaries.

1568

1. The general of the Jesuits, San Francisco de Borja, designates Father Juan Bautista Segura, Jerónimo Ruíz Portillo, Antonio Cedeño, Gonzalo del Alamo, Brothers Pedro Linares, Agustín Báez, Juan Carrera (from Ponferrada, León), and eight postulants as Florida missionaries. They leave with Menéndez in April, and in June they reach Florida, where the Jesuits lodge in a shack made of palm leaves and begin their missionary work. Father Segura, in his capacity as vice provincial, appoints Father Cedeño and Brother Báez to Santa Catalina, Georgia. Father Rogel goes to Santa Elena, South Carolina, where twenty-five caciques promise to become Christians. He spends a couple of months there in his missionary work and then goes with Father Cedeño to Havana, bringing some young Güales to have them educated in a Jesuit school.

2. When Menéndez returns to Havana, he takes over as governor of Cuba and Florida. He summons Tocompaba, cacique of Calus (Charlotte Harbor), who heeds the order, promises to convert to Christianity, and shortly thereafter accompanies Menéndez to Calus. There he forswears his idolatry and publicly burns his idols. However, this is only a sham. The tension begins to rise, and there is a fight between the natives and the Spanish. The cacique dies, along with several others from both sides. As a result of this skirmish, the missionaries withdraw. Menéndez, along with Fathers Segura and Cedeño, leaves for Tequesta (Miami). They are received by Diego, the brother of the cacique who had been baptized in Seville, the cacique himself, and a number of natives. The cacique promises to convert, making a large cross which is set up in the town and worshiped by all. Menéndez and the two Jesuits sail toward St. Augustine to bring back some thirty soldiers to Tequesta, thus protecting the area and the missionaries, and also to repair the mission and the garrison. During this time, Menéndez 2travels constantly between Florida, Cuba, and Spain in search of aid from the crown, including personnel and provisions.

3. Dominique Gourges from Bordeaux, France, leaves with three ships and some 180 men toward Florida to avenge the expulsion of the

141

French two years before. He makes a surprise attack on three Spanish settlements and flees, having savagely killed the majority of their residents and destroyed the San Mateo Fort.

1569

1. The Jesuits, faced with hostility and difficulty in converting the natives of Tequesta, Calus, and Tocobaga, concentrate in the region of Georgia and South Carolina. They encounter many difficulties there as well, due to the savage practices and unrestrained immorality of the natives. In four months, the Jesuits learn the Güale language and work hard, using a variety of methods to convert the natives. However, after a year of work, the results are minimal, due in large part to the Indians' nomadic way of life, their immoral practices, and wide-ranging vices. Father Rogel teaches them to plant corn in order to settle them, but they mock him and pay little attention. At this place Brother Agustín Báez writes his grammar of the Güale language, the first book written in the United States. In November, Brother Báez dies as a result of an epidemic.

2. At the end of this year, the City of St. Augustine loses its importance. The main center of operations becomes Santa Elena, South Carolina, where captain Esteban de las Alas receives 270 colonists to fortify the town.

1570

1. Forced by the inspectors of the crown, Menéndez de Avilés gives the order in June to withdraw from Florida all soldiers with the exception of the 150 paid by the king. The soldiers leaving Florida arrive to Spain in October.

2. In a letter to San Francisco de Borja in February, Father Avellaneda writes that Father Luis Quirós and Brothers Gabriel Gómez and Sancho Ceballos are accompanying Menéndez on one of his expeditions to Florida. In Havana, Brother Pedro Linares and the catechists Cristóbal Redondo, Alonso Méndez, Juan Menéndez, and Gabriel Solís join them. Also included is Don Luis, the brother of the cacique of Axacan, who has been educated in Spain and Mexico for several years. Father Rogel continues working tirelessly for eleven months in Orista (South Carolina) so that the natives form a town. He follows them through the fields, gives them gifts, and builds twenty houses which they later abandon to continue their nomadic life. They reject Christian teaching and tell him that the devil is best because he makes them strong for war. Discouraged, Father Rogel returns to Santa Elena on July 13, after having worked there several months without obtaining any results. A similar situation occurs with Brother Villarreal in Tupiqui.

142

3. Fathers Segura and Quirós, three brothers, four catechists and Don Luis, the brother of the cacique of Axacan, leave Florida for Virginia. Father Segura puts his trust in Don Luis and uses him as guide, interpreter, and catechist. They come upon the Potomac River, thinking it is the passage to the Pacific, and disembark on September 10. With Don Luis as a guide, they continue and reach the Rappahannock River. There, close to the city of Chiskiac, after having played several tricks, the native Don Luis asks the missionaries, who had gone without military protection, for the axes they were carrying. He kills all but the catechist Alonso Méndez, who arrives in Santa Elena and recounts what happened. When Menéndez learns about the murders of Father Segura and his companions, he leaves with Father Rogel, Brother Villarreal, and the catechist Méndez toward Chesapeake Bay with thirty soldiers. He demands the natives hand over the traitor Don Luis in five days. Since they fail to comply with this term, he hangs eight of them as punishment for the crime committed and as a lesson for the future. Menéndez plans to establish his field house and ranch in Guatari, North Carolina, and summons his wife, daughter, son-in-law, and servants to Santa Elena.

1571

During the past six years, Menéndez has traveled to Spain and also to the Spanish territories of the Caribbean, looking for settlers, soldiers, missionaries, provisions, and ammunition to develop and protect his colony. He can truly be called the "Father of Florida.

1572

1. As a result of the deaths of the five Jesuits in Virginia, the authorities of the Society decide to withdraw Jesuits from Florida and have them head toward Mexico to work in that missionary field. The order to withdraw from Florida is given by San Francisco de Borja, then general of the Society of Jesus.

2. Menéndez de Avilés, after seven years of intense colonizing efforts in Florida, also returns to Spain. The king entrusts to him the preparation of the invincible Spanish Armada.

1573

1. Spain decides to forego an armed conquest in order to achieve its mission in the Americas. It adopts the philosophy of pacification, which consists of coming into a territory peacefully to evangelize and occupy the territory. Force should only be used in case of armed resistance or as a response to an attack. At the same time, new legislation

called *"Nuevas Ordenanzas de Descubrimiento y Población" (New Ordinances on Discovery and Population)* is issued. This legislation seeks to consolidate Spanish sovereignty over the conquered territories and the establishment of numerous urban settlements along the borderlands, motivated by economic and social incentives.

2. A royal charter orders that eighteen Franciscans be brought to Florida to replace the Jesuits, but only nine arrive. Their work will shortly extend throughout Florida, Georgia, and the Carolinas.

1574

1. After governing Florida for seven years, the great Pedro Menéndez de Avilés dies on September 16 in Santander, Spain, where Philip II has summoned him to occupy a distinguished position in the Spanish navy. On September 8, shortly before his death, in a letter to his nephew in Florida, he says: "After the salvation of my soul, there is nothing I desire more than to be in Florida and there end my days saving souls. . . . This is my desire and it means all my happiness. May the Lord bring it about as He can, if He sees it necessary."

2. At this time, there are approximately nine thousand towns of Indians, with some five million inhabitants throughout Spanish America. Many books have already been printed in the Americas in twelve different indigenous languages.

1575

1. Catalina Menéndez, daughter of Don Pedro Menéndez de Avilés, appeals to the Council of the Indies that the agreements made with her father be fulfilled, along with what is established in his will. In spite of the king's order, a slow and costly lawsuit follows. Catalina remains in Grado, Asturias, instead of going to live in Madrid as she had desired.

2. This year witnesses the death of Don Francisco Ibarra at the age of thirty-seven. He was governor of Nueva Vizcaya, which included all the northwestern territories of Mexico, New Mexico, and Arizona.

3. Father Alonso Reynoso and several Franciscans arrive in Florida. They work at the Mission Nombre de Dios and have a number of converts.

4. A cacique of South Carolina, his wife, and their children are baptized in Santa Elena. This is an indication of missionary work done there. Diego de Velasco states in a letter that there are no more Christian Indians mostly because of the small number of missionaries.

144

1576

The natives of Santa Elena, South Carolina, kill Sergeant Hernando Boyano. When Captain Solís wants to punish those found guilty, some two thousand Indians kill twenty more soldiers in an ambush. They set fire to and destroy the fort. Through the courage and determination of the new governor, Pedro Menéndez Marqués, Santa Elena begins to recover.

1577

1. Governor of Florida Menéndez Marqués rebuilds Santa Elena Fort, which had been destroyed by the natives the year before. Now he builds it in another area and calls it San Marcos Fort.

2. The natives of the area of Saint Augustine revolt and attack the city, causing large-scale destruction.

1578

Captain Diego de Ordoño and seventeen soldiers sent to Santa Elena are taken by surprise and killed by the Indians on Sapelo Island. The same fate awaits Captain Gaspar Arias and his squadron in Tolomato, Georgia.

1579

1. Juan Ponce de León II is appointed governor of Puerto Rico. He is an intelligent and cultured man, and puts forth great effort building the town hall, courthouse, and jail.

2. The pirate Francis Drake attacks and captures several Spanish ships sailing on the Pacific carrying goods between Peru and Spain. At the same time, French pirate Nicholas Estrozi, who used to raid Spanish settlements along the Atlantic Coast, is captured in Georgia by Pedro Menéndez Marqués, together with a band of twenty-two other corsairs. Taken to St. Augustine, Florida, they are judged and executed.

1580

1. In July a battle is waged in Florida, with Menéndez Marqués defeating the French forces led by Gilbert Gil. This defeat ends France's plans of entering Florida.

2. In the city of St. Augustine, one fourth of all marriages performed are between Spaniards and native women.

3. Father Alonso Reynoso and several Franciscans arrive this year in Florida to work at the Name of God Mission. They begin to get a significant number of converts.

1581

Captain Francisco Chamuscado, ten soldiers, nineteen Christian Indians, ninety horses, and six hundred cows, along with sheep, goats and pigs, depart from Mexico for Cíbola, New Mexico. The Franciscan Fathers Agustín Rodríguez, Francisco López, and Juan de Santa María also join the expedition. They reach the area of Bernalillo and establish themselves in Puaray, near Albuquerque. After some time there, the soldiers decide to return, but the missionaries choose to stay and evangelize the natives. According to Hernando Gallegos, one of the survivors, the three friars have died as martyrs at the hands of the Apaches. Father Agustín Rodríguez is the first person to have given the current name to that region, calling it "New Mexico of Santa Fe of San Francisco."

1582

1. Antonio Espejo, a wealthy merchant from Córdoba living in Mexico, asks permission to organize a rescue of the missionaries remaining in New Mexico. He leaves in November with Father Bernardino Beltrán, fourteen soldiers, and some Christian Indians as guides and interpreters. After reaching the area, they learn that the missionaries have been martyred. Thus it is proved once again that evangelization without military protection is not successful. The expedition continues exploring the area. They go on to Arizona and discover the famous silver mines of Prescott. They continue into Zuñi territory, up to the Río Grande Valley, and head south to return to Mexico after a year of exploration, having covered roughly four thousand miles.

2. The revised calendar of Pope Gregory XIII is adopted by Spain, Portugal, and France. Later it will also be adopted by the rest of the world.

1583

1. With the intensification of pirate attacks, Spanish authorities decide to reinforce the Morro Castle in San Juan, Puerto Rico. A new semicircular parapet is built, in which six more cannons are installed below the existing ones.

2. A royal order commands the viceroy of Mexico to extend his territory farther north. Though some individuals show no interest whatsoever, the viceroy dares to spend money in the enterprise.

1584

1. Britain's Sir Walter Raleigh sends to the Indies an expedition headed by Philip Amadas, Arthur Barlowe, and Simon Fernandez, a Portuguese pilot. They take a route via the Canary Islands, arrive at Roanoke Island on July 4 and explore the area for a month. They return to England with the idea of falling upon any Spanish ship they may find along the way.

2. An average of 375,000 pounds of sugar is produced in Puerto Rico this year. Don Gonzalo Rodríguez owns two sugar mills, one in Yabucoa and another on Vieques island.

1585

1. Upon his return from the Philippines, the Spanish navigator Francisco de Galí arrives near the San Francisco Bay. He explores the coast of California and continues his trip down toward Acapulco.

2. Father Alonso Reynoso and another thirteen Franciscans reach the city of St. Augustine, Florida, where they are received by Governor Menéndez Marqués. They begin their missionary work in the various missions of the region.

1586

1. England tries again, through the expeditions of Richard Grenville, John White, and Ralph Lane (with the help of Pedro Díaz, a captured Spanish pilot), to establish a permanent settlement in the Chesapeake Bay area. The hostility of the Indians, however, and the fear of being caught by the Spaniards, who claim sovereignty of the territory extending from the peninsula of Florida to the Santa María Bay (Chesapeake), prevent these attempts from materializing.

2. Walter Raleigh establishes a colony on Roanoke Island, North Carolina. The group disappears shortly after, and their fate remains unknown.

3. Among the various products that the Spanish bring to Spain is the potato. However, it will take many more years before it will become a staple food in the Spanish diet.

1587

1. The pirate Francis Drake, with a fleet of twenty ships and two thousand men, attacks St. Augustine, Florida, plunders it, and sets fire to the city, levelling it completely. He goes on to Santa Elena, South Carolina, to similarly plunder and rase it, but a strong storm stops him. All the efforts of the inhabitants of St. Augustine over fifteen years are

wiped out by that disgraceful action of piracy promoted by a foreign government. With help from Havana, the rebuilding of the city is begun once again.

2. The map of Richard Hakluyt shows clearly the regions of Quivira (Kansas), Tiguex, and New Mexico.

3. A royal decree authorizes Father Francisco Reinoso to take twelve Franciscans to Florida and orders the House of Trade of Seville to give Father Reinoso four hundred ducats to buy bells, chalices, Mass books, and other needed articles for the missions. Each missionary is to be given personal clothing, a mattress, a blanket, a pillow, and one and a half reals a day for his support during the thirty days' Atlantic crossing. The last names of the missionaries given in verse by Father Juan Escobedo are Reinoso, Vigo, Ojeda, Antonio, Bustamante, Corpa, Manzano, Torquemada, Oviedo, Gómez, López, Ruiz, and Escobedo. On October 5, they arrive in St. Augustine, Florida, where they are warmly welcomed by Governor Pedro Menéndez Marqués, and shortly after they are assigned to the various mission places.

4. Bishop Diego de Salamanca promotes agriculture and education, takes an active role in the founding of Ponce, decides to change the sites of San German and Coamo to the present sites, and appeals often to the king on behalf of Puerto Rico, telling him that it is "the key to the Caribbean." After governing the diocese of San Juan for ten years, he will soon resign and retire to the Augustinian Monastery of Madrid, where he will die. He can rightly be called one of the fathers of Puerto Rico.

1588

1. Through an order of Philip II, Pedro Menéndez Marqués sends Captain Vicente González to search for the presence of an English post on the Santa María Bay (Chesapeake). On May 30, González embarks with soldiers. He reaches latitude 39°, searches both sides of the bay, and finds no settlement. As he is leaving the bay, a powerful storm forces him to enter a small inlet where he finds clear evidence of English presence. He arrives in St. Augustine and tells of his finding. His report is confirmed by two Spanish pilots, Alonso Ruiz and Pedro Díaz; both had been captured by the British, were in that place, and now are free.

2. After leading his congregation as bishop of San Juan, Puerto Rico, Augustinian Don Diego de Salamanca ends his pastoral ministry of ten years. He has strongly promoted evangelization on the island.

3. In Florida, Father Alonso Escobedo writes the first poem written in what will be the United States, entitled "La Florida."

4. The Spanish navy suffers a fatal blow through the rout of the Spanish Armada. This episode will soon bring negative results to her colonies in America.

1589

Governor of Florida Menéndez Marqués visits Chesapeake Bay, which the Spanish call "Santa María." Other Spanish before and after also visit and describe the place in detail, placing it at 38° latitude. There a baptized native named Vicente is found. He is brought along to Spain, but he dies during the crossing. They bury him in a monastery at Santo Domingo, Dominican Republic.

1590

1. Without having obtained the permission required by the Laws of the Indies, Gaspar Castaño, governor of Nuevo León, organizes an expedition and moves north with 170 men. He reaches the Río Grande and heads for Texas.

2. Another twelve Franciscan missionaries leave Spain for Florida with Father Reinoso. The royal accountant of Florida, Bartolomé Argüelles, says that of the twelve that left Spain, six remained at the various ports where the ship stopped.

1591

From Eagle Pass, Castaño de Sosa enters by Pecos River and goes as far as the town of Pecos, whence the natives flee. He continues to the Río Grande, having won submission from thirty towns, and establishes the town of Santo Domingo. He attempts to comply with regulations regarding the protection of the natives. He sends emissaries to Mexico to notify authorities that he has settled on land never occupied by another conquistador, and to ask for acknowledgement from the viceroy. In response, he receives a warrant of arrest for having left without due permission. Later, he is sent to China in exile.

1592

1. The new governor, Don Rodrigo del Junco, arrives in Florida, but his stay is short and is followed by Domingo Martínez de Avendaño. With missions increasing and missionaries becoming scarce, Father Bernardino de San Cebrián asks the Superiors to send more friars.

2. Juan de Fuca, a Greek navigator in the service of Spain, heads an expedition to the Pacific North coast. He explores the bay that bears his name between the State of Washington and the Island of Vancouver.

1593

The Franciscans send Father Miguel Añón and Brother Antonio Badajoz to Santa Catalina Island, Georgia, to invigorate the mission; a garrison has been there for years. The Franciscans establish other missions on Cumberland Island which become very successful in a short time.

1594

Domingo Martínez de Avendaño, appointed governor of Florida, presents his credentials to the governor of Cuba and makes a request for some soldiers and laborers to boost the fortifications of Florida. He also writes to the Franciscan Superior, based in Santo Domingo, to send Father Juan Mesquita back to Florida because he is fluent in the language of the Indians. From Havana the governor takes the dynamic Father Francisco Marrón to replace Rodolfo García Trujillo, an old diocesan priest who for twenty-eight years has been the pastor of St. Augustine's parish. Avendaño immediately writes to the king requesting more missionaries for Florida.

1595

1. Captains Francisco Leyva Bonilla and Antonio Gutiérrez Omaña are sent by the governor to subdue some rebel tribes in the North. They arrive in New Mexico and continue up to Quivira (Kansas). They have several encounters with the natives, and the two die with most of their troops in the place called Matanza. Only a few survive to recount the incident.

2. The navigator Sebastián Rodríguez Cermellón leaves the Philippines for America with the intention of finding a good port on the northern coast of the Pacific. He arrives on his ship *San Agustín* at the port named San Francisco in Drake's Bay. The helmsman of the *San Agustín*, Francisco Bolaños, will return to this bay years later with Vizcaíno.

3. A royal letter orders the House of Trade to provide for the transportation of twelve Franciscans and two helpers to Florida. The House makes arrangements to transport the friars and their belongings with Pedro Sedeño, owner of a ship, who receives 815 ducats in payment. The names of the missionaries are Juan Silva, Blas Montes, Pedro Bermejo, Pedro Fernandez Chozas, Pedro de San Gregorio, Pedro Auñón, Francisco Pareja, Pedro Ruiz, Francisco Ávila, Francisco Berascola, Francisco Bonilla, and Pedro Viniegra. They arrive on September 23, and some days later Father Marrón assigns the missionaries to various places. Governor Avendaño goes with the mis-

sionaries to each place, and in the presence of the Indians he kneels before them, asks for their blessing, and says farewell to them.

1596

1. The Spanish navigator Sebastián Vizcaíno explores the coast of California accompanied by Father Diego Perdomo and other Franciscan missionaries. But hostility from the natives prevents them from continuing the exploration by land.

2. Doña María, cacique of the Timucuas in the area around St. Augustine, Florida, marries the Spanish soldier Clemente Bernal, and they will have three children.

1597

1. Governor of Florida Gonzalo Canzo sends the veteran soldier Gaspar Salas and the Franciscans Pedro Chozas, Francisco Berascola, and thirty Indians to explore the region of Tama, Georgia, where they arrive after an eight-day journey. They find a fertile plain, precious stones, and metals. They visit the Ocute and Guaque regions, and after interesting exchanges with the natives they return to St. Augustine.

2. The Franciscans work with true devotion for the conversion of the Güale Indians. They try to make them abandon some of their customs which are incompatible with Christian ethics, among them polygamy. Father Pedro Corpa calls attention to this matter to Juanillo, brother of the cacique of Tolomato. This angers the native chief, who swears to destroy all the missionaries. He organizes some natives and, on September 13, kills Father Corpa in Tolomato by decapitating him and placing his head on a pole near the bay. He then kills Father Blas in Tupique, Father Añón and Brother Badajoz on Santa Catalina Island. He takes more precautions with Father Berascola, called "the Cantabrian Giant," since he is very tall and strong. But they surprise and kill him in ambush on San Simón Island. They take Father Ávila and another seven Christian prisoners. Finally, the Indian chief of Asao, a friend of Canzo, besieges the town of Yfusinique and kills Juanillo, who has taken refuge there. The death of these martyrs occurs around September 13 and is caused by the missionaries' preaching against polygamy, which is deeply rooted among the Indians.

3. Father Richard Arthur, an Irish priest, is named pastor of St. Augustine and episcopal vicar of Florida.

1598

Juan de Oñate arrives in the Río Grande region near El Paso, Texas, erects a cross, and takes possession of the land with these words: "I want to take possession of this land today, April 30, 1598, the Day of the Ascension of Our Lord." Oñate is the son of Count Oñate, governor of Nueva Galicia and one of the richest men in Mexico. He is married to a granddaughter of Hernán Cortés, and has distinguished himself throughout the conquest. He is prepared to invest a great deal of money in the colonization of New Mexico. He promises the viceroy to finance two hundred soldiers and colonists, many of them with their families; a number of Christian Indians of Mexico, and seven thousand head of livestock, including cows, horses, mules, sheep, goats, pigs, and many other smaller animals. The caravan is formed by eighty-three wagons carrying provisions, ammunition, tools, plants and seeds of wheat, oats, rye, onions, chili, peas, beans, melon, almonds, walnuts, hazelnuts and olives. Later, it will bring grapevines, orange trees, and lemon trees which will be cultivated in the missions. Oñate invests approximately one million dollars in this expedition. The viceroy promises to pay the expenses of six missionaries, provide various pieces of artillery, and grant a loan of six thousand pesos. He will also give him the title of governor and then "Adelantado," which is an honorific title given by the king to men of special merit in the conquest. The Franciscan missionaries, Father Alonso Martínez, Father Cristóbal Salazar, Brother Pedro Vergara, and five others also go on the expedition. After Oñate takes possession, Mass is offered, and the entire group gathers later for a banquet of thanksgiving to God for having allowed them to arrive there after so many hardships along the way. They prepare a meal with fish, game, fruits, and vegetables, which captain Gaspar Pérez de Villagrá describes in his diary: "On April 30, 1598, not very far from El Paso, all of us survivors gathered together around a great fire, in which fish, meat and fruit was being roasted to commemorate the sufferings and to thank God for the happy outcome of so much agony; all of us were very happy." A true thanksgiving dinner! The expedition now heads north up the banks of Río Grande and in June arrives to the confluence of the Río Grande and the Chama, where they establish themselves and begin the foundations of the town of San Juan, a large church, and, a short distance farther up, the Mission of San Lorenzo de los Picuries. Mass is offered, the first bullfight is organized, and a play about Moors and Christians is presented, written by Captain Marcos Farfán. An irrigation canal is built, and Oñate meets with the caciques of the area. In a short time, the town moves to San Gabriel de los Españoles, which constitutes the headquarters for Oñate and the place of departure of missionaries. These missionaries, this same year, establish the Missions of the Assumption in Sia, the Assumption in Gipuy Viejo, and San Lorenzo in Taos. Oñate immediately begins to send explorations to establish friendship agreements with the natives. He puts himself in charge of one of them and heads toward the north, crosses Oklahoma, arrives in Wichita, Kansas, and probably reaches southern Nebraska. He entrusts his nephew, Vicente Zaldívar, with an exploration toward the northeast and arrives in northwest Texas in the Great Plains. He contemplates the herds of buffalo which Cabeza de Vaca had already seen before.

1599

1. The Pueblo Indians living on a fortified hill called the Rock of Acoma treacherously kill Juan Zaldívar and his small escort. His brother Vicente leaves to call those of Acoma to account. They put up a strong resistance. However, after three days of intense battle, the Spanish climb that almost impregnable rock using thick ropes, attack the city, and capture five hundred Pueblo warriors to be tried. Punishment is severe in order to teach a lesson. Except for occasional skirmishes, the next eighty years witness peace. This will allow colonization, missionary work, the establishment of towns, and the development of agriculture, cattle-raising, and mining to advance. The Spanish bring with them from Acoma sixty young girls and send them to Mexico to be educated in schools run by nuns. Then Father Francisco Zamora establishes the San Jerónimo Mission in the town of Taos, famous for its two-story houses made of a special type of clay. Later, in Taos and the entire region of New Mexico, the Brotherhood of the Penitents will begin. They will have their own meeting places, churches, and their special devotions. They practice several penances and flagellate themselves, especially during Lent. They seem to derive from the Flagellants of Europe. (Today they have houses in Alcalde, Taos, Sandoval, San Miguel, Colfas, Valencia County, and even in the southern part of Colorado.)

2. In this year Franciscan missionaries continue increasing their efforts with the natives of New Mexico. They establish the Missions of Santa Ana in Tamayo and Fernandez in Taos.

3. The chronicles of the Dominicans state that during the sixteenth century forty-eight Dominicans who had graduated from the University of Salamanca have left for the Americas. Among these is Father Gregorio Beteta, who worked in Florida and declined his appointment as bishop to be able to continue his missionary work.

4. By this year, thirty thousand books have reached Mexico from Spain over the past three decades. This number does not include the books that were printed in Mexico since 1535.

153

El Castillo de San Marcos, the fortress of St. Augustine, begun by Menéndez de Avilés, is the oldest in the U.S., a national monument

1600-1650:
Vitality and Corsairs

Colonization and missionary work is intensified. Pirates continue their pillaging.

1600

1. Pedro de Vergara leaves for Mexico in search of provisions for New Mexico and more missionaries. He returns to San Gabriel bringing with him seven Franciscans, seventy new colonists, and the provisions Oñate has asked for.

2. Meanwhile, Vicente Zaldívar, during an exploration, arrives at the actual site of Denver, Colorado, and baptizes the Platte River with the name of "Río Chato."

1601

In June, Oñate leaves with seventy soldiers, two missionaries, seven hundred horses and mules, eight wagons, four cannons, and some Christian Indians. He walks eight hundred miles through lands of New Mexico, Kansas, and the borders of Nebraska and Missouri. This exploration takes him five months, and then he returns to San Gabriel. Here he finds a crisis among the settlers. Most of them demand to leave New Mexico because of its poverty. Some of them make accusations against Oñate to the point that the authorities of Mexico are on the verge of ordering the return of the whole expedition. What stops this decision is the argument that returning to Mexico would mean leaving the natives of New Mexico without the Gospel. This argument had a great power in royal decisions.

1602

Philip II orders the Viceroy of Mexico to explore the Northern Pacific Coast. Sebastián Vizcaíno leaves Acapulco in May with a frigate, two other boats, and 130 men. His purpose is to find a secure port for the commercial ships sailing between America and the Philippines. Besides pilot Francisco Bolaños and cosmographer Jerónimo Martín Palacios, he is accompanied by Discalced Carmelites Andrés de la Asunción, Tomás de Aquino, and Antonio de La Ascensión as writer and cartographer. Upon departure, the whole crew goes to confession and receives Holy Communion. On November 19, they arrive at a bay which they name San Diego; they come ashore, where Mass is offered, and later they sail north. A few days later, they pass Santa Catalina Island, naming the ridge

"Santa Lucia." On December 16, they enter a bay which they call Monterey in honor of the viceroy, running into a river which they name Carmelo because the missionaries were Carmelites. Here they offer Mass beneath a huge oak and remain for seven months exploring the region and spending the Christmas season.

1603

1. After seven months of exploring the Monterey area of California, Vizcaíno and his expedition continue north. They name the cape "Mendocino" in honor of Viceroy Mendoza. They surmount the coast of Oregon, naming the capes they discover "San Sebastián" and "Capo Blanco." The river seen flowing is named Santa Inez. At this point, with many of the men sick and forty-eight dead, they return to Acapulco after almost a year away. They have met their objective in finding the Bays of San Diego, Monterey, and San Francisco as stated on the map drawn. Spain considers California part of her sovereignty. However, having conducted these explorations, she will not occupy the bays shown on her maps for the next 160 years out of a lack of personnel and resources. Her huge domains besides those in Europe, stretch in the Americas from Cape Horn in Argentina to Chesapeake Bay and the Colorado Mountains, and from the Pacific Coast to the Philippines. Naturally, this absorbs all her personnel and economic resources. At this time, Spain has a population of some nine million people. The commercial route between America and the Philippines continues to include Manila, California, and Acapulco, but without an established port in the newly discovered bays.

2. Governor Canzo of Florida visits the towns and missions of Georgia. He arrives at Cumberland Island, reestablishes a beautiful mission, and leaves Indian chief Doña Ana in charge, confirming her supreme authority. He meets with twenty-eight Indian chiefs of the area and establishes a garrison for the protection of the Christian natives.

1604

In October, Oñate, thirty soldiers, and two Franciscans depart San Gabriel, New Mexico, for the West in search of a passage to the Pacific Ocean. He passes through Arizona and arrives at the Colorado River (Bill Williams Fork). They set out on the lower Colorado River through Yuma until they reach the Gulf of California, and the expedition returns again to San Gabriel. Although the expedition is a success for the new territories discovered, they do not find the passageway to the Pacific Ocean, nor mines, nor fertile lands for agriculture. In

156

Mexico, discontent grows, fueled by the high cost of maintaining the colony of New Mexico. Oñate, however, tries to keep hopes high, given the possibilities of the new lands.

1605

1. Through this year Father Cristóbal Quiñones and his Franciscan confreres of New Mexico found the Missions of San Francisco, Santa Ana, San Felipe, and Santo Domingo near present-day Albuquerque.

2. In Florida, the Franciscans also restore the Mission of the Island of Amelia. The first project that Father Miguel undertakes is to remove the remains of Father Miguel Añón and Brother Antonio Badajoz, who had died as martyrs eight years before in Asopo. They had been buried by the native people at the foot of a cross. He placed the remains in a more dignified place.

1606

1. The bishop of Santiago, Cuba, Juan Cabezas Altamirano, takes his leave with great solemnity; he departs Cuba for Florida in a boat that he himself has bought and arrives at St. Augustine in the middle of March. He celebrates the Rites of Holy Week, and on Holy Saturday he ordains 21 priests. Some have come with him; others were born in Florida and educated in the Franciscan Seminary of St. Augustine. Here on Easter Sunday he confirms 350 people. The following Sunday at the Mission "Nombre de Dios" he confirms Chieftainess María, her sons, and 213 more people. On April 13 on Cumberland Island he confirms five tribal chieftains and 308 people. He baptizes the chiefs of San Juan, Santo Domingo, Tocoya, and Puturibato. In Talaxe, the chiefs of Asao, Tasquiche, Aluque, Yfulo, Cascanque, and Tuque give a banquet of typical foods for the bishop, and he confirms them on April 22 together with another 262 natives. These have been prepared by Father Diego Delgado. In Tolomato Mission, four native chiefs welcome him with a great feast in a palm house, and he confirms the chief of Salchiches and 208 of his people. On the Island of Santa Catalina they welcome him with just as much festivity; 286 people receive Confirmation, and eight chiefs of the neighboring peoples are present for this event. Back in Cumberland Island on May 9, he confirms 482 more persons, and later the bishop undertakes his mission with the Timucuas. In all, 370 Spaniards are confirmed as well as 2,074 native people of the Güales and Timucuas. The success of the bishop's trip is extraordinary, since from this visit several thousand more native people and 28 chiefs of the Timucuas, Güales, and Apalaches are converted.

2. The superior of the Franciscans, who had asked Philip III to send a bishop to Florida, sends six more Franciscans as well for these missions.

1607

1. Father Francisco Pareja and Alonso Péñaranda work with the Apalache Indians in the area of Tallahassee and report having several thousand converts at one time. They ask for more missionaries.

2. A little farther north, the colony of Jamestown is founded at the mouth of the James River, Virginia, with a group of some hundred English colonists; among them are Captains Newport, John Ratcliffe, and John Smith.

1608

1. The king of Spain is at the point of signing the order of withdrawal from the colony of New Mexico due to the high cost of maintaining it and the few possibilities of the region. When Father Lazaro Jiménez arrives in Spain with the report that in the last few months the number of converts has doubled, the king changes his mind. Not only does he not order the withdrawal, but also makes New Mexico into a new royal province.

2. Oñate is forced to resign; he returns to Mexico, and lives meagerly, having spent his fortune in the colonization of New Mexico. Oñate is one of the greatest men for his courage and the importance of his exploration and colonization for ten years in the Southwest.

3. The Franciscans are enthusiastically welcomed by the Indians of the area of Ivitachuco, Florida, who send their chieftain to visit the Spanish governor at St. Augustine.

1609

1. The king names Pedro de Peralta royal governor of New Mexico to replace Juan de Oñate. In addition, dynamic Father Francisco Escobar resigns as commissary of the Franciscans of New Mexico. He has the satisfaction of seeing that the Gospel is spreading, for by this time there are some 8,000 native Christians in the region.

2. Father Cristóbal Quiñones is the first music teacher in New Mexico; he installs an organ and teaches the Indians of San Felipe to sing and to play musical instruments.

1610

1. Governor Pedro de Peralta begins the construction of the City of Santa Fe in New Mexico and designates it as the capital, replacing the former capital, San Gabriel. Also in New Mexico the Mission of San

Miguel is constructed; its church is still in use today, perhaps the oldest church in the United States. It has a bell which was cast in 1356 and two paintings by an Italian artist completed in the year 1287. Also this year Captain Gaspar Pérez de Villagrá writes his poem "The History of New Mexico," in which he narrates the events of the conquest of this region.

2. Father Pedro Ruiz, commissary of a Franciscan expedition to Florida, makes a request to the Council of Indies for 24 missals, 30 breviaries (prayer books), 24 manuals, seven hymnals, seven Mass books, seven small bells, 30 sets of holy oils, six iron molds to make hosts, and altar stones. Father Ruiz attests before Gaspar Reyes, a notary of Seville, that these articles are needed.

1611

A Spanish caravel with three navigators enters the St. James River in Virginia. The colonists of Jamestown take them prisoners and keep them in the colony for the next five years. In spite of this situation, the prisoners devise ways to inform the king of Spain about the situation in Jamestown.

1612

1. A contingent of twenty-three Franciscans arrives in Florida with Father Luis Jerónimo de Oré, a native of Peru and a great theologian. In that year the general chapter of the Franciscans, celebrated in Rome, establishes the Franciscan missionaries of Florida and Georgia into a province called Santa Elena. They name Father Juan Bautista Capilla as the first provincial, and from then on a great expansion of the missions begins while the number of native converts grows. This Franciscan province encompasses Florida, Georgia, and Carolina.

2. At this time Father Francisco Pareja writes two books in the Timucuana language: *Grammar and Pronunciation in the Timucuana and Castilian Languages* and *Confessional Guide in the Timucuana and Castilian Languages*.

3. Two Dutch ships arrive at the Island of Manhattan (New York), trading with the native people, and in a short time the Hollanders establish a place for commerce. Later they will buy the island from the Indians for merchandise valued at about twenty-six dollars.

1613

1. Father Alonso Peinado and eight other Franciscans work arduously in missions of the area of Santa Fe, New Mexico, where the Christian natives number eight thousand.

2. A reinforcement of eight more Franciscans arrives in Florida in order to strengthen the new Franciscan Province of Santa Elena.

3. The tobacco plant is brought to Florida for cultivation.

1614

Because of a serious conflict between Father Isidro Ordóñez, missionary of Taos, and Governor Peralta concerning the treatment of the native people, the governor is replaced by Admiral Bernardo Ceballos; at the same time, Father Ordóñez is called to Mexico, and another missionary is named in his place.

1615

1. By now some twenty missions have been founded in the region of Florida. Suddenly a great epidemic strikes the region, and thousands of people will die during the three years that this outbreak lasts.

2. The second part of the famous work of Miguel de Cervantes, *Don Quixote de la Mancha*, is published. The first part was published ten years earlier.

1616

1. Some missions are established in Güale land (Georgia): Santa Isabel, San Pedro de Athuluteca, San Diego de Satuache, and San Felipe de Alabe.

2. Father Jerónimo de Oré makes an official visit to the Franciscans of Güale, gathering them in the Monastery of San José de Sapelo. After the meeting, Father Oré makes a report of his visit through this area.

3. Father Antonio de San Francisco builds the Mission of Santa Clara de Tupiqui, a place where the chiefs of Espogoche and Tupiqui will frequently meet. In many of these missions of Florida, there are centers where adults are taught to read and write. On the other hand, the missions are rather poor and have to be maintained to a great extent from Havana. Just about the only foods produced are corn and beans.

1617

The Missions of Pecos, Santa Cruz in Galisteo, San Buenaventura in Cochiti, and San Ildefonso are established in New Mexico.

1618

1. It is reported this year that New Mexico has eleven missions with churches, fourteen thousand indigenous Christians, and many others preparing for baptism. Living in Santa Fe presently are forty-eight soldiers and colonists.

2. In a report on Florida, it is said that the Franciscans have already established some fifty missions or settlements with their churches and that some sixteen thousand natives had been baptized.

3. Father Juan Rogel, S.J., who had worked so arduously in Florida and Georgia, dies in the city of Veracruz, Mexico.

1619

1. The governor of Florida explains, in a letter to the viceroy of Mexico, the need to reinforce the Fort of St. Augustine because of the constant threat of the English. The viceroy, seeing the importance of the matter, notifies the king and sends Juan Salinas, governor of Florida, a monetary subsidy for a quick arrangement.

2. The first black slaves arrive on a Dutch ship in United States territory, to be sold in the English colony of Jamestown, Virginia.

1620

1. At the Mission of Nombre de Dios, near St. Augustine, the chapel dedicated to Our Lady of the Milk and of Happy Delivery (*Nuestra Señora de la Leche y del Buen Parto*) is established. It is the first shrine in the United States.

2. Father Antonio de la Ascensión, O.C., who had accompanied navigator Sebastián Vizcaíno as a cosmographer, publishes his book titled *Brief Report* on the discoveries of exploration along the northern Pacific Coast.

3. Pilgrims arrive at Plymouth, Massachusetts, aboard the ship *Mayflower*. The Puritans, under William Brewster, begin the establishment of a town and the construction of a separate church.

1621

In Holland, the West Indies Company is created with state and private funds. Its purpose will be to attack and take over the Spanish possessions in America, among them Puerto Rico, the Virgin Islands, and Santo Domingo.

1622

The Spanish galleons *Santa María de Atocha* (550 tons) and *Santa Margarita*, members of a flotilla of 23 ships, are shipwrecked and sink near Cayo Hueso, Florida. They have been wrecked by a violent hurricane. (These two galleons have recently been discovered.)

1623

Father Alonso de Benavides, O.F.M., goes to Spain in search of missionaries. He succeeds in securing fifty friars for the Franciscan missions of New Mexico. It costs eighteen thousand pesos to transport them.

1624

1. French corsairs attack the small Spanish forces defending the islands of Guadalupe and Martinique, and they defeat them. Shortly after, the English do the same with San Cristóbal (St. Kitts).

2. The governor of Florida, Juan Salinas, orders an expedition, composed of soldiers and friendly Indians. Its mandate is to investigate rumors about European settlers in inland Georgia and Carolina. The explorers scout more than three hundred miles, but they fail to find any white men riding on horseback, as reported by the Indians.

3. The Dutch buy from the Manhattan Indians the island of the same name that had been previously visited by Corterreal, Cabot, Gómez, and Verrazano. They pay them sixty guilders and call the stony isle "New Amsterdam." Soon after, they begin construction of a broad way (Broadway) to reach the farms on both sides and to connect the island in the north with the continent.

1625

In this year, since the number of missionaries increase, other new missions are founded, bringing the number to about fifty; at the same time, the number of converts is also increasing. Churches are designed, inspected, and built under the supervision of the missionaries; the greater part of the expenses will be charged to the royal treasury.

1626

1. Father Alonso Benavides establishes, among the Pyres Indians of New Mexico, several missions in Sevilleta, Pilabo, and Senecú. Here Father Benavides obtains the conversion of Sanaba, chief of the Gila Indians, and thus clears the way for the evangelization of these people.

2. Franciscan Fathers Jerónimo Zárate, Francisco Porras, and Cristóbal Quirós learn the language of the Indians of New Mexico, catechize them, and celebrate religious services for the native Hopi, Querez, and Jemez.

1627

1. Father Alonso Benavides founds the Mission of the Assumption in New Mexico. This same missionary brings from Spain an image of Mary called *La Conquistadora*, venerated in the Cathedral of Santa Fe, New Mexico. It is the oldest image of Mary venerated in the United States.

2. Near Cuba a fleet of Dutch pirates captures some ships of a Spanish commercial fleet and scatters others to the coast of Florida.

1628

1. English pirates attack the Islands of Barbados and Nevis and occupy them. The Dutchman Piet Heyn at this time surprises a Spanish fleet as it leaves Cuba and confiscates all the merchandise.

2. Father Juan Ramírez founds, on the Rock of Acoma, the Mission of San Esteban Rey. At first, the Indians receive him with hostility, but they finally accept him and later begin to love him as a true father. He will remain there living with them for many years, teaching them the Christian religion. He will build a great church on "The Rock" and die after having spent some thirty-five years with this tribe. The stone stairway used to climb the Rock of Acoma is still in use today and is called "The Road of the Father."

1629

1. Sister María de Agreda, a Poor Clare nun living in Spain, frequently visits the Jumano Indians of Texas while in ecstasy and instructs them in the faith. For twelve years these Indians come from the northwest of Texas to Santa Fe, New Mexico, and ask the missionaries to baptize them. The missionaries are surprised that the Indians know the Christian doctrine and prayers so well. They tell the missionaries that a beautiful lady, dressed in blue, has converted them to the Catholic faith. Fathers Diego López and Juan Salas, with three soldiers and the Indians, leave and journey some two hundred miles to the East of Santa Fe. The group arrives at the settlement of the Jumanos, where they are received with a great cross adorned with wild flowers, and all ask to be baptized. The missionaries spend some time with them and return to New Mexico astounded. There is a consensus on the description of Sister María de Agreda in Spain, examined by Father Benavides and other witnesses, and that of the Jumanos.

2. Several missions are founded in New Mexico, among them the Mission of La Concepción in Hawikuh, the Mission of San Miguel in Tajique, the Mission of St. Gregory in Abo, and that of Gran Quivira.

3. Fathers Francisco Porras, Andrés Gutiérrez, and Cristóbal de la

Concepción establish the Missions of San Bernardino in Awatobi, San Francisco in Oraibi, San Bartolomé in Shongopovi, San Buenaventura in Mishongopovi, and that of Walpi in Arizona.

1630

1. According to a report, there are in New Mexico twenty-five missions, ninety villages, fifty Franciscans, and some sixty thousand Christian Indians. The city of Santa Fe has one thousand people, and there are twelve Franciscans. In the area of Querez, the town of San Felipe is founded. There are three missions with monasteries and beautiful churches, and some four thousand native Christians who are taught how to read, write, do manual work, and play various musical instruments. Having made so much progress, Father Alonso de Benavides, Franciscan superior of New Mexico, asks the king of Spain and the Pope to create the Diocese of Santa Fe, to be cared for by the Franciscans.

2. In the interior region of Georgia are mentioned for the first time the Missions of San Agustín de Urica and Santa María de los Angeles de Arapala, where missionaries say it is necessary to go on horseback in order to do the work.

1631

1. Father Alonso de Benavides, on his trip to Spain, visits Sister María de Agreda, abbess of the Monastery of Agreda, Soria. These revelations are written in her book titled *Mystical City of God*. She tells him that for twelve years, transported in spirit, she has been visiting the Jumano Indians of Texas. She describes them and also the missionaries, the territory, the dangers, the conversions, and the martyrs. Father Benavides is astonished and convinced of the truth of the related facts.

2. At this time, Father Pedro Miranda dies a martyr in Taos, and the same happens to Father Domingo Zaraoz.

1632

1. Fathers Diego Ortega and Juan Salas, with a group of soldiers, return to visit the Jumano Indians of Texas. Father Ortega remains six months with them while the others return to New Mexico.

2. Father Francisco Letrado, who was in charge of the Mission of Hawikuh, New Mexico, is riddled with arrows while on his knees with a crucifix in his hands praying for his executioners. Father Martín Arvide suffers the same fate, in February, on his journey to Zipia, Arizona.

3. Permission is granted to Cecil Lord Calvert to settle Maryland. The first non-Hispanic Catholic population of the Thirteen Colonies, called St.

Mary's, would settle there. Two years later, a group of Catholics will arrive in Maryland on two ships, the *Ark* and the *Dove*.

1633

1. This year begins with the construction of the *Camino Real* (Royal Road) between St. Augustine and St. Mark, Florida, which is almost completed at the end of the century. Along the road, a chain of missions will be founded in this century: Santa Fe, San Francisco (Gainesville), Santa Catalina de Ajuyca (Hildreth), San Juan de Guacara, Santa Cruz (O'Brien), San Pedro de Potohiriba, Santa Elena de Machava, San Mateo de Tolopatafi, San Miguel de Asile (Lamont), San Lorenzo de Ivitachuco (Tallahassee), Concepción de Ayubale, San Francisco de Ocone, San Juan de Aspalaga, San José de Ocuia, Santa Cruz de Capola, San Martín de Tomole, Purificación de Tama, San Pedro y Damián de Escambe, San Carlos de los Chacatos, San Pedro de los Chines, San Luis de Tamali. These missions will serve the Apalache, Yamasees, and Chatoto Indians. By means of this Royal Road, cattle and grain will be transported from coast to coast in Florida.

2. Father Francisco Porras, working with the Hopi Indians in Walpi, Arizona, is hated by the sorcerers of the tribe because of his prominence. They poison him, and he dies a martyr on June 28.

3. Also in this year, Captain Alonso Vaca and a group of soldiers cross the Río Grande from the area of Santa Fe, head toward the northeast and explore again the territory of the Gran Quivira (Kansas).

1634

1. Father Benavides asked, years before, for the erection of a bishopric in New Mexico. Now the plan is finalized, but the viceroy of Mexico is strongly opposed to the plan and it does not materialize.

2. At the same time it is reported that in Florida some thirty-five Franciscans serve forty-four missions.

3. Fathers Pedro Muñoz and Francisco Martínez make a great effort to establish a permanent mission in the Apalache region of Florida. They are respected and held in great esteem by the Indians. It seems that the mission is St. Louis Inihayca.

4. Spain cedes Curaçao to Holland.

1635

1. Captain Iñigo de la Mota y Sarmiento, from the noble family of the count of Salvatierra, is named governor of Puerto Rico. He takes possession of his charge and will govern the destiny of the island efficiently for six years.

2. Spain loses the Virgin Islands.

3. In Florida, Father Gregorio Mabilla, O.F.M., translates Cardinal Bellarmine's book *Explanation of Christian Doctrine* into the Timucuana language of Florida. He also writes "Short Form for Administering the Sacraments to the Indians and to the Spaniards Who Live Among Them."

1636

The bishop of Cuba, Jerónimo Manrique, with a letter dated in September, reaffirms his jurisdiction over St. Augustine in Florida. The letter states that he is in charge of the priests of the city and chaplain of the fort, exercising all pontifical services.

1637

1. Again, Bishop Manrique asks the crown for tithing of the Church of St. Augustine, Florida. The king agrees, but then reminds him of the economic burdens that he has to assume regarding the administration and the support of the personnel.

2. An expedition is planned to subject the natives of West Florida; its outcome is successful.

1638

1. Damián de la Vega Castro is named governor of Florida and directs the activity of the region for six years. In that time the Apalache Indians will attack a settlement, but the governor with a group of soldiers will be able to repel the attack.

2. The governor of Florida plans to establish a trade line by sea between the city of St. Augustine and a port in the Apalache area, and the following year he will send a frigate. This port, expected to carry on trade with St. Augustine, is used by the missionaries to trade the products of Apalache with other regions as well; this causes serious disagreements between the governor and the missionaries.

1639

1. With the growing aggressiveness of pirates throughout the Caribbean, the reinforcement of the Castillo del Morro in San Juan, Puerto Rico, is necessary. Governor Mota y Sarmiento raises a wall around the front side, and about two million ducats are spent in its construction.

2. The missionary effort of the Franciscans in Florida is changing the hostile attitude of the Indians, and the number of converts continues to grow.

3. The chieftain of the village of Cupaica becomes a Christian, peace among warring tribes is restored, and communication by water is estab-

lished between Apalache and St. Augustine, where food supplies will be arriving.

1640

1. Starting this year and throughout the decade, attacks of Dutch pirates on Puerto Rico, Trinidad, and other Caribbean Islands intensify so much that the people are terrorized.

2. Pierre LeGrand, a French pirate, takes over the vice-admiral ship of a Spanish fleet near Florida by taking advantage of the carelessness of the sailors. LeGrand takes the ship to France, where he remains to enjoy the booty.

3. Serious difficulties arise between the missionaries of New Mexico and the governor, whom they accuse of provoking a rebellion among the natives. Governor Rosas loses his life, and disturbances continue for some time.

1641

1. Spanish forces of the Caribbean decide to respond and attack the French pirates who have occupied the islands of Tortola, Santa Cruz, and Vieques; they force the corsairs to abandon the islands immediately.

2. A strong missionary expansion begins in the Apalache region of Florida; there are many conversions, including eight chieftains of the main villages, who invite the missionaries to build missions there.

1642

Tension continues between the civil and religious authorities of New Mexico. The missionaries claim almost absolute power in their work with the natives, while the governor also wants to exercise his authority over them; he therefore accuses the missionaries of interfering with his authority. Then Alfonso Pacheco de Heredia is named governor of New Mexico with instructions to punish those responsible for the death of Governor Rosas and to eradicate the problem. He will govern the region for three years.

1643

1. Don Fernando de la Rivera Agüero, knight of a military order, is named governor of Puerto Rico. He settles in to govern the Island for seven years.

2. Governor Pacheco of New Mexico, a short time after his arrival, orders the execution of eight soldiers who participated in the death of Governor Rosas and grants amnesty to others less blameworthy. How-

ever, he has a conflict with the missionaries for ordering Sandoval buried in the church cemetery.

3. In Florida, the Franciscans found the Mission of Achalaque and shortly afterward baptize the chief, thus marking the beginning of spreading the faith among the Cherokees. Years later, the Englishman Bristock will visit this mission and relate that he was well received and that it was thriving.

1644

1. Don Fernando de Argüello Carvajal, named governor of New Mexico, takes over his post and will govern the region for the next four years, trying to reestablish tranquillity.

2. Father Pérez de Ribas in his book *Historia de los Triunfos de Nuestra Fe* ("History of the Triumphs of Our Faith") says that in the area of Sonora, Mexico, there are thirty-five missions established by the Jesuits. Each of them serves from one to four Indian villages, and the baptismal records show the names of thirty thousand baptized Indians. These missions will serve as a base to begin the colonization and evangelization of Arizona a few years later.

1645

1. A synod is celebrated in Puerto Rico. Among the various topics discussed are the frequency of attending Mass and the distance one has to travel in order to determine the obligation to attend.

2. The governor of Florida asks the crown to name a deputy governor for the Apalache region, citing the distance from St. Augustine, the fact that there are several missions and towns there, and that the area is an important source of food provisions for St. Augustine. Shortly after, Claudio Luis de Florencia is appointed and arrives in the area, but some time later he and his family will be assassinated by the Indians in a revolt.

1646

1. Damián López de Haro, bishop of Puerto Rico, moves religious life forward all over the island with the publication of the synod's decrees, approved by the crown. They deal with parish organization, clergy and faithful, economic matters, teaching, and various other subjects.

2. This year the village of Coamo tallies a population of one hundred families.

3. England attacks and takes over the Bahama Islands, which have been under the sovereignty of Spain since the arrival of Columbus.

1647

1. Transportation of provisions between Mexico City and New Mexico is of enormous importance. Articles are brought to New Mexico that are neither produced nor crafted there, and diverse products are carried from there. Caravans are formed that consist of some thirty-two wagons pulled by mules. Because of the enormous distance, a caravan is formed once every two years, and it will be useful for changes or transfer of personnel. The arrival of a caravan is an occasion of great joy, a day of festivity. Father Francisco de Ayeta is an expert organizer of these caravans and will lead several in these years. Father Ayeta's help from El Paso will be vital for the fugitive population of the Santa Fe area in the rebellion of the Pueblo Indians years later.

2. The Indians of the Apalache area rise in a revolt, kill the deputy governor, his family, and three missionaries, destroying seven missions; the uprising is quelled, some rebel leaders are executed, and peace returns to the area.

1648

1. From this year on, the Dutch tactic of attacking Spanish colonies will change to doing business with them; but at the same time, the English continue raiding the colonies. Faced with this situation, the governor of Puerto Rico, Riva Agüero, creates the People's Militia, composed of farmers; he trains the people in the use of arms in order to make use of them in case of pirate attacks on Puerto Rico.

2. The Franciscan Order obtains a royal expedient by which they can increase from forty-three to seventy the number of missionaries to serve the missions of Florida. As a result of this grant, Father Pedro Ruiz leaves for Florida with twenty-seven more Franciscans.

1649

1. Canon Diego Torres Vargas writes a book in Puerto Rico entitled *A Description of the Island and the City of Puerto Rico* with interesting anecdotes of the period.

2. An epidemic begins in Florida that will last ten years, causing the death of thousands of people, Indians as well as Spaniards.

Equestrian statue on the grounds of the Arizona state capitol in Phoenix shows Father Eusebio Kino, an Italian-born Spanish Jesuit who worked principally in Mexico and Arizona in the late seventeenth and early eighteenth centuries, founding mission towns and protecting the interests of Indians (Henry Unger photo)

1650-1700:
Growth and Martyrdom

The number of settlements and missions increase; rebellion of the natives makes many new martyrs.

1650

Captains Hernán Martín and Diego del Castillo together with a group of soldiers go up the Nueces River, visit the Indians, and stay with them for six months. They continue down the river, finding pearls which they send to the viceroy, and finally arrive at the land of the Texas Indians, which means "friends."

1651

The Franciscans continue their intense missionary work in Georgia and South Carolina. They establish the missions of San Miguel de Asile, San Luis de Xinayca, and others near the Rivers Combahee, Edisto, Ocmulgcee, and Oconee. At the same time, they advocate that the labor given to the Indians at St. Augustine not be excessive.

1652

1. According to a report, there are three main villages in Puerto Rico at this time besides San Juan: Coamo with a hundred families, San Germán with the same number of families, and Arecibo with approximately fifty families.

2. The Franciscans have established several missions near the Apalachicola River in Florida over four years and now begin to sow and harvest wheat in the area of Asile and Apalache.

1653

1. Captain Alonso de León arrives from Cerralvo, Mexico, at the Río Grande and explores it until he reaches the Atlantic Ocean. Along the four hundred miles he discovers fertile lands, an abundance of fish, and he makes contact with several Indian tribes living in that area of Texas.

2. Spain sends, as governor of New Mexico, Don Juan Samaniego y Jaca, who remains for a term of four years.

1654

Once again, Captain Diego de Guadalajara, with thirty soldiers, visits the Indians near the Nueces River in Texas and begins trading buffalo and deer skins with them. During that trip the company is attacked by the Cuitoas tribe and battle with them the whole day. Finally they return to their base at Santa Fe in New Mexico.

1655

The Franciscans establish several missions in Florida and Georgia: San Ildefonso de Chaminí, Santa Cruz de Cachipile, San Francisco de Chuaguin, Concepción de Ayubale, San Francisco de Oconí, San José de Ocuia, San Juan de Aspalaga, San Pedro de Patale, and others. To protect the missions in the area of Tallahassee, they depend on Fort of San Luis de Appalache. This year there are forty-four missions with seventy Franciscans tending to approximately twenty-eight thousand Christian natives in that area. The chain of missions stretches from St. Augustine to Tallahassee to the west, and to Santa Elena, South Carolina, to the north. Since there was much progress in the missions, the Franciscans ask that a diocese be established in Florida.

1656

1. A disagreement between Diego Rebolledo, governor of Florida, and the Franciscan missionaries prompts an insurrection of the natives. They destroy several missions, causing some missionaries to escape to Cuba. This rebellion lasts eight months and is finally controlled with the execution of some of the chiefs.

2. The Council of the Indies finds Governor Rebolledo of Florida guilty of mistreating the Indians; it advises that he be arrested and taken prisoner in one of the Havana castles.

2. Jamaica, under Spain since 1493, falls to England. Because of its strategic location, England will use it as base for trade, smuggling, and attacking more Spanish colonies of the Caribbean and Florida.

1657

1. The Pope names Don Francisco Arnaldo de Issasi bishop of San Juan, Puerto Rico. He will exercise his pastoral ministry for four years.

2. Governor Diego Rebolledo visits the area of Apalache, Florida, its ten missions, and two dozen of other surrounding villages; at this time the San Luis Fort is also reinforced.

3. A royal decree is issued by which Diego Rebolledo is removed as governor of Florida in view of the accusations of the Franciscan superior

and the uneasiness of the Indians. Rebolledo is to be taken to Cuba and locked up in a castle, but he dies before reaching Havana.

1658

1. A group of Sephardic Jews of Spanish origin establish themselves in Newport, Rhode Island. Later they will build the first synagogue in the United States.

2. Good reinforcement for the missions of Florida comes with the arrival of twenty-nine Franciscan missionaries. Father Pedro Moreno Ponce de León makes the arrangements for their transportation from Seville to St. Augustine, Florida. The House of Trade gives him 509,052 reales, from which he spends 7,354 to buy the provisions needed aboard: one case of syrups, waters and ointments, 20 *quintales* (5,000 lbs.) of biscuits, 60 *arrobas* (240 gallons) of wine, three arrobas (12 gallons) of vinegar, eight arrobas (32 gallons) of oil, two cows in dried meat, 300 pounds of ham, four rams, one *fanega* (two bushels) of chickpeas, three quintales (750 lbs.) of codfish, one quintal (250 lbs.) of noodles, 250 reales of sugar, cinnamon, and other spices, one quintal of rice, one quintal of raisins, 220 reales of eggs, 12 whole cheeses, four big copper pans, kitchen utensils, silverware, dishes, pans, frypans, and other accessories. His report is kept in the Archive of the Indies and is quoted by Pedro Borges in his book *El Envio de Misioneros a America* (The Sending of Missionaries to America).

1659

1. A church and a monastery under the title of Our Lady of Guadalupe are built in El Paso, Texas.

2. In the same year, Bernardo López de Mendizábal is named governor of New Mexico, and Father Juan Ramírez is named superior of the Franciscans. They go to New Mexico in the same caravan, and from the start they disagree about their respective roles. As a result, ten new Franciscans who were coming with them return to Mexico.

1660

1. Bands of Apache and Comanche warriors ford the Río Grande and wage a surprise attack on the villages of Monterey, Saltillo, and Casas Grandes in Mexico. They lay siege to the dwellings and property, rustling a large herd of livestock.

2. Two more missionaries arrive to continue the work begun by Fathers Juan Letrado and Martín Arvide among the Zuñis of New Mexico. Before long they are beaten after unceasing labor and are forced

to return to Parral, Mexico. They soon come back, however, and found the mission of San Pedro del Cuchillo and some others.

1661

The Council of the Indies selects Diego Peñalosa as governor and captain of New Mexico. Immediately there arises a disagreement between the missionaries and the governor-elect concerning the right of sanctuary. The superior of the Franciscans is arrested, and his case is transferred to Mexico, where the governor is reprimanded harshly.

1662

Governor Peñalosa sends an expedition of eight soldiers and a thousand native allies, along with Padres Miguel Guevara and Nicolás Freitas, who will write a report. They reach Nebraska and meet there with seventy Indian chiefs of that region. In their expedition they come upon the Escanjaques, who are warring with the Quiviras. The Spaniards are constrained to battle the Escanjaques, and later on they start their return to Santa Fe. About four months later the Quiviras journey to Santa Fe to thank the Spaniards for their assistance, presenting them with assorted gifts.

1663

Approximately one hundred colonist soldiers of various villages of northern Mexico which have been previously attacked cross the Río Grande in the vicinity of Eagle Pass and with eight hundred horses initiate a bloody battle. They defeat the Comanches, slaying about a hundred of them, take some one hundred fifty others prisoners, and put them to labor in the silver mines of Zacatecas.

1664

1. Governor Peñalosa of New Mexico explores the region bordering on the Grande and Mississippi Rivers. Alonso de León, at the same time, is seeking information about a reported French settlement by the Bay of Espíritu Santo in the Gulf of Mexico.

2. The Duke of York, with an army, takes over the Dutch city of New Amsterdam (Manhattan), which was poorly defended. He expels the Dutch, changes its name to New York, and builds a wall (Wall Street) to protect the city against Indian raids.

1665

1. The Comanches ford the Río Grande anew and lay waste the villages on the Mexican side. Then they withdraw. Supported by the Boboles Indian tribe of Coahuila, the Spaniards cross northward, open up a fierce fight with the Comanches, and rout them. A Comanche woman plays a flute to stir up the others while the battle rages. The Boboles request permission to eat her, but the Spaniards, of course, deny the request. Having captured, however, a young male Comanche, they offer him in sacrifice and consume him secretly.

2. In the meantime Fernando Villanueva is elected governor of New Mexico, where he will rule for three years.

1666

1. Because of the vast expanse of its territories in the New World, its small population, and the repeated attacks of the European powers, Spain is unable to control all the explored lands. Therefore, the expanse of Florida, which originally extended as far as Chesapeake Bay, begins to shrink in size.

2. John Yeaman settles a cluster of colonies in North Carolina near Cape Fear. This occurrence, coupled with the frequent attacks against the city of St. Augustine, forces Spain to construct a powerful bulwark there.

1667

The restlessness created by Governor Peñalosa in New Mexico and the inability of the authorities to suppress the uprisings of the natives embolden the Comanches, who present a constant menace to peace during the administration of Fernando Villanueva.

1668

1. Governor Peñalosa is punished for speaking against the Holy Office and is forced to walk publicly through the streets of Santa Fe while carrying a green candle. He leaves New Mexico and travels to England, where he proposes a plan to surrender the territories of New Mexico to the British.

2. The city of St. Augustine in Florida is besieged by the pirate John Davis, who disembarks from a captured Spanish ship. He enters the city with a large band of pirates, occupies it, sets it ablaze, and slaughters many inhabitants. With the pirates, Henry Woodward escapes, having pretended to convert to Catholicism, lived in the parish house for some months, and performed as surgeon in the city. Woodward leaves knowing the secrets of government in St. Augustine. From then on it is decided to construct a stone

fort to protect the city. Its magnificence and impenetrability, the effort of the military engineer Ignacio Daza, can still be seen today.

3. It is reported that the Spaniards have begun working gold mines in northern Georgia; this news stirs expectations in Spain.

1669

An epidemic caused by widespread drought in the regions of Arizona and New Mexico encourages the Comanches of Mescalero to raid the various villages of the Christian Indians. They take the inhabitants prisoner to sacrifice them to their gods and eat them.

1670

1. England and Spain sign the so-called Treaty of Madrid, whereby both countries pledge to respect the territories they now occupy; Santa Elena, South Carolina, is retained by England.

2. Padre Pedro Ávila, O.F.M., is seized by the Apaches of Hawikuh, New Mexico, stripped naked, scourged, and finally assassinated with a tomahawk on the seventh day of August.

3. Some 2,700 Spaniards commit themselves to agriculture and cattle-raising this year in the vicinity of Santa Fe, New Mexico.

1671

Over the years some tribes living in the northern sector of the Río Grande, Texas, have visited the missionaries of the villages on the Mexican side. They ask to be baptized and declare that a lady had appeared to them. Something of the same nature happened to the Jumanos some years before. Padre Juan Larios will minister to them for three years on the southern side of the Rio Grande.

1672

1. The task of constructing the fortification of St. Augustine, Florida, is undertaken with materials of coral-rock taken from the depths of the ocean. It will replace the wooden fort and require twenty-five years for completion. The Fort of San Marcos has a wall 336 feet long and nine feet high, with a parapet twenty-five feet high, and is equipped with fifty cannons.

2. Founded this same year are the Missions of Santa Cruz of Capoli and Candelária de Tama in the Apalache region of Florida.

1673

1. Construction of a fort on the Island of Santa Catalina is initiated. It will be completed in fourteen years.

2. Antonio Menéndez Marqués is selected accountant of the Exchequer of the Royal Arks in Florida.

3. Father Sebastián Izquierdo, Jesuit procurator before the Council of Indies, says that this year the assistance of European missionaries to the Spanish Missions of America, including Florida and New Mexico, was the following: 6,601 from Germany (Germany, Austria, Bohemia, Lowlands), 2,937 from Italy, and 2,040 from Spain.

1674

1. Most Reverend Gabriel Vara y Calderón, bishop of Cuba, visits Florida and stays there for ten months. He makes a pastoral visit to the missions, confirms 13,152 Christian natives, and ordains seven priests.

2. This year are founded the missions of San Carlos de los Chacatos, San Nicolás de Tolentino, and Encarnación de Sabacola in the region of the Apalachicola River. Fathers Miguel Valverde, Rodrigo Barrida, and Juan Ocón minister to them. The missionaries report that there are three hundred Christian natives and several chiefs in that region.

1675

1. Fathers Juan Larios and Dionisio Buenaventura, along with Lieutenant Fernando del Bosque, ten Spaniards, two Indian chiefs, and 120 Christian natives, cross the Rio Grande near Eagle Pass and enter Texas. They erect crosses and find a Spaniard captured by the Indians. On May 16 Padre Larios, having built an altar on the bank of the river near San Isidro, celebrates the first Mass on this region of Texas. Some 1,700 natives request baptism, and sometime later the Fort of Sacramento will be built nearby.

2. The sorcerers and religious guides of the Indian villages of New Mexico call an assembly to plan a sedition against the Spaniards and Christian natives. The Governor, Juan Francisco Treviño, once informed, imprisons forty-seven of them including Popé. He releases the majority after punishing them and issuing a stern warning. Those religious leaders were attempting to keep alive their superstitions and ancestral beliefs. They deeply resent Indians becoming Christian, therefore making their conversion difficult. Popé goes back to Taos, where he organizes a group of followers. For some years he will plan in detail the extermination of all the Spaniards, men, women, and children as well as missionaries, and the obliteration of the missions.

3. Padre Alonso Gil Ávila and a group of Christians are martyred that same year at the hands of the Apaches in Senecu.

4. Seven new missions are opened or appear for the first time in Florida: Asunción del Puerto, San Simon, Ocotonico, Santa María de los Yamasee, San Felipe (Cumberland), San Felipe, and Santa Clara (Amelia). By this year the Franciscans have founded sixty-six missions in Florida and Georgia. Near San Luis in the Apalache a village composed of Spanish families is also established.

1676

1. In search of assistance for New Mexico, Padre Francisco de Ayeta leaves for Mexico. He is granted 50 additional soldiers, 1,000 horses, and ten men to bring in. He also brings cows, sheep, arms, and provisions worth 14,700 pesos. A caravan is organized, and they set out for New Mexico.

2. The Apaches destroy several towns and churches in New Mexico and kill a few Spaniards and Christian Indians; their leaders are caught and executed.

1677

1. Antonio de Otermín is chosen to succeed Don Juan F. Treviño as Governor of New Mexico, and will rule for six years. By this time there have been erected some fifty churches of stone and other compact materials, along with ornamentation, vestments, and standard equipment.

2. Father Juan Paiva is able to convince a group of Indian leaders of the Apalache area to suppress a soccer-like sport; the fights and even deaths that resulted from the game have moved the missionary to take action.

1678

1. The people of New Mexico complain that they do not have sufficient arms and resources to defend themselves against the incursions of the Apache. Once more Father Ayeta departs for Mexico in search of more reinforcements. He pleads for a hundred soldiers, which are denied him. He will spend part of the following year gathering and buying provisions and munitions to bring to New Mexico in twenty wagons.

2. The Indian Chief of Ajoica in Florida announces that he has given permission to Nicholas Suárez to start a cattle ranch.

1679

1. Up to this year, and throughout the preceding seventy, the public treasury has spent one million gold pesos to support the missions of New

Mexico. This reveals the high degree of interest that Spain has in the religious aspect of maintaining these missions situated in a poor territory. The colonization of this region is due to an essentially religious motive; as an economic investment, it has been bad business.

2. Father Juan Ocón and two confreres are sent to the area of Apalachicola to establish a mission at Sabcola on the banks of the Chattahoochee River. Aware of this, the chieftain of the Coweta Indians comes down to the place and forces the departure of the missionaries. The purpose of establishing a mission here is both to evangelize the natives and to stop the advancement of the British explorers.

1680

1. Popé, the spiritual leader, in concurrence with the Indian chiefs of the Pueblo Indians of New Mexico, launches a surprise assault on the Spanish and Christian natives on the tenth of August. They surround the city of Santa Fe and cut off the supply of water. They assassinate some four hundred men, women, and children, among them twenty-one Franciscan missionaries. They destroy the missions, dwellings, and property, but about 2,500 people, protected by a sparse number of soldiers, manage to flee southward. Governor Otermín, along with the survivors, takes refuge near El Paso.

2. By this year, according to a report, there are in New Mexico some eighty thousand Christian natives in forty-six villages and thirty Franciscan monasteries with one hundred twenty missionaries in residence. The Franciscans have toiled unceasingly for a hundred years among the Apaches, Navajos, Pueblos, Picuries, Zuñis, and many other tribes. Now they see all their efforts come to a halt. Once the Spaniards depart from New Mexico, Popé becomes a tyrant among his own tribesmen and wages a bloody civil war against the natives. The Spaniards receive visits from some messengers a short time later, requesting that they return.

3. A chronicle of the events of this year in Florida reveals that there are nine missions in the region of the Apalache, among which San Luis is the principal mission serving as a base of operations. There is also a fort here to defend the region.

4. The English, supported by native allies, attack the island missions of Jekyll, Sapelo, San Simon, and Santa Catalina in Georgia.

5. A synod convened in Santiago, Cuba, mandates the following: "Pay careful attention and be vigilant for the welfare and kind treatment of the Indians of Florida, and do not tolerate the mistreatment of them by any person, ecclesiastical or secular, in word or deed."

1681

1. Governor Otermín, accompanied by 146 soldiers and Indians, arrives at Isleta with the intention of reconquering Santa Fe, where 1,500 Indians, terrified by other natives, welcome them hospitably. Otermín heads north and reaches a point 25 miles west of Santa Fe, but he realizes that he is not properly prepared to battle the rebellious Pueblo tribe. He then returns to El Paso with a large number of natives who beg him to allow them to return with him.

2. At the same time, Padre Ayeta, seeking aid, confronts the bureaucracy of Mexico. He is given a letter, dated a year and a half earlier, in which King Carlos II directs that he be granted the necessary assistance to save the region of the Río Grande.

3. Governor Juan Marqués Cabrera from Florida again sends to the region of Sabacola, Georgia, two missionaries, now escorted by a company of soldiers, in order to establish a mission. After a few months of work, he leaves the place because of the hostility of the Indians, turns back south, and establishes among the Sabacola Indians the Mission of Santa Cruz near the junction of the Chattahoochee and Flint Rivers.

1682

1. Spaniards and Christian natives who two years before were able to escape the massacre set up a settlement close to El Paso. They establish three villages with their own missions; the villages of Senecu with native Piros, Isleta with Tiguas, and Socorro with Piros and Jemex are now part of Texas.

2. Diego de Peñalosa, former governor of New Mexico, travels from England to France and, once there, has an interview with Robert Cavalier Sieur de La Salle, the pirate Grammont, and Beaujen. They plot the overthrow of Spain in the northern area of Mexico and the territory between the Grande and Mississippi Rivers, i.e., Texas. Peñalosa proposes the construction of a fort at the mouth of the Río Grande, and to set up a post there with one thousand soldiers. Peñalosa's conspiracy encourages the explorations of La Salle south of the Mississippi.

1683

1. At the request of the Jumano Indians, Fathers Juan Domínguez de Mendoza and Nicolás López begin an exploration of the Nueces River region. They spend some time with the Jumanos, explore the area, and return to El Paso with five thousand buffalo skins. This is the result of a bargain with the natives after they are promised to come back the following year with missionaries and colonists.

2. With the approval of Pope Innocent IX, Father Antonio Linaz, O.F.M., institutes the College of Santa Cruz of Queretaro, Mexico, which is the very first of the "Propagation of the Faith" in the New World. Many of the missionaries of Texas will be alumni of this college, among them Father Margil de Jesús, who will found the College of Zacatecas years later.

3. Pirate Nicholas Agramont raids the missions of St. Catherine Island, Georgia. He takes away the tower bells and church ornaments and murders the Christian Indians. Many flee to the forest inland, and the end of this old mission begins. A short time later, pirate Hinckley makes another raid and forces the soldiers and the native Christians to withdraw from Jekyll Island.

1684

Francisco Padilla is chosen bishop of San Juan, Puerto Rico. He is aware of the scarcity of inhabitants and asks the king to send one hundred families from the Canary Islands, whose people are known for their working habits and pleasing temperament. They will provide great assistance to the island. A few years later an epidemic will break out and take the lives of a large number of people. Twenty-one of the twenty-four priests will succumb to the disease.

1685

1. Antonio Matheos, commander of the Tallahassee region, chases after the Britisher Henry Woodward, who pretended to be a friend of the Spaniards and feigned interest in becoming Catholic. Gleaning information on the Spanish condition in Florida, he has slipped away with some English pirates. Matheos goes northward from Tallahassee by river until he reaches Columbus, Georgia, with a force of soldiers and 250 Indians to seize Woodward. He goes into hiding, and they cannot find him. Because of the frequent incursions of the English in the Columbus area, various expeditions are dispatched. Governor Quiroga finally orders that a fort be built in Coweta along the Chattahoochee River. He posts twenty soldiers and twenty Indians there.

2. To forestall French plans to occupy the Gulf of Mexico, the king commands the governor of Florida and the viceroy of Mexico to lend support to Martín Echegaray in occupying Espíritu Santo Bay (Matagorda), Texas. It is at this time that a French expedition headed by La Salle arrives at the Bay of Espíritu Santo and builds a fort. However, internal rivalry, hostility of the natives, and epidemics wipe them out.

1686

1. Tired of the constant raids of British pirates on the missions of Georgia, governor Juan Marqués Cabrera sends three ships from Florida with soldiers under commander Tomás de León to Port Royal, South Carolina. De León destroys the English settlement, takes several settlers as prisoners, and shoots a few others, among them the chieftain who protected Henry Woodward. He also raids the plantation of Governor Morton, burns a few others, and takes some prisoners and a booty estimated at about three thousand pounds sterling. De León then heads for Charleston, but a violent hurricane sinks two of his ships, and the third arrives finally at St. Augustine in very bad shape. The Spaniards have now paid the British back with similar coin.

2. Alonso de León, setting out from Texas, crosses the Río Grande and leads five expeditions to locate the French fort on the coast of the Gulf of Mexico. He arrives by land at the mouth of the Colorado River in Texas. Juan Enríque Barroto and Andrés Pérez pursue the same goals in their expedition, but they find only the wreck of one of the French ships.

1687

1. Fathers Eusebio Kino, Antonio Salvatierra, and other Jesuits open Mission Dolores by the bank of the San Miguel River in northern Mexico. This mission will become the center of operations for Father Kino and all his apostolic enterprises in that region. The mission of San Gabriel of Guevavi, Arizona, is founded this same year.

2. Pedro Reneros Posada reenters New Mexico with a company of soldiers and by a heroic feat takes hold of the village of Santa Ana, built above the rocks; a short time later he is forced to withdraw.

3. The first black slaves escaping from the plantations of South Carolina are six men, two women, and one infant. They arrive in St. Augustine, Florida, in a stolen canoe, ask to be baptized in the Catholic faith in order to be free, and beg not to be returned. The plantation owners demand of the Spanish authorities that the slaves be returned. The Spanish respond that the slaves have already been baptized and therefore are free under Spanish law. They marry, are hired with salaries, and begin a settlement. Thus the first town of free black people is born in Florida. Such towns have been in existence already for a hundred years in other Spanish territories such as Cuba, Santo Domingo, Puerto Rico, Colombia, and Venezuela. These towns were called *palenques*.

1688

In order to recapture Santa Fe, Domingo Jironza de Cruzate arranges an expedition out of El Paso. They come in contact with the forces of the rebellious Pueblo tribe in the village of Zía, and engage in a bloody battle that claims the lives of six hundred Indians. Cruzate, realizing that he does not have the necessary forces to pursue the recapture of Santa Fe, withdraws to El Paso.

1689

1. Separate expeditions to explore the coast of the Gulf of Mexico were undertaken in previous years, but now Alonso de León sets out by land with Father Damián Massanet and a strong contingent of troops to survey the coast by land. Arriving at the Bay of Matagorda, they discover the remains of the French encampment there. Heading northeast, they upon two Frenchmen living with the Indians who inform them about the French expedition there and its disappearance. Alonso de León returns to Mexico and urges the king to occupy this area of Texas with soldiers and missionaries.

2. Governor Quiroga of Florida orders the construction of a fort in Coweta on the banks of the Chattahoochee River, near present-day Columbus, Georgia. He entrusts the plroject to Captain José Primo de Rivera, who completes the fortress in a period of three months, with a palisade, ravine, parapet, and four bastions. Commander Fabian Angulo and twenty soldiers are assigned to this place.

1690

1. Alonso de León, the Franciscans Damián Massanet, Miguel Fontcuberta, Francisco Casañas, Antonio Bordoy, and one hundred men come to the Neches River, Texas, near the Bay of Espíritu Santo. Soon the chief of the Texas tribe invites them to a village by the Trinity River. On May 23, the Spaniards open up a village, erect a chapel of wood, celebrate Mass, and thereby found a mission which they name San Francisco de los Tejas. They also found the mission of Santa María in the same locality. With soldiers to protect him, Padre Fontcuberta remains at the head of the mission. De León, returning to Coahuila, Mexico, leaves livestock and horses for breeding.

2. The provincial of the Franciscans dispatches Father Salvador Bueno to Macaya, Florida, to serve the Mission of San Salvador, which has begun to flourish.

1691

1. The Spanish crown establishes Texas as a new province and selects Domingo Tern de los Ríos as its first governor. Tern and Father Massanet organize the colonization of Texas, bringing with them soldiers, colonists, and livestock. Enduring severe trials on the journey, especially fording the Trinity River, they come upon the area of the Bay of Galveston and the Mission of San Francisco de los Tejas, which were founded a year earlier. Two groups make up this expedition, one by land and one by sea, and they meet each other at the bay. The party led by Padre Massanet arrives overland with nineteen Franciscans for the purpose of serving the missions they hope to found. Arriving at the actual site of San Antonio on June 13, they are welcomed by the natives of the Yanaquana. Some three thousand natives of various tribes led by chief Papaya, some of them mounted on horseback, go together to welcome Father Massanet. They carry a large banner with the image of the Virgin of Guadalupe that the Padre had given to them the year before. The expedition travels to the site of the bay, where Tern will remain for two years, establishing new villages and missions.

2. Diego Vargas, of a noble and prosperous Mexican family, becomes governor of New Mexico and plans to invest his fortune to reconquer it. Arriving in September with eight hundred soldiers, colonists, and Christian Indians, he begins the reconquest of New Mexico. He approaches Santa Fe, and after a two-day battle he overcomes. He blockades the Mesa Negra de San Ildefonso for eight months and occupies it. He directs his attention then to the Indians of Potrero Viejo, the Peña of San Diego de Jemez, and the Roca de Acoma (the Gibraltar of New Mexico), where the Indians are entrenched. By authentically heroic feats of military strategy, Vargas routs his enemies. Once reestablished in Santa Fe, he undertakes the task of reconstruction. The missionaries busy themselves with the rebuilding and renovation of the missions. Within a short time they baptize two thousand children born in the last ten years. They toil to establish new villages, cultivate new land, increase the livestock, and expand production of manufactured goods.

1692

James Moore plunders various missions, among them those of Potohiriba, Isla Amelia, and Fort George, and destroys them. His main objective is to round up Indians to sell them as slaves to landowners of Carolina and Virginia.

1693

1. Governor Vargas returns to Mexico to seek reinforcements in order to colonize New Mexico once again. With the aid of the viceroy, Vargas sets out with a hundred soldiers, seventy families, eighteen Franciscans, nine hundred head of cattle, and two thousand horses. He arrives at the region of Santa Fe, where he meets with the opposition of the natives. Only after waging a fight is Vargas able to enter the capital of New Mexico with his entourage.

2. On April 8, Don Andrés de Pes and Father Carlos Siguenza, professor of mathematics at the University of Mexico, arrive in the area of Pensacola, Florida, aboard a frigate and another vessel. Exploring the bay, they disembark and sing the *"Te Deum"* before a cross which has been erected in a place chosen for the settlement of a village. The construction of Pensacola will be undertaken five years later.

1694

1. A reinforcement of sixty-six families under the leadership of Father Francisco Farfán, assisted by Father Antonio Moreno, sets up and founds the new village of Santa Cruz (La Cañada) to the North of Santa Fe. (A beautiful statue of Our Lady of Mount Carmel, dating from the seventeenth century, is venerated today in the church of this mission.) Father Juan Hurtado takes up residence in Bernalillo with forty families to bolster the life of this village. Losing no time, the governor leads an expedition with Father Juan Alpuente and explores the southern region of Colorado.

2. Father Eusebio Kino, from his base in Sonora, Mexico, expands the colonization of southern Arizona as far as the Gila and Colorado Rivers. An expert builder and rancher, he founds the Mission of Tucson, the Visita of San Javier del Bac, and he will later construct a church with the title of San José de Tucson. Here the Franciscans will establish a school of arts and crafts to educate the natives. The Fort of Tubac is moved to Tucson, and a wall is built around the village to defend it from the frequent attacks of the Apaches. About the same time, the missions of San Cayetano de las Calabazas is founded to christianize the Papago Indians, and also that of San José de Tumacacori, which will produce a large quantity of wheat, cattle, and sheep. In one of their attacks, the Apaches will burn the church and the houses, but they will be rebuilt again.

1695

1. The Council of the Indies approves the dispatch of fourteen Franciscans to Florida, with the condition that eight of them be assigned to the missions of Mayaca, Anacapi, Jororo, and La Concepción.

2. At the end of the year, there prevails an atmosphere of restlessness in the native population of New Mexico. The missionaries warn Governor Vargas to take precautions.

1696

1. A new rebellion breaks out on June 14 in fifteen villages of New Mexico. Five Franciscans and twenty-one other Spaniards die. Many churches and dwellings likewise are pillaged and burned. Vargas successfully quells the revolt after three months of fighting, and he chastises those responsible. There follows a long period of peace, while agriculture and livestock prosper. The Apaches, Navajos, and Hopi, however, are not completely submissive, and every now and then they provoke hostilities.

2. Juan Uribarri, on a new exploration with forty Spaniards and one hundred Indians, reconnoiters southern Colorado, the Arkansas River, the Animas, and the neighborhood of Pueblo. He takes possession of the land in the name of the king.

3. In Florida Father Luis Sánchez Pacheco, a Franciscan missionary born in Cuba, earns the crown of martyrdom at the hands of the Jororo Indians.

1697

1. The Franciscan missionaries provide lodging for Jonathan Dickinson in the mission of Santa María de Sena, Georgia. He has been shipwrecked in this area and will relate later the flourishing of the mission and the great work of the Franciscans with the natives. Judging by the discovered ruins, Santa María de Sena had an impressive edifice and fortress.

2. Once the Indian revolt in New Mexico is over, the viceroy of Mexico sends to the survivors the following provisions: 1,400 *fanegas* (2,100 bushels) of corn, 1,500 meters of fabric, 1,245 meters of flannel, 2,000 blankets, 2,000 goats, 3,000 sheep, 600 cows, and 200 bulls.

3. Three months later, the new governor of New Mexico, Pedro Rodríguez Cubero, arrives to replace Diego de Vargas. The latter refuses to give up the government, but Cubero takes possession, beginning an investigation of the tenure of Vargas, and a legal battle ensues that will last six years before it is resolved.

1698

By order of the viceroy of Mexico, Andrés de Arriola of Veracruz sets sail from Mexico with three ships, 200 men and 18 cannon. He lands at the Bay of Pensacola and begins the construction of the Fort of San Carlos, which measures 110 feet on each side and is still in existence today. From this moment he inspires the building of the city of Santa María de Pensacola, Florida.

1699

Fathers Kino, Adan Gil, and Captain Juan M. Manje, along with Captain Diego Carrasco and a band of soldiers, eighty horses, twenty-five mules with provisions, and thirty-six cows, set out from Dolores, Mexico, and travel northward. They arrive at the junction of the Gila and Colorado Rivers, discovering the place, named San Pedro, which they consider suitable for a mission. They are well received by the natives and continue to explore the area of the Gila as far as Casa Grande, whence they return to Dolores once again.

Father (now Blessed) Junípero Serra, builder of the California missions, also has a statue in the United States Capitol Rotunda

1700-1750:
Expansion and Splendor

Work is extended to Texas, and the missions and settlements flourish.

1700

1. The construction of San Javier del Bac, near Tucson, Arizona, is started on April 28 to evangelize the Sobaipuris Indians. Father Eusebio Kino and his military escort, Captain Manje, bring seven hundred head of cattle from Dolores, and thus cattle raising and agriculture begin in this area. Father Kino, puzzled by the finding of some shells in this region, tries in several explorations to find a trail from Arizona to the Pacific.

2. According to a report, in Florida there are thirty-four cattle ranches besides the missions. However, at this time Florida is not self-sufficient and has to be subsidized by Spain with one hundred thousand gold pesos every year. The crown assumes this cost because Florida is strategically located for the defense of commercial ships that sail between America and Spain.

1701

With the arrival of the new governor of New Mexico, Pedro Rodríguez Cubero, things change for Diego Vargas, who is taken prisoner. The Franciscan superior notifies the viceroy of this fact, and he in turn notifies the king. The king then orders that Vargas be returned his honor and gives him the title of "marquis." Afterwards, he is again named governor and captain general of New Mexico.

1702

1. Santa Fe Mission in Florida is destroyed by English settlers of South Carolina and their Apalachicola Indian allies. Governor Zúñiga sends Captain Francisco Romo Uriza with a group of soldiers and eight hundred Timucua Indians to punish the Apalachicola Indians and the English. Caught in an ambush, the troops of Uriza are defeated, and the Appalache missions remain in great danger.

2. Colonel James Moore, with a fleet of twelve ships, attacks the city of St. Augustine. He burns the church, the library, the Franciscan convent, and several houses close to San Marcos fort. Unable to take the fort, he withdraws.

1703

1. The missions of San Juan Bautista, San Francisco Solano, and San Bernardino are founded at the border of Río Grande, Texas.

2. A horde of Apalache Indians destroys the mission of San José de Ocuia, Florida, and their devastation continues in the Timucuan territory.

1704

James Moore attacks the Apalache region in the Tallahassee area, defeats the weak native and Spanish garrison, destroys the fourteen missions with another twenty-four settlements, and tortures Franciscan friars Juan Parga, Manuel Mendoza, Angel Miranda, Tiburcio Osorio, Agustín Ponce de León, and Marcos Delgado. First Father Parga's leg is cut off, and then he is beheaded. Father Manuel Mendoza is pierced with pieces of wood, forming a cross on his body. After the tortures are inflicted, they slowly burn everyone. Also tortured are soldiers Pedro Marmolejo and Baltasar Francisco, and the Christian Apalaches Antonio Enixa, Cui Domingo, and Indian Chief Cui Feliciano. They bravely confess their faith, giving unequivocal proof of their Christian courage. Moore takes twelve thousand Christian natives prisoners and sells them as slaves in Charleston, South Carolina. As a result of these attacks, all missions of Georgia together with Christian settlements and cattle ranches of the Apalache area are destroyed. The efforts and labor of many people for more than a hundred years are reduced to ashes.

1705

1. Upon Father Kino's request, the silver and potassic salt mines close to Phoenix and Tucson are exploited. Later, the mines of "*Bolas de Plata*" (silver nuggets) and brass in Ajo and the gold mines in Quijotoa and Arivaca will also be worked.

2. The precarious trade situation forces Spaniards and Indians to improve their relations. The most common trading articles in New Mexico are food products, fuel, fabrics, and livestock. Selling of horses and firearms to the Indians is prohibited, because of possible danger to the Spanish. This trade interchange, begun by Governor Vargas, helps to improve relationships among the settlers of New Mexico.

1706

1. Governor Francisco Cuervo founds the city of Albuquerque with fifty families brought from Santa Fe, New Mexico. About this time, the neighboring towns of Los Padillas and Los Lunas are also established. Twenty-one missionaries work in the area of New Mexico, each serving

two or three towns. The number of Christian natives is increasing, and in spite of many difficulties, they help the missionaries with work as indigenous catechists.

2. Through an order of the governor, Commander Roque Madrid heads an expedition of soldiers and allied Pueblo Indians in order to pacify the Moqui tribes of northern Arizona. As a result, two Moqui villages are subdued and settled. At the same time, another expedition led by captain Juan de Ulibarri heads to northeast New Mexico toward the Arkansas River to subdue some hostile Pueblo Indians. He arrives at Cuartelejo (Colorado) and there establishes a settlement to protect the southern territories.

1707

1. James Moore attacks and destroys the town of Pensacola but is unable to take the fort because reinforcements arrive. He also attacks the Mission of Ayubale of the Timucuanos, and ignoring a poor Franciscan who comes out barefoot at the entrance of the town interceding for the natives, he pushes them to the other side of the St. John River, where they form the town of Timucuos. Spain in reprisal directs an attack against Port Royal, but without any major consequences.

2. Wealthy Frenchman Antoine Crozat, in spite of the British attacks in the region, is able to maintain his presence in Mobile, Alabama, and other places in the area, thanks to his personal fortune.

1708

José Chacón, marquis of Peñuelas and governor of New Mexico, receives orders from Viceroy Albuquerque to give increased protection to the towns against Apache raids and to protect the Indians against the abuses of colonizers and soldiers; at the same time he asks him to lower the expenses in the administration because the $76,000 annual subsidy that he has been receiving is a heavy burden to the royal treasury. He suppresses the military installation of Albuquerque. The Apaches, aware of the situation, appear in the area, steal livestock, and commit atrocities. The people defend themselves as best they can without the governor's help.

1709

1. An expedition led by Father Antonio Olivares explores the area of Texas and New Mexico, journeying along the Rivers of San Marcos, Nueces, Sarco, Hondo, Chapa, Chiltipique, Robalos, Mediana, Guadalupe, Garrapatas, Salado, San Antonio, San Pedro, and León. The expedition proves of great geographical value.

2. Father Dionisio Resinó, born in Cuba, is named auxiliary bishop of Santiago to serve the territory of Florida and is consecrated in Yucatan, Mexico. He arrives in Florida on June 26 and gives the sacrament of Confirmation to a large number of people in St. Augustine. On July 10 he begins an official visit to this part of the diocese.

1710

1. The Mission of Saint Augustine (still in use today) is founded in Isleta, New Mexico. A chronicle of this same year states that in the area of Santa Fe there are 20,000 inhabitants paying taxes, missionaries, and 120 soldiers in the military post.

2. Governor Marquis of Peñuelas organizes a military expedition to put an end to the Navajo Indians' hostility. They pose a constant threat against Christian Indians of the Zuñi and Acoma regions. The operation is a success, and a period of peace follows.

1711

1. Father Eusebio Kino, after twenty-four years working as a missionary in northern Mexico and Arizona, founding missions and fostering farming and cattle raising, dies. His confrere, Father Juan Salvatierra, and other Jesuits continue his work and establish missions between Loreto and the Pacific.

2. Aware that the missions of eastern Texas are receiving little attention from the Mexican authorities, Father Francisco Hidalgo writes a letter on January 17 to the French governor of Louisiana, requesting his intervention in pacifying the tribes of Texas. The good Father hopes that with the appearance of the French in Texas, the Spanish authorities will send reinforcements to the military posts and more missionaries to the area.

1712

1. Texas Governor Pedro Fermin de Echevers arrives and will remain in office for two years.

2. Juan Ignacio Flores Mogollón is installed as governor of New Mexico. He reinforces the defenses of Albuquerque, adds more soldiers, and forbids horse trades and the sale of firearms to the Indians as a measure of security. He also forces the implementation of the policy of not allowing anyone to leave New Mexico without a permit. During his term, the Suma Indians rebel, but they are put down by Captain Antonio Valverde and settle in Realito de San Lorenzo, near El Paso.

1713

1. The viceroy of Mexico orders Captain Domingo Ramón, in charge of San Juan Bautista Fort in Texas, not to allow either merchants or foreign merchandise into Spanish lands, while transgressors are to be imprisoned.

2. The king of Spain gives Miguel Enríquez the titles of "Captain of Sea and War" and "Commander of the Privateers of Puerto Rico" as a reward for his valor and astuteness in the struggle against the attacks of pirates and for expelling them from the island of Vieques.

1714

1. Louis of Saint-Denis, with three other Frenchmen and three Indians, leaves Mobile, Alabama. They cross Texas and, after a six-month journey, present themselves to Captain Domingo Ramón. They claim that they want to buy cattle from the missions. The captain, observing the rules, puts them under arrest and holds them at his house to await orders from Mexico. During this time of waiting, Saint-Denis falls in love with the captain's daughter, marries her, and is named Spanish official in charge of provisions. This time order is given to revive the missions of the eastern part of Texas, near Louisiana.

2. By order of the viceroy of Mexico, explorations are begun to the north of the Río Grande, Texas, near an existing fort. Sergeant Trasviña, fifty soldiers, twenty Indians, and Fathers Gregorio Osorio, José Arransegui, Andrés Ramírez, and Juan A. García come to the area and found the towns and missions of San José de Los Puliques, San Antonio, and San Cristóbal. When the expedition returns to Mexico, Fathers Osorio and García remain behind with abundant supplies.

1715

1. There is a severe hurricane off the cost of Florida, near Fort Pierce, that sinks ten Spanish galleons leaving Cuba for Spain; they carry a large cargo of gold, silver, and other metals, as well as products coming from various parts of Spanish America.

2. In South Carolina and Georgia there is a general revolt of Yamasee, Creek, Choctaw, and Cherokee Indians against unfair trade practices used by the authorities of Charleston, South Carolina. This insurrection is known as the "Yamasee War." The English defeat the Indians, and a great number of them seek refuge in Florida under the protection of the Spaniards whom they have constantly fought, as allies of the English. Some forty Creek chieftains meet with the Spanish authorities in Pensacola and sign a peace treaty. Seven of them are taken

to Mexico City, where they make an oath of fidelity to the king of Spain and are caught up in the beauty and magnificence of the city.

1716

Captain Domingo Ramón, with twenty-five soldiers, forty colonists, eleven Franciscans from the College of Queretaro, among them Fathers Isidro F. Espinosa and Francisco Hidalgo, and some Christian Indians, leaves for northeastern Texas. As they advance, they are warmly received by the natives. They arrive at Neches River with a thousand head of cattle, sheep, equipment to build a fort and a mission, and tools for plowing. Mass is celebrated daily, and marriages take place. Construction begins on the missions of San Francisco de los Tejas, near the Neches River; Purisima Concepción, near the Angeline; Guadalupe, with Father Margil de Jesús in Nacogdoches; and San José, with Father Isidro Felix Espinosa, for the Nazone Indians. In a short time, on the other side of the Sabine River, nea778r the present Robeline, Father Margil founds the Mission of San Miguel of the Adaes and constructs Fort Pilar not far from Natchitoches.

1717

1. Father Margil de Jesús and his companions begin their missionary work in the four recently founded missions in the area of the Neches River. They encounter great difficulty in converting the natives because of their nomadic character and almost exclusive livelihood from hunting. The San Miguel Mission operates as capital of Texas until it is transferred to San Antonio.

2. The viceroy of Mexico appoints Antonio Valverde Cossío as governor of New Mexico. Felix Martínez, who had been appointed temporary governor after Flores Mogollón's term, refuses to give up his authority. The case is taken to Mexico City, where a two-year litigation ensues. Finally, Valverde is confirmed as legitimate governor.

1718

Father Antonio Olivares advises Baltasar de Zúñiga, marquis of Valero and viceroy of Mexico, about the advisability of establishing a fort and town between the Río Grande and the missions of northeast Texas in the Neches River area. The project is approved, and San Antonio River is selected as the best site. Martín de Alarcón, governor of Coahuila, and Father Olivares arrive at the site on April 25 with 50 colonists, seven pairs of mules, 548 horses, and a good number of cattle. Alarcón begins the construction of Fort San Fernando de Bejar, while Father Olivares starts the Mission of San Antonio de Valero (the Alamo). The city is established between the fort and the mission and given the name San Antonio de Bejar. Some time later, 16 families will come from the Canary Islands to settle there.

1719

1. Governor Jean Baptiste Bienville of Louisiana attacks the Spanish population of Pensacola, Florida, and burns the town, the fort, and the church; finally, the community surrenders. The following year the city will be rebuilt on the same location.

2. At the same time, Louis de Saint-Denis, commander of Natchitoches, attacks and captures Fort Pilar de los Adaes; later, the natives will destroy the Mission of San Miguel.

3. On the Atlantic Coast, the Spaniards, French, and Yamasee Indians attack the English colonies. Because of his inability to halt these attacks, Robert Johnson is removed from his post and replaced by James Moore.

1720

1. Captain Pedro de Villasur leaves Santa Fe, New Mexico, for the northeast, with Father Juan Mínguez, forty-two soldiers, and sixty Indians. They cross Colorado and Kansas and arrive in Nebraska, to see if the French are trying to come toward the west. They are also to establish friendly relations with the Comanches of the Great Plains. They encounter the Pawnee Tribe and are subjected to severe hostility. The natives take the Spanish camp by surprise, drive away the horses, and kill two thirds of the group. The survivors are able to get to Santa Fe.

2. The mission of San José is founded near San Antonio, Texas. It has granaries, shops, living quarters for the friars and Indians, and barracks for soldiers.

1721

1. By order of the marquis of Aguayo, Captain Domingo Ramón, with forty men, begins the construction of Fort Loreto on the Bay of Espíritu Santo at the mouth of the San Antonio River; on the same site, La Salle, thirty-seven years earlier, established a post. The purpose of this fort is to supply provisions by sea to the city of San Antonio from Veracruz, Mexico, and to establish the Mission of Espíritu Santo.

2. Don José Azlor Virto de Vera, marquis of Aguayo, is named governor of Coahuila and Texas. By order of the viceroy, Valero, he leaves Monclova, Mexico, for San Antonio with five hundred men to fortify the settlements and missions of northeastern Texas. He crosses the

Guadalupe, Colorado, and Trinity Rivers, and by August, he arrives at Neches in the area of the missions and settlements. By November, Aguayo will construct Fort Pilar, and Father Margil de Jesús will build the mission of San Miguel de los Adaes that he founded five years before. It was located at a site some twelve miles from Natchitoches, where the French and indigenous natives had attacked them. With his task completed, Aguayo returns to Mexico, leaving behind in Fort Pilar a hundred soldiers and six cannon to thwart any possible French advance into Texas territory.

3. Franciscan Brother José Pita dies a martyr in Carneceria, Texas, while hunting buffalo to provide food for the Mission of San Antonio. Apaches fell upon him north of the Camino Real and killed him.

4. A royal decree is given that public schools are to be established in New Mexico.

5. The English pirate Blackbeard (Edward Teach) has attacked the coast of Florida on several occasions. He is finally captured and hanged.

1722

When the marquis of Aguayo leaves for Mexico, Fernando Pérez de Almazán remains as leader of the Texan establishments, choosing San Miguel de los Adaes as his governor's residence. He promotes friendly relations with the natives and spearheads development of San Antonio Bay and the area of San Miguel de los Adaes. By this date, there are in Texas ten missions and four forts, with 268 soldiers and four settlements.

1723

1. Commander Alejandro Wauchope, sent by the viceroy of Mexico, arrives at the island of Santa Rosa in Pensacola Bay, Florida, and constructs a garrison and more than fifty houses.

2. Immediately after he is sworn in as governor of New Mexico, Juan Domingo Bustamante forbids the sale of firearms and horses to hostile Indians. This practice was begun through scarcity of financial resources of the administration. Since the soldiers in Santa Fe Fort were poorly paid and sometimes not paid at all, they resorted to such trade to compensate for their small income. Another of Bustamante's first activities is to undertake a campaign against the surprise raids of Indians against Christian towns, but he does not accomplish much. Once the Ute, Apache, and Comanche Indians raided the towns by surprise, they would escape to the mountains of Colorado or the plains of Western Texas or Kansas, making it almost impossible to find them.

1724

1. Captain Domingo Ramón, who had distinguished himself in various endeavors to establish garrisons and missions in Texas together with the marquis of Aguayo, dies at the Bay (Port Lavaca), Texas, as a result of wounds received in a conflict with the Karankawa Indians.

2. Governor Juan D. Bustamante of New Mexico orders all trade with foreigners to cease immediately. Legislation prohibits all trade with foreign citizens. In the last few years, products and persons of apparent French origin were present at the north of New Mexico and West of Texas. The French policy in America is not the formation of Indian settlements and their evangelization in Missions like the Spanish policy, but rather it consists of extending trade with the Indians without investing time, money, or effort in their civilization and evangelization. For this they try to gain their friendship by means of gifts and good public relations. This commerce in territories considered of Spanish sovereignty is illegal and of great concern to the authorities of New Mexico as well as the viceroy of Mexico, Marquis de Valero.

3. The Comanche Indians attack the Apaches of northeastern New Mexico and southern Colorado who are friends of the Spaniards. They take away half of their women and children, kill all male Apaches, except for 69 survivors, and then burn their villages. In response, the governor of New Mexico sends a military force of a hundred soldiers to punish the Comanches, but they cannot find them throughout the immense Texas plains.

1725

1. At the confluence of the Grande and Conchos Rivers, the natives capture two missionaries, bind them, gather around them to dance, and later decapitate them. They give them time to receive the sacrament of Penance from each other. Suddenly, a group of soldiers arrives and the natives flee. The missionaries are taken to Chihuahua, Mexico, where their survival is celebrated by the whole town.

2. British forces, commanded by Colonel John Palmer, make an attack on San Marcos Fort at St. Augustine, Florida, but are unable to conquer it.

1726

Captain Pedro Rivera, in his *Diario y Derrotero*, mentions that Albuquerque, New Mexico, is a town populated by Spaniards, mestizos, and mulattos, and that many of these are scattered throughout the ranches. Rivera reinforces the garrison and leaves eighty soldiers, each with an annual salary of four hundred pesos. At the same time, the Jesuits decide to convert the Moqui Indians of Arizona after obtaining a royal letter and permission of the viceroy for the undertaking. The Moquis, nonetheless, resist, because conversion symbolizes abandonment of their way of life.

1727

1. By order of the Marquis de Valero, viceroy of Mexico, General Pedro Rivera makes a survey of all military installations in Arizona, New Mexico, and Texas, noting the number of garrisons and soldiers, their effectiveness, administration, and interrelationship. As a result of his recommendations, some garrisons are eliminated and the number of soldiers diminished, with a saving to the crown of sixty thousand pesos. This causes a great protest on the part of the governor, missionaries, and Christian Indians, but without any result.

2. Bishop Benito Crespo of Durango, Mexico, visits Arizona, which is part of his diocese. Seeing the great need for missionaries, he writes to King Philip V requesting the establishment of three missions at his own expense. Four years later, three Jesuits, among them Father Ignacio Keller, will arrive at Guevavi to promote missionary work in the area.

1728

Because of tension produced by the war between England and Spain, conflicts arise in the North American territories of each. The colonists of South Carolina attack the Spaniards, while the Spaniards protest the English military establishments in the region. An English military contingent penetrates Florida and destroys the Christian Indian population near Saint Augustine.

1729

As a result of his official visit to Texas, Pedro Rivera recommends to the king not to bring colonists from the Canary Islands to Texas because it would be too costly. He also recommends the reduction of train caravans which cross the Camino Real from San Miguel de los Adaes to San Antonio, Saltillo, and Mexico City for the distribution of provisions and ammunition to the missions, settlements, and forts. He recommends they be sent only four times a year; on the first days of January, April, July, and November. Each caravan should be protected by ten armed soldiers on horseback. Those who travel must adjust to this schedule if they want protection. The recommendations are not well received by the missionaries and settlers.

1730

1. Sixteen families from the Canary Islands and other families from Mexico arrive to settle in the town of San Fernando de Bejar. The best known of the settlers from the Canary Islands is Juan Leal Goraz, who travels several times to Mexico, seeking help for the settlers. Captain Juan A. Almazán names him regional representative. Later, Leal is elected mayor of the city.

2. Because of repeated pirate attacks on the city of St. Augustine, Florida, the forts of Mantanzas, Diego, and Mosa are constructed north of the city.

1731

1. Father José de la Garza arrives as pastor of San Fernando de Bejar (today the cathedral of San Antonio, Texas). With the arrival of more Franciscans, the missions of Purisima Concepción, San Francisco de la Espada, and San Juan Capistrano are established.

2. Father Francisco Martínez y Tejada is named auxiliary bishop of Santiago, Cuba, with residence in Florida, to serve the people of the province.

1732

1. The warrant given to Georgia permits grantees to award land and liberty of conscience to all except Catholics. The colony of Georgia is created as a refuge for Protestants persecuted in the north and as a buffer zone against the attacks of the Spanish from Florida and the French from Louisiana.

2. Gervasio Cruzat y Góngora, governor of New Mexico, issues several decrees: he forbids gambling, alcoholic beverages, and prostitution in Indian villages. He also prohibits vagabonds and vagrants in the province, as well as the sale of Apache prisoners to the Pueblo Indians. He also orders the building of a bridge on the Chama River. His government shows signs of economic prosperity demonstrated by the fact that permission is granted to build a new and larger church.

1733

1. Benjamin Franklin studies Spanish and later will make it part of the curriculum at the Academy of Philadelphia. For the rest of his life he will read books printed in Spanish.

2. Father Mariano de los Dolores arrives in Texas, makes frequent visits to the Tonkawans near the Brazos River, and does extraordinary missionary work in the area.

1734

1. Don Miguel Sandoval is named eleventh governor of Texas, a position he will hold for three years.

2. Father Gaspar Steiger works arduously in the Jesuit mission of San Javier del Bac, Arizona.

3. Several court cases take place in Santa Fe, New Mexico, where some mayors, among them those of Bernalillo and Acoma, are accused of mistreatment and abuse of the Indians. In both cases the mayors are removed from office and punished. Spanish law imposes stiff penalties for this crime because it is a cause for Indian revolt.

1735

1. Father Francisco B. Martínez y Tejada, a native of Seville, is consecrated auxiliary bishop of Santiago, Cuba, and arrives in Florida, where he will reside for the next ten years. He is the first resident bishop of the United States. He attends to the faithful, promotes education, helps fugitives, and gives hope to the people during the siege of James Oglethorpe on the city of St. Augustine. After his pastoral visit to Florida in 1745, he will be designated Bishop of Yucatan, Mexico.

2. The French transfer their fort of Natchitoches more to the west along the Red River. José González, commander of San Miguel de los Adaes Fort, opposes this move and cuts off all traffic and communication with Natchitoches.

1736

The governor of Florida sends Don Pedro Lamberto and Don Manuel D'Arcy to Jekyll Island as his delegates, to discuss with an English delegation the question of sovereignty of Georgia's coast. After lengthy discussion, it is decided to leave the decision to the courts of Spain and England.

1737

1. Bishop Martín Elizacoechea of Durango, Mexico, visits the area of Gallup, New Mexico, and engraves his name on the Rock of El Morro on the 28th of September.

2. Governor Carlos de Franquis of Texas has some conflicts with the missionaries, who accuse him of using Christian natives for his own personal interests and those of other colonists. The viceroy sends a visitor to investigate the matter. This results in Prudencio Orobio being named as temporal governor, replacing de Franquis.

1738

1. The town of Manati is founded in Puerto Rico, and construction is begun in Texas on the Church (now the Cathedral) of San Fernando in the city of San Antonio. It is built on one side of the main plaza, with the fort to its west.

2. The governor of Florida sends an expedition to the destroyed areas of Apalache and Fama, Florida, to weigh the possibility of rebuilding the places.

3. Manuel de Montiano y Sopelena, governor of Florida, orders unconditional freedom for all black slaves arriving from Carolina. He places them in a settlement north of St. Augustine which he calls *"Gracia Real de Santa Teresa de Mose"* (Royal Grace of St. Teresa of Mose). Seeing themselves free and in their own town, these black persons show their gratitude to Governor Montiano and promise him "to defend, to the last drop of their blood, the Crown of Spain and the holy Catholic Faith." They form a militia with Francisco Menéndez, also a freed black slave, as its commander and build Fort Mose to protect St. Augustine against enemy attacks. In a short time, forty black settlers will live there, served by priests in their spiritual needs. Captain Menéndez will stay as head of the town and Fort Mose for over twenty-five years. This is how Montiano reflects Spanish policy, influenced by Catholic values. This policy, contained in the *"Siete Partidas"* (Seven Decrees) of King Alfonso X el Sabio, was retained by the Laws of the Indies, which recognized the human, juridical, and moral personhood of black slaves, their right to have property and enjoy security, their condition as children of God, the responsibility of the Church to instruct them in the faith and to give them the sacraments, and their right to have a family, with masters frequently witnesses of their marriages and sponsors of their children. All this was in deep contrast with British policy, in which slaves were just chattel property, devoid of rights.

1739

1. The so-called "War of Jenkins's Ear" begins between Spain and England over the control of Georgia. It takes this name from the fact that bootlegger Robert Jenkins appears before the English Parliament with an ear cut off. The Spanish coast guard has caught him trading illegally. According to him, the captain of the Spanish cut off his ear, handing it over to him, and now he shows his ear in a bottle before the assembly. This incident gives origin to a war that will last fourteen years in which the Creek, Chickasaw, and Choctaw Indians ally themselves with the English while Vice-Admiral Edward Vernon takes Portobello and several other

Spanish points of the Caribbean are attacked. In reality, this war is just a small sample of a bigger struggle between Spain and England to stretch their dominions and to control international trade.

2. After crossing the source of the Missouri and Platte Rivers, the Mallet brothers — Pierre and Paul — cross over the Colorado Mountains and arrive at New Mexico. Governor Gaspar D. Mendoza interrogates them and gives them the choice to remain in New Mexico or to go back to Louisiana. At the same time, it is discussed whether the purpose of the Mallet brothers was a simple exploration or establishment of a trade route with New Mexico. After a stay of over one year in New Mexico, they return to Louisiana. Two French companions of their group decide to remain there.

1740

1. In Stone, South Carolina, a revolt of black slaves takes place. Slaves from Angola try to escape to St. Augustine, Florida, but they are captured. British authorities blame Spanish policy for the insurrection, because it offers sanctuary and refuge to slaves arriving in Florida. In reprisal, James Oglethorpe, with the help of the Cherokee and Creek Indians, raids Florida in January and is able to take over the Fort of San Francisco de Pupo and Fort Picolata. He lays siege to the city of St. Augustine, courageously defended by its Governor-Captain Don Manuel de Montiano. The Basque governor, firmly entrenched at San Marcos Fort with 750 soldiers, resists the cannonade and overcomes the long siege placed by the more numerous forces of Oglethorpe. After reinforcements arrive from Havana, Oglethorpe withdraws his troops, unable either to defeat Montiano or take over the city.

2. A violent hurricane in Puerto Rico causes disaster to crops and livestock. This calamity is particularly difficult because only two years before Puerto Rico was devastated by another hurricane and is just beginning to recover.

1741

1. Since Oglethorpe failed to conquer St. Augustine, Florida, Admiral Edward Vernon gets 3,500 soldiers from the colonies north of Carolina, while 9,000 more are sent from England in a huge fleet never seen before in America. Its main purpose is to take over Havana, but waiting there is Admiral Torres with a powerful fleet too. Seeing this, Vernon gives up and heads toward Cartagena (Colombia) but also fails. He then turns towards Santiago (Cuba) to take it over by land but is unable to do so. Frustrated by these failures, he gathers his decimated fleet and seeks

refuge in Jamaica. Now the Spaniards take the offensive using the same methods as the English. Many individuals and armed groups begin to raid English plantations and settlements all along the Atlantic Coast.

2. Governor Mendoza of New Mexico undertakes a military campaign against the Comanche Indians to prevent their raids on towns of the Río Grande valley. He realizes, however, that looting non-Christian Indian villages is prohibited and heavily penalized by Spanish law. It seems that the outcome of this expedition is rather meager, because Mendoza advises the mayors of New Mexico to keep a vigilant eye for possible raids of Comanche Indians.

3. Spain, in accord with its policy of pacification, orders the commanders of the garrisons of Texas to engage in military activity against the Comanches only as a defensive measure.

4. Csarret Noel issues, in New York, the first Spanish grammar published in the Thirteen Colonies, under the title *A Short Introduction to the Spanish Language*.

1742

To punish Oglethorpe, who had laid siege to St. Augustine, Florida, a fleet of fifty Spanish ships disembarks a contingent of 3,000 soldiers in the area of Brunswick, Georgia, on the orders of Governor Manuel Montiano; a battle ensues with Oglethorpe's troops. Given the marshy conditions of the area, Spanish soldiers have difficulty receiving supplies and support from the sea. This prompts Montiano to retreat to St. Augustine, Florida. The event will be known as the Bloody Marsh War.

1743

1. James Oglethorpe again tries to take over St. Augustine and attacks the city with considerable force. Spanish soldiers, entrenched in the fortress of San Marcos with six cannon, force him to give up and retreat.

2. Jesuits José M. Monaco and José J. Alana arrive from Havana, to establish a small mission in the south of Florida, near Florida Cape and the Ratones River. The missionaries struggle against the pagan customs of the Indians, such as human sacrifice, lustful behavior, and robbery. They manage to form a small Catholic community that will last until the Seminole War.

1744

1. Father Mariano de los Dolores of San Antonio Mission visits the Cujanes, Karankawas, Manos de Perro, and Piquique tribes of Texas on the banks of the Guadalupe River. Baptismal registers of the mission list

baptisms of people from at least forty different tribes who reside in the land between the Río Grande and the Colorado River.

2. Records in New Mexico show that at this time there are 771 homes of colonists with some 10,000 people, and 25 missions, each with 30 to 100 native families. The four principal cities are Santa Fe, Santa Cruz, Albuquerque, and El Paso; the last, according to Antonio Villaseñor in his book *Teatro Español*, has some 300 families.

1745

1. One chronicler of the mission of San Antonio, Texas, records that there are 311 Christian families there. The mission consists of two rows of adobe houses. Through the middle of them for some distance there is a water channel, with a street on both sides. There is also a monastery where three missionaries live, a blacksmith shop, a carpentry shop, and a workshop for various crafts such as the weaving of linen and cotton. The mission has good land where cotton, corn, beans, watermelons, muskmelons, and pumpkins are grown to sustain the natives. As for livestock, there are 23 yoke of oxen for farming, 2,302 head of cattle, 1,317 sheep, 344 goats, and 40 horses. Other missions of the area of San Antonio have similar situations, although struggling to settle the nomadic Indians. Father Ortíz writes that it is impossible to instruct the Indians in their native tongues since, in the region of the Río Grande alone, there are about 200 dialects, each unique to its tribe.

2. The Franciscans write an old and interesting history of Texas, in which they record the ways and customs of the Indians of the region.

1746

1. Don José Escandón, mayor of Queretaro, Mexico, is named viceregal governor of Texas, receiving orders to populate the Gulf of Mexico from the Río Grande to the Mississippi River.

2. The mission of Cebolleta is founded in New Mexico.

1747

General José Escandón, with some eight hundred soldiers, begins to settle the area along the Río Grande, establishing fourteen villages with five hundred families who volunteer for the endeavor. They are given land and loans. Many places such as Dolores (San Ignacio), Río Grande City, Roma, and Laredo are established. The territory between the Río Grande and Nueces is cultivated, converts are made, and the area will become an important cattle center in Texas.

1748

1. Antonio Villaseñor publishes his book *American Theater*, which mentions that at this time the native Indians of New Mexico are well dressed; there are industry, peace, and abundance in the settlements, and the churches are such that they should not envy those of Europe.

2. Father Mariano de los Dolores establishes the missions of San Ildefonso in Texas, which include 349 Indians, and San Francisco Xavier de los Horcasitas on a height over the Rio San Gabriel (near present Thorndale). Shortly after, a fort is built to protect the missions against the fierce hostility of the Comanches.

1749

1. Some four hundred Apaches with their four chiefs arrive at San Antonio, Texas, and sign a peace treaty with the Spaniards. All attend Mass, followed by a barbecue feast held to celebrate the treaty. The missionaries in Texas give evidence of great valor and apostolic zeal by extending their efforts to the territories of the Cocos, Osages, and Missouri Indians. One of them, however, loses his life, and another escapes after capture.

2. Apostolic activity is extended to the area between the San Marcos and Brazos Rivers, where Father Mariano de los Dolores is the central figure. The Bay Mission of Nuestra Señora del Espíritu Santo, established in 1721 by the Marquis de Aguayo, is transferred to Goliad on the banks of the San Antonio River. Nearby, the Fort of Our Lady of the Angels is built. This is a very prosperous mission with extensive lands and thousands of cattle and horses. Agriculture is abundant, yielding good crops of corn, potatoes, melons, figs, and cotton. Nonetheless, the Franciscans have great difficulty settling the indigenous natives, given the Indians' propensity for nomadic life.

Juan Bautista de Anza, born into a military family in the Arizona territory, blazed a trail from that area all the way to California, establishing in 1776 a settlement that became San Francisco with its Mission Dolores. Thereafter he was appointed governor of New Mexico, which included the territories of Arizona and Colorado. He He fought battles against the Comanche Indians, with whom he signed a historic treaty in Santa Fe in 1786 (courtesy Mercaldo Archives)

1750-1800:
Spain and the Birth of a Nation

Spain helps the United States in its independence. She extends her work to Louisiana and California.

1750

1. Thomas Vélez Capuchín, governor of New Mexico, fights a fierce battle against Comanches who attack the town of Galisteo to steal horses. He kills 101 and takes 44 prisoners.

2. This year and in the next few years, the settlements of Dolores, Peñitas, and La Lomita will be founded on the banks of the Río Grande, Texas. This is to be followed by the granting of lands like "King Ranch," Brownsville, and Corpus Christi.

3. Also during this year, Padre Island is assigned to Father Nicholas Balli, so that he may undertake the conversion of the Karankawa cannibals who inhabit the island.

1751

1. The Indians of Arizona start a rebellion, and two Jesuits are martyred.

2. Missionaries bring from Santo Domingo to Louisiana the first sugar cane to be cultivated in the United States.

3. Governor Vélez Capuchín receives three Frenchmen who arrive at Santa Fe with the purpose of establishing trade. The three are allowed to reside at Santa Fe, where they remain working in their professions as tailor, barber, and blood taker. A short time after, another four Frenchmen arrive and are sent to Chihuahua, Mexico, for interrogation. A few months later, another two are apprehended and their goods confiscated and sold. With the cash, they are sent first to Mexico and then to Spain with a warning that their entrance into Spanish territory is illegal.

1752

1. Captain Juan Bautista de Anza, with fifty soldiers and about four hundred colonists, establishes the settlement of Tubac, where a fort and the Church of St. Gertrude are built.

2. Father José Ganzábal receives the crown of martyrdom in Texas. Because of his death, the missions of San Ildefonso and the Candelaria on the banks of the Río San Gabriel will suffer great disturbances.

1753

José Vázquez Borrego, a Spanish rancher from Texas, starts a ferry service with two boats and four oarsmen to cross the Río Grande from the Texas side to the Mexican settlement of Dolores. Later, Tomás Sánchez, pioneer of the city of Laredo, starts another transportation service. At the same time, Escandón founds the city of Mier, and says, "The northern part of the Río Grande is colonized."

1754

Close to La Bahía (the Bay), Texas, Father Juan de Dios Cambreras establishes the Mission of Our Lady of the Rosary, not far from the San Antonio River. In the years that follow, the mission will prosper to the point of having thirty thousand head of cattle, then later will decline. However, the mission will continue until 1831, when it will be secularized.

1755

1. On May 15, taking advantage of fording the Río Grande and a fertile prairie to the north where the city of Laredo is located, José Escandón moves a group of families there to develop the land for agriculture. Farther north, several families of the Tlaxcalteca Indians of Mexico are sent to start a settlement on the banks of the Trinity River.

2. The Mission of San Francisco de Asís is built in Rancho de Taos, New Mexico. The church is 108 feet long and has two high towers at the entrance.

3. A group of disgusted English colonists, led by Edmund Graig, cross the Altamaha River and settle on the banks of the Satilla River in Georgia in a place called New Hanover. This action goes against the recent agreement between Spain and England, which considers the region between the Altamaha and St. Mary's Rivers neutral territory. The governor of Florida sends a group of soldiers to tell the English to leave said area. English authorities, fearful of Spanish reprisals, also order the colonists to return north of the Altamaha River.

1756

1. The viceroy of Mexico orders construction of the "Mission of Our Lady of the Light" on Galveston Bay at the mouth of the Trinity River. Franciscans Bruno Chivara and Marcos Zataraín, with the help of Governor Francisco García and a group of Indians who had come from Tlaxcala, work eagerly. The site, near the present Anahuc in Chambers County, is not a good one and therefore does not prosper. Close to the

mission, the garrison of San Agustín de Ahumada is built in what will be Wallis.

2. The city of Pensacola, Florida, is built on the banks of the Escambia River and a stockade is erected to protect the Christian Indians of the area.

1757

1. Pedro Romero de Terreros donates 150,000 pesos for the establishment of a mission, a garrison, and a village near the San Sabas River in Texas. Colonel Diego Ortíz Parrilla builds the San Luis de las Amarillas Fort close to the present Menard. A little further down, the Mission of San Sabas is established, as well as the settlement. It is hoped that the Apaches, persecuted by the Comanches of the North, will become friendly with the Spaniards and settle in the village. To this purpose, a group of Christian Tlaxcalteca families is brought in. One reason for the settlements is to exploit the silver mines recently discovered on the banks of the San Sabas River.

2. Father Andrés Burriel, S.J., writes a book titled *News from California*, published in Spain. Because of the information it contains, it is translated into French, Dutch, English, and German. This publication awakens interest and ambition in some European nations, including Russia. For this reason, Spain decides to occupy and settle upper California, which has previously been explored and included in the maps as a territory of her sovereignty.

3. A number of families from the Canary Islands arrive in Florida to engage in farming. They are met with constant raids by the Indians allied with the English. These attack San Diego Ranch and the town of Monte del Puerco, burn houses, slaughter livestock, and murder six civilians and two soldiers. A short time later they kill another three soldiers, ambush a group of seven cavalrymen in Santo Domingo, and capture a group of German colonists at Tolomato Island, five miles North of St. Augustine, Florida.

1758

The Mission of San Sabas near Menard, Texas, after a prosperous start, is destroyed by a ferocious Comanche attack. On March 16 they murder Father Alonso Giraldo de Terreros and Father José Santiesteban. Father Miguel Molina and two soldiers, who remain buried under the rubble until midnight, survive and flee in the shadows of the night.

1759

1. The Comanches continue threatening various missions and towns of Texas. Colonel Parrilla departs from San Antonio with 380 soldiers, 90 Indians of the Mission, 30 Indians from Mexico, and 134 Apache friends. He arrives at San Sabas and chases the Comanches to the Colorado River. Here, near the present city of Ringold, he is met by two thousand more Comanches, many riding horses and equipped with firearms provided by French merchants of Louisiana. After a four-hour battle, the Spanish, seeing the impossibility of victory, begin retreating gradually after losing 60 men. In order to protect their Christian Apaches, the Spanish will soon establish the missions of La Candelaria and San Lorenzo a little more to the west, on the banks of the Nueces River.

2. Bishop Francisco Martínez Tejada, now bishop of Guadalajara, Mexico, makes a visit to the missions of the area of Río Grande and San Antonio, Texas. He inspects the parish books, the buildings, and also confirms 644 persons, both Spanish and Apache.

3. Charles III becomes king of Spain at the death of his brother Ferdinand VI. The event is celebrated a few months later in the capital city of Florida with most of the people gathering in the main square. Before the flag, displayed by the second lieutenant major, the crowd shouts, *"Viva el Rey!"* ("Long live the King") repeatedly; a solemn Mass is said, and the celebration goes on for two days with music, dramatizations, and dances. A report by Father Juan José Solana states that this year the city of St. Augustine, Florida, has 303 homes, housing 462 families and a total of 2,446 persons. Among said families some 40 came from the Canary Islands, sent for the purpose of farming. At Fort Mose there are also 33 black soldiers, some with their families, who reside at the fort to protect the city of St. Augustine in case of a northern attack.

1760

1. Captain Blas de la Garza receives a royal charter of 975,000 acres of land in Texas. He settles with his family, colonists, and soldiers in the place that he names "King Ranch of Santa Petronila." He begins a center for the development of agriculture and cattle-raising, which becomes a bulwark against the dreaded Comanches. Later this ranch will be highly renowned for the meat industry and the number and quality of its cattle.

2. Bishop Pedro Tamarón Romeral of Durango, Mexico, makes a pastoral visit to the province of New Mexico. He confirms 2,973 in El Paso and 11,371 in the northern part of the region. After visiting all the towns he is satisfied with the situation of the missions, but remarks that Spanish is to be taught to the Indians so that they may go to confession

and receive the other sacraments. After his visitation he publishes an interesting report together with a census of the population.

3. According to a report, the forces that defend Florida this year, consist of three infantry companies commanded by captains Alvaro López de Toledo, José Gemmir, and Ventura Díaz with a total of 340 soldiers. The cavalry is composed of 50 mounted soldiers and 46 dragoons. The artillery has 45 men and 148 pieces of equipment, the great majority of them located at St. Augustine.

1761

1. In order to protect the Mission of San Antonio, Texas, against Apache attacks, a high wall is built around the mission. Above the entrance they build a tower equipped with three cannons, munitions, and mechanisms to place the arquebuses.

2. Father Diego Jiménez and Captain Felipe Rábago y Teran begin the foundation of San Lorenzo Mission, called "The Canyon" (*El Cañon*), on the banks of the Nueces River, close to present Barksdale. Nearby, they also build the Candelaria Mission near today's Montell. These two missions do not have a fort for the protection of missionaries and new Christian natives against attacks of savages from the north. They are established here because four hundred Apache friends take refuge in this place; the initiative to rebuild the destroyed Mission of San Sabas will start from here.

3. Comanche Indians sieze the town of Taos. Manuel Portillo, acting governor, gets there with some four hundred soldiers, and a fierce battle ensues, in which about four hundred Comanches are killed. Seeing Spaniards and Comanches battling each other, the Ute Indians from southern Colorado take advantage of the occasion, stampede the cattle, and take about a thousand horses that belonged to both parties. The outcome of this battle is a rough lesson for the Comanche tribe.

1762

1. Father Mariano Martí is appointed bishop of San Juan, Puerto Rico. He builds schools in Guaynabo, Bayamón, and other places. There are also educational centers at the monasteries of the Franciscans and Dominicans and at the Cathedral.

2. The British take over Havana, Cuba, and take Bishop Agustín Morell of Santiago into exile in Charleston, South Carolina, and later in St. Augustine, Florida. The bishop remains here for several months, provides pastoral care to the Catholic community, and bestows the sacrament of Confirmation on 639 persons.

3. Forced by the pact of the Bourbon family, Charles II of Spain sides with France in the war she wages against England. Aware of this action, England declares war on Spain on January 1. As a result of this war, England will occupy Havana and Manila.

1763

1. As a result of the war that France and Spain fought against England, the Treaty of Paris is signed. England gives Havana back to Spain in return for Florida and Georgia, while France cedes Louisiana to Spain as compensation for the help received in this war and the loss of Florida. England then expels from the area of St. Augustine all Christian natives and takes away their land. The Indians go to the West and take the name of Seminole.

2. Through kinship between royal houses and the help that Spain provided France in the war against England, France cedes to Spain the territory of Louisiana stretching from the Mississippi to the Sabine River. England keeps the region east of the Mississippi. Many of the French from the east side of the river now move to the west side because the Spanish are Catholic. Thus the situation of this region undergoes a big change. Spain now has the British instead of the French as neighbors in the eastern part of her territories. Her subjects in Louisiana are of French origin, the Indians have not been formed under the mission system, and the territory is excessively large. Spanish borders now stretch from the Strait of Magellan in the South to the Mississippi River in the North, a territory too large to be civilized, evangelized, and defended by a nation like Spain, which at this time has but ten million people. This year, Louisiana counts some ten thousand people. The strategic situation also changes. Spain now controls New Orleans and the navigation of the Mississippi River at its mouth and along its western bank. This will be of vital importance for the Thirteen Colonies in the War of Independence, since it will be, practically speaking, the only way of getting provisions from the outside.

1764

After Louisiana comes under the sovereignty of Spain, the merchant Pierre LaClede, with a group of other people, moves his fur company from Fort Chartres to the west bank of the river and settles at the confluence of the Mississippi and Missouri Rivers. Thus begins the city of St. Louis, Missouri, where the Spanish establish their headquarters to protect the upper Mississippi River and found a commercial center for trading furs obtained along the Missouri River and its tributaries. Shortly after, a lieutenant governor is named because of the strategic position of the city. The first parish is built, and Father Bernardo Limpasch is appointed first pastor of the city.

1765

1. An expedition commanded by Captain Juan Rivera goes across the Rocky Mountains for the first time. He explores the basin of Gunnison River in Colorado, and the expeditionaries engrave crosses and names on the trees, leaving clear proof of their presence precisely in the middle of that immense chain of mountains.

2. A large number of English colonists arrive in Florida; they get farm land, begin to establish small industries and enterprises, and a great economic activity follows.

1766

1. Juan Alonso Ulloa, a scientist, officer of the Royal Navy, and writer, arrives in New Orleans on March 5 and is sworn in as governor of Louisiana. He places military garrisons at Balize, Iberville, across from Natchez, and in Missouri. In New Orleans he installs the first astronomical observatory and the first laboratory for the study of metals. Ulloa is a man of science but as governor and politician is somewhat wanting.

2. Charles III orders a review of the military situation of New Mexico and appoints two visitors: José de Gálvez and Cayetano Pignatelli, marquis of Rubi. Pignatelli leaves for the North and inspects the military garrisons and forts of New Mexico and Texas. Afterwards, he makes a recommendation to set up a military defensive line from the Gulf of California to the mouth of the Guadalupe River in East Texas, and to establish a fort every forty leagues. This measure will result in the elimination of some military posts and the building of new ones. According to his proposal, the crown will save some eighty thousand pesos annually.

1767

1. Charles III, by a decree signed on February 27, orders the expulsion of the Jesuits from all Spanish territories. This action is apparently motivated by his liberal philosophy influenced by the Enlightenment movement of the time; by his decision to subject the Church to his absolutist policy, considering the Jesuits an obstacle to this goal; by the pressure exercised upon him by some of his powerful ministers, and by the maneuvers of secret organizations hostile to the Church. The Jesuits are blamed for plotting the famous Esquilache Riot, and this serves as the basis for their expulsion. Because of this ban from Spanish territories,

they also leave sixteen missions in Arizona, and these are placed under the guidance of Franciscans.

2. Shortly after Pedro de Mendinueta, the new governor of New Mexico, arrives, a serious flood takes place in Santa Fe. The overflowing river causes serious damage in the city. Thanks to the tireless efforts of its citizens, many works are saved. A few months later, Mendinueta orders the establishment of a military post on San Antonio Hill, near Ojo Caliente in southern Colorado, to protect the valleys of St. Louis and Rio Grande against the raids of the Ute and Comanche Indians. Also this year, the Mission of Nuestra Señora de Belén is established in the county of Belén, New Mexico, while another mission is being erected in St. Louis, Missouri.

1768

1. Notified by his ambassador in Russia that Catherine II is in the process of establishing commercial posts and friendly relations with the natives of the northern coast of the Pacific, King Charles III of Spain gives orders to the viceroy of Mexico. He is to send a military expedition to Upper California to cover that coast with forts and missions and to repel any Russian attempt to settle in those lands.

2. A royal envoy and the viceroy of Mexico organize the expedition to occupy Upper California. Two ships depart, the *San Carlos* and the *San Antonio*. The *San Carlos* leaves La Paz in Lower California with twenty-six seamen, Father Fernando Parrón as chaplain, one physician, and one engineer. The *San Antonio* pulls out from La Paz also with twenty-six seamen and Franciscans Father Francisco Gómez and Father Juan González Vizcaíno. Two other expeditions march on land. One leaves from Velicata headed by Captain Juan Rivera, with Father Juan Crespi as historian. The other expedition, led by Captain Gaspar de Portolá and Father Junípero Serra, takes off from Loreto and meets the first one in the area of San Diego Bay on July 1. After a few days, the two ships finally show up. All men but two from the *San Carlos* have died of epidemic on the trip, while eight have died on the *San Antonio*, and those who survive are very sick. Once the four groups have gathered, Father Serra raises a cross on Presidium Hill, and on July 16 the first mission of Upper California, called San Diego, is established. The main purpose of the expedition is to establish the headquarters of the operation at Monterey Bay and to secure a harbor to providing safety and supplies for the Manila galleon on its way back from the Philippines. Portolá decides to go forward while the major contingent and Father Serra remain there to establish the town and Mission of San Diego. Portolá, Captain Rivera, Fathers Crespi and Gómez, twenty-six soldiers, and seven mules loaded with provisions

march on their way to Monterey. They cross the Bears Canyon (Cañon de los Osos) and the Santa Lucia Mountains and gorges. After a true adventure, they finally reach the dreamed-about Bay of Monterey in the first days of October. A few days after, Captain Rivera with a group of soldiers continues the exploration toward the North, arrives, and gazes at the beautiful Bay of San Francisco. Father Crespi says in his diary that this bay is so big that there is room in it not only for the fleet of Spain, but of all Europe also. Portolá, after exploring the area of Monterey, returns to San Diego. This is how exploration and colonization begin in California, where Franciscan Fathers Junípero Serra, Fermin Lasuén, Francisco Palou, Juan Crespi, and confreres will establish twenty-one missions and towns along the "Camino Real" (Kings Highway).

3. Some 1,255 immigrants from Menorca Island arrive in the city of St. Augustine, Florida, and settle near Mosquito River in a place called New Smyrna. Two priests come with them: Father Pedro Camps, a doctor of theology, and Father Bartolomé Casanovas, an Augustinian.

1769

1. Alejandro O'Reilly, with a fleet of 24 ships and 2,600 soldiers, arrives in New Orleans as the second Spanish governor of Louisiana. He is sworn into office, and a "*Te Deum*" in thanksgiving is sung at the Church of St. Louis. The population swears loyalty to Spain while they cry five times, "*Viva el Rey!*" (Long live the King). O'Reilly is a military officer of Irish origin, educated in Spain. He has participated in Spanish military campaigns in several places of Europe. Appointed governor of Louisiana at the age of thirty-two, he reforms political life, commerce, the army, and represses an insurrection with a strong hand. In his time, great buildings like the Cabildo will be constructed in New Orleans.

2. Father Francisco Garcés arrives in New Mexico; he explores and evangelizes the region for six years. A little later, he joins Juan de Anza on the trip to California, but he decides to remain in the area of the Colorado River. He walks through deserts and mountains some four thousand miles, crosses the Grand Canyon of Colorado by the pass known as *Vado de los Padres* (Padres' Pass). Throughout his years as a missionary in the region, he will work with some twenty different groups of Indians and finally die a martyr.

1770

1. Portolá and Father Crespi with a group by land, and Father Serra with another group aboard the *San Antonio*, arrive at the Bay of Monterey. They formally take possession of the place, attend Mass, and

sing the hymn "*Te Deum*" in thanksgiving. They also begin construction of a fort with a chapel and a mission. A few months later they are moved a little farther up near the Carmel River because of differences between Father Serra and Captain Pedro Fages. The Mission is called San Carlos Borromeo.

2. A report on the Mission of the Holy Spirit in Goliad, Texas, states that in the current year there are forty thousand longhorn cattle. Nearby, the El Rosario Mission has about thirty thousand head. The non-branded cattle are called "*mesteño*," where the name mustang originates. Also in Texas, the Fort of San Elizario is built near El Paso and gives the name to the town.

1771

On July 14, Father Serra founds the Mission of San Antonio de Padua by the river of the same name; its church is 130 feet long (and totally restored today). In the best days it will raise 8,000 cattle, 12,000 sheep, and good crops of grain; it will also be known for its good grapes and wine. On September 8, Father Serra also initiates the San Gabriel Mission near the present city of Los Angeles. It will enjoy great prosperity through the next 60 years. In the last inventory made by the Franciscans, they will report that it has 16,500 head of cattle. It must be remembered that this prosperity, and that of other missions, is what makes them self-sufficent for their Christian native population.

1772

1. Father Serra establishes the San Luis Obispo Mission in California, and the complex is formed by many buildings for the housing of indigenous Christians. It will become prosperous under the care of Father Luis Martínez. The chronicles of the missionaries record that there are many bears in the area.

2. Through an order of the viceroy of Mexico, Captain Pedro Fages with fourteen soldiers, explores San Francisco Bay carefully. He passes through Santa Clara, arrives at the Sacramento River, turns South and goes back to Monterey through the San Joaquin Valley.

3. The bishop of Santiago, Cuba, sends Father Cirilo de Barcelona with four other Capuchins to New Orleans to minister to the Catholics of Louisiana, now under his jurisdiction. Father Barcelona is named vicar general of Louisiana, and the other four are named pastors in New Orleans, St. Louis, and Iberville. Shortly after, another six Capuchins will also arrive.

1773

1. Count Laci, Ambassador of Spain in Russia, alerts the Spanish king that the Russians are making preparations to establish a post on the Northwest Coast of the Pacific for fur trading. Charles II orders Viceroy Bucarelli of Mexico to occupy the coast north of Monterey to 60° latitude. Should they find a foreign settlement, they are to go even farther north, establish a settlement, take possession of the area, and plant a cross; under the cross they are to bury a pitch-sealed bottle containing documentation stating that said land belongs to Spain.

2. Antonio Gil y Barbo (born in Burgos, Spain) and his descendants establish the city of Nacogdoches in northeast Texas.

1774

1. To carry out the order of King Charles III, Viceroy Bucarelli orders Juan Pérez, a frigate lieutenant, to explore and occupy the coast of the North Pacific to the 60° parallel. On January 25, Pérez departs from the port of San Blas, Mexico, aboard the ship *Santiago*. He arrives in Monterey in June, explores the coast of Oregon, Washington, British Columbia, and arrives at Prince of Wales Island (55°). There Pérez trades with the indigenous people, whom he describes as "strong, joyful, and of beautiful eyes." He arrives in Alaska and then turns back. Pérez enters the Bay of Nootka at Vancouver Island, goes even farther into Seattle Bay, and then continues his journey south to Monterey, where he stays several days. After a rest, he continues south to arrive in San Blas November 3. Through his remarkable journey, Pérez draws a detailed map and takes possession of those places for Spain.

2. Juan Bautista de Anza receives an order from the viceroy of Mexico to look for a route to connect Arizona with California. Anza, born in Tubac, Arizona, is the captain of Tubac's fort; he is intelligent, brave, and familiar with the region. On January 8, Anza leaves Tubac with Fathers Francisco Garcés and Juan Díaz, California Indian Sebastián, and 33 soldiers. They take with them 35 mules loaded with provisions, 140 horses, and 65 cows, arriving in the area of Yuma, where the Colorado and Gila Rivers join. They also meet Indian Chieftain Palma, who is very cooperative. Anza and his people continue across the desert and the Sierra Nevada until they finally arrive at San Gabriel near Los Angeles. After a few days' rest they continue the trip to Monterey. From here, they return by the same route to Tubac, Arizona, where they arrive in July after covering over eight hundred miles. They open land communication between Arizona and California — indeed, between the Atlantic and the Pacific — for the first time in the present territory of the United States.

3. The first Spanish women arrive in California, among them the wife of Francisco Ortega. In the following year, she gives birth to the first European born in California.

4. England realizes the restlessness prevailing in the population of the Thirteen Colonies, giving orders to guard gunpowder deposits and carefully monitor its import into the territory.

1775

1. Viceroy Antonio Bucarelli of Mexico gives orders to Juan B. de Anza to establish the city of San Francisco in California. In October, Captain Anza departs from Tubac, Arizona, with 240 soldiers and settlers, plus Franciscan Fathers Francisco Garcés, Pedro Font, and Tomás Eixarch, 695 horses, and 355 head of cattle. They follow the route of the Gila River to its confluence with the Colorado River at Yuma. There Fathers Garcés and Eixarch decide to remain with the Yuma Indians and Chief Palma. Father Font, who is an astronomer and journalist, continues with the Anza expedition. They spend Christmas in the desert and will finally arrive at San Gabriel Mission in January 1776. After a brief stay there they will continue to Monterey, where Fathers Francisco Palou and Benito Cambon will join them, and a few days later they will arrive at the fabled bay. There Anza will establish the city of San Francisco at the tip of the peninsula, the Mission of Dolores and a fort equipped with two cannons to protect the entrance to the bay. Anza will then return to Arizona and leave Lieutenant Moraga in charge of the settlement.

2. An Indian war party attacks the San Diego Mission and kills Father Luis Jayme, a blacksmith, and a carpenter. Since the mission, through a decision of Father Serra, is about six miles from the Fort, the soldiers do not know about the attack and are therefore unable to prevent it. Captain Rivera searches and tries to capture the murderer, who seeks refuge inside the church. Rivera breaks in and apprehends him. Father Serra, in turn, judging that Rivera has violated the law of sanctuary, excommunicates him. This incident stops construction work, but after some time the activity is resumed. The construction of San Juan Capistrano Mission is initiated also on October 30 of this year.

3. Worried by the possible presence of Russia on the North Pacific Coast, King Charles III appoints naval Commander Bruno de Heceta and another six naval officers, among them Juan Bodega y Quadra, Juan Pérez, and Francisco Mourelle, to conduct another expedition to the North Pacific Coast. Viceroy Bucarelli gives them the frigate *Santiago* and two other ships with a plentiful crew, and abundant provisions for the missions and towns of San Diego and Monterey. In June they arrive at

Eureka Bay, which they carefully inspect. They sail on to Trinidad, where they land, take possession of it, and Father Miguel Campa, O.F.M., says Mass and preaches. Bodega y Quadra draws the map and takes note of the customs of the natives, with whom he also exchanges merchandise. After ten days there, they continue north on the Oregon coast. In August, they arrive at the mouth of the Columbia River, which Heceta calls Río San Roque, and Assumption Bay, which he carefully surveys. They sail north and enter Grayes Bay (Aberdeen). There some sailors go ashore to get some drinking water, and seven of them are killed by the Indians. They continue their voyage bordering the Olympic Peninsula and land on Vancouver Island. Father Solís cannot say Mass because of bad weather, but they plant the cross and take possession of the place with the usual ritual in the presence of the natives, with whom they also trade. Heceta continues his voyage and arrives at Forrester Island, then on to Prince of Wales. He calls a harbor "Guadalupe," a river "Remedios," and a bay "Bucarelli" in honor of the viceroy of Mexico who has sent him. He heads north and arrives at Krussoh Island. He carefully draws a detailed map of all visited places and, not finding any European settlement or organized nation, takes possession of that zone on behalf of the king of Spain, registering it in Spanish sovereignty. In October, he heads south and arrives in Monterey, California, where he rests for three weeks. Then continuing south, he arrives at San Blas, Mexico, whence he departed eight months earlier, and gives a report of his expedition.

4. In this year, the population of Puerto Rico is 72,331. In the following years there will be a sizcable increment in the population due to an increase in commerce, a larger military presence, and growth in agriculture.

5. Since the Thirteen Colonies do not have their own money, the Continental Congress orders the issuance of bills worth two million dollars which should be redeemed with Spanish dollars, "a sum not to exceed two million Spanish milled dollars." The Spanish dollar takes that name from the Bohemian "thaler," for the place in Bohemia where Spain used to coin her money. The name of "thaler" later became "Spanishized" and its pronunciation sounded like the word dollar, which is how it was written in Spanish afterwards. The Thirteen Colonies adopt the Spanish dollar because it is the money used in all the territories surrounding them: Cuba, Louisiana, Mexico, and the rest of America. It is with these territories that commerce will be conducted, since England has ceased to trade with her colonies and has withdrawn the pound sterling. The wording on the bill reads: "Three dollars. The bearer will receive three Spanish milled dollars according to the resolution of Congress taken in Philadelphia on May 10, 1775." This way, the Thirteen Colonies adopt the Spanish dollar based on

the decimal system, the "$" sign is the abbreviation of the plural "Pesos," and the two pillars with the motto *"Plus Ultra"* are taken from the Spanish imperial blazon.

6. Thomas Jefferson begins to speak almost perfect Spanish, and he promotes its study at Williamsburg College and the University of Virginia.

1776

1. England lays siege to the Thirteen Colonies. She is in control of the Illinois and Missouri Rivers northwest to the Mississippi's east bank; in the South with the Forts of Mobile, Pensacola, and St. Augustine, and in the East with a blockade of the Atlantic by the British fleet. The siege is such that nothing can be exported or imported, nor provisions or munitions brought. Practically the only supplies received from outside by the revolutionaries of Washington arrive via the west bank of the Mississippi River in ships bearing the Spanish flag. These vessels are loaded with all kinds of supplies in New Orleans and other Spanish ports, and then are guided up the west side of the river to tributaries that reach West Virginia and western Pennsylvania. This activity takes place amid frequent protests of the British consul in New Orleans and of Commander Peter Chester, who commands British forces in the South.

2. In January, George Gibson, a captain at Fort Pitt, carries via the Mississippi River a letter from General Charles Lee to the Spanish governor of Louisiana, Luis Unzaga, who resides in New Orleans. In the letter, Lee distressfully asks for a shipment of arms and quinine. Unzaga sends him ten thousand pounds of gunpowder, via the Mississippi and Ohio Rivers, thus saving the fort from falling. Gibson later gives a thousand pounds of this gunpowder to General Morris. He also gives Virginia's Committee of Security the valuable information that the king of Spain and the governor of Louisiana, though officially neutral in the conflict, are firmly supporting the cause of independence with arms, clothing, and medicines. A few months later, Gibson again takes from the Spanish arsenals of New Orleans another thousand pounds of gunpowder for Philadelphia, where it is desperately needed. At the same time, Charles III gives orders to help as much as possible and without delay Washington's revolutionaries to receive arms, munitions, and clothing from Havana, Louisiana, Texas, and Mexico.

3. The Congress of Virginia sends Benjamin Franklin, Arthur Lee, and Silas Deane to Spain, where they ask the crown to declare war on England and to help the Thirteen Colonies with supplies. The Spanish Crown answers that for political reasons Spain has to remain neutral in

the conflict for the moment, but that she will provide substantial help to the Thirteen Colonies. Most of the activities will be conducted not through political channels but through commercial arrangements between the Spanish ambassador in Paris and the Spanish firm of Diego Gardoqui in Philadelphia.

4. As documented on September 7, the count of Aranda, Spanish ambassador in Paris, by order of Charles III opens an account for one million torinese pounds to help North American independence. The money is used to buy 216 cannons, 27 mortars, 209 cannon carriages, 29 locomotives, 12,826 bombs, 51,134 bullets, 30,000 rifles with bayonets, 4,000 camp tents, 30,000 military uniforms, and a great quantity of gunpowder and lead to make bullets. These munitions are sent through the Rodríguez and Hortalez Company, specifically created to carry this merchandise and to finance the trip of Baron Von Steuben and of General Marquis de Lafayette.

5. About one hundred Spanish men, fighting for independence with Washington's revolutionaries, are taken prisoner by the British in New York. Juan Miralles, the Spanish delegate in Philadelphia, intercedes and they are freed.

6. Jorge Farragut, a Spanish merchant born in Menorca, joins the cause of independence. As a captain in the navy, he fights in South Carolina and Georgia, is captured in Charleston, and later is freed. Later on, he will take part in the battles of Cowpens and Hamilton. Finally, he will retire to Tennessee and marry Elizabeth Shine. From this union, his son David G. Farragut will be born, and he will be the future first admiral of the U.S. Navy during the Civil War.

7. On October 23 Charles III of Spain issues a decree stating the right of the Thirteen Colonies to their sovereignty and not to be considered rebels against an established goverment. This decree is published in spite of strong opposition from the British ambassador in Madrid.

8. Franciscan Fathers Silvestre Vélez Escalante and Atanasio Domínguez leave Santa Fe, New Mexico, with eight soldiers, a cartographer, and an Indian interpreter seeking to find a good pass to California. They scout through the western part of Colorado near Mesa Verde, pass through the Spanish Fork and arrive at Utah Lake, which they call *"Nuestra Señora de La Merced de los Timpanogotzis"* (Our Lady of Mercy of the Timpanogotzis). They continue on Río Verde near the present Dinosaur Quarry and think of turning westward, but heavy snow that has fallen makes it impossible. They descend toward Arizona, crossing for the first time from East to West in the Grand Canyon, which Father Garcés crossed four months earlier from West to East through the

"Vado de los Padres" (Fathers' Pass). They come down to Zuñi territory until they finally return to Santa Fe after walking some 1,800 miles in five months. This is a deed worth mentioning in all history books. Father Escalante writes an interesting diary on the places, plants, and animals of this region. This good Franciscan will spend twenty-five years of his life exploring the lands of New Mexico, Arizona, and Colorado, and evangelizing the Yuma, Comanche, Apache, Laguna, Tirangapuy, Moqui, Zuñi, Navajo, and Pueblo Indians.

9. As a result of the visitation to New Spain by José de Gálvez, now president of the Council of Indies, Charles III orders that the northern territories of New Spain be separated from the jurisdiction of the viceroy of Mexico and become a semiautonomous region with the name "Internal Provinces." Texas and Nuevo León will constitute the Eastern Internal Provinces, while New Mexico and Arizona will be the Internal Provinces of the West. The region will be governed by a general commander with powers similar to those of the viceroy. The king appoints Teodoro de Croix to this position, who in the future will not be a governor but a military commander. De Croix is a nephew of the former viceroy of Mexico.

10. Captain Fernando Rivera heads a group of settlers from Arizona walking to California to settle at San Gabriel. On the way they are ambushed by Yuma Indians, and almost all of them are murdered.

11. Father Palou and Lieutenant Joaquin Moraga continue in San Francisco, building the Mission Dolores by the lake which they dedicate on October 4. This mission will never enjoy great prosperity because of lack of proper farming land. The chronicles state that the Indians of this mission, once they become Christian, often escape from it.

1777

1. The young new Spanish governor, Captain Bernardo Gálvez, arrives in New Orleans. He is a captain of infantry grenadiers in Seville and has a brilliant military record from operations in Mexico and France. He is the son of the viceroy of Mexico and nephew of Don José Gálvez, president of the Council of Indies. In April after his arrival, he apprehends eleven British ships and orders all British subjects to leave Louisiana within fifteen days. At the same time, he opens the Mississippi River to free navigation and trade with the people of the Thirteen Colonies. England protests vigorously without getting any response. As a friend of Oliver Pollock, the financier of the revolutionaries, he defends and protects him in New Orleans against the order of arrest given by British Governor Chester. Gálvez sends a letter to the Continental Con-

gress saying that they have an open door in the Spanish territories to buy any supplies. Pollock will be the liaison between him and those fighting for independence.

2. Gálvez sends a load of arms, munitions, and provisions through the Mississippi River to James Willing, who had been sent by Robert Morris, a member of the Continental Congress. In addition, he makes available to him a building in New Orleans to sell and store products and collect funds for the cause of independence. The method used by Gálvez to sneak American ships into New Orleans, avoiding the search of the British frigates posed at the entrance, is to apprehend them on the high seas, bringing them into New Orleans as captured boats and, once they are out of danger, setting them free. Gálvez also sends ships under the Spanish flag loaded with clothing, shoes, quinine, other medicines, and munitions to Virginia and Pennsylvania for the armies of Washington and Lee. Throughout this year, he sends $74,000 and a load that had arrived from Spain containing six cases of quinine, eight cases of medicine, 108 cotton bales, 15,000 pounds of gunpowder, and 300 rifles with bayonets. Because of this help, Gálvez becomes, together with Clark and Pollock, one of the three most important persons in the independence of the Northwest.

3. Arthur Lee, representing the United States, arrives in Spain, and before he reaches Madrid, Prime Minister Marquis de Grimaldi meets him and has an interview with him at Burgos. Lee asks that Spain recognize the United States as a nation and declare war on England. Grimaldi responds that there are plenty of munitions and provisions at the Havana warehouses to supply the United States, and that other supplies will be sent from Spain through Gardoqui's trading firm located in Philadelphia. With this assurance, the Continental Congress notifies Clark that his military campaign will be financed with credits given to Oliver Pollock by Bernardo Gálvez, the governor of Louisiana. Pollock will frequently receive munitions and sundry other supplies on credit given by Gálvez, his successor Leyba, and José Vigo, a wealthy Spanish merchant in Missouri. Patrick Henry also requests from Gálvez an urgent loan of 150,000 gold dollars, offering him in exchange "the gratitude of this free and independent country."

4. Benjamin Franklin is appointed representative of the United States to Spain.

5. The persecution and hostility of the British and their allies, the Chickasaw, Creek, and Cherokee Indians, toward the American colonists of the eastern side of the Mississippi, prompt thousands to cross over the river and seek refuge in Louisiana under Spanish protection. Because of this hostility, Gálvez petitions the Spanish govern-

ment for two additional frigates to defend the Mississippi River and Louisiana.

6. There is an invoice at the National Historical Archives of Madrid, dated in September, where the costs are given for the following supplies sent to the United States: eight warships, copper and tin for cannons, thirty thousand military uniforms, one thousand rifles and cannons, sixty thousand pairs of shoes, ten tons of gunpowder, eighty thousand blankets, eighty thousand shirts, and three thousand horse saddles. The total of the invoice is $7,730,000. The merchandise is carried by ships from Spain, Cuba, Mexico, France, and Holland.

7. One of the most valuable helps to the United States is to make the port of Havana available and free for repairing and supplying U.S. ships with all kinds of munitions, clothing, and provisions. Because of the tight blockade that the British fleet keeps over the Thirteen Colonies, it would be almost impossible for them to maintain the revolution if Spain closed her ports. But Spain does not do that. She opens them as places of haven, repair, and supply for the American ships. This is vital for the cause of independence, since only Spain can provide this type of help in America.

8. The capital of California is moved from Loreto, Lower California, to Monterey, and Felipe de Neve is appointed first governor. In January, Neve sends Lieutenant Joaquín Moraga and Fathers Tomás Peña and José Munguía to establish the town and the Mission of Santa Clara on the banks of the San José River with fourteen families from Monterey and San Francisco. Many natives are instructed in the faith and baptized. This marks the beginning of the city of San José, which in a matter of months is already a municipality. It will quickly prosper thanks to the good farming land, cattle raising, and osier (willow basket) weaving.

1778

1. Governor Gálvez grants permission for James Willing to return and sell in New Orleans all merchandise that he obtained from British ships and properties. The profit from this sale is a great relief for the revolutionaries, whose resources are almost exhausted. It is sent to them through Oliver Pollock. Another shipment of munitions, gunpowder, muskets, clothing, and provisions worth 100,000 gold dollars is sent by Gálvez aboard the ship *Morris*. This shipment comes from Spain via Mexico to help the Americans. About this time also, twelve thousand rifles are sent from Spain and delivered in Boston.

2. With his private fortune, Spanish businessman José M. Vigo helps General George Rogers Clark to capture the city of Vincennes, Indiana.

3. King Charles III of Spain provides funds for moving a group of

colonists from the Canary Islands to Louisiana. They settle and found New Iberia. They engage in cattle raising and start plantations of flax and hemp.

1779

1. On June 22, Spain closes her embassy in London, declares war on England, alleging the capture of Spanish ships and damages to Spanish lands, and recognizes openly the sovereignty of the Thirteen Colonies. England then offers to return Florida, Gibraltar, and fishing rights in Terranova to Spain on the condition that she not get involved in this war, close Spanish ports to the insurgents, and join troops with the British to fight them. The response of Spain is negative, and she joins France in behalf of the American cause. George Washington, once he learns of this decision, writes a letter to his friend John Sullivan on September 3, telling him, "I have the pleasure to inform you that Spain finally has taken a decisive part . . . it is expected that this formidable bifurcation of the House of Bourbons will not fail to establish the independence of North America in a short time. . . ."

2. Spain puts her navy into action. General Antonio Barceló blockades Gibraltar, thus preventing the British navy from leaving to fight Washington's forces. The Spanish navy attacks the Bahama Islands, while Admiral José Solano with twelve ships, guards the coasts of the Thirteen Colonies. Lieutenant General Luis Córdoba captures seventy British ships at Espartel Cape.

3. In July, General Gálvez calls all his military officers of Louisiana to a war council: Captain Francisco Cruzat of St. Louis, Missouri, Captain Juan D'Elavillebeuvre of the South, Captain Alejandro Coussot of Arkansas, Captains Pedro Favrot, Hilario Estenoz, Joaquin Blanca, Manuel Nava and Martín Monzun, Colonel Manuel González, Lieutenant Colonel Esteban Miró, Commander Pedro Piernas, and Commander Jacinto Panis. Gálvez notifies them that Spain has declared war on England and that the British in turn will most likely attack Louisiana "as a result of the Spanish recognition of American independence." Therefore he asks them for their decision. Unanimously, all answer: "We will offer our lives and would give our fortunes if anything of them would remain."

4. In September, Gálvez with 1,427 men takes Fort Manchac, strongly defended by the British, in an assault. About fifteen days later, Gálvez marches against the strategic fort of Baton Rouge, defended by Lieutenant Colonel Alexander Dickson, 550 heavily armed men, and 13 cannons. After nine hours of heavy cannonade and crossfire between the armies, Dickson surrenders the fort and Gálvez takes over Baton Rouge.

At the same time, in order to avoid more deaths, Dickson also cedes Fort Pan Muré in Natchez, and Gálvez sends Captain D'Elavillebeuvre and fifty soldiers to take it over. Thus Gálvez is now in complete control of the Mississippi River. He also apprehends eight British ships bringing munitions and reinforcements to the captured forts.

5. Lieutenant Ignacio Arteaga, in command of the frigate *Princesa*, and Juan F. Bodega y Quadra, in charge of the frigate *Favorita*, depart on February 11 from San Blas, Mexico, with 195 men to survey once again the Pacific Coast to the north of California. After eighty-two days sailing, they arrive at Bucarelli Bay (55°) on May 13, go ashore, and Father Juan Riobo offers Mass, plants the cross, and calls the place "*Puerto de la Santa Cruz*" (Port of the Holy Cross). They explore the area for a month and then continue north, arriving on July 16 at "*Cabo y Monte San Elías*" (Mt. Logan, 58). They sail northwest, enter a bay, and go ashore. On August 2, they take possession of the place and call it "*Ensenada de la Regla*" (Shelicoff Strait). Five days later they decide to return, and on September 14 they arrive in San Francisco, where they remain a month and a half, resting and drawing charts and maps of the explored lands. They leave San Francisco on October 30, arriving at San Blas on November 21, after nine months of navigation.

6. British adventurer William Bowles leads an expedition, arrives at the area of Apalache (Tallahassee), Florida, and declares the independence of Muscogee State. With the help of some Indians he takes Fort San Marcos, but shortly after is captured and sent to Cuba, where he will die.

7. Governor Juan B. de Anza departs from New Mexico with soldiers looking for Comanche Indians, who constantly raid the towns, stealing horses and cattle. He arrives at the central part of Colorado, near Salida, where he finds them and inflicts a severe defeat. Years later, delegates of the Comanches will arrive in Santa Fe to sign a peace treaty with Anza.

8. Franciscan Fathers Francisco Garcés and Juan Díaz, helped by Commander Teodoro Croix, establish a mission, a fort, and a town in Yuma, Arizona.

1780

1. Gálvez makes preparations to attack the Bay of Mobile. He counts on twelve ships of his own and eight hundred men. The following reinforcements arrive from Havana: one Infantry battalion of Spain, 41 soldiers from Principe Battalion, 50 from Havana Battalion, 141 from Louisiana Battalion, 14 artillerymen, 26 musketeers, 223 militiamen, 107 mulattos, and 26 Americans. All these come in four ships. Gálvez enters the bay with his fleet, exchanging greetings and exquisite gifts with Colonel Elias

Durnford, the British commander. After these military courtesies, Gálvez politely asks for the surrender of the city,which is refused by Durnford. Gálvez now begins to lay siege to the bay and the city that are strongly protected by Fort Charlotte. Through 20 days of siege, Gálvez shoots cannons from sea and land until finally Durnford and his 1,400 men surrender and give up the city of Mobile and the fort on February 12. The Spanish enter the city and give the church (today a cathedral) the name of Immaculate Conception. Soon after there will be 13 priests working in the city.

2. The British decide to conquer the city of St. Louis, a strategic point for the control of the upper Mississippi River and a passage through which the revolutionaries receive their supplies. Afterwards, they also intend to take the rest of the Spanish forts on the west bank of the river. General Sinclair, with an army of 300 British soldiers and 900 Indian warriors, attacks St. Louis and Fort Pencourt. Lieutenant Governor Leyba is able to gather 25 soldiers and 289 civilians who present a ferocious resistance, until the attackers opt to withdraw to Canada before the reinforcements sent by Gálvez arrive. This victory of Leyba, his ally, allows General Clark to continue his fighting more easily on the eastern side of the Mississippi River. Leyba is now able to help Clark with 100 well-equipped soldiers, boats, arms, artillery, and provisions. Thanks to this help, Colonel Richard Montgomery marches up the Missouri River to get to Peoria and subdue the Sauk and Fox Indians. These submit, and from then on relations with Louisiana's Spanish people also improve. Leyba begins the construction of Fort San Carlos to protect the city from British attacks and to help General Clark in the fight for the independence of the Thirteen Colonies.

3. Captain Baltasar de Villiers, with a detachment of soldiers from Arkansas, takes possession of what will become the state of Mississippi. This territory will remain under Spain for the next twenty years. Among the commanders of this territory under the governor of Louisiana are Carlos Grand Pré, Pedro Piernas, Esteban Miró, and Manuel Gayoso.

4. Operations west of the Alleghenies are decisive in the triumph of independence. The three main factors are the supply of Clark's troops, the expedition of Willing through the Mississippi, and the action of Clark in Illinois. These three are substantially financed by Gálvez.

1781

1. John Jay, appointed colonial plenipotentiary before Spain replacing Arthur Lee, writes to the Spanish Prime Minister Count Floridablanca: "I find myself constrained to beseech Your Excellency to think a little of my

situation. Congress flatter themselves that the offers they have made would certainly induce His Majesty, at least, to assist them with some supplies. The residue of the bills drawn upon me remain to be provided for. Those payable in the next month amount to $31,809. Would it be too inconvenient to Your Excellency to lend us this sum?" The Spanish crown at this time lends 88,000 Spanish gold dollars. John Jay answers Floridablanca: "The impression made in the United States by the magnanimity of the conduct of Your Majesty toward them . . . causes the United States to guarantee Your Catholic Majesty all your domains in North America."

2. General George Washington, his wife, and his children lodge during the winter at the home of Francisco Rendón, the Spanish representative in Philadelphia.

3. Governor Gálvez continues to help Oliver Pollock with the purchase of provisions, but he meets some problems with the merchants because the continental currency does not have much value. While some merchants of New Orleans do not accept it, others accept it only if backed by Spain. Thus Pollock writes to Congress: "I would have sunk completely if I had not convinced Don Bernardo de Otter, the accountant of Louisiana, to lend me $40,000. I went to him asking for money from the public treasury, but having no authority to do that, it was impossible to get it. However, his friendship toward me and his consideration for the interest of the United States moved him to give me an advance from his private fortune."

4. Spanish Commander Francisco Cruzat, who had replaced Fernando Leyba as deputy governor in St. Louis, Missouri, orders the conquest of the British Fort St. Joseph on the shores of Lake Michigan. To this end, he appoints Captain Eugenio Purré and Captain Carlos Tayón, who march North with a detachment of soldiers defying snow and low temperatures. They take over the fort by surprise, and Captain Purré takes possession of it with the following words: "I annex and incorporate to the domains of his Catholic Majesty the King of Spain, my Lord, from now on and for always, this establishment of St. Joseph and its accessories, and of the river of the same name which flows into the Mississippi." This fact is of great importance because the area of the Ohio River from Michigan down to the Mississippi is now under Spanish control. The British force will cease to be a threat to the region, and Generals Clark and Montgomery can now continue to take control of the region between the Alleghenies and the Mississippi with ease.

5. Gálvez's target now is Pensacola, where most of the British southern forces are concentrated and where the two forts, Barrancas

Coloradas and George, make this place almost impregnable. About 10,000 British soldiers and Indian warriors are defending Pensacola. Gálvez receives reinforcements from Spain through Havana, and he is able to secure 49 ships and 3,800 men. At the time when he is organizing his fleet, a strong hurricane scatters the ships, sinking some them, but Gálvez is able to recover immediately. He gets another 1,300 men from Havana to strike from land and decides to march on Pensacola, where he arrives on March 9 and begins the battle. The British frigates protect the entrance to the bay, and cannons open fire. The Spanish cannons respond, and with a display of uncommon audacity, Gálvez storms into the bay with several ships. Once inside, he shoots from both inside and outside. During the night he unloads several cannons on land and keeps attacking from land and sea. A lucky cannon shot hits the gunpowder dump of Fort Barrancas, and this strategic bastion is blown up. Gálvez, who had been seriously wounded, personally commits all his troops to the assault. There are bayonet fights, and finally he takes over Fort Barrancas. Once there, he continues with the artillery shots on the rest of the British positions. General John Campbell surrenders, and on May 21 he gives Gálvez Fort Barrancas, Fort George, and the city. At the end of the battle another 20 ships arrive at the scene from Havana. The whole British army of the South, composed of some 14,000 men, both British and natives, is now out of combat, and prisoner of Gálvez.

6. American revolutionaries, protected now on the west and south by Spain, can, concentrate their forces to achieve independence. The battle of Pensacola had lasted two months and the defeat of the British army here has definitely redounded in favor of the Thirteen Colonies. Gálvez now appoints Arturo O'Neill as Commander of this region east of the Mississippi. At the same time, King Charles III orders that Pensacola Bay be named "Bay St. Mary's of Gálvez," that Fort Barrancas be called "Fort San Carlos," and Fort George, "Fort San Miguel." The king also rewards Gálvez by appointing him as lieutenant general and captain general of Florida and Louisiana. He gives him the title of count and allows him to place on his coat of arms a brigantine with the motto "*Yo Solo*" (I alone).

7. While Gálvez seizes Pensacola, his uncle José Gálvez orders an attack on the British forces in Central America. General Miguel Cajigal captures the Bahama Islands, and Spanish forces attack Gibraltar. The brilliant performance of young General Gálvez spreads everywhere and captures the admiration of people in all countries. His contribution, though, to the cause of independence of this country has not yet been valued enough, and his name is never included along with other heroes of the Revolutionary War. Gálvez later will be appointed

governor of Cuba, and then viceroy of Mexico, where he dies at the age of forty.

8. At a time when the revolutionary army remains without resources to continue the war, General Rochambeau sends three frigates to Havana to desperately seek help. Miguel Cajigal, the governor of Cuba, orders a public collection in Havana and raises 1,200,000 torinese pounds, arms, clothing, and munitions. Twelve ships leave Havana to deliver the shipment. This vital help allows Rochambeau's army to move forth and to finance the battle of Yorktown, whose outcome crowns the independence of the United States.

9. Because of problems between the native Indians of Yuma in Arizona and the Spanish settlers, the Indians rise and attack the Missions of San Pedro, San Pablo, and Conception. On July 17, they murder Franciscan Fathers Francisco Garcés, Juan Barreneche, and José Moreno. They also kill Captain Fernando Rivera and all males, while they take women and children captive. Three expeditions ordered by Pedro Fages, Antonio Romeu, and Teodoro Croix, respectively, rescue some seventy-five captives and a thousand horses, while two hundred Indians die in the battle. This rebellion is a setback to the missions of the area.

10. Felipe Neve, governor of California, founds the city of Los Angeles with eleven families that Captain Rivera has brought from Lower California, Mexico. Each family is given a plot of land on which to build its house. Later on, a chapel is built in honor of Our Lady of the Angels (*Nuestra Señora de los Angeles*).

11. Father Cirilo de Barcelona is consecrated a bishop. He will be an auxiliary to the bishop of Santiago, Cuba, with residence in New Orleans and will take care of the Catholics of Louisiana and Florida. He is the first resident bishop in Louisiana. He organizes the church there, administers the sacrament of Confirmation, and appoints pastors in Pensacola and Mobile. He also invites two Irish-born priests educated in Spain, Fathers Thomas Hassett and Michael Reilly, to serve both the English and the Spanish-speaking people of Florida. To cover the expenses of pastoral visitations to Mobile and Pensacola, the king of Spain orders that $4,000 be allocated to the bishop.

1782

1. Father Serra establishes the Mission of San Buenaventura at the place where Cabrillo had arrived in 1542. Father Serra builds the Mission for the Indians, ignoring the instructions of Governor Neve, who wanted rather to establish a town for Spanish settlers. Sergeant José Francisco Ortega, through an order of the governor, also begins the construction of

a fort in the Santa Barbara area, on a higher place one mile away from the beach. The mission will be built a few years later.

2. England intends to gather all her forces in the Bahamas in order to recover the Thirteen Colonies, but the Spanish navy battles Admiral Maxwell, defeats him, and maintains the islands under the sovereignty of Spain.

1783

1. As a result of the British defeat at Pensacola, Florida is returned to Spain, and Manuel de Céspedes is appointed governor. He holds this position in East Florida for seven years.

2. Juan Bautista Filhiol, with a group of soldiers and settlers, moves from New Orleans and settles near the Onachita River to begin the town of Monroe, Louisiana, where he also builds Fort Miró.

1784

1. Father Junípero Serra dies in California after years of vigorous missionary activity establishing towns and missions. He is buried at San Carlos Mission, where his confreres Fermin Lasuén, Juan Crespi, and Julián López will be buried also. His biography will be written by his companion Father Francisco Palou.

2. The construction of the beautiful Mission of San Javier del Bac in Arizona is initiated. It is a beautiful example of baroque style.

3. The Continental Congress names John Adams, Benjamin Franklin, and Thomas Jefferson the plenipotentiaries before the Spanish Court. Franklin is also chosen as the first academic journalist of the Royal Spanish Academy of History.

1785

1. Spanish businessman Andrés Almonester funds the cost of the Church (today, Cathedral) of St. Louis, the Cabildo, the Presbytery in the French Quarter, a hospital, a public school, and the chapel of the Ursuline Sisters in New Orleans.

2. King Charles III of Spain funds the construction of St. Peter's Church in New York, the first Catholic church in the city, and George Washington attends the dedication. Previously, Catholics of the area had to gather for the Mass said on Sundays at the chapel of the Spanish Consulate.

1786

1. Taking into account the opportunities that Spain offers to the United States for trading with her colonies of America, and the payment in gold and silver so needed to reinforce the value of the currency of the new nation, Congress, on a secret ballot, grants Spain control of both shores of the Mississippi River for twenty-five years.

2. Spanish authorities order Pedro Vial to explore a way to link San Antonio, Texas, with Santa Fe, New Mexico. Vial leaves San Antonio in October with only one companion, and after spending a few weeks with the Tawaknoni and Comanche Indians, he arrives in Santa Fe in May of the following year. He shows Governor Concha the diary of his trip, and the map proving to him that a link was possible by land for all Spanish provinces north of Rio Grande.

3. On December 4, Father Fermin Lasuén begins the construction of Santa Barbara Mission in California called the "Queen of Missions" because of its beauty and its size. The governor at the time is Pedro Fages. The quantity and the quality of its products make it impressive. In a few years, there are in the mission 1,700 Indians under instruction to be baptized, living in 250 adobe houses.

4. Francisco Dunegant establishes the town of San Fernando de Florissant, Louisiana, near St. Louis, Missouri, where soon after a church is built in honor of the holy king, conqueror of Seville.

1787

1. Attempts are made to create the new independent Franklin State with territories taken from West Virginia, North Carolina, Georgia, Alabama, and Tennessee. John Sevier is named governor, and through James White he asks help from Diego de Gardoqui, Spain's ambassador in New York, from Bernardo de Gálvez, captain general of Havana, and from Esteban Miró, governor of Louisiana. Sevier argues that because of neglect on the part of the eastern-region states and the need to open trade through the Mississippi River in order to take out their products, it would be more advantageous to the people of the new state to join Spain. Sevier writes to Gardoqui: "The people of this region are aware which is the nation from whom their happiness and safety will depend in the future, and foresee that their interest and prosperity are thoroughly linked to the protection and liberality of your government." Spain, though sympathizing with the idea, does not provide the requested help, and the idea of secession dies.

2. James Wilkinson, a prominent person of Kentucky, promotes an independence movement due to the abandonment of the region west of

the Alleghenies by the federal government and to the lack of protection in the face of constant attacks of the Indians. He writes twice to the king of Spain and even swears fidelity, asking for his help and the exclusive right of trade through the Mississippi River. The Spanish government, not wanting any friction with the new nation, disregards the request and opens the Mississippi River to Americans for trade. Wilkinson then returns to the American army.

3. On June 20, the Spanish government gives permission to thirty families of the United States to settle in Camden County, Arkansas.

4. In July, Governor Concha of New Mexico sends José Mares, with two companions, to travel the road from Santa Fe, New Mexico, to San Antonio, Texas. They arrive in October, and soon after they return through northern New Mexico, which makes the trip much shorter.

5. At the request of the chieftain of the Comanche Indians, Anza establishes the town of San Carlos of Jupes on the banks of the Arkansas River in Colorado. He sends personnel for construction, farming equipment, sheep, oxen, and seeds.

6. Father Fermin Lasuén founds the Purisima Concepción Mission in California. Father Mariano Payeras follows and completes the construction. A short time later the Indians seize it, but soon it is recovered and restored.

7. The diocese of Santiago, Cuba, is divided and the diocese of Havana is newly created, to which now belong Louisiana and Florida. Father José Trespalacios is appointed bishop of the new diocese, and he is given Father Cirilo de Barcelona as auxiliary bishop, still serving Louisiana and Florida. King Charles III orders that some bilingual Irish priests be sent to West Florida to minister to English-speaking Catholics in their own language; shortly after, four diocesan Irish priests, trained in Spain, arrive in Florida to work in three parishes projected for English-speaking Catholics. Some time later, another three Irish priests arrive in St. Augustine from Spain: Father Michael Crosby, O.P., Father Michael Wallis, O.P., and Father Constantine McCaffrey, O.C. Father Hassett is appointed episcopal vicar for East Florida with residency in St. Augustine. At the same time, it is proposed that three parishes for English-speaking Catholics be designated in East Florida and another three in West Florida.

8. Father Hassett establishes a school for children in St. Augustine, Florida. Writing, reading, mathematics, and geography are taught by Father Francisco Traconis and Mr. José A. Iquiniz. The school is run with specific high standards, and it seems to be the first free school in the United States.

233

1788

1. When the king of Spain is notified that Russia has established four trading posts on the West Coast of North America, he appoints graduate Lieutenant Esteban Martínez and Pilot Gonzalo López de Haro to head an expedition on the frigate *Princesa* and the *Filipino* to search the coast to parallel 61°. Martínez departs from San Blas, Mexico, on March 8. He arrives at Prince William Cove (60°), continues to Flores Strait and Port (now Shelikoff), and on May 28 he takes possession of the place. On June 24 they watch Miranda Volcano, and two days later they arrive at Trinidad Island. At Three Saints, Haro visits a settlement of sixty Russians. Chief Delarof tells him that there are six Russian posts to latitude 55° and about four hundred men engaged in fur trading. Martínez continues northwest until he reaches Unalaska, one of the Aleutian Islands. He disembarks on its north side, and with the cross on high and his sword unsheathed, he takes possession of the region in the name of the king of Spain on July 28. He remains there with his people until August 18, then undertakes his return to San Blas, where he arrives on December 5 and gives a report on his expedition.

2. Traveler Pedro Vial now walks the road from Santa Fe, New Mexico, to Natchitoches, Louisiana. From there he goes on to San Antonio, Texas, and returns to Santa Fe after walking 2,500 miles. With the roads opened by Hernando de Soto, Pedro Vial, José Mares, and Juan Bautista de Anza, the southern route across the United States is now complete. It links St. Augustine, Florida, New Orleans, Nacogdoches, San Antonio, Santa Fe, Yuma, and Los Angeles; this is the famous "Spanish Trail" connecting the Atlantic Ocean and the Pacific Ocean.

3. Bishop Cirilo de Barcelona leaves New Orleans for a pastoral visitation to Florida and praises the excellent work done by the two priests at St. Augustine.

1789

1. The king of Spain is informed that Russia is planning to settle Nootka Bay and orders the viceroy of Mexico to protect the place. The viceroy calls again on Esteban Martínez to take another expedition and build a fort on Nootka Bay on the "Isla de Quadra" (Vancouver Island). In the meantime, the king sends a protest to the Russian court because of the settlements on the coast of North America. The royal treasury advances $30,000 to prepare the expedition, and Martínez leaves with two frigates, 195 soldiers, settlers, arms, munitions, and medicines. Three missionaries also accompany the expedition: Fathers Inés López, José Díaz, and Nicolás López. They arrive at Nootka Bay on May 5, disem-

bark, and mount ten cannons. They apprehend two American ships, the *Columbia* and *Washington*, one Portuguese, and two British vessels. Martínez, escorted by his people and in the presence of the captains and crew of the foreign boats, takes official possession of Santa Cruz of Nootka. They all shout "Long live the King of Spain!" (*Viva el Rey de España*), placing documentation inside a sealed bottle, and immediately after, Commander Martínez gives a banquet for all guests. Then he sets free the American and Portuguese ships and sends the British ships with Captains James Colnett and Washson, to San Blas, Mexico. Martínez now begins the structure of the fort on a hill near the entrance to the bay and calls it "*Bastion de San Miguel de Nutka*" (St. Michael's Bastion of Nootka), where he sets up the ten cannons. He builds barracks, houses, shops, a small hospital, and a bakery.

2. Governor Esteban Miró gives permission to George Morgan to establish a town in Louisiana. Morgan departs from Pittsburgh with four boats and seventy colonists. They settle on the west bank of the Mississippi River, giving birth to the city of New Madrid. Later, disagreements between Morgan and the Spanish authorities will compel him to withdraw from the established city.

3. The day of the inauguration of George Washington as President of the United States, Spanish Ambassador Diego de Gardoqui stands at the right of Washington. The Spanish warship *Galveston* guards the entrance of New York Bay.

1790

On February 3, Pedro Alberni departs for Nootka with Captains Francisco Eliza, Salvador Fidalgo, and Manuel Químper. They go aboard three ships: the frigate *Princesa* with 160 men, 22 cannons, 20 rifles, 40 pistols, gunpowder, and provisions for ten months; the frigate *Princesa Real* with 31 men, several short range cannons, rifles and pistols; and the frigate *San Carlos* with 100 men, 14 cannons, rifles, and munitions. They arrive at Nootka on April 3 and continue their expedition northward, arriving at Prince William Bay (61°), where Alberni gives names to several places like Menéndez, Volcán Fidalgo, Valdés, Revillagigedo, Mazarredo, and Isla del Conde. They visit one Russian settlement near Cook River and, at Two Heads Cape they visit another one. After this, they return to Nootka, Monterey, and finally San Blas.

1791

1. Commander Alejandro Malaspina and José Bustamante, by a royal order, undertake a scientific expedition to the North Pacific and try to find

a passage from the Pacific to the Atlantic Ocean. They leave from Spain taking two corvettes, *Descubierta* and *Atrevida*, and head toward Montevideo, Strait of Magellan, Santiago de Chile, Callao del Peru, Panama, and Acapulco. After a few days' rest, they leave from Acapulco on May 1, taking aboard a good number of astronomers, cartographers, botanists, naturalists, and other persons skilled in the various sciences. They arrive at the Sitka area (Edgecombe Cape) and continue to Yakutat Bay. They discover the big glacier that they call Malaspina. They pass Cordoba, enter Prince William Bay, and here they do interesting studies on geography, botany, zoology, customs of the natives, and their cannibalism. They continue heading northwest until they reach the Bering Strait, and from here they can see the sun at midnight, as they say. Once they realize that there is no passage to the Atlantic Ocean, they return to Nootka. Here the naturalist José M. Moziño remains among the Indians of Nootka, researching and writing on the plants, animals, and customs of the natives. His writings will be published later. Malaspina and Bustamante, who was born in Santander, return to Acapulco taking with them about twenty children that they have bought to free them from the cannibal Indians.

2. Spaniard Francisco Marín arrives in Hawaii. Marín, whom the natives call "Mianini," brings to the islands many new plants, flowers, and fruits never seen before. He processes many of the natural products, gives instructions on the Catholic faith, baptizes many of the natives, and is highly esteemed by the Chieftain Kamehameha.

3. Near the San Lorenzo River in California, the Mission of Santa Cruz is established. Not too far from there, the town of Branciforte is formed, where Indian and Spanish houses are planned to alternate as a way to assimilate the natives to a new way of life. A large square is built in the center of town, with houses on all sides and also a racetrack. Land is divided and apportioned among the settlers. On October 9 in California, Father Lasuén founds La Soledad Mission, which will never become very prosperous, although it will be very active for the next forty-five years.

4. Francisco Hector, baron of Carandolet, is appointed governor of Louisiana, in whose time the New Orleans Channel is built and the first theater is dedicated.

5. The Catholic Church ministers in their language to the English-speaking people residing in St. Augustine, Florida, by means of several Irish-born priests educated in the Irish Royal College of Salamanca University and other places of Spain.

1792

1. Commander Jacinto Caamaño departs from Mexico on May 23 aboard the frigate *Aranzazu*, also heading north. He delivers supplies at Nootka and continues to Port Bucarelli. He remains one month exploring bays and the Islands of Prince of Wales, Queen Charlotte, Revillagigedo, and Aristizabal. He enters through the Dixon Strait, passes between Queen Charlotte and the continent, and returns to Nootka. A few days later, on June 5, Captains Dionisio Galeano and Cayetano Valdés, aboard the ships *Sutil* and *Mexicana,* leave from Nootka. On Fuca Strait they see the frigate *Princesa*, commanded by Captain Fidalgo, who is safeguarding the strait. They get deep inside the bay and explore all its inlets from south (Seattle) to north, Fonte Channel, Cordoba and the central Rosario Channel. A British ship commanded by Captain George Vancouver arrives and invites Spanish Captains Galeano and Valdés to go aboard, and together they continue exploring the area for a month. When they leave, the Nootka Indian chieftain Tetaku asks the Spanish captains to take him with them, which they do with pleasure. Throughout the exploration, he shows a great interest in the Spaniards' way of life. The reports on all Spanish explorations to the Pacific Coast of North America are published with many details.

2. Traveler Pedro Vial, accompanied by Vicente Villanueva and Vincent Espinosa, leaves Santa Fe, New Mexico, in May. They follow the course of the Canadian and Arkansas Rivers, and are taken captive by the Kansas Indians. Soon they are set free by other Indian friends of the French. They now take the course of the Kaw River in Kansas and follow it to its confluence with the Missouri River. There they find a fur merchant who gives them information on the road, and then engage in conversations with the Osage and Missouri Indians. In October they arrive at St. Louis, where they are warmly received by Deputy Governor Zenon Trudeau. The following June, on their way back, they board a ship going up the Missouri River to southeast Nebraska. Here they go ashore, walk back to the Canadian River, and arrive in Santa Fe in November. As a result of this trip, Pedro Vial inaugurates the so-called "Santa Fe Trail" and a new route is opened to trade.

1793

1. On August 11, Captain Juan Martínez Zayas aboard his Mexican schooner reaches the mouth of the Columbia River on the West Coast, explores it with several of his men, goes up fourteen miles, and returns to the schooner after being harassed by the Indians. At this point he turns south, and on the way visits capes such as Lookout, St. Gregory, Toledo,

Diligencia, San Sebastián, Puerto Trinidad, Mendocino and Vizcaíno; he also visits Puerto Bodega, San Francisco, Monterey, and San Diego. He arrives on November 4 at San Blas, Mexico, his point of departure.

2. The Diocese of Louisiana and Florida, taken from Havana, is established, and Father Luis Peñalver y Cardenas is appointed as first bishop; he is a native of Havana and vicar general of the diocese.

3. A report mentions that throughout this year 162 United States ships have anchored at Cádiz Harbor in Spain. This fact gives an idea of the heavy trade between the two countries.

1794

1. Sovereignty over Nootka Bay raises a serious conflict between England and Spain, to the point that both countries put their fleets on high alert. They finally come to an arrangement and opt to declare Nootka Bay neutral. Some time later, Commander Juan Bodega y Quadra, in the name of Spain, cedes to England, in the person of Captain George Vancouver, Nootka Bay and Quadra Island (now Vancouver). This arrangement greatly upsets chieftain Macuina and his people, who felt very identified with the Spaniards.

2. Baron Carandolet, governor of Louisiana, orders that trade be intensified along the Missouri River. The deputy governor of St. Louis, Zenon Trudeau, goes up the river with nine merchants and several boats. They arrive at Platte River, continue to the land of the Sioux Indians, and trade with them. They proceed along the White River and arrive at the land of the Arikara Indians in central South Dakota. They establish friendly relations with the Cheyenne near the White River. The purpose of the trip is to look for and increase fur trade.

3. Father Juan Bautista Zengotita is appointed bishop of San Juan, Puerto Rico. He gives an impetus to church work. On the island there are now 38 parishes and 35 shrines (*ermitas*), among them Porta Coeli in San German and Monserrate in Hormigueros. There are also 97 confraternities, three hospitals, and three monasteries of Franciscan, Dominican, and Carmelite nuns. At the end of the century, there are about 140,000 people on the Island and 89 diocesan priests.

1795

1. On October 27, the United States and Spain sign the Pinckney Treaty at San Lorenzo de El Escorial. Spain cedes to the United States all her ports and forts on the eastern side of the Mississippi. She also opens the river to free American navigation, grants them a post in New Orleans for product trading, and the border between both countries is set at Paral-

lel 31°· At this time, Governor Carandolet builds forts on the Mississippi in Natchez, San Fernando, and Barrancas de Marot.

2. James Mackey, a Spanish citizen of Scottish origin, is appointed lieutenant governor of St. Louis. He departs from St. Louis and continues up the Missouri River with four boats of the Missouri Fur Company carrying plenty of gifts and commodities to trade with the Indians. He builds a fort among the Oto natives, spends the winter with the Omaha Indians, and builds Fort Carlos. He proceeds up the river trading with the Arikara and Cheyenne Indians, and together with John Evans of the Missouri Fur Company, another Englishman in the service of Spain, arrives at the territory of the Mandan natives, where they establish a post and raise the Spanish flag. They ask the Indians for a passage to the Pacific Ocean, explore the area of the Yellowstone River, and decide to return to St. Louis after a trip that has lasted two years. In following years, other Spanish merchants will keep increasing trade along the Missouri River.

3. A good part of the funding for the missions, founded by the Franciscans, is coming from the "Pious Fund" established by the Jesuits in Lower California, to which many private individuals give donations.

4. On April 25, Father Luis Peñalver is consecrated first bishop of Louisiana and Florida, and on July 24 he takes possession of the new diocese, whose limits stretch from Mexico to Baltimore, Maryland. New Orleans is chosen as its See, and Father Thomas Hassett is brought in from Florida to be the vicar general.

1796

Governor Carandolet authorizes Julián Dubuque to work the silver mines of Iowa. Dubuque now fights the British and defeats them at Prairie du Chien, forcing them to retreat from the area. Once he obtains the charter from the king of Spain, he establishes the city of Dubuque, where he also builds a fort.

1797

1. This is a year of heavy missionary activity in California. The construction of San Juan Capistrano Mission, designed by engineer Isidro Aguilar, is renewed. It will have many stone-carved decorations and a tower 115 feet high. On June 11, Father Lasuén, helped by several soldiers, founds the Mission of San José de Guadalupe. From the beginning, the missionaries will find great difficulty in the conversion of the native Indians. On June 24, Father Lasuén also establishes the San Juan Bautista Mission with a large convent, a granary, soldiers' barracks, and houses for the Christian natives. Later, a large church will be built; soon there

will be about 500 Indians living at the mission, which also will be the origin of the town of St. John the Baptist.

2. On July 25, San Miguel Arcangel Mission is initiated. It is surrounded by large extensions of farmland and will become very prosperous under the leadership of Father Juan Cabot. Soon there will be about 1,000 Indians at this mission, Christian or in the process of becoming Christian. Many are also trained in various skills and crafts, blacksmiths, masons, carpenters, tanners, and soapers. Hundreds farm the fertile lands, grow grapes, and make charcoal for their kitchens. On September 8, Father Lasuén founds San Fernando Rey Mission, which, in addition to evangelization, will be well known for its large herds of livestock and its agricultural products and crops. On its best days it will have 13,000 cattle, 8,000 sheep, and 2,300 horses. The mission also has a small hotel to lodge travelers along the "Camino Real" (King's Highway).

1798

1. On June 13, Father Lasuén, a native of Vitoria, Spain, initiates the San Luis Rey Mission, which will be continued by Father Antonio Peyri. It is square-shaped with a 500-foot wall on each side and 32 arches inside. One side is used for dormitories for single young girls and the other for single young men. Its great church is attached to the convent, and it possesses a large quantity of farmland where grain, vegetables, and fruit trees are planted. In its best days there will be 26,000 horses. Some of the harvest will yield 395,000 bushels of grain and 2,500 casks of wine. When Father Peyri leaves the mission, harrassed by Mexican civil authorities during the secularization, more than 500 Indians run to the Port of San Diego, tearfully begging him not to leave them.

2. Governor Manuel Gayoso builds his residence near Fort Pan Muré, Louisiana, and grants Daniel Boone a permit to settle in Louisiana.

1799

1. Phillip Nolan, a protege of General James Wilkinson, swears fidelity to the king of Spain and is sent to Texas by the Governor of Louisiana to buy horses in order to protect Louisiana. Nolan stays a long time in Texas, establishes friendly relations with the Indians, draws maps, buys horses, and finally returns to Louisiana. But there are suspicions of his being a spy who passes information about the Spanish forces in Texas to the colonists east of the Mississippi River, hungry for land on the west side. It is proved that he is a traitor; he is apprehended and killed in Waco, Texas.

2. On October 16, William A. Bowles declares the State of Muskogee in western Florida independent. Bowles fought in the American Revolution against Washington, was a friend of Alexander McGillivray, and a leader of the Creek Indians. He was a prisoner of the Spaniards in Havana for five years. Supported now by the Creek and Cherokee Indians, he seizes Fort San Marcos of Appalache. Vicente Folch, the Spanish governor of Pensacola, reacts immediately to the takeover and orders the recapture of the fort. Bowles and his followers flee to the jungle, where he will continue to raid Spanish territories the next three years, but his adventure of independence will not last long. Finally, the Creek themselves will hand him over to the Spaniards, who will send him to Havana. Placed in the Castle of El Morro, he will die two years later.

3. The census taken by Spain in Louisiana registers 42,375 persons, of whom two thirds are located in the southern part of the region.

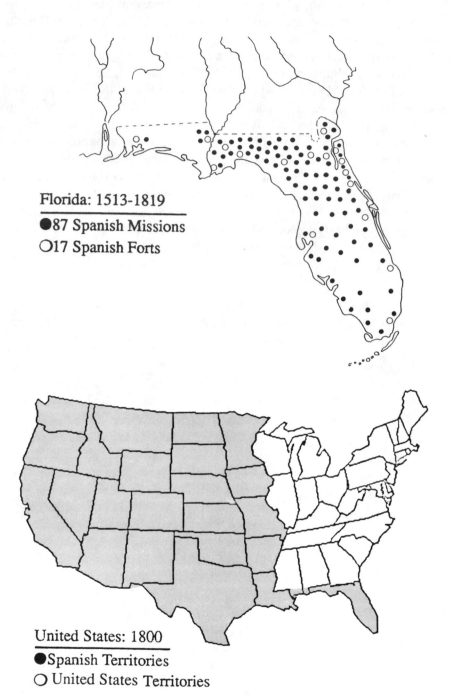

Florida: 1513-1819
● 87 Spanish Missions
○ 17 Spanish Forts

United States: 1800
● Spanish Territories
○ United States Territories

1800-1850:
Decadence and Development

While Spain loses its territories, the United States quadruples its original size.

1800

1. The Mission of San Diego has 50,000 acres of land, with 10,000 head of cattle, 20,000 sheep, 1,250 horses, and abundant vineyards. This is one of the first nine missions established by Father Junípero Serra during his 15 years of work in California. The Christian natives who live there are many. By this time there are a great number and variety of animals in the California missions. The missions of New Mexico, Texas, and Arizona find themselves also in a time of high prosperity.

2. Lieutenant Colonel Carrisco discovers the copper mine of St. Rita, near Silver City, New Mexico.

3. The missions of Florida receive a strong reinforcement with the arrival here of thirty-seven Franciscan priests.

1801

1. The royal treasury grants the governor of New Mexico, Fernando Chacón, a subsidy to reinforce the town of Cebolleta and protect it against frequent attacks of the Navajos.

2. David G. Farragut, the first admiral of the United States Navy, is born. His father is Captain Jorge Farragut, a native of Menorca, Spain.

1802

1. Daniel Boone settles in Missouri. He pledges fidelity to the king of Spain and is named a public official of Femme Ossage in the area of St. Charles. He is granted nine hundred acres of land.

2. Pressured by France, Spain closes the Mississippi River to American navigation, and the friendly relations of the two countries become strained.

1803

1. Louisiana territory, which stretches from the Mississippi River in the East to the Sabine River in the West and the Missouri River on the North, colonized and governed by Spain since 1763, becomes part of the United States. During Spain's government, 1,463,333 acres of land have

been distributed, but only half of the acreage has been confirmed by the Spanish governor of Louisiana.

2. According to a report, there are 24,544 Christians in the missions of California, counting both Spanish and natives. They own 103,143 head of cattle, 36,794 horses, 2,962 mules, 539 donkeys, 132,654 sheep, 3,501 goats, and 131,000 pigs. The harvest in bushels includes 53,758 of wheat, 18,353 of corn, 3,005 of barley, 10,271 of beans, and 31,239 of chick-peas and lentils.

1804

1. The vice-governor of St. Louis, Missouri, when giving his farewell and surrendering Louisiana to the United States, pronounces these words: "The new father will maintain and defend the land, and will protect all the white people and the redskins residing here. You will live as happy as if the Spanish were still here."

2. The Mission of Santa Inez, California, is founded on September 17 and from the beginning enjoys great prosperity. During its most prosperous times, it has 768 Christian natives, 10,000 head of cattle, and 15,000 bushels of harvested grains. Two large reservoirs are constructed for irrigation. Some of the mission buildings will be burned in a rebellion and damaged in the earthquake of 1812 and in a fire, but later they will be restored.

1805

1. Count Nicolai P. Rezanov, representative of the Czar of Russia, plans to establish a post on the West Coast of North America. He arrives in California and falls in love with Conchita Argüello, the daughter of the governor. Count Rezanov returns to Russia to obtain imperial permission for the wedding, but he dies on the way. Conchita, hearing of her lover's death, enters a convent. For the present, the Russians will not attempt to open a post in California.

2. In New Mexico and Arizona, measles and whooping-cough epidemics develop. Doctor Larrañaga, with the governor's help, conducts a massive vaccination campaign against the epidemic. This is opposed by the population, who are ignorant of this practice.

1806

1. Spanish Governor Luis Argüello, through an official notice, rejects the petition of Russia for permission to fish and hunt in California. Count Rezanov had requested this permission the previous year.

2. Many Spanish settlers of Louisiana become disappointed by the Spanish cession of this region to France. A good number of settlers of

New Gálvez, Iberia, Valenzuela, and other cities decide to leave Louisiana and move to Veracruz, Mexico, where they settle down.

1807

1. Spanish fur trader Manuel de Lisa and forty-two men go up the Missouri River in search of furs. They arrive at the Yellowstone and Big Horn confluence, near Billings, Montana. There he builds a trading post which he calls Fort Ramón in memory of his son.

2. Father Nicolás Balli is given a long, narrow island on the southern coast of Texas so that he might give himself to the conversion of the frightful Karamkawa Indians, who are cannibals; from this comes the name "Padre Island," which it still bears today.

3. Joaquin R. Alencaster, governor of New Mexico puts Zebulon M. Pike under arrest for intruding into Spanish Territory; he is taken prisoner in San Luis Valley near the Conejos River and sent to Santa Fe. He will be released shortly after.

1808

1. Manuel de Lisa gives great impulse to the fur trade along the Missouri River, and his business, the Missouri Fur Co., experiences great prosperity. He explores Nebraska, marries a princess of the Omaha tribe, provides the natives with a variety of seeds, and teaches them the methods to grow them. He builds Fort Lisa north of the city of Omaha and dies a few years later.

2. Napoleon invades Spain; this action has great repercussions in the Spanish territories of America. It will give rise to independence movements throughout the hemisphere.

1809

The council of the Spanish government issues a decree giving all Spanish territories of America, and therefore New Mexico, Texas, California, and Florida, the privilege of electing a delegate to represent them in Madrid before the Spanish *Cortes* (Parliament).

1810

1. The people of New Mexico elect Pedro Bautista Pino as their delegate before the Spanish Parliament. Along with rendering his report, he requests from the Parliament a larger number of forts, a bishopric for New Mexico, and the establishment of an educational system.

2. Some rebels rise in Baton Rouge, capture the fort, take Governor Carlos H. DeLassus prisoner, and on September 23 proclaim the inde-

pendence of the West Florida Republic. They appoint Judge Fulmar Skipwith as president and hoist their flag (blue background and a silver star in the middle). President James Madison protests this proclamation to Governor Claiborne of New Orleans and tells him to put an end to the insurrection. Claiborne takes over the cities of St. Francisville and Baton Rouge, and the independence of the West Florida Republic is over seventy-four days after it began.

3. Don Miguel Hidalgo, the Creole priest of the town of Dolores, Mexico, rises with a group of followers. At the cry of "Long live Fernando VII and down with the bad government!" he begins a rebel movement against the government established by Napoleon in Spain. This movement of Father Hidalgo is the beginning of a process that leads to the independence of Mexico. It will also bring substantial changes to the territories now part of the United States.

1811

1. A group of rebels, called the patriots, attack and take over Amelia Island, Florida. Commander Justo López resists, but, because of the larger number of the enemy, he surrenders the city of Fernandina where San Marcos Fort stands to protect the area. Some time later the whole island will go to the United States.

2. Dr. Samuel Lathan Mitchell, an expert in Spanish Literature, gives a report to the United States Congress in order to promote cultural exchanges with developing Latin American countries.

1812

1. Several American traders, Robert McKnight, Samuel Chambers, and James Bird among others, arrive in the area of Santa Fe, New Mexico, to establish trading with the people there. They bring six mules loaded with a variety of merchandise. Because of their illegal entrance into Spanish territory, they are arrested, their merchandise is confiscated, and they are put in jail.

2. Taking advantage of the chaotic situation of the Spanish government, the United States takes over the bay and city of Mobile, Alabama, and West Florida.

3. Father Andrés Quintana dies as a martyr in the Mission of Santa Cruz, California.

1813

1. Encouraged by the independence movement of Mexico, Bernardo Gutiérrez de Lara, with some help from Anglo settlers, leads an insurrec-

tion near San Antonio, Texas, against Governor Manuel Salcedo. He takes him prisoner and executes him along with some others. He declares Texas an independent republic, but troops sent from Laredo suppress the rebellion four months later.

2. The first newspaper of Texas, called *El Mexicano*, is published in Nacogdoches.

1814

1. The war fleets of Spain and England clash near Cape Canaveral, Florida. Immediately, English ships take over the city of Pensacola, but they are expelled soon after. Peace between the countries is restored with the signing of the Treaty of Ghent, Belgium, in December.

2. British ships capture the American frigate *Essex* in Valparaiso Bay, Chile, after a three-hour battle. Many American sailors are left dead, but David G. Farragut, who at that time is thirteen years old, is one of the survivors.

1815

1. George Gordon Meade is born in Cádiz, Spain, where he will live his first years with his family. His father has been sent by the United States government to work at the Navy Base in Cádiz. because of commercial and legal problems, the Meade family will return to the United States, and young George Gordon will enter West Point Academy. He will later play an important role during the Civil War at the battle of Gettysburg and several other military campaigns.

2. In the academic field, Abiel Smith establishes a chair for the teaching of Spanish at Harvard University. It will be occupied in the future by such distinguished academic men as Henry Longfellow, James R. Lowell, and others.

3. A report on California shows that the San Diego Mission at this time has 50,000 acres of land, 20,000 sheep, 10,000 cattle, 1,250 horses, and is also known for its excellent wine production.

1816

1. José Miguel Carrera seeks United States support for Chile in its war against England. He meets with Commodore Porter and President James Madison, and with the help of Joel Poinsett manages to buy some ships, but American help is not very significant.

2. At the request of the State of Georgia, American troops attack and destroy Apalachicola Fort in Florida, which is inside Spanish territory. This neglected fort has been used by the Seminole Indians and other hostile groups.

1817

1. Gregor McGregor, a Scottish military man who has fought alongside Simón Bolivar in South America, arrives at Amelia Island, Florida, with two ships and 150 soldiers. Commander Francisco Morales, believing that the invaders are far superior in number, delivers Fernandina City without firing a shot. McGregor proclaims the independence of the McGregor Republic on June 29 and raises the new nation's flag (white background with the green cross of St. George). Soon after, José Coppinger, the new Spanish governor, drives the adventurers away. Not a long time elapses before pirate Louis Aury takes Amelia Island and proclaims the independence of the Republic of Amelia Island. Aware of this, President James Monroe sends some troops who drive the pirates from the island and end the life of Amelia Island Republic.

2. Franciscan Fathers Vicente Sarriá and Luis Gil establish the Mission of San Rafael Archangel in California. With his medical expertise, Father Gil takes care of the sick Indians of the San Rafael Mission, which is attached to the Mission of Dolores. San Raphael is practically a hospital where all the sick Indians of the region are cared for. Soon the mission will prosper, with about a thousand Indians living there.

1818

1. An insurrection of the Indians in the Apalache area, near Tallahassee, Florida, causes General Andrew Jackson and his troops to take over the San Marcos Fort, but the United States government orders him to vacate it and return it to the Spanish garrison. Shortly after, this fort and all Florida will go to the United States.

2. Father Felipe Arroyo de la Cuesta, who headed the San Juan Bautista Mission in California, writes two books on the Mutsumi language. It is said that this missionary is able to understand twelve Indian languages and to speak seven of them fluently.

1819

1. By the Treaty of Adams-Onis, signed on February 22, Spain cedes Florida to the United States; more than a purchase, it is a donation, since the five million dollars received from the United States is given to private individuals for compensations and claims. This way, Spain leaves Florida after a stay there of three hundred years. She now turns over to the United States a territory that is explored, colonized, and evangelized, with cities like Jacksonville, St. Augustine, Miami, and Gainsville in addition to Tampa, Tallahassee, and Pensacola, which were passed over the previous

year. From now on, the Diocese of Charleston, South Carolina, will take care of East Florida.

2. James Long, at the head of a small army of soldiers and colonists of Natchez, thirsty for Texan lands, crosses over the Sabine River, arrives in Nacogdoches, and proclaims the independence of the Republic of Texas. Long is named president, the lone star flag is raised, and a government council is formed. Among the members is Bernardo Gutiérrez de Lara. Antonio Martínez, the Spanish governor, dispatches a company of soldiers to control the situation. The rebels flee, but Long is captured, led to Mexico, and, when he tries to escape from prison, is shot by a guard and dies.

1820

1. The Spanish Parliament issues a decree encouraging American colonists to come over to Texas. They are promised generous grants of land provided they become Spanish citizens. Moses Austin accepts this offer, promises to give up his American citizenship, and becomes a subject of the king of Spain. Shortly after, he becomes a Catholic. This authorizes him to come to Texas, where he settles with three hundred families, establishing the town of Austin, the future state capital.

2. A fort is built near Sangre de Cristo (Blood of Christ) Pass in Walsenburg, Colorado, to protect the Spanish colonists of that area.

1821

1. President James Monroe sends General Andrew Jackson to Pensacola to arrange with Colonel José Callava, the Spanish governor, details of turning Florida over to the United States. Callava, who had a brilliant career of military achievements, resorts to delaying tactics that make Jackson lose his patience. The latter does not show his credentials personally, but tries to arrange details through middlemen. The former does not feel obliged to respond to Jackson, who pressures Callava to withdraw his troops from Pensacola. The proud Callava answers that he will leave on July 17 and not one day sooner. On July 17, at ten o'clock in the morning in Pensacola, Jackson and Callava sign a document turning Florida over to the United States. The Spanish flag begins to be lowered while the United States flag starts to rise. At half mast both flags meet, while a 21-gun salute is fired in honor of both nations. The following day the Spanish troops leave for Havana. According to a census ordered by Callava a few days before his departure, there were in Pensacola at that moment 695 persons: 441 white and 254 free blacks.

2. Mexico issues the "Plan de Iguala" and declares itself an inde-

pendent nation. A short time later, the Mexican government gives a grant of 73,000 acres in Cochise County, Arizona, to Ignacio Pérez. There is a mission at this place, where the San Bernardino Ranch, famous for its excellent cattle, is established.

1822

1. Spain cedes to Mexico the territories of Texas, New Mexico, Arizona, Colorado, Utah, and California with all the missions, forts, and institutions existing there. Since the time Spain of Spain's arrived in Florida in 1513, 205 missions have been built. Each of them, normally, is composed of convent, church, housing for the natives, warehouses, shops, and extensive land for farming and grazing. Some 70 forts have also been built. Out of the hundreds of missionaries who labored in this land, some 80 have shed their blood for the sake of Christ.

2. This year, El Paso, Texas, has population of 8,384. From this number 2,072 are farmers, 681 artisans, 269 laborers, six industrialist, five merchants, three students, and six soldiers.

3. Luis Antonio Argüello, the first Mexican governor, arrives in Monterey, California, the capital city, and on December 8, La Placita Mission in Los Angeles is dedicated.

4. The Cathedral of the Assumption is dedicated in Baltimore, Maryland.

5. Antonio J. Martínez is ordained a priest in New Mexico and is assigned to the parish of Taos. While serving here, he builds schools for Hispanic children, imports a print shop, and publishes the newspaper called *El Crepusculo de la Libertad* (The Twilight of Freedom).

1823

1. On December 2, the United States issues its "Monroe Doctrine." It proclaims that European countries do not have the right to interfere in the affairs of the American Hemisphere.

2. The Mission of San Francisco Solano is founded in Sonoma. It is the last of the Franciscan missions established in California to evangelize the natives. Its church still exists today.

1824

1. Mexico adopts a form of federal government and allows the territories of Nuevo León, Coahuila, and Texas to form three separate states. Disturbances and rebellions that occur cause Mexico to forbid public meetings and assemblies.

2. Martín de León, born in Burgos, Spain, establishes the city of Vic-

toria, Texas. The Oblate Fathers build a chapel and plant a large orange grove, which is the first in the southern part of the Rio Grande.

1825

1. Joel Poinsett is appointed ambassador to Mexico. On his return, he will bring a plant with red leaves that will become popular during the Christmas season; it will be called poinsettia. He promotes the purchase of Texas among Mexican liberal politicians and brings into Mexico the freemasonry of the York Rite to offset the political influence of that of the British Rite that was supported by the Ambassador of England.

2. Mexico issues a law opening the doors of East Texas to American colonists.

3. A commercial treaty is signed by the United States and the Central American nations of Costa Rica, El Salvador, Guatemala, Honduras, and Nicaragua.

4. The opera *El Barbero de Sevilla* ("The Barber of Seville") is presented in the famous Park Theater of New York. Heading the cast is the Spanish tenor Manuel García.

1826

1. The Universities of Harvard, Virginia, and Bowdoin begin the teaching of the Spanish language. Yale will follow them a little later.

2. Anglo colonist Hayden Edwards proclaims the independence of "Fredonia" (Texas), but he is immediately arrested by the Mexicans.

1827

1. Secretary of State Henry Clay authorizes the American ambassador to offer Mexico a million dollars to extend the American border to the banks of the Rio Grande.

2. The great patriot Ramón Betances is born in Puerto Rico. All his life he will pursue the federation of all Caribbean islands into one nation, although respecting their natural differences.

1828

1. The United States and Mexico sign a treaty setting the border between both countries at the Sabine River, thus reaffirming a previous treaty signed by the United States and Spain.

2. Gold mines are discovered at a place about thirty miles southwest of Santa Fe, New Mexico.

1829

1. On August 25, President Andrew Jackson makes a proposal to Mexico to buy Texas, and he gives as a reason that some American colonists are already living there. Mexico rejects the proposal and forbids slavery, which the Anglo colonists of Texas are trying to introduce into their farms.

2. Father Juan Rafael Rascón is sent by the Bishop of Durango to visit the vicariate of New Mexico. Father Rascón sees the need of forming priests in the area, and establishes a house for the formation of native priests.

1830

1. Seeing the political restlessness prevailing in Texas, Mexico forbids the entrance of more Anglo colonists into that state and also reaffirms its position of not allowing the import of black slaves.

2. The Mexican population in Chicago, Illinois, is estimated at approximately twenty thousand people.

1831

Argentina captures some American boats that are fishing near the Falkland Islands (Malvinas) and takes them to Buenos Aires. The American ambassador protests this action, and the warship *Lexington* is sent there. This is the beginning of a dispute on the sovereignty of these islands that has not been solved yet.

1832

1. The United States and Chile sign a commercial treaty that later will be approved by the Senate.

2. Seeing the need for priests in the Eastern part of Texas, the bishop of Monterey, Mexico, sends Father José A. Díaz to Nacogdoches, and he works there for a year. One day he is mercilessly murdered by some savage nomad Indians.

3. The settlement begun by Stephen Austin in Austin, Texas, shortly after the independence of Mexico now numbers eight thousand Anglo colonists, far surpassing the number of Mexican people in the area. In October, the Anglo colonists gather at San Felipe and decide to turn Texas into a state separated from Coahuila. They form a commission and send Stephen Austin to Mexico to request the entrance of Texas into the Federation of Mexican States. Austin is arrested and sent to prison, where he remains for some months.

1833

1. On January 15, twelve Franciscan missionaries arrive in California to strengthen the missions. Up to this year some eighty-eight thousand native Indians have been baptized, and twenty thousand of them are still living there. They have been trained in a variety of skills and are now living in towns. But this same year the Mexican Congress issues a law forcing the secularization of all missions of California. The lands of the missions will become property of the Indians through previous distribution, and the church will become the parish of the town. What happens, however, is that a short time later political leaders and unscrupulous people will take over the mission lands and their belongings, giving them away to their relatives and friends. When they try to use the Indians to till the lands, they disappear from the area.

2. Most Reverend Antonio Zubiria, bishop of Durango, Mexico, arrives in New Mexico to make a pastoral visit to all the parishes under his jurisdiction. He is enthusiastically received by the people and stays in the area for several months, giving the sacrament of Confirmation and encouraging the people. He will return later on two other occasions.

3. The first vein of gold is discovered in the Gold Mountains, now known as Ortíz Mine, New Mexico.

4. The city of Las Vegas is established in Nevada.

1834

1. There are in California this year 21 missions with some 20,000 Christian Indians living there. These missions own 396,000 head of cattle, 62,000 horses, 321,000 hogs, some 200,000 sheep and goats. The harvest amounts to 123,000 bushels of grain yearly. This year a process of deterioration begins, and the missions will almost disappear because of the secularization policy applied by the Mexican government. In addition, since the missions are not subsidized now by the government, the number of missionaries will begin to decrease, the buildings to deteriorate, and the care of the Indians to lessen.

2. The people of the United States begin to eat the tomato, which is a product native of Mexico. There was previously a belief that it was poisonous, while in Italy people thought it to be an aphrodisiac.

1835

Political relations between the United States and Mexico begin to deteriorate with the declaration by President Antonio López de Santa Ana of Mexico that he is the president of all Mexicans, including those of Texas. Throughout this year there are clashes between the colonists of

Texas and the troops of Mexico. A group of soldiers headed by colonel Ugartechea demands from the people of González City the return of a cannon that had been lent to them for their defense. With the rejection of the demand a battle follows, and several persons are left dead. Another group in Goliad rises in rebellion, taking the arms and ammunition of the depot. Several hundred colonists seize the city of San Antonio. Mexican general Martín P. Cos comes to face them, but after a few days of skirmishes Cos yields to the pressures of the colonists who demand that Texas be a State separated from Coahuila. He is forced to do the same thing in Anahuac, a town on the Texas border, where the military garrison is forced to cross south of the Rio Grande. A group of Anglo colonists, headed by William Travis, has taken over the Mexican Fort of Anahuac, and some other disturbances take place.

1836

1. On March 2, Texas, which since the sixteenth century has been explored and colonized by Spain and was ceded in 1821 to Mexico, declares itself an independent Republic. It takes over several official institutions, among them the Mission of San Antonio de Valero, called El Alamo. General Santa Ana, with an army, comes up to recover El Alamo, defended by two hundred entrenched Texans, and wins it back after a bloody battle. General Santa Ana goes right away to Goliad to quench the revolt. He is ambushed on the way by a sizeable group of rebel colonists headed by Sam Houston, attacking while the Mexican troops are taking a siesta after dinner. Unable to react, Santa Ana is defeated and captured on April 21 at the place called San Jacinto. "Remember the Alamo!" is the battle cry of the people commanded by Houston. In order to recover his freedom, Santa Ana is forced to sign the independence of Texas, which just a month earlier had been proclaimed by Houston and his followers at the village of Washington of the Brazos, Texas. Houston enacts a constitution, legalizes slavery, and asks for the annexation of Texas to the United States. Unwilling to endanger its relations with Mexico, the United States does not accept the annexation.

2. This year the well-known writer William Prescott publishes his book titled *Ferdinand and Isabella*. Though brilliant, this writer is influenced by the Black Legend in his writings about Spain.

1837

1. On March 3, President Andrew Jackson of the United States, with the approval of Congress, recognizes the independence of the Republic of Texas.

2. Centralization of power and high taxes cause a revolt in New Mexico, where the governor is assassinated.

1838

An epidemic of measles and repeated Apache attacks, with Mexican authorities providing no attention, force the people of Pecos, New Mexico, to abandon the town. For 250 years it has been home for native Indians, Spaniards, and missionaries. The church building, however, still remains there as a perennial witness of the work performed in the place.

1839

Bishop Antoine Blanc of New Orleans, under instructions from the "Propaganda Fidei" Congregation, sends Father John Timon to visit Texas and seek information about the situation of the Church there. Father Timon visits Galveston and Houston and returns to New Orleans to inform the bishop.

1840

1. At the request of the Mexican Congress, Pope Gregory XVI establishes the Diocese of California comprising both Lower and Upper California. Father Francisco García Diego, O.F.M., a native of Mexico, is consecrated as bishop and places the See in Monterey.

2. A few months later, on July 8, the apostolic prefecture that comprises the whole Republic of Texas is established. Father John Timon is appointed apostolic prefect, enjoying an authority similar to that of a bishop.

1841

1. A caravan of forty-eight wagons, with a large number of immigrants, arrives in Sacramento, California, via the route of the Humboldt and Sierras Rivers.

2. Texan President Mirabeau Lamar heads an expedition of some 350 to invade New Mexico. Aware of this move, Governor Manuel Armijo comes out to meet Lamar and inflicts a painful defeat on him.

1842

1. Encouraged by the defeat of Lamar, Mexican authorities of New Mexico attempt to recover the cities of San Antonio and Corpus Christi. They are successful. Sam Houston, however, regains those positions.

2. On March 6, Father John Odin is consecrated in New Orleans as first bishop of the apostolic vicariate of the Republic of Texas.

3. The famous writer William Prescott publishes his book *The Conquest of Mexico*.

1843

1. President Santa Ana of Mexico notifies the United States that an attempt to annex Texas will be considered a declaration of war against Mexico. At the same time, on June 15, a pact of mutual understanding is signed by Mexico and Texas.

2. Some thirty-two diocesan priests serve the Catholic population of New Mexico this year; seventeen of them have been born in the area.

1844

1. A treaty of annexation is signed between Texas and the United States but the Senate does not give its approval. Relations between Texas and Mexico, at the same time, become progressively more strained. Once Santa Ana has ceased to be president of Mexico, his successor, Joaquin Herrera, promises to accept the independence of Texas. Shortly after, both the House and the Senate sign the annexation of Texas to the United States.

2. The United States appoints Thomas O. Larkin as its consul in Monterey, California. At the same time, Bishop García Diego opens the first seminary of the California's diocese near Santa Inez Mission. A short time later there will be thirty-three students there.

1845

In a joint resolution, the United States Congress approves, on March 1, the annexation of the Republic of Texas which is signed by President John Tyler. General Almonte, the Mexican representative in Washington, protests this decision. Soon after, General Zachary Taylor is ordered to occupy a position in Texas near the border on the Río Grande to protect the annexation. Taylor stations his troops to the west of the Nueces River, and in December Texas becomes part of the Union.

1846

1. Once Texas is annexed, the Mexican army crosses over the Río Grande and lays siege to Fort Texas. It is defeated at the battles of Palo Alto and Resaca de la Palma, and it is forced to cross the Río Grande back to Mexico. Soon after, General Taylor crosses the river and takes over the cities of Matamoros and Monterey. Throughout this year also a movement begins to seize New Mexico, Arizona, and California which will take two years to complete. The taking of this vast region by the

United States is not like coming into an uncivilized land, but into a territory that is explored and unified. It is a territory with a language and culture deeply rooted in its people and cities. Also, this is a territory with mining, agriculture, cattle raising, and economy in progress. It is a territory with its Indian population, to a large extent, settled, civilized, and christianized from a slow but steady labor of Spain for over three hundred years. It is also a great legacy of Spain, which is now an integral part of its geographical, anthropological, and cultural identity. To realize that, one only has to formulate this question: "Would the United States be the same without Texas, New Mexico, Arizona, Colorado, and California?"

2. A group of American colonists of the area of Sacramento, California, after some riots, rebel and on September 15 proclaim the independence of the Republic of California. They appoint William B. Ide president, and raise the new white flag with a red stripe, a star, a bear, and the inscription "California Republic." A month later, Commodore John D. Sloat arrives in the harbor of Monterey, raises the United States flag, and declares California annexed to the United States.

3. Cuban-born Father Felix Varela, residing in the archdiocese of New York, attends the Council of Baltimore, representing the archdiocese.

1847

1. American General Winfield Scott, with ten thousand soldiers, occupies the city of Veracruz. He marches on toward Mexico City and defeats the Mexican army in Cerro Gordo, Churubusco, Molino del Rey, and takes over the Chapultepec Castle, valiantly defended by a group of heroic youths (*niños heroes*).

2. Domingo Faustino Sarmiento, a great writer and statesman, travels to the United States. He analyzes the success of this country, writes articles in newspapers and magazines and a number of books. He can be considered "The Father of Public Education" in Argentina and Spanish America.

1848

1. After the independence of Mexico, a series of years follow characterized by political instability and disorganization in its governments. Mexico loses all its territories north of the Río Grande, and on February 2 the government signs the Treaty of Guadalupe-Hidalgo, by which all the territories north of the Río Grande officially become part of the United States. In exchange, Mexico receives the amount of fifteen million dollars. The said Treaty includes three conditions for its validity: respect for

the property of its present owners; keeping of the Spanish language, culture, and customs of its people; and freedom to practice their Catholic faith. None of these conditions will be respected in the years to follow. It is important to remember that up until now the border between the United Stated and Mexico has been the banks, not of the Río Grande, but of the Sabine River, and that therefore Mexicans are used to going from south to north and north to south without any immigration problems.

2. Gold is discovered on the property of John Sutter of California. As a result of this news, "Gold Fever" begins and a huge wave of immigrants heads west to California.

3. Colombia and the United States sign a treaty by which the United States is granted the right of way through the Isthmus of Panama, under the condition that the zone remain neutral.

1849

1. The legislature of New York legally incorporates the "Panama Railroad Company," and it will begin to operate regularly a few years later.

2. There are twelve priests this year to serve the twenty thousand Catholics of the entire State of Texas. At the end of the year, the Oblates of Mary Immaculate arrive in the area of Brownsville.

David Glasgow Farragut followed his father, the Spaniard Jorge Farragut, as a career officer in the U.S. Navy, supporting the Union cause at the outbreak of the Civil War. He was the hero of engagements at Mobile Bay, New Orleans, and the Mississippi (like Bernardo de Gálvez before him) and was the first American naval officer to be named an admiral of the fleet by the U.S. Congress

1850-1900:
The Spanish Roots Abated

Spain leaves North America, but the Hispanic heritage remains: people, language, and culture.

1850

1. During the years that follow the signing of the Guadalupe-Hidalgo Treaty, Anglo immigrants take part of the land belonging to the Mexicans. At this time the laws are changed, and many Mexicans do not know them. Furthermore, since the majority do not have their properties registered or pay taxes, and the titles they have are not recognized by the new law, they lose not only their land but their political power as well. As a result, they are socially segregated. Though their presence is rejected, their roots continue to be strongly attached to the United States.

2. The seventh United States census registers in the country a population of 23,191,876 inhabitants, 100,000 of which are of Hispanic origin.

3. The Catholic hierarchy is structured in the old Spanish territories with some appointments. The Spanish Dominican Father José Sadoc Alemany is named by Pope Pius IX as bishop of Monterey, California. He will exercise his pastoral ministry there for three years, until he is transferred to San Francisco as archbishop. Among Bishop Alemany's classmates in Barcelona and in Rome were St. Antonio Maria Claret, philosopher Jaime Balmes, Blessed Francisco Coll, and Father Jean Baptiste Lacordaire. In New Mexico, Pius IX establishes the Diocese of Santa Fe and names Jean Baptiste Lamy as the first bishop. Lamy will be succeeded by four other bishops of French origin.

4. Spanish Dominican Father Francisco Villarrasa founds a monastery in Monterey, California. Shortly after, six Catalan youths arrive to start their novitiate, and four years later the monastery will be moved to Bernicia, California. Twenty years later, there will be twenty Dominicans, Spaniards and Irish, working in California.

5. Basque Spaniards, looking for gold, arrive in California. Later on, some more will arrive and begin to shepherd in Idaho, Nevada, Oregon, Montana, Wyoming, and Colorado.

1851

1. A group of about five hundred Americans and Spanish refugees, commanded by Narciso López, against the order of the United States, leave for Cuba to annex it and divide among themselves a large portion of

the territory. The adventure is defeated, and López is executed in Havana.

2. A few settlers from Taos, New Mexico, arrive in Colorado with some priests and settle in the village of San Luis. Three years later they build a church. This settlement is followed by the settlements of San Pablo, Acacio, and Chama on the banks of the Culebra River.

3. With the help of Bishop José Alemany, three Dominican nuns establish the convent of Santa Catalina in Monterey, California. A few days later they open a school for girls, and in six months, 70 girls will be registered. This congregation, called Sisters of the Most Holy Name of Jesus, will have 20 houses and 259 professed religious in 1890.

1852

1. Governor James Lane arrives in New Mexico to pacify the Indians who have rebelled. He runs for congress but is defeated by Father José Manuel Gallegos and leaves New Mexico.

2. Bishop Jean Lamy finally takes possession of the diocese of Santa Fe on January 10. Immediately after his appointment, he begins to have difficulties with the Hispanic clergy because of cultural differences. His problems with Father Antonio Martínez, Father José M. Gallegos, and Father Mariano Lucero are noteworthy.

1853

1. Bishop José Sadoc Alemany is transferred from Monterey to San Francisco as archbishop. He builds the cathedral and 150 churches. At the time of his arrival in San Francisco there are 500 Catholics, but they will number 250,000 when he dies. His remains are kept in San Francisco.

2. Father Felix Varela dies in St. Augustine, Florida. He was a learned man, a professor at the University of Havana. He represented Cuba in the Parliament of Spain and was a promoter of Cuba's independence. During his thirty-year exile in New York, he published a Spanish newspaper and was named vicar general of the archdiocese.

1854

1. Pierre Soule, United States ambassador to Spain, sends to Secretary of State William Marcy a recommendation called the "Ostend Manifesto" to acquire Cuba, paying Spain the sum of one hundred and thirty million dollars. If the offer is rejected, they will have to take Cuba by force. Marcy rejects the proposal.

2. The Presidential Report of November 13 states: "The Pueblo or the semi-civilized Indians of this territory (New Mexico) live in a satisfactory condition from all points of view. They live in villages established on

plots of land given by the government of Spain and Mexico, and sustain themselves comfortably with the farming of the land, cattle raising, and flocks of several kinds. Many of them speak Spanish fairly well. . . . Each town or village has its church. When disputes arise among them, the matter is brought to the territorial governor and his decision is invariably accepted as final."

1855

William Walker, supported by the trade interest of some Americans who looked for a route across the Isthmus of Panama, takes advantage of an internal political disturbance in Nicaragua and proclaims himself dictator of that nation. Walker remains there for two years, keeping control over the country.

1856

1. Pablo de la Guerra, a Californian legislator, states before Congress: "They (Mexican-Americans) are foreigners in their own country. I have seen old men in their sixties and seventies crying like children because they have been rooted out from the land of their ancestors. They have been humiliated, insulted, and denied the privilege of drinking water from their own wells."

2. Father Tadeo Amat, a Spanish Vincentian born in Barcelona, is appointed bishop of Monterey, California. He criticizes the style of the Mexican people's Catholicism and orders the Franciscans to leave the Apostolic College of Santa Barbara, approved by Bishop Alemany, his predecessor. This decision starts a controversy that will ensue for several years.

1857

Lola Martínez, a famous artist who says she is of Spanish origin, though she was born in Ireland, returns to the United States after making a popular tour around the world. She sings, dances, gives conferences, and writes books. Among them, there is one called *The Art of Beauty*.

1858

1. Father José M. Gallegos, a representative of New Mexico before Congress, writes to the Bishop of Durango, Mexico: "The Cabinet here keeps looking for a way to start a war with Spain, to get away with Cuba."

2. Narciso Gener González, a prominent writer and reporter, is born in Cuba. He founds *The State*, a newspaper published in Charleston,

South Carolina, and becomes an ardent fighter against child labor. He also defends the rights of women and black people, and exposes political corruption. He is assassinated by a politician named James Tillman, who is later declared innocent.

1859

1. Luis Muñoz Rivera is born in Puerto Rico. He will become a conspicuous politician and seek the independence of the island, first from Spain and later from the United States. As a pragmatic solution for Puerto Rico, he works out the idea of a "Free and Associated State" that later his son, Luis Muñoz Marín, will successfully complete.

2. Bishop Tadeo Amat of Monterey, California, transfers the diocesan See to Los Angeles and starts building the Cathedral of Santa Vibiana.

3. The Church of Our Lady of the Pillar opens in Brooklyn to serve Spanish-speaking Catholics of that area of New York City.

1860

1. Domingo Faustino Sarmiento returns to the United States as ambassador of Argentina, a position that he will hold for three years. He displays an intense activity at all levels to make Latin America known to the people of the United States. He develops strong public relations with many people in this country and finally returns to Argentina, where he is elected president.

2. A group of Spanish people from the Basque region arrive in Nevada and engage in sheep tending. Later on they will spread to neighboring states.

1861

1. Abraham Lincoln appoints Henry Connolly governor of New Mexico. Miguel A. Otero is named secretary and becomes a prominent figure in state matters; later, he will also become governor.

2. On June 17, Spain, seeing the approaching Civil War in the United States, declares herself neutral in this internal conflict.

3. Once the Civil War breaks out, some ten thousand Hispanics get involved in the rift; some fight for the Union, others for the Confederacy.

1862

David G. Farragut, of Spanish origin and in command of a flotilla, takes over New Orleans, Baton Rouge, and Natchez, later opening up Mobile Bay in Alabama. For his outstanding action during the Civil War he will be named vice-admiral, and later the first admiral of the American Navy.

1863

1. General Nathaniel P. Banks, with six thousand soldiers, arrives in Brownsville, Texas, which is held by the Confederate forces. He sends a message to the forty thousand French who are in Mexico giving support to Archduke Maximilian, that they should not even think of sending troops to the northern border.

2. The Jesuits return to the Mission of San Javier del Bac, Arizona, after being evicted from the area almost one hundred years before by a decree of Charles III of Spain.

1864

An army of five thousand French soldiers arrives at the city of Matamoros, Mexico. General Juan N. Cortina meets them and makes them back up. He later takes Brownsville from the Confederates and offers it to the commander of the Union forces.

1865

United States Secretary of State William H. Seward warns Napoleon III on December 16 that his ambitions in Mexico will endanger relations between the nations.

1866

The United States, through its secretary of state, notifies France to set a time limit for taking its military force out of Mexico. The last French troops will depart from Mexico one year later.

1867

Admiral David G. Farragut, commanding his frigate *Franklin*, enters the Spanish harbor of Mahon, Menorca Island, where his father was born. He pays a visit to the cathedral and reads the baptismal record of his father, kept in the archives. The city offers him a great party that lasts all night long, honoring him as a distinguished fellow countryman.

1868

1. Inspired by Ramón Betances and counting on some firearms they have bought, a group for independence start a small rebellion in Puerto Rico with the so-called *Grito de Lares* ("Lares Cry"), proclaim-

ing the independence of the island. This attempt, though, does not succeed.

2. A strong earthquake rocks the city of San Francisco, California, causing the collapse of many buildings and seriously damaging the missions of the area.

1869

1. Carlos Juan Finlay, a famous Cuban bacteriologist of the United States Academy of Science, finds out through research that Yellow Fever is transmitted by a mosquito.

2. Construction of the present Cathedral of Santa Fe, New Mexico, is begun.

1870

1. Puerto Rico becomes a Spanish province and is given the right to send a delegate to the Parliament.

2. David G. Farragut, of Spanish ancestry and first admiral of the United States Navy, having played an outstanding role during the Civil War, dies at Portsmouth, New Hampshire.

1871

1. The governor of New Mexico destroys the colonial archives, where important documents related to land distribution and other historical matters were kept.

2. Julián Blanco, a native of Vega Baja, Puerto Rico, is elected representative of the island before the Parliament in Madrid, together with his compatriot Manuel Cochado.

1872

1. The representative of the United States in Bolivia writes to the U.S. secretary of state, informing him of a dispute between Bolivia and Chile over control of some silver mines that were recently discovered.

2. George Gordon Meade, who was born and raised in Cádiz, Spain, dies. He played a prominent role during the Civil War.

1873

1. The Spanish warship *Toronado* captures the American ship *Virginius* carrying arms and munitions to the rebel forces of Cuba. Eight Americans are judged and executed.

2. The Mexican writer Ricardo Flores Magón is born. After being exiled from Mexico, he will go to Los Angeles, California. There he

will begin the newspaper *La Regeneración* ("The Regeneration") and develop a social-anarchist ideology. Because of his underground activities, he will be jailed and will die in prison years later.

1874

The Diocese of San Antonio, Texas, is created, and Father Antonio Pellicer is appointed its first bishop. During his six years of service there he will dedicate fifteen new churches, seven chapels, twenty-five parish schools, one college for boys, and one hospital. The Catholic population of the Diocese at this time is about forty-eight thousand faithful.

1875

A group of Sisters of Charity, expelled by the Mexican government, arrive in Brownsville, Texas. Bishop Dominic Manucci decides that they cannot remain in the diocese. The Mexican-American community, however, opposes the decision and will not allow the sisters to leave, preventing the train's departure. The bishop promises the people that he will invite the sisters back again, and with that the sisters leave the city, but they will never be invited to come back again.

1876

Laws on the reform of land property enacted by Mexican President Porfirio Díaz precipitate a wave of emigration of people to the United States. Once they arrive, these immigrants engage in farmworking and are employed on the railroads.

1877

Donaciano Vigil is born in New Mexico. He will later become involved in politics through the first years of New Mexico as a state of the Union. He will be named territorial secretary, governor, and later will serve as assemblyman for many years.

1878

A conflict arises on the right to use of some salt mine of a few lakes about one hundred miles east of El Paso, Texas. From time immemorial, the people on both sides of the Río Grande (now a frontier) make use of the salt with no problems. Now there are restlessness, threats, and deaths. With the establishment of the military base of Fort Bliss in the area, peace returns to the region.

1879

Chile, Bolivia, and Peru become involved in a war for control of the nitrate on Bolivian soil. Mr. Pettis, the United States representative in Bolivia, tries to mediate the problem, but with scant results.

1880

José Martí, the prominent Cuban patriot, arrives in New York. He will reside there for the next fifteen years and will write for several newspapers of the area.

1881

On July 3, the United States and the European nations meet for a conference in Madrid, Spain, to restrict the extraterritorial protection of the citizens of Morocco.

1882

American architect Henry Richardson travels to Spain and is greatly impressed by Spanish architecture. This impact is reflected in Trinity Church of Boston, the Cathedral of Albany, and other structures that will later be built. Richardson's style will also influence the architects of his time.

1883

1. The University of Columbia in New York begins to offer a course in Latin American history. It is taught by Professor Daniel de León.

2. The Jesuits install an excellent meteorological observatory in Santurce, Puerto Rico.

1884

The United States and Spain sign an agreement to abolish discriminatory trade rights in the ports of Cuba, Puerto Rico, and the United States. This agreement is signed by José A. Elduayen for Spain and John W. Foster for the United States.

1885

On April 24, the United States sends five hundred Marines to the Isthmus of Panama to protect American property.

1886

1. France presents the gift of the Statue of Liberty to the United States, and it is placed on a small island at the entrance of New York harbor.

2. The Supreme Court of the United States declares that a foreigner is a person according to law.

3. Spanish businessman Vicente Martínez Ibor comes from Cuba and establishes a tobacco factory in Tampa, Florida, which gives origin to the tobacco industry in this region. This factory provides work for many people and builds an important Spanish nucleus in that city.

1887

A bill is introduced before the United States Congress to admit New Mexico in the Union, but it is not approved. During this time, on June 18, Congress approves a pension for veterans of the war with Mexico.

1888

1. Bishop Claude Neraz of San Antonio, Texas, builds a school for children of Mexican origin because of the exclusionist policy of the educational system of that state. This year also, the San Fernando Cathedral School is built, and the majority of its students are of Hispanic origin.

2. Lucrecia Bori, a famous opera singer, is born in Valencia, Spain. She will come to New York, where she will perform for fifteen years at the Metropolitan Opera House. She will constantly receive applause and admiration from her audience.

1889

The first Conference of American States takes place in Washington, D.C., with delegates attending from eighteen countries. The purpose of the meeting is to provide some unity to customs, to establish uniformity in weights and measures, to build an intercontinental railway, to create an international American bank, and to offer some type of mediation to international conflicts; but no agreement is signed. This conference is the start of the Organization of American States (OAS).

1890

1. The United States gives orders to its representatives in Chile, Bolivia, and Peru to hold a meeting with representatives of the above-mentioned nations in order to seek a solution to their dispute over the nitrates. They meet aboard the United States ship *Lackawana* at Arica Bay, Chile, but they do not reach an agreement.

2. Mariano Vallejo, who was born in Monterey, California, dies. He did remarkable work as an assemblyman, as a delegate to the constitutional convention, and as a member of the Senate.

3. New Mexico and Arizona are denied entrance into the Union because of an internal problem. The Anglos of the South fear the Hispanic leadership in the North of the State. In addition, the United States Congress has another reason: "The Roman Catholic population seemed un-American."

1891

Pedro Albizu Campos is born in Puerto Rico; he will graduate from law school at Harvard University, and later he will question the legality of both the Spanish-American agreement of 1898 and the annexation of Puerto Rico. At the same time he will justify the use of force in the legitimate defense of the island against foreign occupation.

1892

1. Father Pedro Verdaguer is appointed apostolic vicar of Brownsville, Texas. During his ministry there, the number of Catholics will greatly increase; the apostolic vicar will dedicate new parishes, schools, and hospitals, and the number of priests will also expand.

2. A great celebration takes place in New York to celebrate the fourth centenary of the discovery of America. Three Spanish ships bring a replica of the three caravels. A large regatta is organized, with ships from the United States, Spain, and other countries. This is followed by a colorful parade along Fifth Avenue in New York City.

1893

On October 30, the world's fair held in Chicago, Illinois, on the occasion of the fourth centenary of the discovery of America closes after joyful celebrations take place on the shores of Lake Michigan. Art works, industrial, agricultural, mining, and sea products are exhibited. The fair is held in an area of 644 acres, and the government assigns a budget of $22,000,000 to cover the expenses. Seventy-two countries participate and 27 million people visit the fair.

1894

1. Members of the Autonomist Party gather at an assembly at San Juan, Puerto Rico. There is division among them, but, thanks to the steadfast work of José Celso Barbosa, the problem is solved at a meeting held in Ponce, where a new directorate is elected.

2. Bishop Toribio Minguella, O.A.R., is named bishop of San Juan, Puerto Rico, and he will remain there, zealously taking care of the

Church, until the Spanish-American War is over. He is the last bishop of Spanish origin to head the Church in Puerto Rico.

1895

1. Argentina and Brazil get into a territorial dispute over their borders. The United States intervenes and makes a decision in favor of Brazil.

2. England and Venezuela get involved in a harsh quarrel over the boundary between Venezuela and British Guyana. The United States intervenes and invokes the doctrine of national security along with that of Monroe.

3. A political turmoil arises in Cuba. President Grover Cleveland of the United States advises not to help the rebels but to remain neutral in the tumult.

1896

1. On May 22, Spain rejects the mediation offered by the United State because of an internal turmoil in Cuba. At the same time, she affirms that the island has one of the most liberal governments in the world.

2. A group of engineers hands President Cleveland a negative report over the proposal to build a transoceanic channel across Nicaragua. The President submits the report to Congress.

1897

On May 20, the United States Senate approves a resolution stating the war situation in Cuba. At the same time, the Senate urges the President to propose to Spain a peace settlement in Cuba by giving the island independence.

1898

The American warship *Maine* explodes in the Bay of Havana. A team of Spanish experts concludes that the explosion was due to some work inside the ship. The United States declares war on Spain and lays siege to Cuba. President William McKinley asks for 200,000 volunteers. Congress appropriates $400,000,000 dollars and 17,000 soldiers to take over Guantanamo and Santiago. After a fierce battle in which 323 Spanish soldiers and just as many Americans die, the city surrenders. The war comes to an end with the Treaty of Paris. As a result, Cuba, Puerto Rico, the Philippines, and Guam pass over to the United States after 400 years of Spanish colonization.

1899

1. A furious hurricane devastates Puerto Rico, where two thousand people die.

2. The United Fruit Company begins to organize in the United States. This Company will later extend to several countries of Latin America and will exercise a tremendous influence over the politics and economy of these nations.

*The church and the beginning of the long, graceful gallery at the
Mission Santa Barbara, called "Queen of the California Missions,"
as it looked before its restoration in the 1960s. Established in
1786 and completed in 1820, the mission is considered the largest,
most beautiful, and most successful of the many missions built by
the Franciscan Fathers along the Pacific Coast of California and
across the Southeastern and Southwestern areas of the United States*

1900-1950:
Resurgence of Spanish Roots

After a period of darkness, "Hispanidad" starts making its reappearance.

1900

1. Some Puerto Ricans begin to leave the island. A good number of them settle in Hawaii where they work in the pineapple plantations; and still some others go to the area of New York.

2. The United States census this year registers 75,999,575 inhabitants. The main census office is located in Columbus, Indiana.

1901

1. On December 1, José Luis Girao is born in Almería, Spain. He is the son of José Girao and Isabel Mendoza. The Giraos will emigrate to Chicago with their two small sons, who will suddenly be left orphaned. Mr. Elias Disney will adopt little José Luis and give him his surname; some years later he will become the famous Walt Disney.

2. The Seton Hospital opens in Austin, Texas; here, Father J. O'-Reilly and Sister Julia give great service to the Hispanic people in matters related to health and other social concerns.

3. The Second Pan-American Conference takes place in Mexico City, where it is decided that an arbitration, whether compulsory or voluntary, should be established for cases of financial dispute among member nations. From now on the permanent chairman of the conference will be the representative of the United States.

1902

1. On May 20, the United States recognizes the independence of Cuba. The Cuban flag is raised in Havana, and the first president of the new nation is sworn in.

2. The parish of Our Lady of Guadalupe is established in New York City. This is the first parish opened to take care of the pastoral needs of the Hispanic community. The parish is entrusted to the Assumptionist Congregation, which soon begins its ministry also in the parish of Our Lady of La Esperanza. Later, two more parishes will be established in the same city for the spiritual care of Spanish-speaking people: La Milagrosa and Santa Agonía, both of which are entrusted to the Vicentian Fathers.

1903

1. Cuba signs a treaty with the United States on February 23. By this agreement Cuba surrenders Guantanamo and Bahía Honda to the United States for the establishment of naval bases there.

2. On January 22, Colombia signs the Hay-Herran Treaty, by which the Panama Canal is ceded to the United States for a period of 99 years. Panama ratifies the treaty, and with the help of the United States, she obtains her independence from Colombia. Panama is to receive $10,000,000 plus $250,000 annually. The United States Senate approves the treaty with Panama, but it is rejected by the Colombian Congress when Panama becomes independent.

3. The University of Puerto Rico, which had started three years before as a normal school, is officially established in Río Piedras.

1904

1. Archer M. Huntington founds the "Hispanic Society of America." Soon a beautiful building will be constructed in New York City to house a library and a museum, where there are valuable collections of books related to Hispanic culture, a collection of historical documents, and art objects.

2. Racial segregation in the schools of the southern states is a common practice. Mexican-American children are not allowed to attend the same schools as American children of European origin; they must attend the Mexican school. On the other hand, the Supreme Court declares on January 4 that Puerto Ricans are not foreigners and therefore they are not subject to the laws that restrain immigration.

3. The United States forms a committee of thirteen engineers, and the majority of them vote in favor of building a sea-level canal. Chief engineer John L. Stevens, however, is in favor of a lock canal.

1905

A protocol is signed between the United States and the Dominican Republic. By this agreement, the United States takes charge of the Dominican customs and their international debt, while at the same time she will guarantee Dominican integrity. The Senate, though, does not ratify this protocol. President Theodore Roosevelt continues, however, with said agreement. This is another sign of the "Manifest Destiny" ideology.

1906

1. At the request of the first president of Cuba, Tomás Estrada Palma, American troops arrive in Cuba to quell a rebellion that has erupted as a result of political elections. American troops take over the government of Cuba.

2. Mexico and the United States sign an agreement on May 21, by which the waters of the Río Grande are fairly distributed between the two countries.

3. The Third Pan-American Conference takes place on July 23 at Rio de Janeiro, Brazil, where the policy of the "Good Neighbor" is introduced and developed and a commission of jurists is created.

1907

1. The United States sends the Marine Corps to Honduras to protect American lives and property during a time of political turbulence.

2. The Mercedarian Nuns open a school in Peñitas, Texas, for the education of Hispanic children. After this foundation is established, several others follow in cities of the South. At the same time the Sisters of the Sacred Heart, founded in Mexico, come to Laredo, Texas, where they establish a house to care for orphan children.

1908

As a consequence of a previous meeting held in Washington, D. C., Central American countries establish, on May 25, the Central American Court of Justice with the head office at San José, Costa Rica.

1909

On May 31, American troops, who had come to Cuba three years before because of the political turmoil resulting from the elections, leave the island.

1910

1. Francisco Madero starts a revolutionary war in Mexico to over-throw President Porfirio Díaz. The revolution has been in preparation since the previous year, and it marks the beginning of a revolutionary process that will last for the next twenty years. Due to this upheaval, a steady flow of Mexican immigration begins to move toward the United States. It is estimated that about 800,000 Mexicans will cross the Río Grande to the North through the coming years.

2. The Society of the Sisters of St. Teresa come to San Antonio, Texas, and establishes the parish school of Our Lady of Guadalupe.

1911

1. On January 10 the government of the United States signs an agreement with Honduras requiring the former to assume the foreign debt of the latter in exchange for the right to collect customs duties. The senate does not approve the agreement.

2. Dr. Luis C. Álvarez is born in San Francisco, California. Medicine and research will be his professional field. He will teach at the Universities of San Francisco, Stanford, and California and the Mayo Clinic of Minnesota and will receive many awards and recognitions for his writings and lectures. Among others we may mention the Nobel Prize of Physics in 1968, the "Ground Control Approach," and many other scientific discoveries.

3. The First Mexican Congress is established to defend the civil rights of Hispanic workers and to fight against racial discrimination.

1912

1. In February, in order to preserve American property, it is asserted, the United States sends five hundred marines to Honduras. A short time later the same procedure is followed in Nicaragua and in the Dominican Republic.

2. The Hispanicist Archer Huntington builds Our Lady of Esperanza (Hope) Church in New York City, located next to the Hispanic Society of America.

3. The Sisters of Notre Dame take charge of the parish school of St. Gerard and give themselves with great dedication to work with the Hispanic people of San Antonio, Texas.

1913

1. On October 27, in Mobile, Alabama, President Woodrow Wilson enunciates his philosophy toward Latin America and declares that he will neither mingle in its matters nor attempt to take a foot of its territory. Three days later he will demand that the president of Mexico, Victoriano Huerta, resign from the government of the country.

2. The Spanish language daily newspaper *El Diario* is founded; it still continues at present and is one of the few Spanish dailies in the country.

1914

1. The United States finishes the building of the Panama Canal. It holds a zone of land with a military base there and a strip of land five miles wide along each side the canal. The cost of building the canal was $366,650,000.

2. After some American soldiers are arrested in Tampico, Mexico, President Wilson orders the use of force. American troops occupy the City of Veracruz and demand the resignation of President Huerta. Through the mediation of Argentina, Brazil, and Chile, the troops depart from Veracruz.

3. A new organization is formed in Arizona called "The Protection League" (*La Liga Protectora*), whose purpose is to fight the laws that discriminate against Mexican-Americans in the workplace.

1915

1. A Conference of Latin American countries assembles in Washington, D.C., on August 5 to resolve the political turmoil prevailing in Mexico. Attending are representatives of Argentina, Brazil, Bolivia, Chile, Guatemala, Uruguay, and the United States.

2. The Panama Canal opens officially in July. The long-sought passage from one ocean to the other is now a reality.

3. The parish of San José (St. Joseph) is established in Fort Worth, Texas, to serve the Hispanic people of the area; it is administered by the Vincentian Fathers.

1916

1. The Mexican revolutionary Pancho Villa, with 1,500 followers, attacks Columbus, New Mexico, and kills 120 Americans. As a response, the United States sends General John Pershing, who arrives in Carrizal, Mexico, and engages the Mexican troops in a battle where 17 American and 38 Mexican soldiers are killed. The American Army will stay there for some time.

2. Prominent Puerto Rican statesman Luis Muñoz Rivera dies. He has resided in New York for fifteen years, founded a newspaper and wrote in many others, like the *Puerto Rican Herald*. He was appointed resident commissioner in Washington, D.C., and helped frame the "Jones Act" (see 1917, #2, below).

3. Spanish academician Federico de Onís arrives in New York, teaches at Columbia University, and is appointed director of the Hispanic Institute of that university.

4. Octaviano Larrazolo, a Mexican lawyer, is elected governor of New Mexico. During his term of office he fights for the rights of the Hispanic people and supports the teaching of Mexican-American culture and of the Spanish language in the public schools. Later he will serve in Washington, D.C., as a senator.

1917

1. As a result of the Mexican revolution and of the persecution of the Catholic Church, a large member of Mexicans flee toward California, Arizona, New Mexico, and Texas. Venustiano Carranza is elected President of Mexico and President Woodrow Wilson recognizes him immediately. After this, General Pershing and his ten thousand American cavalry soldiers leave Mexico.

2. On March 2, with the passage of the "Jones Act" bill, the U.S. Congress gives American citizenship to all persons born in Puerto Rico. A system of government similar to that of the United States is established. Though the governor and other officials are still appointed by Washington, Puerto Rico will be represented in the Congress by a commissioner elected by the people. This same year one hundred twenty thousand young Puerto Ricans register for the United States Army and many of them will fight in World War I.

3. The Order of the Augustinian Recollects arrives in Omaha, Nebraska. Later it will spread to Kansas, Missouri, Texas, California, New York, and New Jersey. It will choose pastoral work with Hispanic people as its special apostolate.

1918

1. The famous Puerto Rican patriot José de Diego dies in New York. All through his life he fought for the cultural identity of Puerto Rico, for its independence, and for the formation of an Antillian country made up of Cuba, the Dominican Republic, and Puerto Rico.

2. A wave of Spanish immigrants begins to arrive in Elizabeth, New Jersey, and shortly after will settle in Newark. Franciscans of the Third Order Regular (TOR) care for their pastoral needs at the Church of St. Joseph.

1919

Once World War I is over, many Puerto Rican soldiers remain in New York City and thus, with some others who were already there, give rise to the first Hispanic concentration in the city, called "El Barrio," These will be joined by others who will come from the island in subsequent years.

1920

1. The Archdiocese of San Antonio, Texas, is experiencing a remarkable growth. Up to this year some eighty new churches have been constructed, in addition to schools and other institutions.

2. The Sisters of the Sacred Heart open the Orphanage of the Sacred Heart in El Paso, Texas, and do excellent pastoral work there and in other areas of the southern United States.

1921

On April 20, Colombia and the United States sign a treaty of friendship by which they review their diplomatic relations. It is approved by the United States Senate, and the United States pays twenty-five million dollars to Colombia in compensation for the loss of Panama.

1922

1. The *Bulletin of the Pan-American Union* reports in January that the United States has imported from Latin America during the year 1920 goods in the amount of $72,087,969.

2. On July 20 a border conflict arises between Peru and Chile that takes them to the brink of a war. The rift is referred to U.S. President Warren Harding, who tries to give a solution to the case.

1923

1. On March 25 the Latin American Countries and the United States participate in the Fifth Pan-American Conference at Santiago, Chile. The agreement signed previously, to resolve peacefully all conflicts arising among them, is reinforced at this conference.

2. The League of United Latin American Citizens (LULAC) is established at Corpus Christi, Texas. Its goal is to further education, participation, and integration of Hispanics in the life of the nation at all levels. It puts out a bulletin with the title "LULAC News."

3. The Bethlehem Steel Co. of Pennsylvania brings some one thousand persons of Mexican origin from Texas to work in the steel industry, thus beginning another Hispanic settlement in the Northeast.

1924

The United States removes its army from the Dominican Republic after having been in that land for the past eight years because of internal political disturbances. The countries sign a new treaty, which is approved by the Senate, and the Dominican government is allowed to request loans up to the amount of twenty-five million dollars.

1925

1. The United States removes its marines from Nicaragua after having occupied the country for the past thirteen years.

2. The famous Spanish poet Federico García Lorca arrives in New York to pursue special studies. During his stay here he writes his famous work *Poet in New York (Poeta en Nueva York)*.

1926

1. American troops arrive again in Nicaragua to dissolve an uprising headed by César Augusto Sandino against Emiliano Chamorro, who is in power. Two months later the troops, led by Admiral Julián Latimer, leave the country.

2. The Theatine Fathers arrive in Denver, Colorado, to take care of Hispanic people. They establish the parish of St. Cajetan, which begins serving the Hispanics of the area.

1927

1. On May 3 a Pan-American Trade Conference takes place in Washington, D.C., to seek ways that might facilitate commercial cooperation among the countries of America. President Calvin Coolidge attends the opening and gives a welcome to all delegates.

2. The Confederation of Mexican Unions of Workers is established in California and organizes the first strike in the Imperial Valley.

1928

1. Charles Lindbergh, in his famous "Spirit of St. Louis," tours several countries of Latin America and the Caribbean. Some months later, new President Herbert Hoover also undertakes a journey of friendship through some Latin American nations.

2. By this date there are in the area of Chicago, Illinois, and Gary, Indiana, some thirty-five Hispanic societies, like "The Mutualista," which helps its members in economic difficulties. Several of them are sponsored by Catholic organizations.

3. Twenty-three Sisters of Charity of the Good Shepherd arrive in El Paso, Texas, fleeing from the bloody religious persecution started by President Plutarco Elías Calles of Mexico. Bishop Anthony Schuller, S.J., receives them kindly, and they establish a house for delinquent girls in the city.

4. Famous Spanish ophthalmologist Ramón Castroviejo arrives in New York City and establishes his well-known clinic.

1929

1. On May 17 President Herbert Hoover announces that the border conflict between Peru and Chile, after difficult negotiations, has been resolved with the signing of the Tacna-Arica Pact.

2. In October of this year the New York Stock Exchange plummets and the Great Depression begins. This will affect not only the United States but also all Latin American countries.

1930

Hispanicist Archer Huntington establishes the Hispanic Foundation in the Library of Congress in Washington, D.C. This foundation will collect books and documents related to Hispanic culture and history.

1931

1. Almost all Catholic churches that provide services in Spanish to the Hispanic people of Texas begin to establish confraternities and religious associations. One of the most popular is that of the Our Lady of Guadalupe.

2. A massive deportation of persons of Mexican origin begins in California. Many of those deported are United States citizens sent back to Mexico, and this practice will continue for the next three years.

1932

1. Luis Muñoz Marín is elected a member of the Senate of Puerto Rico.

2. Bishop Rudolph A. Gerken of Amarillo, Texas, is appointed as archbishop of Santa Fe, New Mexico. Soon after, he begins recruiting Hispanic vocations to the priesthood and establishes a seminary.

1933

1. On January 2, the United States begins to withdraw its marines from Nicaragua after being in the country for the past twenty years. Also this year, representatives of all Latin American countries assembled in Rio de Janeiro, Brazil, sign an anti-war and non-aggression treaty which is ratified by the Senate of the United States. Two months later a Pan-American Conference takes place in Montevideo, Uruguay.

2. The Confederation of Unions of farm workers of California go on strike against the strawberry growers. They get a raise in wages and better working conditions. In the future Mexican workers will develop a closer unity to defend their interests.

1934

On April 27, twelve Latin American nations and the United States meet in Buenos Aires and review the anti-war treaty. Some months later the United States abrogates the "Platt Amendment," ends its protectorate over Cuba, retains Guantánamo Bay, and both nations sign a commercial agreement.

1935

1. Mexican muralist David Alfaro Siqueiros opens an exposition of paintings in New York; to create them he uses special materials.

2. Hispanic candidates begin to be ordained priests in New Mexico, and at the same time some new parishes are established to minister to Hispanic people, among them that of Chaperito.

1936

1. A civil war begins in Spain, and though the government of the United States is not involved, hundreds of Americans march to Spain to help the government of the Republic and its leftist ideology. The forces of General Francisco Franco, however, will prevail in the rift. Later the United States will recognize the new government.

2. The Pan-American Conference assembled on March 2 in Buenos Aires, with President Franklin D. Roosevelt attending, issues an agreement by which the countries represented there commit themselves to consult with one another before going to war. In addition, Panama and the United States make an agreement to defend the Panama Canal.

1937

In Delaware Spanish philanthropist Elías Ahuja establishes "Good Samaritan, Inc.," an educational institution to help Spanish youths who wish to study in the United States. Mr. Ahuja, who was born in Cádiz, immigrated to the United States, graduated from the Massachusetts Institute of Technology, and occupied a high executive position in the Dupont Company.

1938

1. On March 18, President Lázaro Cárdenas of Mexico signs an executive order directing the government of the country to expropriate the lands of all foreign oil companies; many of them are American, and their assets were worth four hundred fifty million dollars.

2. On December 24, representatives of twenty-one American countries meet at Lima, Peru, and commit themselves to mutual consultation in case of aggression or attempts against their territorial sovereignty.

1939

1. In the face of World War II, foreign relations ministers of all the American countries come together in Panama on October 3; they agree on a security maritime zone around the whole continent.

2. Prominent Spanish architect José Luis Sert arrives in the United States, settles in this country, begins teaching, and develops several projects at Yale and Harvard Universities.

1940

1. Foreign relations ministers of the United States and Latin American countries meet at Havana, Cuba, on July 30 and issue a declaration of solidarity to protect those European colonies in America that might be in danger of being taken over by Germany.

2. The famous philosopher George Santayana, born in Madrid, publishes his book *The Realm of the Spirit*. He has previously published works such as *The Sense of Beauty, The Life of Reason, The Realms of Being*, and many others. Because of his philosophical work, he deserves to be remembered as one of the most prolific writers of the United States.

3. Raquel Welch is born in Chicago. Her real name is Raquel Tejada; her father came from Bolivia and her mother from England; Raquel will be internationally famous for her beauty and for her many starring roles in movies.

1941

1. The naval ministers of eleven Latin American countries arrive in the United States on May 4 to visit the naval bases on both seacoasts of this country. At the same time, Mexico and the United States reach an agreement to compensate American Oil Companies whose properties were expropriated two years before.

2. The famous Spanish painter Salvador Dalí arrives in the United States and remains in this country for a number of years. Many of his works will be painted here.

3. As soon as World War II breaks out, some 400,000 Hispanic Youths enroll to serve in the armed forces of this country. Many of them perform in an outstanding manner, as is testified to by the numerous medals awarded for their valor and courage.

1942

1. The foreign relations ministers of twenty-one American countries meet in Rio de Janeiro on January 15 and resolve to cut off diplomatic relations with Germany, Italy, and Japan.

2. Because of the shortage of workers caused by World War II, the government of the United States establishes the "Bracero Program" for Mexican laborers to work in the farm and food industries. As a result of this program, more than 2,500,000 Mexican workers come to the United States and most of them remain here.

3. The United States spurs a campaign of economic development in Puerto Rico with "Operation Bootstrap," giving tax exemption and other incentives to investments of foreign companies. A strong process of industrialization begins on the island.

1943

Luis Flórez, born in New York of Spanish parents, receives the Collier Trophy. Flórez is the inventor of a synthetic system for the training of pilots, in addition to thirty other inventions related to aeronautics.

1944

1. The United States and Mexico reach an agreement on February 3 for a fair use of the waters of the Río Grande, the Colorado, and the Tijuana rivers by both countries.

2. Puerto Rico sends to Washington Jesús T. Piñero as its resident commissioner.

1945

1. All the American countries, with the exception of Argentina, assemble in Mexico City to discuss war issues and sign a pact of mutual protection in case of aggression.

2. Up to this date there are about 97,000 Puerto Ricans in the New York area.

3. An office to care for the religious needs of Hispanic people of this country is established, which is the origin of the present Secretariat for Hispanic Affairs of the National Conference of Catholic Bishops.

1946

1. President Harry Truman appoints Jesús T. Piñero, the resident commissioner of Puerto Rico in Washington, D.C., as governor of the island. He is the first native Puerto Rican to hold this position since the Spanish-American War.

2. The GI Forum is established to defend the interests of Hispanic war veterans and their families. They offer several programs for their members and publish a monthly bulletin with the name *The Forerunner*.

1947

1. President Harry Truman of the United States visits Mexico City on March 3; he meets with President Miguel Alemán and once again reaffirms his "Good Neighbor" policy.

2. The Inter-American Conference of Countries of this Continent gathers at Rio de Janeiro, Brazil, and delegate countries reaffirm their mutual help and protection to preserve peace. President Truman addresses the assembly at the closing.

3. The United States Congress amends the "Jones Act" to grant the Puerto Rican people the power to elect the governor of the Island.

1948

1. The Puerto Rican people hold elections for the first time to choose their governor, and Luis Muñoz Marín of the Popular Party is the winning candidate. During his term of office he fosters education and works hard to build low-income housing.

2. The National Conference of Catholic Bishops reinforces its office in Washington to improve the religious care of Hispanic people in this country. The office publishes its bulletin called *En Marcha* ("On the March") every other month.

1949

1. The Ninth Pan-American Conference of nations decides to create a new entity called the "Organization of American States" (OAS), which still continues today.

2. The Latin American Educational Foundation is established in Denver, Colorado; its goal is to create opportunities for the education of young Hispanics through financial and technical assistance.

3. Four priests of the Archdiocese of San Francisco organize a movement to help the farm workers of California. For the following twelve years they help raise consciousness on more just salaries, union rights, and the social doctrine of the Church.

"Our Lady of the Navigators" or *"Mary Mother of Sailors,"* after
"La Virgen de los Navegantes" of the Reales Alcázares of Seville

1950-1992:
'Hispanidad' — the United States Today

"Hispanidad" keeps growing apace; it is a constituent element of this nation.

1950

1. Congress approves a law allowing the annual entry of 250 Spanish immigrants from the Basque region, who will engage in sheep herding. This is the origin of a wave of immigrants who have become fairly successful. It is estimated that there are actually some three thousand Spanish people of Basque origin in the Northwest.

2. Rita Moreno, a famous Puerto Rican theater artist, makes her debut with a movie titled "So Young, So Bad." This is followed by a few others, including "West Side Story," which will be very successful.

1951

1. This could be considered the initial year of the great American exodus of Puerto Ricans to New York. It is prompted, to a great extent, by a high index of unemployment that prevails on the island.

2. The Department of Immigration of the United States begins a campaign of massive deportation called "Operation Wetback." In a period of four years, some four million Mexican and Mexican-American people are deported from the country.

1952

1. On July 25, Puerto Rico is officially declared a commonwealth of the United States, a free and associated state.

2. Many Hispanics have joined the armed forces and fight in the Korean War. They are distinguished by their valor, and nine of them are awarded medals by the United States Congress. Special mention will be made of the 65th Infantry Regiment, entirely composed of Puerto Ricans.

1953

The United States and Spain sign a military and economic agreement on September 26. Spain allows the United States to have military bases on her soil for the defense of Europe, and the United States offers economic help in exchange.

1954

1. In March, the Organization of the American States meets in Caracas, Venezuela, to examine the expansion of communism in their respective countries.

2. Guatemalan Colonel Carlos Castillo Armas, helped by the Central Intelligence Agency (CIA), leaves Honduras. He leads a military insurrection in Guatemala and takes power on June 18. The United States helps his government with some six million dollars.

1955

The United States and Panama once again sign an agreement on January 25, mutually agreeing to cooperate in anything related to the Panama Canal, and the yearly payment for the canal increases from $430,000 to $1,930,000.

1956

According to the stipulations of the Organizations of American States, President Dwight D. Eisenhower and eighteen other heads of state sign the Declaration of Panama on July 22.

1957

1. Gabriela Mistral, a Chilean writer of international fame, dies in the United States. She published the book *Desolation* under the auspices of Teacher's College of the University of Columbia in New York City; was consul of her country in California, where she resided for over ten years; frequently delivered lectures at various American universities, and received the Nobel Prize for Literature.

2. The Archdiocese of New York establishes the Institute of Spanish Language and Culture to train clergy. Cardinal Francis J. Spellman sends a great number of seminarians to study Spanish at the Catholic University in Ponce, Puerto Rico. This practice will continue for years to come and will be extended to Colombia and the Dominican Republic.

3. The Puerto Rican Forum, which pursues the socioeconomic advancement of Hispanics through professional training and employment, is established in New York. It maintains offices in several states in the Northeast and the Midwest.

4. The first *Cursillo de Cristiandad* (Short Course in Christianity) is given in Waco, Texas. It is brought into this country by two Spanish Air Force cadets training in Texas and by a Franciscan priest. This movement has become very popular both in English and Spanish and at present is established in some 160 dioceses.

1958

1. Carlos Castañeda, prolific historian and writer who was born in Mexico, dies. He was a graduate of the University of Texas, and wrote the six-volume work *Our Catholic Heritage in Texas.* He authored another twelve books and eighty-five articles in different publications. History is the theme of his life.

2. The famous Spanish writer Juan Ramón Jiménez, who spent over twenty years of his life in the United States, dies in Puerto Rico. He was awarded the Nobel Prize for Literature, taught at the University of Maryland, and lectured at the Universities of North Carolina and Duke, residing in Coral Gables, Florida.

3. A group formed by several lay persons and a priest coming from Texas gives the first *Cursillo de Cristiandad* (Short Course in Christianity) in New York City. Seventeen candidates, several of them employed at the United Nations, attend this event. Because of the success of this program, Cardinal Francis Spellman charges the Augustinian Recollects with its direction, and soon the movement will spread to the whole Northeast region.

1959

1. Fidel Castro seizes power in Cuba, imposes a communist regime, and expropriates property worth of over two billion dollars that belongs to American citizens. This marks the beginning of the exodus of Cubans who will abandon the island and head to the United States, concentrating mostly in the area of Miami, Florida, and Union City, New Jersey.

2. The statue of Father Junípero Serra is placed in the rotunda of great Americans in the Capitol at Washington, D.C.

3. Severo Ochoa, a famous Spanish scientist residing in the United States, is awarded the Nobel Prize for Medicine because of his research on RNA and DNA.

1960

1. President Dwight D. Eisenhower makes a visit to several Latin American countries — Brazil, Argentina, Uruguay, and Chile — as a gesture of friendship and cooperation.

2. Entrance of the United States into the Vietnam War causes many Hispanics to join the Armed Forces and participate in the fight. An information source will show that one fifth of all dead or wounded soldiers from the South were of Hispanic origin.

1961

1. President John F. Kennedy presents to Congress the Alliance for Progress program, and it is approved. Six hundred million dollars are budgeted to aid Latin America. A few months later, the foreign assistance bill is passed and four billion dollars are allocated for economic and military assistance.

2. The Archdiocese of New York establishes St. Joseph's Center as headquarters of the *"Cursillo de Cristiandad"* Movement, where thousands of lay persons from the New York area will receive courses in religious formation and leadership.

3. Antonio Pantoja, a Puerto Rican community leader, founds ASPIRA of America, in New York. It is an institution to encourage Hispanic students to pursue higher studies. It operates with federal and state funds and with grants provided by foundations and corporations.

4. From the end of World War II up to the present, 847,000 Puerto Rican persons have arrived in the continental United States. A high percentage of them remain in the area of New York City. Sometime later, sizable groups will concentrate also in Chicago and Los Angeles.

5. A force of some fifteen hundred Cubans who have left Cuba in the past two years organize and make an attempt to overthrow the communist government of Fidel Castro with the so-called "Bay of Pigs" invasion; but the promised American support does not arrive, the expected internal revolt does not happen, and the attempt to liberate Cuba fails.

6. The Association of Cuban Engineers is established with the purpose of keeping technical standards and making contacts with Latin American engineers; it has branches in several states, sponsors bimonthly workshops, and publishes a newsletter titled "Bulletin of Cuban Engineers."

1962

1. The Soviet Union installs nuclear rockets in Cuba; President Kennedy blockades the island and warns Russia that he will not lift the blockade until the rockets are dismantled and taken out. While the world remains in suspense, afraid of a nuclear conflagration, Russia finally decides to dismantle the rockets, and Kennedy orders a total embargo to Cuba of all American products.

2. The United States breaks diplomatic relations with Peru because of a military overthrow, canceling economic and military aid. A month later, diplomatic relations are renewed.

3. Dennis Chávez, assemblyman of New Mexico, U.S. representative and senator, dies. Throughout his years in the Capitol, he stood out for his

concern on matters related to health and preservation of a clean environment.

1963

1. On February 14, President Kennedy announces his Peace Corps program, formed by groups of young Americans who volunteer their services to help people in depressed areas of the third world. Many of them head for Latin America.

2. The nations of Central America and President Kennedy announce the Declaration of San José to form a Central American Common Market, signing an agreement in Costa Rica.

1964

1. The United States and Panama break diplomatic relations after riots caused by the flags of the United States and Panama flying in the Canal Zone; three months later normal relations will be resumed.

2. The National Conference of Catholic Bishops strengthens its office in Washington, D.C., to improve the pastoral care of the Hispanic people of the country.

3. Congress cancels the "Bracero" program by not renewing the bill that gave birth to it. The wave of Mexican farmworkers to the North, however, continues with the same or even greater intensity.

1965

1. On April 28, the United States sends a force of twenty thousand soldiers to the Dominican Republic to protect American life and property. Political quarrels have caused internal turmoil, and a quasi-civil war ensues. Several months later, the United States recognizes a provisional government that has been set up.

2. Pedro Albizu Campos, a dedicated defender of the independence of Puerto Rico, dies this year.

3. The Latin Chamber of Commerce of the United States (CAMACOL) is established; its purpose is to promote trade among Hispanic people and to spur tourism.

4. César Chávez, who has initiated the struggle on behalf of the cause of farmworkers with the National Association of Farmworkers, calls for a strike against the growers of farm products in the area of Delano, California.

5. The program called "*Maquiladora*" is also established this year. Products from the United States are taken to Mexican border towns for elaboration, finishing, or ensemble. Articles like electronic devices, office

equipment, or clothing are part of the operation of this program. Some twenty years later, the program will number about 600 factories employing 130,000 workers who receive some $2,000,000,000 a year in wages.

6. Fidel Castro allows departure from the island of Cubans who have relatives in the United States. These departures give origin to the so-called "freedom flights" that bring some four thousand persons a month into the United States.

7. Joseph Montoya, well known for his defense of the interests of the Hispanic people, is elected a member of the U.S. Senate and will remain in that position for three consecutive terms.

1966

1. The National Union of Farmworkers, headed by César Chávez, is recognized on April 16 as a negotiating agency on behalf of Schenley Industries workers.

2. The Colorado Migrant Council is formed in Colorado to assist Hispanic farmworkers with labor training, and also assists their families in their needs by offering several programs related to food, energy, and cattle raising. Its quarterly bulletin is called "Farm Workers Journal."

3. The Committee of Spanish-speaking of Virginia is formed to help with economic aid to the Hispanics of Virginia and to establish projects concerned with education, voter registration, and assistance to the elderly. It counts a membership of twenty thousand persons, and its bulletin is called "*Información.*"

1967

1. On April 12, all the presidents of Latin America and Lyndon Johnson of the United States meet at Punta del Este, Uruguay, where they decide to form the Latin American Common Market, improve trade, and eliminate unnecessary military expenses.

2. On October 28, the United States and Mexico reach an agreement, whereby the United States gives back to Mexico the "*El Chamizal*" area that was left on the North side of the border when the Río Grande changed its course in 1850 near the city of El Paso, Texas. Presidents Lyndon Johnson and Gustavo Díaz Ordaz attend and sign the agreement.

3. A group of descendants of Spanish and of Mexicans, called the "Federal Alliance of Free People," headed by Reyes López Tijerina, rises up in Tierra Amarilla, New Mexico, and takes over the county court on June 5. They claim twenty-five hundred square miles of land that, according to them, the Crown of Spain had granted their ancestors, which were taken away by Anglo colonists after 1846.

4. The population of Puerto Rico votes on the political status of the island. Sixty per cent of the votes reject the idea of becoming a state of the union.

5. In July, the first Marriage Encounter is given at St. Joseph's Center in New York by Father Gabriel Calvo, founder of the program, and a couple from Mexico City. The following week, another Marriage Encounter is given, attended by bilingual couples of the region, and this marks the beginning of the movement that later will spread throughout the United States, both in English and Spanish.

1968

1. The National Council of La Raza is established, formed by more than one hundred organizations from all over the country. Its purpose is the educational, economic, and social advancement of the Hispanic community, helping more than one million people through its organizations. The bulletin that it publishes is called "Agenda."

2. The Mexican-American Legal Defense and Education Fund (MALDEF) to provide legal and educational assistance to Hispanics is established in San Francisco, California, for the purpose of giving encouragement to Hispanics to pursue law studies and to raise awareness of their Hispanic heritage. Its bulletin bears the name of "MALDEF Newsletter."

3. The city of San Antonio, Texas, celebrates the 200th anniversary of its founding on April 6, and Hemisfair 68 takes place there, attracting many visitors to the celebration. Several structures of artistic and cultural interest are built in the city on this occasion.

4. On October 30, the Nobel Prize for Physics is awarded to Dr. Luis W. Alvarez of the University of California at Berkeley for his research on subatomic particles.

1969

1. A serious conflict arises between the National Association of Farmworkers and the agricultural product growers of California. In order to help solve the problem, the United States Catholic Conference forms an ad hoc committee.

2. The organization *Católicos por la Raza* (Catholics for the Race) is formed in California. It is composed, to a large extent, of young people demanding civil rights and social services.

3. After a preliminary meeting held a few weeks before in Tucson, Arizona, on October 7 the organization PADRES is formed by priests of Mexican origin born in this country. Its purpose is to play an advocacy

role for the rights of Hispanics who are ignored. At this meeting they approve several resolutions that they send to the National Conference of Catholic Bishops.

1970

1. Rev. Patricio Flores is appointed auxiliary bishop of the Archdiocese of San Antonio, Texas, and is the first Mexican-American to achieve such a position. In 1990 there will be twenty-one bishops in the United States of Hispanic origin.

2. The National Economic Development Association is established to help Hispanic businessmen and entrepreneurs get loans for the development of their businesses, also providing for technical assistance. It publishes, every two months, a bulletin under the name "*Impacto*."

3. Herman Badillo, a Puerto Rican leader born in Caguas and a resident of New York for many years, is elected a member of the U.S. House of Representatives in Washington, D.C.

4. José Angel Gutiérrez founds *La Raza Unida* ("Race United"), seeking the participation and victory of Hispanic candidates in political life.

1971

1. The Mexican-American Cultural Center (MACC) is established in San Antonio, Texas. to foster Christian leadership and to train people in the Spanish language and culture through regular courses, workshops, and conferences. It provides an outstanding service to Catholics throughout the country.

2. The National Coalition of Hispanic Mental Health and Human Services Organizations is established, doing psychological and sociological research in health matters related to the Hispanic community. It is composed of over three hundred organizations and publishes a monthly magazine titled, "COSSMHO Roadrunner" and "COSSMHO Reporters."

3. President Richard Nixon appoints Ramona A. Bañuelos as treasurer of the United States, the first Hispanic person to occupy such a position.

1972

1. The First National Hispanic Encounter takes place in Washington D. C., assembling bishops, priests, religious, and lay representatives of the Hispanic Catholic community from the entire country. Its main purpose is to raise awareness of the Hispanic presence in the Church, to unify objectives, and to improve pastoral service to the people. Soon

regional centers, diocesan offices, and pastoral institutes will be established throughout the nation.

2. The Puerto Rican Legal Defense and Education Fund is founded in New York to protect the legal rights of the Puerto Rican community. Also this year, the American Association of Spanish-speaking Certified Public Accountants is created in Washington, D.C., giving an annual scholarship for the formation of Hispanic accountants and publishing its bulletin with the name "*La Cuenta.*"

3. At the age of ninety-five, famed Spanish cellist Pablo Casals gives a premiere presentation of his "Hymn to the United Nations" and receives the Peace Medal from the U.N.

4. George I. Sánchez, famous writer born in Albuquerque, New Mexico, who studied at the Universities of Texas, New Mexico, and California (Berkeley), a pioneer in matters related to bilingual education and author of numerous books and reports, writes *The Forgotten People* and dies at the age of sixty-six.

1973

1. The government of Spain, in memory of forty years of Spanish presence in Louisiana, donates a million dollars for the construction of a Spanish-style plaza at New Orleans.

2. The Latin American Manufacturers Association is established in Washington, D.C., to encourage the participation of Hispanic businessmen in the contracts of government and corporations. It publishes a quarterly bulletin called "LAMA."

3. The National Association of Farmworkers Organization is formed to improve work and housing conditions of the farmworkers. Its bulletin is called "The National Farmworkers."

4. The organization COPS is formed in San Antonio, Texas; it seeks to improve the social services to the Hispanic community through economic and political pressure. It achieves great success and spreads to other cities.

1974

1. It is revealed that the Central Intelligence Agency (CIA) was involved in the operations to overthrow the president of Chile, Salvador Allende, and that eight million dollars were spent in that matter. The senate committee will declare the following year that the CIA did not have a direct participation in the fall and death of Allende.

2. A regional encounter of Hispanic Catholics from the northeastern part of the country takes place in Holyoke, Massachusetts. This is con-

sidered of great importance to improve religious service to the Hispanics of the area. As a result of this event, the Northeast Pastoral Center is established in New York.

3. Father Roberto Sánchez, appointed archbishop of Santa Fe, New Mexico, is the first Mexican-American to occupy such a position in the Catholic hierarchy of the United States.

4. The Society of Hispanic Professional Engineers is established to help the advancement of Hispanic students and engineers through scholarships and employment. It publishes a bulletin every other month under the name of "SHPE National Newsletter."

1975

1. The Association of Hispanic Arts is formed to gather and spread information on Hispanic Arts such as drama, music, and dance. It receives funds from the National Endowment for the Arts and publishes, every two months, a bulletin called "Hispanic Arts."

2. The National Association of Latin Elected and Appointed Officials (NALEO) is established in Washington, D.C., for the purpose of raising consciousness and promoting political representation of the Hispanic community. Its bulletin is called "Washington Report."

3. Another organization that comes to light this year is the National Association of Pro-Aging Persons (AMPPM). It has as its goal to see that the elderly Hispanic persons receive the services guaranteed them by law and to correct possible deficiencies.

4. Jerry Apodaca, a Mexican-American, is elected governor of the State of New Mexico, while Raul Castro is elected governor of the State of Arizona.

1976

1. The Hispanic Organization of Professionals and Executives (HOPE) is established to increase the number of Hispanics in businesses and professions and to provide managerial and technical assistance to Hispanic businessmen and professionals. Its headquarters are in Washington, D.C.

2. The National Association for Bilingual Education is established by educators, businessmen, and paraprofessional people, seeking to promote bilingual education among Hispanics through training of bilingual educators. It also pursues quality education and publishes a bulletin titled "NABE Journal."

1977

1. Presidents James Carter of the United States and Omar Torrijos of Panama sign a Treaty by which the administration of the Panama Canal will be transferred to Panama in the year 2000. The agreement is brought before Congress in both countries and is approved.

2. The Congressional Hispanic Caucus is organized in Washington D.C., to introduce legislative measures to satisfy the needs of the Hispanic community. It is composed of 145 Congressmen and persons of Hispanic origin representing zones of dense Hispanic population. Its bulletin bears the name "AVANCE."

3. The Second National Hispanic Encounter takes place in Washington D.C., and assembles twelve hundred Hispanic Catholic delegates, including bishops, priests, religious and lay people from all over the country. The encounter is the culmination of a process of reflection and dialogue that lasted a whole year, with the participation of over one hundred thousand people.

4. In Miami a group of young and capable Hispanic architects organizes the association called "Arquitectonica." Arquitectonica is a project to develop the architectural talents of young Hispanics and will erect outstanding buildings on several locations of the United States.

1978

1. Joseph Montoya, a descendant of those Spanish who had settled New Mexico, is elected a member of the U.S. Congress. He is concerned with matters affecting ethnic groups, especially Hispanics and American Indians.

2. The Hispanic Higher Education Coalition is established, with headquarters in Washington, D.C., by a number of prestigious Hispanic organizations. It looks to encourage Hispanic youth to move to higher studies, while it assists them with information and technical help.

1979

1. The United States breaks its diplomatic relations with Nicaragua on February 8 to pressure dictator Anastasio Somoza to negotiate with the revolutionary groups that are fighting him, and economic restrictions are also applied. The revolutionary groups overthrow Somoza and the Sandinista group seizes power, putting in place a Marxist regime instead of a democratic one as it had promised.

2. The National Association of Spanish Broadcasters is established in Washington D.C., to promote broadcasting in Spanish by radio and television stations. It puts out a bulletin named "News/*Noticias*."

3. The United States Hispanic Chamber of Commerce, a coalition of chambers of commerce of the various states, is formed in Washington D.C. Its primary goal is to assist Hispanic merchants in everything related to trade.

1980

1. About 140,000 Cubans leave the island from the port of Mariel with the implicit consent of Fidel Castro, arriving in Florida by boat. This massive exodus is a clear rejection of the Marxist government imposed by force of arms on the island twenty years before.

2. In the field of communications, though the volume of mass media is not in proportion with the number of Hispanic people in the country, some twenty-three television stations and five hundred radio stations broadcast in Spanish. In addition, there are over one hundred newspapers printed in Spanish.

3. Scientist Francisco Álvarez, who was born in Mexico, dies this year. He graduated from Harvard University and was research chairman of Syntex in California. He made noteworthy contributions in medical and chemical research and is mentioned as inventor of eighty patents in the United States and author of fifteen scientific publications.

1981

1. A group of directors of Spanish-language publications meets in New York and establishes the "Hispanic Media Council MSA." Its objective is to further media communications in Spanish and to prove to publicity agencies that the Spanish Press is a good means of publicity. There are presently twenty-one publications represented by the Council.

2. The city of San Antonio, Texas, elects Henry Cisneros as its first Mexican-American mayor.

3. This year the famous painting "Guernica" by Pablo Picasso is taken from the Museum of Modern Art of New York and placed in the museum of El Prado in Madrid, Spain.

1982

1. Argentina and England get involved in a war, both claiming sovereignty over the Falkland Islands (Malvinas). The intervention of the United States, siding with England, helps England's victory. At the same time, a feeling of distress toward the United States is evident in all Latin American countries. They perceive that the priority of the United States is not with them, and that the Monroe Doctrine means little on this occasion.

2. The Center for Chicano Studies is formed at the University of

California in Los Angeles (UCLA) and joins the Center for Puerto Rican Studies of the City University of New York (CUNY) to conduct research on demography, immigration, and other related matters.

3. The State of Arizona elects Esteban Torres as its representative to the U.S. Congress. Torres is a native of Arizona and has served as ambassador to UNESCO, counselor to President James Carter, and president of the Hispanic Caucus.

1983

1. The Catholic bishops of the United States issue a pastoral letter titled "The Hispanic Presence: Challenge and Commitment," which brings into prominence the noteworthy presence of the Hispanic community in the Church of this country, its values and importance, as well as the commitment to pastoral service.

2. Luis Muñoz Marín, illustrious politician of Puerto Rico, dies. He spent a good part of his youth in the United States and wrote in magazines like *The Nation* and *New Republic* among others. He helped to consolidate the status of the Commonwealth of Puerto Rico and was the driving force behind "Operation Bootstrap." He is eighty-five years old at the time of his death.

1984

1. The International Court at the Hague in Holland examines the complaint of the Nicaraguan government against the United States, and determines that the United States should refrain from mining and blockading its seaports. The United States responds that it is under no obligation to abide by this declaration.

2. Archbishop of Newark Peter L. Gerety entrusts Bishop David Arias with the responsibility of undertaking a research study on the religious and social situation of the large Hispanic community of that area of New Jersey. After four years of research, the study is completed and presented, together with a plan of action, to the new Archbishop Theodore E. McCarrick, who gives his approval and orders its immediate implementation.

1985

1. The Third National Hispanic Catholic Encounter takes place in Washington, D.C., with delegates from the whole country including bishops, priests, religious, and lay people. The assembly is preceded by a year of preparation by tens of thousands of people participating in parishes and institutions. A result of the encounter is the decision to es-

tablish a national pastoral plan to improve religious care to the Hispanic people.

2. The city of Miami, Florida, elects an Hispanic mayor, Javier Suárez, a young Cuban graduate of the Universities of Villanova and Harvard.

1986

1. The United States Congress approves the new "Immigration and Reform Control Law" on November 5, to control the arrival in the country of persons who do not have legal documentation. It issues an amnesty for the people who arrived before January 1, 1982, and requires sanctions for the employers who hire undocumented aliens. It is expected that about two and a half million undocumented persons, many of them Hispanics, will be able to legalize their residency as a result of this law.

2. Congress rejects the proposal to provide one hundred million dollars to help the contra-revolutionaries of Nicaragua in their fight to liberate their country, and two days later twenty million dollars is approved to help Honduras in her protection against Nicaragua. Three months later, the International Justice Court declares that all help to the contra-revolutionaries would be a violation. The American delegation responds that the United States does not recognize the jurisdiction of the court in this case.

3. Roberto Martínez, a prominent politician of Spanish origin, is elected Governor of Florida. He is the first Hispanic to hold this position since Florida became part of the United States.

1987

1. Pope John Paul II, in his second official visit to the United States, tours areas with a dense Hispanic population like Miami, New Orleans, San Antonio, Phoenix, Los Angeles, and San Francisco, and addresses the people in English and Spanish. His visit and talks help bring to a higher awareness the presence of the Hispanic people in the nation.

2. The National Conference of Catholic Bishops approves a pastoral plan to better serve the religious needs of the Hispanic people of the country. It is now up to the local dioceses and parishes to adapt it to their particular situation and implement it.

1988

On September 25, Father Junípero Serra is declared Blessed by Pope John Paul II. Father Serra was a tireless Franciscan missionary who spent his life and all his efforts in the evangelization of California, seeking the human and religious promotion of the American Indian. He is the first person of Hispanic origin in this country to be declared Blessed.

1989

1. Vice-President J. Danforth Quayle visits several countries of Latin America and attends the swearing in of the president of Venezuela, Carlos Andrés Pérez. Four months later he will meet with the presidents of Guatemala, Honduras, El Salvador, and Costa Rica.

2. The five Presidents of Central America meet at San Salvador and sign an agreement to seek ways to bring peace to Nicaragua, deciding that military help to the contra-revolutionaries by the United States should stop. Nicaragua promises to hold free elections in February of the coming year.

3. The United States invades Panama to arrest General Manuel Noriega, who is accused of being responsible for dealing in and bringing drugs into the United States. Noriega seeks asylum in the Nunciature of the Vatican, but a few days later gives himself up and is brought to the United States to stand trial.

4. President George Bush appoints four persons of Hispanic origin to be members of his Cabinet: Eloy Cabazos, Secretary of Education; Manuel Lujan, Secretary of the Interior; Antonia Novello, Surgeon General; and Catalina Villalpando, Treasurer of the United States.

1990

1. After dictator Anastasio Somoza was overthrown, the Sandinista Front took power in Nicaragua, and put in place a Marxist-Leninist regime, which faced a great deal of opposition from a good percentage of the Nicaraguan people, the Church, and the United States. A period of ten years of quasi-war followed. Pressured by his Central American colleagues and other international powers, Daniel Ortega agrees to call a democratic election, and on February 25 a free and democratic election takes place in Nicaragua, with the result being a resounding defeat of the Sandinista Front and the victory of a coalition of national parties (UNO). Violeta Chamorro is elected president of the country.

2. The prestigious Nobel Prize for Literature is awarded to Octavio Paz, a renowned Mexican writer, lecturer, and honorary doctor of Harvard University.

1991

1. On January 15, the United States declares war on Iraq for its invasion of Kuwait. After forty days of fighting the war ends with the vic-

tory of the United States and several allied nations. Of the 475,000 American soldiers participating in this war some 25,000 are of Hispanic origin.

2. On March 14, the Senate of Puerto Rico declares Spanish as the only official language of the Island. The House of Representatives approved the same bill the year before. It had been determined in 1902 that both Spanish and English would be the official languages; that determination is now abrogated. However, teaching of the English language in all schools will continue to be mandatory.

1992

1. October 12 of this year marks the fifth centenary of the arrival in America of Christopher Columbus and his 105 sailors aboard the three caravels *Santa Maria, Pinta, and Niña*. A great variety of scientific, cultural, and social activities are taking place to commemorate the event. There is a national committee appointed by former President Ronald Reagan and many other state committees involved in organizing a variety of events, while several cities such as Chicago, Columbus, Los Angeles, Miami, New York, San Francisco, and Washington have been designated sites for special commemorative activities.

2. The National Conference of Catholic Bishops has established an "ad hoc" committee for the celebration of five hundred years since the coming of the faith to the Americas. They have also published a pastoral letter called "Heritage and Hope," addressed to the Catholic people of the United States on the occasion of this fifth centenary. Both the committee and the pastoral letter are spearheading a number of activities at national, diocesan, parish, and university levels which will bring to a higher awareness the development of the Catholic faith in the United States during the past five hundred years.

CONCLUSION

This summary view of the history of a particular people in this country brings us to the conclusion that "Hispanidad" is not a new phenomenon that has appeared in the United States in recent years, but it has been so since the first years after the discovery of America by Spain. Since then, "Hispanidad" has been present here through constant explorations throughout these national territories, attested to by maps and other documents. "Hispanidad" has been involved in the colonization of these lands and in the civilization of its indigenous people. It has been engaged in a task of evangelization which is not yet achieved. "Hispanidad" has consisted of building this country, fighting for its independence, and participating in its national formation. It has been present here in people of great stature who deserve to be remembered by the citizens of this country as heroes, in no way inferior to others popularly acclaimed. "Hispanidad" has been like a seed that, planted in the beginning of the sixteenth century, has grown steadily and has formed a plant which still waits to bear its best flowers and fruits. This is why it can be said that "Hispanidad" is an integral part of the United States of America, and so also its history.

APPENDIX

Governors of Hispanic Origin in the United States

This list is based on those provided by Federico Ribes Tovar (*Puerto Rican Heritage Encyclopedia*), Vito Alessio Robles (*Coahuila and Texas*), and Carlos Fernandez Shaw (*Presencia Española en Estados Unidos*).

PUERTO RICO

1505, Vicente Y. Pinzón
1509-1511, Juan Ponce de León
1511-1513, Juan Cerón
1513, Rodrigo Moscoso
1513-1514, Cristóbal Mendoza
1514, Gonzalo de Ovalle
1514-1519, Sánchez Velázquez
1519-1520, Antonio de la Gama
1520-1522, Pedro Moreno
1522-1524, Alonso Manso
1524-1528, Pedro Moreno
1528-1529, Antonio de la Gama
1529-1536, Francisco de Lando
1536-1537, Vasco de Tiedra
1537, Gerónimo de Ortal
1537-1545, Alcaldes Ordinarios
1545, Gerónimo Lebrón
1545-1546, Iñigo López C.
1546-1550, Antonio de la Vega
1550-1554, Luis de Vallejo
1554, Alonso Estévez
1555-1564, Diego de Carasa
1564-1569, Francisco Bahamonde
1569-1576 Francisco de Solís
1575-1579, Francisco de Obando
1579, Juan Ponce de León II
1580, Gerónimo Agüero
1580, Juan de Céspedes
1580-1583, Juan López Melgarejo
1582-1593, Diego Meléndez
1593-1597, Pedro Suárez C.
1597-1598, Antonio de Mosquera
1598-1602, Alonso de Mercado

1602-1608, Sancho Ochoa
1608-1614, Gabriel Rojas Páramo
1614-1620, Felipe de Beaumont
1620-1625, Juan de Vargas
1625-1631, Juan de Haro
1631-1635, Enrique Henríquez S.
1635-1641, Iñigo Mota Sarmiento
1641, Agustín Silva F.
1641-1643, Juan de Bolaños
1643-1650, Fernando Riva Agüero
1650-1656, Diego de Aguilera
1656-1661, José de Novoa M.
1661-1664, Juan Pérez Guzmán
1664-1670, Jerónimo de Velasco
1670-1674, Gaspar de Arteaga
1674, Diego Robledilla
1674-1675, Baltasar Figueroa
1675-1678, Alonso Campos E.
1678-1683, Juan Robles L.
1683-1690, Gaspar Martínez A.
1690-1695, Gaspar Arredondo
1695-1698, Juan Fernández F.
1698-1699, Antonio Robles S.
1699-1700, Gaspar Arredondo
1700-1703, Gabriel Gutiérrez R.
1703, Diego Jiménez V.
1703, Gaspar de Olivares
1703, Andrés Montañez
1703-1705, Francisco Sánchez C.
1705-1706, Pedro Arroyo G.
1706, Francisco Calderón
1706, Fernando Castilla
1706-1708, Juan López Morla
1708-1713, Francisco Granados

1713-1716, Juan de Rivera
1716, José Carreño
1716-1720, Alonso Bertodano
1720-1724, Francisco Granados
1724, José A. de Isasi
1724-1731, José de Mendizábal
1731-1743, Matías de Abadía
1743, Domingo Pérez H.
1743-1750, Juan José Colomo
1750-1751, Agustín Pareja
1751-1753, Esteban Bravo R.
1753-1757, Felipe Ramírez E.
1757-1759, Esteban Bravo R.
1759-1760, Antonio Guazo C.
1760, Esteban Bravo R.
1760-1766, Ambrosio Benavides
1766-1768, Marcos de Vergara
1768-1769, Coronel José Tentor
1769-1776, Miguel de Muesas
1776-1783, José Dufresne
1783-1789, Juan Dabán
1789, Francisco Torralbo
1789-1792, Miguel A. Urtáriz
1792-1793, Francisco Torralbo
1793, Enrique Grimarest
1795-1804, Ramón Castro G.
1804-1809, Toribio Montes
1809-1820, Salvador Meléndez
1820, Juan Vasco Pascual
1820-1822 Gonzalo Aróstegui
1822, José Navarro
1822, Francisco Linares
1822-1837, Miguel de la Torre
1837-1838, Francisco Moreda
  Prieto
1838-1841, Miguel López Baños
1841-1844, Santiago Méndez Vigo
1844-1847, Rafael Arístegui V.
1847-1848, Juan Prim (C. Reus)
1848-1851, Juan Pezuela C.
1851-1852, Enrique España T.
1852-1855, Fernando Norzagaray
1855, Andrés García Gamba
1855-1857, José Lemery

1857-1860, Fernando Cotoner
1860, Sabino Gamir
1863-1865, Félix de Messina
1865-1867, José M. Marchessi
1867-1868, Julián Juan Pavia
1868-1870, José Laureano Sanz
1870-1871, Gabriel Baldrich
1871-1872, Ramón Gómez Pulido
1872, Simón de la Torre
1872-1873, Joaquín Eurile
1873, Juan Martínez P.
1873-1874, Rafael Primo Rivera
1875, José Laureano Sanz
1875-1877, Segundo Portilla
1877-1878, Manuel Serna Pinzón
1878, José Gamir
1878-1881, Eulogio Despujol D.
1881-1883, Segundo Portilla
1883-1884, Miguel Vega Inclán
1884, Carlos Suances C.
1884, Ramón Fajardo
1884-1887, Luis Dabán y Ramírez
1887, Romualdo Palacios
1887-1888, Juan Contreras
1888-1890, Pedro Ruíz Dana
1890, José Pascual Bananza
1890-1893, José Lasso y Pérez
1893-1895, Antonio Dabán R.
1895-1896, José Gamir
1896, Emilio March
1896-1898, Sabas Marín
1898, Ricardo de Ortega
1898, Manuel Macías Casado
1898, Ricardo de Ortega
1921, José Benedicto
1939, José E. Colón
1940, José M. Gallardo
1946-1948, Jesús T. Piñero
1948-1964, Luis Muñoz Marín
1964-1968, Roberto Sánchez Vilaya
1968-1972, Luis A. Ferré
1972-1980, Rafael Hernández Colón
1980-1984, Romero Barceló
1984-, Rafael Hernández Colón

FLORIDA

1512, Juan Ponce de León
1519, Alonso Álvarez Piñeda
1524, Lucas Vázquez Ayllón
1527, Pánfilo de Narváez
1537, Hernando de Soto
1558, Tristán de Luna
1563, Angel Villafañe
1565-1574, Pedro Menéndez A.
1575-1577, Hernando de Miranda
1577-1578, Pedro Menéndez M.
1578-1589, Pedro Menéndez M.
1589-1592, Gutiérrez de Miranda
1592-1594, Rodrigo de Junco
1594-1595, Domingo Avendaño
1596-1603, Gonzalo Méndez Canzo
1603-1609, Pedro de Ybarra
1618-1623, Juan de Salinas
1624-1629, Luis de Rojas Borja
1630-1631, Andrés Rodríguez V.
1633-1638, Luis Horruytiner
1639-1645. Damián Vega Castro
1645-1650, Benito Ruiz Salazar
1650-1651, Nicolás Ponce Léon
1651-1655, Pedro B. Horruytiner
1655-1659, Diego de Rebolledo
1659-1663, Alonso Aranguiz C.
1664-1670, Francisco de la Guerra
1670-1673, Manuel de Cendoya
1674-1675, Nicolás Ponce Léon
1675-1680, Pablo Hita Salazar
1680-1687, Juan Marqués Cabrera
1687-1693, Diego Quiroga Losada
1693-1699, Laureano Torres A.
1699-1706, José Zúñiga Cerda
1706-1716, Francisco Córcoles
1717-1718, Juan Ayala Escobar
1718-1734, Antonio Benavides
1734-1737, Francisco del Moral
1737, Manuel J. Justis
1737-1749, Manuel Montiano
1749-1752, Melchor Navarrete
1752-1755, Fulgencio García S.
1755-1758, Alonso Fernández H.

1758-1761, Lucas de Palacio
1762-1763, Melchor Feliú
1986-1990, Roberto Martínez

FLORIDA EAST

1783-1790, Manuel de Zéspedes
1790-1795, Juan Quesada
1795, Bartolomé Morales
1795-1811, Enrique White
1811-1812, Juan de Estrada
1812-1815, Sebastián Kindelán
1815-1816, Juan de Estrada
1816-1821, José Coppinger

FLORIDA WEST

1781-1793, Arturo O'Neill
1793-1795, Enrique White
1795-1796, Francisco Gelabert
1796-1811, Juan Folch
1811-1812, Francisco St. Maxent
1812-1813, Mauricio de Zúñiga
1813-1815, Mateo González M.
1816-1819, José Masot
1819-1821, José Callava

NEW MEXICO

1598-1608, Juan de Oñate
1608-1610, Cristóbal de Oñate
1610-1614, Pedro Peralta
1614-1618, Bernardino Ceballos
1618-1625, Juan de Eulate
1625-1630, Felipe Sotelo O.
1630-1632, Francisco Silva Nieto
1632-1635, Francisco Mora Ceballos
1635-1637, Francisco Martínez Baeza
1637-1641, Luis de Rosas
1641, Juan Flores Sierra
1641-1642, Francisco Gómez
1642-1644, Alonso Pacheco H.
1644-1647, Fernando Argüello
1647-1649, Luis de Guzmán
1649-1653, Hernando de Ugarte
1653-1656, Juan Samaniego Jaca
1656-1659, Juan Manso Contreras

1659-1661, Bernardo Mendizábal
1661-1664, Diego Peñalosa B.
1664-1665, Juan Miranda
1665-1668, Fernando Villanueva
1668-1671, Juan Medrano Mesia
1671-1675, Juan Durán Miranda
1675-1677, Juan Francisco Treviño
1677-1683, Antonio de Otermín
1683-1686, Domingo Jironza C.
1686-1689, Pedro Reneros Posada
1689-1691, Domingo Jironza C.
1691-1697, Diego Vargas Zapata
1697-1703, Pedro Rodríguez C.
1703-1704, Diego Vargas Zapata
1704-1705, Juan Páez Hurtado
1705-1707, Francisco Cuervo Valdés
1707-1712, José Chacón Medina
1712-1715, Juan Flores Mogollón
1715-1717, Felipe Martínez
1717-1717, Juan Páez Hurtado
1717-1722, Antonio Valverde C.
1722-1731, Juan Domingo B.
1731-1736, Gervasio Cruzat G.
1736-1739, Enrique Olavide
1739-1743, Gaspar Domingo M.
1743-1749, Joaquín Codallos R.
1749-1754, Tomás Vélez Cachupín
1754-1760, Fco. Marín Valle
1760-1760, Mateo A. Mendoza
1760-1762, Manuel Portillo
1762-1767, Tomás Vélez Cachupín
1767-1778, Pedro Mendinueta
1778-1778, Francisco Trébol N.
1778-1788, Juan Bautista de Anza
1788-1794, Fernando Concha
1794-1805, Fernando Chacón
1805-1808, Joaquín Real A.
1808-1808, Alberto Máynez
1808-1814, José Manrique
1814-1816, Alberto Maynez
1816-1818, Pedro María Allende
1818-1822, Facundo Melgares
1822, Francisco X. Chávez
1822-1823, José A. Vizcarra

1823-1825, Bartolomé Baca
1825-1827, Antonio Narbona
1827-1829, Manuel Armijo
1829-1832, José A. Chávez
1832-1833, Santiago Abreu
1833-1835, Francisco Sarracino
1835-1837, Albino Pérez
1837-1844, Manuel Armijo
1844-1844, Mariano Chávez
1844-1844, Felipe Sena
1844-1845, Mariano M. Lejanza
1845-1845, Mariano Chávez
1845-1845, José Chávez
1845-1846, Manuel Armijo
1846-1848, Donaciano Vigil
1897-1906, Miguel A. Otero
1917-1919, Ezequiel Cabeza de Vaca
1919-1921, Octaviano Larrazolo
1975-1979, Jerry Apodaca
1983-1987, Antonio Anaya

TEXAS
1522-1523, Francisco Garay
1526-1528, Pánfilo Narváez
1528-1530, Nuño de Guzmán
1538-1543, Hernando de Soto
1691-1692, Domingo Terán Ríos
1692-1697, Gregorio de Salinas
1698-1702, Francisco Cuervo Valdés
1703-1705, Mathías de Aguirre
1705-1708, Martín de Alarcón
1708-1712, Simón Padilla C.
1712-1714, Pedro F. Echevers
1714-1716, Juan Valdez
1716-1719, Martín de Alarcón
1719-1722, Marqués de Aguayo
1722-1727, Fernando Pérez A.
1727-1730, Melchor Media Villa
1730-1734, Juan Bustillo Z.
1734-1736, Manuel de Sandoval
1736-1737, Carlos Benítez F.
1737-1741, Prudencio Orobio
1741-1743, Tomás F. Wintuisen
1743-1744, Justo Boneo Morales

1751-1759, Francisco García Larios
1759-1766, Angel Martos N.
1767-1770, Hugo Oconor
1770-1778, Barón de Riperdá
1778-1786, Domingo Cabello
1786-1787, Bernardo Bonavía
1787-1788, Rafael Martínez P.
1788-1789, Vacante
1790-1798, Manuel Muñoz
1798-1800, José Irigoyen
1800-1805, Juan Elguezábal
1805-1810, Antonio Cordero
1811-1813, Manuel Salcedo
1814-1817, Cristóbal Domínguez
1817-1817, Ignacio Pérez
1817-1817, Manuel Pardo
1817-1822, Antonio Martínez
1822-1823, José F. Trespalacios
1823-1824, Luciano García
1824-1826, Rafael González
1827-1827, José I. Arispe
1827-1827, José M. Viesca
1827-1827, Victor Blanco
1827-1830, José M. Viesca
1830-1831, Rafael Eca
1831-1831, José M. Viesca
1831-1832,, José M. Letona
1832-1833, Rafael Eca
1833-1833, Juan M. Veramendi
1833-1834, Francisco Vidaurri
1834-1835, Juan J. Elguezabal
1835-1835, José M. Cantú
1835-1835, Marcial Borrego
1835-1835, Agustín Viesca
1835-1835, Miguel Falcón
1835-1835, Bartolomé Cárdenas
1835-1835, Rafael Eca

LOUISIANA
1766-1768, Antonio de Ulloa

1768-1769, Philippe Aubry
1769-1770, Alejandro O'Reilly
1770-1777, Luis Unzaga Amézaga
1777-1785, Bernardo de Gálvez
1785-1791, Esteban Rodrigo Miró
1791-1797, Barón de Carondelet
1797-1799, Manuel Gayoso Lemos
1799-1801, Marqués de Casa C.
1801-1803, Juan Manuel Salcedo

CALIFORNIA
1768-1770, Gaspar de Portolá
1770-1775, Felipe de Barri
1775-1782, Felipe de Neve
1782-1791, Pedro Fagés
1791-1792, José Antonio Romeu
1792-1794, José J. Arrillaga
1794-1800, Diego de Borica
1800-1814, José J. Arrillaga
1814-1815, José Argüello
1815-1822, Pablo Vicente Solá
1822-1825, Luis Argüello
1825-1831, José M. Echeandia
1831-1832, Manuel Victoria
1832-1832, Pío Pico
1832-1833, José M. Echeandia
1832-1833, Agustín M. Zamorano
1833-1835, José Figueroa
1835-1836, José Castro
1836-1836, Nicolás Gutiérrez
1836-1836, Mariano Chico
1836-1836, Nicolás Gutiérrez
1836-1842, Juan B. Alvarado
1842-1845, Manuel Micheltorena
1845-1846, Pío Pico
1845-1846, José Castro
1875-1875, Romualdo Pacheco

ARIZONA
1975-1977, Raúl H. Castro

Spanish Missions in the United States

The following lists are based on those given by John H. Hahn (*The Americas*, v.XLVI), George B. Eckart (*Little Known Missions in Texas*), Carlos Fernández Shaw (*Presencia Española en Estados Unidos*), and Earle R. Forrest (*Missions and Pueblos of the Old Southwest*). The dates may vary since the sources give different dates, depending on the initiation of construction, the dedication, the transfer to another place, or the first time they appear on a list or report. Some of these were "*Visitas*" (Chapels) serviced by the main mission.

PUERTO RICO
1510, Mission of Caparra

SOUTH CAROLINA
1526, San Miguel of Guadalupe
1568, Mission of Santa Elena
1570, Mission of Escamacú

NORTH CAROLINA
1566, Mission of Guatari
1574, Mission of Joada

VIRGINIA
1570, Mission of Axacán

ALABAMA
1560, Santa Cruz (Nanicapan)

FLORIDA
1539, Anhaica, Apalache
1559, Santa María Filipina Ochuse
1565, Mission Nombre de Dios
1567, Mission of Tequesta
1567, Mission of Palican
1567, Mission of Soloy
1567, San Antonio de Carlos
1570, Mission of Tupiqui
1577, San Sebastián
1587, San Juan del Puerto
1587, San Antonio (Enacape)
1587, Santa Ana, Potano
1602, Mission of Tocoy
1602, Mission of San Julián
1602, Santo Domingo (Napa)

1602, Santa María
1602, Mission of Veracruz
1602, Mission of Potayo
1602, San Mateo (St.John River)
1602, San Pablo del Puerto
1602, Mission of Hicachirico
1602, Mission of Chinisca
1602, Mission of Carabay
1602, Cascanque and Ycafui
1602, Mission of Socochuno
1604, Mission of Olatayco
1604, Mission of Molo
1607, San Francisco(Potano)
1610, San Miguel (Potano)
1610, San Buenaventura (Potano)
1610, San Martín (Ayacatu)
1612, San Juan (Guácara)
1612, Santa Cruz (Tarihica)
1616, Santa Fe (Toloco)
1616, San Luis (Acuera)
1616, Mission of Apalo
1630, San Luis (Eloquale)
1633, San Lorenzo (Ivitachuco)
1645, San Diego (Laca)
1647, San Pedro (Patale II)
1651, San Luis (Xinayca)
1651, San Miguel (Asile)
1655, San Ildefonso (Chamini)
1655, Santa Cruz (Cachipile)
1655, San Francisco (Chuaquín)
1655, Santa Catalina (Afuica)
1655, Santa Elena (Machaba)
1655, San Mateo (Tolopatafi)
1655, San Diego (Salamototo)

311

1655, Santa María (Ayubale)
1655, San Francisco (Oconi)
1655, San José (Ocuia)
1655, San Juan (Aspalaga)
1655, San Juan (Aspalaga II)
1655, Ss. Pedro/Pablo (Patale)
1655, San Martín (Tomole)
1655, Santa Lucía (Acuera)
1655, San Salvador (Macaya)
1656, San Damián (Ilcombe)
1656, San Luis (Xinayca)
1657, San Antonio (Bacuqua)
1657, Santa María (Bacuqua)
1657, Ss. Cosme/Damián (Escambé)
1672, Candelaria de Tama
1672, Santa Cruz (Ytuchafun)
1672, S. Pedro Alcántara (Ytuchafun)
1674, San Carlos (Los Chacatos)
1674, San Nicolás de Tolentino
1674, Santa Cruz (Sabacola)
1675, Asunción (Puerto)
1675, San Carlos (Los Chacatos)
1678, Santa Rosa (Ivitanayo)
1680, San Pedro (Los Chines)
1680, San Antonio (Anacapi)
1680, San Salvador (Macaya)
1680, San Felipe (Amelia Is.)
1680, Santa Clara (Amelia Is.)
1686, San Carlos (Los Chacatos)
1689, Santa Cruz (Guadalquini)
1689, San Nicolás (Apalachicola)
1689, Santa Catalina (Is.Amelia)
1693, San José (Jororo)
1694, San Antonio (Los Chines)
1697, La Misión Calusa
1699, La Concepción (Atoyquime)
1699, Mission of Atisme
1704, Mission of Ivitachuco
1717, Santa Catalina (Ibaja)
1717, San Buenaventura (Palica)
1717, Candelaria (La Tamaja)
1717, San José (Jororó)
1717, Misión de los Dolores
1717, Misión de Pocosapa

1717, El Rosario (Jabosaya)
1717, Misión de Pocotalaca
1717, Misión de Tolomato

GEORGIA
1568, Mission of Güale
1570, Mission of Tupiqui
1585, San Pedro (Mocama)
1587, Ss. Pedro/Pablo(Puturibato)
1587, Santa Catalina (Güale)
1587, San
  Buenaventura(Güadalquini)
1587, Santo Domingo (Asao)
1587, Santo Domingo (Is. S. Simón)
1595, Guadalupe (Tolomato)
1595, Santa Clara (Tupiqui)
1597, Mission of Espogache
1597, Mission of Ospo (Tulapo)
1597, Mission of Tulafina
1597, Mission of Ivi
1602, Santa Maria de Sena
1602, San Antonio (Aratabo)
1602, Chica Faya (Magdalena)
1602, Santiago (Ocone)
1605, San José (Zapala)
1609, Mission of Yoa
1616, Santa Isabel (Utinahica)
1616, San Pedro (Athuluteca)
1616, San Diego (Satuache)
1616, San Felipe (Alabe)
1630, San Agustín (Urica)
1630, Los Angeles (Arapaha)
1675, San Simón (Is. S. Simón)
1675, Ocotonico (Is. S. Simón)
1675, San Felipe (Cumberland)
1679 Mission of Savácola
1686 San Carlos de Savácola

NEW MEXICO
1590, San Juan
1591, San Marcos (San Marcos)
1598, San Lorenzo de Picuris
1598, San Jerónimo (Taos)
1598, La Asunción (Zia)

1598, Monastery of Gipuy Viejo
1599, Santa Ana (Tamayo)
1599, Fernandez de Taos(Fernandez)
1601, San Diego Jémez(Gyusiwa)
1605, San Domingo (Huashpatzena)
1605, San Felipe (S. Felipe)
1605, San José Jémez (Patoqua)
1605, San Miguel (Santa Fe)
1608, Mission of Nambe
1610, Santa Ana(Alamillo)
1614, San Francisco(Sandía)
1617, San Buenaventura (Cochiti)
1617, San Ildefonso
1617, Mission of Pecos (Pecos)
1617, Santa Cruz (Galisteo)
1626, Santa Clara (Tuva)
1626, San Luis Obispo (Sevilleta)
1626, Monasterio Socorro (Texas)
1627, San Juan Jémez (Astilakwa)
1627, San Francisco (Santa Fe)
1628, San Esteban Rey (Acoma)
1629, Immac. Conception (Hawikuh)
1629, Halona (Halona, Cíbola)
1629, Immac. Conception (Quaray)
1629, San Miguel (Tajique)
1629, San Gregorio (Abó)
1629, Monte Gran Quivira (Tabira)
1629, San Antonio (Isleta)
1629, San Pascual (Socorro)
1629, San Antonio (Senecú)
1629, Mission of San Lázaro
1630, Our Lady of Navidad (Chilili)
1640, Guadalupe (Santa Fe)
1660, Santa Ana (Alameda)
1661, San Pedro del Cuchillo
1680, San Cristóbal (S. Cristóbal)
1680, Mission of la Ciénaga
1692, Capilla Rosario (Santa Fe)
1692, Iglesia Agua Fría (Santa Fe)
1692, San Juan (San Juan)
1695, Santa Cruz (Santa Cruz)
1699, San José (Laguna)
1699, Mission of Zuñi
1706, San Felipe (Albuquerque)

1706, Guadalupe (Pojoaque)
1709, San Agustín (Isleta)
1746, Mission of Cebolleta
1754, Our Lady of la Luz (Santa Fe)
1767, Our Lady of Belén (Valencia)
1772, San Francisco (Rancho Taos)
1776, Capilla Cementerio (Santa Fe)
1828, Capilla Ortizea (Santa Fe)
1846, Capilla de Vigilias (Santa Fe)

ARIZONA

1629, San Bernardino (Awatobi)
1629, San Francisco (Oraibi)
1629, San Bartolomé (Mishongnovi)
1629, Mission Walpi (Kisakobi)
1687, San Gabriel (Guevavi)
1692, San José (Tumacacori)
1694, San Cayetano (Calabazas)
1699, San Francisco (Ati)
1699, San Marcelo (Sonoita)
1699, San Serafín (S. Javier Bac)
1700, Ss. José/Agustín (Tucson)
1701, San Luis (Guevavi)
1702, San Ignacio (Sonoita)
1702, Mission Arivaca (Guevavi)
1732, Mission Jamac (Guevavi)
1752, Santa Gertrudis (Tubac)

TEXAS

1660, San Antonio (Senecú)
1670, La Concepción (Socorro)
1680, Corpus Christi (Isleta)
1680, Our Lady of Socorro (Socorro)
1684, Santiago (Alamitos)
1684, Navidad de las Cruces
1684, San Clemente
1690, Nombre de María (Texas)
1690, San Francisco de los Texas
1699, San Juan Bautista
1700, San Francisco Solano
1702, San Bernardo
1715, San Cristóbal
1715, San Antonio (La Junta)
1715, San Francisco de los Julimes

1715, San José (La Junta)
1716, Guadalupe (Nacogdoches)
1716, Purísima Concepción (Aynais)
1716, La Misión (Redford)
1716, La Candelaria
1716, San Antonio (Puliques)
1716, N.P. San Francisco
1716, Los Dolores (Los Ais)
1716, San José (Nazones)
1716, Santa María Redonda(Cíbola)
1716, Mission of las Cíbolas
1718, San Antonio Valero (Alamo)
1720, Ss. José/Miguel (Agüayo)
1721, Our Lady of la Bahía
1722, San Francisco Xavier (Nájera)
1726, Espíritu Santo (Zúñiga)
1726, San Pedro A.(Tapalcomes)
1730, San Francisco(Neches)
1731, San Francisco de la Espada
1731, Purísima Concepción (Acuña)
1731, San Juan Capistrano
1748, San Javier de Horcasitas
1749, San Ildefonso
1749, La Candelaria (Milani)
1754, Our Lady of El Rosario
1756, Guadalupe (Río San Javier)
1756, La Luz (Orocoquisac)
1757, Santa Cruz (San Saba)
1762, San Lorenzo (Santa Cruz)

1767, La Candelaria (El Cañón)
1773, El Pilar (Bucareli)
1793, Our Lady of el Refugio

LOUISIANA
1716, San Miguel (Los Adaes)

CALIFORNIA
1769, San Diego de Alcalá
1770, San Carlos (Carmel)
1771, San Antonio (Jolón)
1771, San Gabriel Arcángel
1772, San Luis Obispo
1776, San Francisco de Asís
1776, San Juan Capistrano
1777, Santa Clara
1782, San Buenaventura
1786, Santa Bárbara
1787, Purísima Concepción
1791, Mission of Santa Cruz
1791, La Soledad
1797, S.José Guadalupe
1797, San Juan Bautista
1797, San Miguel Arcángel
1797, San Fernando Rey
1798, San Luis(Oceanside)
1804, Santa Inés(Solvang)
1817, San Rafael Arcángel
1823, San Francisco Solano

Spanish Forts in the United States

This list is based on the ones provided by Carlos Fernandez Shaw in *Presencia Española in the United States* and by Sydney B. Brinckerhoff in *Lancers for the King*.

PUERTO RICO
Castillo del Morro
Fort San Cristóbal

NORTH CAROLINA
San Juan Xualla
Guatari
Cauchi

SOUTH CAROLINA
San Felipe
San Marcos

GEORGIA
Santa Catalina de Güale
Zapala
Espogache

314

Chiaha
Coweta
San Pedro

FLORIDA
San Carlos (Fernandina)
San Mateo
Picolata
Diego
Mosa
San Marcos (San Agustín)
Matanzas
Tequesta
Santa Lucía
San Carlos (Calus)
Tocobaga
San Luis (Apalache)
San Marcos (Apalache)
San Carlos de Austria
San Bernardo (Pensacola)
San Miguel
Sombrero
Merino Fort
Rosario Fort
Nogales
San Esteban de Tombecbe
San Fernando de las Barrancas

TENNESSEE
Manchester
San Fernando de Barrancas

ALABAMA
Esteban
Confederación
Spanish Fort (Mobile)
Carlota

MISSISSIPPI
Nogales
Panmure

LOUISIANA
Spanish Fort (New Orléans)

Manchac
Baton Rouge
Galvestown
Miró
El Pilar de los Adaes

ARKANSAS
Arkansas Post
Esperanza

MISSOURI
San Carlos
Don Carlos Tercero el Rey
Don Carlos Príncipe de Asturias

MICHIGAN
San José (Conquistado)

COLORADO
Sangre de Cristo Pass

TEXAS
Old Stone Fort (Nacogdoches)
Nuestra Señora de los Dolores
San Agustín de Ahumada
Our Lady of Loreto (La Bahía)
San Francisco Xavier Horcasitas
San Luis de las Amarillas
Santa Cruz de San Saba
San Fernando de Béjar
Sacramento
San Elizario
Del Norte
Bucarelli
Arroyo de Cíbolo
Laredo

NEW MEXICO
Taos
Santa Fe
Albuquerque
Socorro
Robledo

ARIZONA
Tubac
San Agustín (Tucson)
Yuma
Quiburi
San Bernardino

CALIFORNIA
Guijarros

San Diego
Santa Bárbara
Monterey
San Francisco (Yerbabuena)

GUAM
Santiago
Santa Soledad
Santa Cruz

Missionary Martyrs in the United States

This list is based on *Heroes of the Cross* by Marion A. Habig, O.F.M. (The date indicates the year of martyrdom.)

1542, Juan Padilla, O.F.M. (Kansas)
1542, Luis Escalona, O.F.M. (New Mexico)
1542, Juan de la Cruz (New Mexico)
1549, Luis Cáncer, O.P. (Florida)
1549, Diego Tolosa, O.P. (Florida)
1549, Hermano Fuentes, O.P. (Florida)
1553, Diego de la Cruz, O.P. (Texas)
1553, Hernando Méndez, O.P. (Texas)
1553, Juan Ferrer, O.P. (Texas)
1553, Juan Mena, O.P. (Texas)
1566, Pedro Martínez, S.J. (Florida)
1570, Juan B. Segura, S.J. (Virginia)
1570, Luis Quirós, S.J. (Virginia)
1570, Juan B. Méndez, S.J. (Virginia)
1570, Gabriel Solís, S.J. (Virginia)
1570, Pedro Linares, S.J. (Virginia)
1570, Cristóbal Redondo, S.J. (Virginia)
1570, Sancho Zeballos, S.J. (Virginia)
1570, Gabriel Gómez, S.J. (Virginia)
1581, Francisco López, O.F.M. (New Mexico)
1581, Agustín Rodríguez, O.F.M. (New Mexico)
1581, Juan de Santa María, O.F.M. (New Mexico)

1597, Pedro de Corpa, O.F.M. (Georgia)
1597, Miguel Añón, O.F.M. (Georgia)
1597, Francisco Berascola, O.F.M. (Georgia)
1597, Blas Rodríguez, O.F.M. (Georgia)
1597, Antonio Badajoz, O.F.M. (Georgia)
1631, Pedro Miranda, O.F.M. (New Mexico)
1631, Pedro Ortega, O.F.M. (New Mexico)
1632, Francisco Letrado, O.F.M. (New Mexico)
1632, Martín Arvide, O.F.M. (Arizona)
1633, Andrés Gutiérrez, O.F.M. (Arizona)
1633, Francisco Porras, O.F.M. (Arizona)
1633, Cristóbal de Concepción, O.F.M. (Arizona)
1647, Three Franciscans (Florida)
1670, Pedro Ávila, O.F.M. (New Mexico)
1675, Alonso Gil, O.F.M. (New Mexico)

1680, Juan Bautista Pío, O.F.M. (New Mexico)

1680, Juan Bernal, O.F.M. (New Mexico)

1680, José Trujillo, O.F.M. (Arizona)

1680, Fernando Velasco, O.F.M. (New Mexico)

1680, Tomás Torres, O.F.M. (New Mexico)

1680, Luis Morales, O.F.M. (New Mexico)

1680, Antonio Sánchez, O.F.M. (New Mexico)

1680, Matías Rendón, O.F.M. (New Mexico)

1680, Antonio Mora, O.F.M. (New Mexico)

1680, Manuel Tinoco, O.F.M. (New Mexico)

1680, Francisco Lorenzana, O.F.M. (New Mexico)

1680, Juan Talabán, O.F.M. (New Mexico)

1680, José Montes de Oca, O.F.M. (New Mexico)

1680, Juan de Jesús María, O.F.M. (New Mexico)

1680, Lucas Maldonado, O.F.M. (New Mexico)

1680, Juan del Val, O.F.M. (New Mexico)

1680, José Figueroa, O.F.M. (Arizona)

1680, José Espeleta, O.F.M. (Arizona)

1680, Agustín de Santa María, O.F.M. (Arizona)

1680, Juan Pedrosa, O.F.M. (New Mexico)

1680, Domingo Vera, O.F.M. (New Mexico)

1682, Francisco López, O.F.M. (New Mexico)

1683, Antonio Guerra, O.F.M. (New Mexico)

1683, Simón de Jesús, O.F.M. (New Mexico)

1683, Manuel Beltrán, O.F.M. (Texas)

1696, Luis Sánchez Pacheco, O.F.M. (Florida)

1696, Francisco Corvera, O.F.M. (New Mexico)

1696, Antonio Moreno, O.F.M. (New Mexico)

1696, Antonio Carbonell, O.F.M. (New Mexico)

1696, José Arbizu, O.F.M. (New Mexico)

1696, Francisco Casañas, O.F.M, (New Mexico)

1704, Juan de Parga, O.F.M. (Florida)

1704, Manuel Mendoza, O.F.M. (Florida)

1704, Angel Miranda, O.F.M. (Florida)

1704, Tiburcio Osorio, O.F.M. (Florida)

1704, Agustín Ponce de León, O.F.M. (Florida)

1704, Marcos Delgado, O.F.M. (Florida)

1704, Domingo Criado, O.F.M. (Florida)

1718, Luis Montes de Oca, O.F.M. (Texas)

1720, Juan Mínguez, O.F.M. (Nebraska)

1721, José Pita, O.F.M. (Texas)

1731, Domingo Saraoz, O.F.M. (New Mexico)

1749, Francisco J. Silva, O.F.M. (Texas)

1751, Francisco Tello, S.J. (Arizona)

1751, Enrique Ruhen, S.J. (Arizona)

1752, José Francisco Ganzabal, O.F.M. (Texas)

1758, Alonso Giraldo Terreros
(Texas)
1758, José Santiestéban, O.F.M.
(Texas)
1775, Luis Jayme, O.F.M.
(California)
1781, Juan Díaz, O.F.M.
(California)
1781, José M. Moreno, O.F.M.
(California)

1781, Francisco Garcés, O.F.M.
(California)
1781, Juan Barreneche, O.F.M.
(California)
1801, Francisco Pujol, O.F.M.
(California)
1812, Andrés Quintana, O.F.M.
(California)
1834, Antonio Díaz de León, O.F.M.
(Texas)

Bishops of Hispanic Origin in the United States

(The date indicates the year of episcopal consecration.)

1709, Dionisio Resinó (Florida)
1731, Francisco Martínez Tejada,
O.F.M. (Florida)
1787, Cirilo Barcelona, O.F.M. Cap.
(Louisiana/Florida)
1793, Luis Peñalver (New Orleans)
1801, Francisco Porro Reinado, O.
Min. (Louisiana/Florida)
1840, Francisco García Diego,
O.F.M. (California)
1850, José S. Alemany, O.P. (San
Francisco)
1854, Tadeo Amat, C.M. (Monterey)
1860, Miguel Domenec, C.M.
(Pittsburgh)
1873, Francisco Mora (Monterey)
1874, Antonio Pellicer (San Antonio)
1890, Pedro Verdaguer (Brownsville)
1934, José Preciado Nieva, C.M.F.
(San Antonio)
1936, Mariano Garriga (Corpus
Christi)
1970, Patricio F. Flores (San Antonio)
1971, Juan A. Arzube (Los Angeles)
1972, René H. Gracida (Corpus
Christi)
1974, Gilberto E. Chávez (San Diego)

1974, Roberto F. Sánchez (Santa
Fe)
1976, Raymundo J. Peña (El Paso)
1977, Manuel D. Moreno (Tucson)
1977, Francisco Garmendia (New
York)
1979, Agustín A. Román (Miami)
1980, José J. Madera, M.Sp.S.
(Fresno)
1980, Arturo N. Tafoya (Pueblo)
1980, René A. Valero (Brooklyn)
1981, Alfonso Gallegos, O.A.R.
(Sacramento)
1981, Ricardo Ramírez, C.S.B. (Las
Cruces)
1983, David Arias, O.A.R. (Newark)
1983, Plácido Rodríguez, C.M.F.
Chicago)
1985, Alvaro Corrada, S.J.
(Washington D.C.)
1986, Enrique San Pedro, S.J.
(Galveston/Houston)
1987, Armando Ochoa (Los Angeles)
1988, Roberto O. González, O.F.M.
(Boston)
1989, Carlos A. Sevilla, S.J. (San
Francisco)

Hispanic Bishops, Resident or on Pastoral Visit

(The date indicates the year of their visitation or residence)

1606, Juan Cabezas Altamirano
(Florida)
1674, Gabriel Díaz Vara Calderón
(Florida)
1727, Benito Crespo (Arizona)
1737, Martín Elizacochea (New
Mexico)
1760, Pedro Tamarón Romeral (New
Mexico)
1762, Agustín Morell (Florida)
1833, Antonio Zubiria (New
Mexico)

Queen Isabella's Proclamation on the Treatment of Indians

"Medina del Campo
"November 23, 1504

"In the name of the holy Trinity: Father, Son, and Holy Spirit. May all those who see this codicil letter as I, Doña Isabel, by the grace of God, Queen of Castile, León, Aragón, Sicily, Granada, Toledo, Valencia, Galicia, Mallorca, Seville, Sardinia, Córdoba, Corcega, Murcia, Jaen, Los Algarbes, Algeciras, Gibraltar, Canary Islands, Countess of Barcelona, Lady of Vizcaya and Molina, Duchess of Athens and Neopatria, Countess of Rosellón and Cerdania, Marquise of Oritan and Goceano, say that I made and gave my testament before Gaspar de Grizio, my secretary. . . .

"At the time when the islands and firm land of the Ocean Sea, discovered and to be discovered, were given to us by the Holy Apostolic See, it was our main intention, when we asked this from Pope Alexander VI of good memory, who gave us this grant, to try to induce to and bring the peoples from there and to convert them to our holy catholic faith, and to send to the said islands and firm land prelates, and religious, and clergy, and other learned and God-fearing persons to teach its citizens and dwellers the catholic faith and to teach and instruct them in good morals, and to do it with great diligence in accordance to the more extensive letters by which this grant was given. Therefore, I ask the King, my lord, with great affection and entrust and command to the Princess, my daughter, and to the Prince, her husband, that thus they act, and fulfill it, and that this ought to be their main goal, and that they put in it a great diligence, and that they should not permit or give an occasion that the Indian citizens and dwellers of the said islands and firm land, acquired or to be acquired, receive any harm in their persons or in their possessions, even more they must order that they should be well and justly treated, and if they have received any harm they should amend it and see to it that in no way they should go beyond what is urged and commanded to us by the apostolic letters of the said grant.

319

"And I say and declare that this is my will which I wish to be valid by way of codicil and if it were not valid by way of codicil I wish to be valid by whatever other means as my last will or by whatever way it might or should be valid. And so that this be firm and there be no doubt, I gave this letter of codicil before Gaspar de Grizio, my secretary, and the witnesses who signed and sealed it with their seals, which was given at the Villa of Medina del Campo, on the twenty-third day of the month of November, the year of the Nativity of our Savior Jesus Christ of one thousand five hundred and four, and I signed it with my name before the said witnesses and I order to be sealed with my seal.

"I, the Queen Isabel" (sig.)

Witnesses:
Don Fadrique de Portugal, Bishop of Calahorra
Don Valeriano Ordoñez, Bishop of Ciudad Rodrigo
Dr. Martín Fernández de Angulo, Royal Council
Dr. Pedro de Oropesa, Royal Council
Lic. Luis Zapata, Royal Council

First Baptized Indians — Certificate

Facsimile of the baptismal certificate of the Indians Cristóbal and Pedro, servants of Christopher Columbus: July 29, 1496 (original kept in the the Royal Monastery of Guadalupe, Cáceres, Spain).

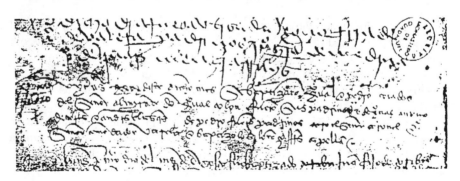

Friday, XXIX of this month, Cristóbal and Pedro were baptized, servants of Admiral Don Cristóbal Colón. Their Godparents were: for Cristóbal, Antonio Torres and Andrés Blazquez; for Pedro, señor Colonel and señor Justice Varela, and they were baptized by Lorenzo Fernandez, Chaplain" (*First Book of Baptisms*).

THE SOURCES: Notes and Bibliography

The information contained in this book comes from many sources. I would like, in particular, to mention some that have served me as the primary base of information, above all for the first part of this work. Aside from these primary sources, I have consulted a great number of other works for the second part which the reader will find mentioned in the Select Bibliography which follows.

A. Part One: Main Sources

CHAPTER I: THE POLICY OF SPAIN IN AMERICA

1. John F. Bannon: *The Spanish Borderlands Frontier*
2. Ricardo G. Villoslada: *Historia de la Iglesia en España*
3. John F. Bannon: *Op. cit.*
4. *Misioneros Extremeños* (Congress, 1986)
5. Charles Lummis: *The Spanish Pioneers*
6. John F. Bannon: *Op. cit.*
7. John F. Bannon: *Op. cit.*
8. Philip W. Powell: *Tree of Hate*
9. Philip W. Powell: *Op. cit.*
10. John G. Shea: *The Catholic Church in Colonial Days*
11. Ricardo de la Cierva: *La Gran Historia de América*
12. Lopetegui L./Zubillaga F.: *Historia de la Iglesia en América*
13. Herbert E. Bolton: *The Mission as a Frontier Institution*; Lewis Hanke: *The Spanish Struggle for Justice*
14. L. Byrd Simpson: *Los Conquistadores y el Indio Americano*
15. Francis Weber: *Catholicism in Colonial America*
    Thomas A. Bailey: *A Diplomatic History of the American People*
    Constantino Bayle: *España en Indias*
    Frank W. Blackmar: *Spanish Institutions of the Southwest*
    Herbert E. Bolton: *Defensive Spanish Expansion*
    Hodding Carter: *Doomed Road of Empire*
    José García Mercadal: *Lo que España Llevó a América*
    Lewis Hanke: *Spanish Struggle for Justice*
    John T. Lanning: *A Reconsideration of Spanish Colonial Culture*
    Charles Lummis: *Los Exploradores del Siglo XVI*
    Frederick Turner: *The Significance of the Frontier in American History*
    Dale Van Every: *Ark of Empire*

CHAPTER II: EXPLORATIONS IN THE UNITED STATES

1. John F. Bannon: *The Spanish Borderlands Frontier*
2. Earle R. Forrest: *Missions and Pueblos of the Old Southwest*
3. Charles Lummis: *Spanish Pioneers*
4. Herbert H. Bolton: *Spanish Explorations in the Southwest*

5. Lucio Mijares: *El Mundo Social de los Conquistadores* (Conf. "La Huella de España en América," 1986)
6. Francisco Morales Padron: *Armas Espirituales y Colaboracionismo Indigena* (Conf. "La Huella de España en America")
7. John F. Bannon: *Op. cit.*
8. Guillermo Céspedes del Castillo: *Economia y Comercio Indianos en el Siglo XVI* (Conf. "La Huella de España en America")
9. Paul I. Wellman: *Glory, God, and Gold*
10. J. Milanich & S. Milbrath: *First Encounters*
11. John F. Bannon: *Op. cit.*
12. Guillermo Céspedes: *Op. cit.*
13. Jerónimo Mendieta: *Historia Eclesiastica* (V; cap.III)
14. John F. Bannon: *Op. cit.*
15. Javier Ybarra y Berge: *De California a Alaska*; Alvaro del Portillo: *Descubrimiento en California*
16. Maria L. Ramos Catalina: *Expediciones Cientificas a California*
17. Herbert E. Bolton: *Colonization of North America*
18. Charles Lummis: *The Spanish Pioneers*
19. Hodding Carter: *Doomed Road of Empire*
20. Arturo Morales Carrión: *Historia del Pueblo Puertorriqueño*
21. Philip W. Powell: *Tree of Hate*
22. Paul E. Hoffman: *A New Andalucia*
23. Javier Ybarra y Berge: *Op. cit.*
24. Alvar Nuñez Cabeza de Vaca: *Naufragios y Comentarios*
25. Paul E. Hoffman: *Op. cit.*
26. John F. Bannon: *Op. cit.*
27. Pedro Borges M.: *Conquista y Evangelización* (Conf. "La Huella de España en America," 1986)
28. Philip W. Powell: *Op. cit.*
    Fidel Blanco Castillo: *Hernando de Soto, el Centauro del Norte*
    John A. Caruso: *Southern Frontier*
    Bernard de Voto: *Spanish Presence in the Northwest*
    Paul Horgan: *Great River*
    Paul Horgan: *Conquistadors in North American History*
    John Jennings: *The Golden Eagle*
    Irving Kull: *American History*
    Francisco Morales Padrón: *Conquistadores Españoles en U.S.A.*
    Irving B. Richman: *The Spanish Conquerors*
    Ronald Syme: *First Man to Cross America*
    H.R. Wagner: *Juan Rodríguez Cabrillo, Discoverer of California*

CHAPTER III: COLONIZATION IN THE UNITED STATES

1. Guillermo Céspedes: *La Economia y el Comercio Indianos en el Siglo XVI* (Conf."La Huella de España en America")

2. Dario Fernandez: *The Spanish Heritage in the United States*
3. Charles Lummis: *The Spanish Pioneers*
4. Luciano Pereña: *Catecismo Limense*
5. John F. Bannon: *The Spanish Borderlands Frontier*
6. Francisco Morales Padrón: *Armas Espirituales y Colaboracionismo Indigena* (Conf. "La Huella de España en America")
7. Maria L. Martínez Salinas: *La Hacienda Indiana en el Siglo XVI* (Conf. "La Huella de España en America")
8. Francisco Solano: *La Fundacion de las Ciudades Americanas* (Conf. "La Huella de España en America," 1987)
9. John F. Bannon: *Op. cit.*
10. Moisés Sandoval: *Fronteras*
11. John T. Lanning: *The Spanish Missions of Georgia*
12. John F. Bannon: *The Spanish Borderlands Frontier*
13. J. Milanich/S. Milbrath: *First Encounters*
14. Julián Marias: *La Integración del Mundo* (Conf. "La Huella de España en America")
15. Maynard Geiger: *The Franciscan Conquest of Florida*
16. John F. Bannon: *Op. clt.*
17. Pedro Borges M.: *Primera Etapa de la Evangelización de America* (Conf. "La Huella de España en America")
18. Maynard Geiger: *Op. cit.*
19. Julián Marias: *Op. cit.*
20. Philip W. Powell: *Tree of Hate*
21. Paul Horgan: *Great River*
22. Julián Marias: *Op. cit.*
23. Arturo Morales Carrión: *Historia del Pueblo Puertorriqueño*
24. Georges Baudot: *Vida Cotidiana en la America Española del Siglo XVI* (Conf. "La Huella de España en America")
25. Carlos Fernandez Shaw: *La Presencia de España en Estados Unidos*
26. Warren Beck: *New Mexico*
27. Guillermo Céspedes: *La Economia y el Comercio en el Siglo XVI* (Conf. "La Huella de España en America," 1986)
28. Herbert E. Bolton: *The Padre on Horseback*
29. Carlos Fernandez Shaw: *La Presencia Española en Estados Unidos*
30. Guillermo Céspedes del Castillo: *Op. cit.*
31. Georges Baudot: *Op. cit.*
32. Carlos E. Castañeda: *Our Catholic Heritage in Texas*
33. Carlos M. Fernandez Shaw: *Op. cit.*; R. Newcombe: *Spanish Colonial Architecture in the United States*
34. Julián Marias: *Op. cit.*
35. Carlos M. Fernandez Shaw: *Op. cit.*
36. John F. Bannon: *Op. cit.*
37. Ricardo de la Cierva: *La Gran Historia de America* (Rev. Epoca)

38. Guillermo Céspedes: *Op. cit.*
39. *Ibid.*; Georges Baudot: *Op. cit.*
40. Carlos Fernandez Shaw: *Op. cit.*
41. Guillermo Céspedes: *Op. cit.*
42. J. Milanich/S. Milbrath: *Op. cit.*
43. John F. Bannon: *Op. cit.*
44. Carlos Fernandez Shaw: *Op. cit.*
45. Jose Garcia Mercadal: *Lo que España Llevó a America*
46. Salvador de Madariaga: *El Auge y el Ocaso del Imperio Español en America*
   Herbert H. Bancroft: *Arizona and New Mexico*
   Herbert H. Bancroft: *The North Mexican States and Texas*
   Warren A. Beck: *A History of Four Centuries*
   Frank W. Blackmar: *Spanish Colonization in the Southwest*
   Herbert Bolton: *Texas in the Middle of the 18th Century*
   Herbert Bolton: *Colonization of North America*
   Edward G. Bourne: *Spain in America*
   Eugene Lyon: *The Enterprise of Florida*, 1976
   Juan F. Cárdenas: *Hispanic Culture and Language in the U.S.*
   Gorton Carruth: *Encyclopedia of American Facts*
   George M. Foster: *Culture and Conquest, America's Spanish Heritage*
   Stanley T. Williams: *The Spanish Background of American Literature*

CHAPTER IV: EVANGELIZATION IN THE UNITED STATES

1. Paul Horgan: *Great River*
2. Pedro Borges: *El Envío de Misioneros a América durante la Epoca Española*
3. John F. Bannon: *The Spanish Borderlands Frontier*; Congreso Internacional 1988: *Los Dominicos en el Nuevo Mundo*
4. John F. Bannon: *Op. cit.*
5. Herbert E. Bolton: *The Mission as a Frontier Institution*
6. Francis Weber: *Catholicism in Colonial America (Homiletic Rev.)*
7. Herbert E. Bolton: *Op. cit.*
8. John G. Shea: *The Catholic Church in Colonial Days*
9. Herbert E. Bolton: *Op. cit.*
10. Pedro Borges: *La Primera Etapa de la Evangelización en América* (Conf. "La Huella de España en América")
11. *Ibid.*
12. John G. Shea: *Op. cit.*
13. Congreso 1986: *Franciscanos Extremeños en el Nuevo Mundo*
14. Herbert E. Bolton: *Op. cit.*
15. Pedro Borges Morán: *Op. cit.*
16. Michael V. Gannon: *The Cross in the Sand*
17. John F. Bannon: *Op. cit.*
18. Herbert E. Bolton: *Op. cit.*; Carlos Alvear A.: *Medio Milenio de Evangelización*

19. Congreso Inter. 1985: *Los Franciscanos en el Nuevo Mundo*
20. Clifford Lewis: *The Spanish Mission in Virginia*
21. Congreso Inter. 1988: *Op. cit.*
22. Congreso Inter. 1985: *Op. cit.*
23. Paulino Castañeda: *La Organización Eclesiástica de América en el Siglo XVI* (Conf. "La Huella de España en América")
24. Congreso Inter. 1988: *Op. cit.*
25. Congreso Inter. 1985: *Op. cit.*
26. John T. Lanning: *The Spanish Missions of Georgia*
27. John F. Bannon: *Op. cit.*
28. Pedro Borges: *Op. cit.*
29. *Ibid.*
30. John F. Bannon: *Op. cit.*
31. Herbert E. Bolton: *Op. cit.*
32. Carlos Fernández Shaw: *Presencia Española en Estados Unidos*
33. John G. Shea: *The Catholic Church in Colonial Days*
34. Congreso Inter. 1985: *Op. cit.*
35. Pedro Borges: *Op. cit.*
36. John T. Lanning: *Op. cit.*
37. Warren Beck: *New Mexico*
38. Congreso 1986: *Franciscanos Extremeños en el Nuevo Mundo*
39. Congreso Inter. 1985: *Op. cit.*
40. John T. Lanning: *Op. cit.*
41. Rafael González Moralejo: *Los Religiosos en la Evangelización de América* (1988)
42. Paul E. Hoffman: *A New Andalucia*
43. Clifford Lewis: *The Spanish Mission in Virginia*
44. John F. Bannon: *Op. cit.*
45. John G. Shea: *Op. cit.*
46. Alvar Núñez Cabeza de Vaca: *Naufragios y Comentarios*; John Caruso: *The Southern Frontier*
47. Warren Beck: *Op. cit.*
48. Herbert E. Bolton: *The Mission as a Frontier Institution*
49. John F. Bannon: *Op. cit.*
50. Alvar Núñez Cabeza de Vaca: *Op. cit.*; John T. Lanning: *Op. cit.*
51. John G. Shea: *Op. cit.*
52. John T. Lanning: *Op. cit.*
53. John Caruso: *Op. cit.*
54. Warren Beck: *Op. cit.*
55. Herbert E. Bolton: *Op. cit.*
56. Maynard Geiger: *The Franciscan Conquest of Florida*
    Herbert E. Bolton: *The Padre on Horseback*
    George B. Eckart: *Missions of Sonora*
    Earle R. Forrest: *Missions and Pueblos in the Old Southwest*

John H. Hann: *Guide to Spanish Florida Missions (The Americas)*
John H. Hann: *Apalache — Land Between the Rivers*
Hildegarde Hawthorne: *California's Missions*
John Tracy Ellis: *Catholics in Colonial America*
Ralph B. Wright: *California Missions*
Zubillaga y Lopetegui: Historia de la Iglesia en America (BAC)

CHAPTER V: SPAIN AND THE INDEPENDENCE OF THE UNITED STATES

1. Buchanam P. Thompson: *La Ayuda de España en la Guerra de la Independencia de Estados Unidos*
2. Juan F. Yela Utrilla: *España ante la Independencia de Estados Unidos*
3. Francisco Morales Padrón: *Participación de España en la Independencia de Estados Unidos*
4. Salvador de Madariaga: *El Auge y el Ocaso del Imperio Español en América*
5. Letter of the North American Emissaries to Count of Aranda, December 6, 1776
6. Buchanam P. Thompson: *Op. cit.*
7. Juan F. Yela Utrilla: *Op. cit.*
8. Manuel Conrotte: *La Intervención de España en la Independencia de Estados Unidos*
9. Francisco Morales Padrón: *Op. cit.*
10. Letter of Grimaldi to Felipe Rivero, Regent of the Crown in Pamplona, February 17, 1777
11. Buchanam P. Thompson: *Op. cit.*
12. Francisco Morales Padrón: *Op. cit.*
13. Letter of Grimaldi to Aranda, June 27, 1776
14. Letter of Aranda to Grimaldi, September 7, 1776
15. Letter of Arthur Lee to Unzaga, May 22, 1776
16. Letter of José de Gálvez to the Governor of La Habana, July 8, 1777
17. Letter of José Gálvez to Bernardo Gálvez, September 24, 1778
18. Francisco Morales Padrón: *Op. cit.*
19. Buchanam P. Thompson: *Op. cit.*
20. Francisco Morales Padrón: *Op. cit.*
21. *Ibid.*
22. *Ibid.*
23. *Ibid.*
24. Bernardo Gálvez: *Relación de los Puestos Ingleses en el Mississippi, Octubre 16, 1779*
25. Buchanam P. Thompson; *Op. cit.*
26. *Ibid.*
27. Letter of George Washington to John Sullivan, September 3, 1779
28. Fulton Sheen: *Spanish Heritage* Booklet (1976)
    Hodding Carter: *Lower Mississippi*
    Manuel Fraga I.: *Aportación de España a la Independencia de Estados Unidos*

Luis García Melero: *Independencia de Estados Unidos y la Prensa Española*
Charles Gayarre: *History of Louisiana*
Mario Hernández Sánchez B.: *Bernardo Gálvez, Militar y Político*
Jack D. Holmes: *Gayoso*
Louis Houck: *The Spanish Regime in Missouri*
Arthur Nussbaum: *A History of the Dollar*
Herminio Portell-Vila: *Los Extranjeros en la Revolución de Estados Unidos*
Mario Rodríguez: *La Revolución Americano 1776 y el Mundo Hispánico*

CHAPTER VI: "HISPANIDAD" IN THE UNITED STATES

1. Florida Treaty, 1819
2. Treaty of Guadalupe-Hidalgo, 1848, III, 8-9
3. R. Cortina/A. Moncada: *Hispanos en los Estados Unidos*
4. Alberto Moncada: *La Americanización de los Hispanos*
5. Herbert E. Bolton: *The Spanish Borderlands*
6. Francis J. Weber: *Catholicism in Colonial America*; Juan Louvier C.: *La Cruz en América*
7. Pedro Borges: *La Primera Etapa de la Evangelización de América* (Conf. "La Huella de España en América")
8. Warren Beck: *New Mexico*
9. Moisés Sandoval: *Fronteras*
10. Herbert E. Bolton: *Op. cit.*
11. Warren Beck: *Op. cit.*
12. Carlos Castañeda: *Our Catholic Heritage in Texas*
13. Manuel Gamio: *Mexican Immigration to the United States*
14. Archdiocese of Newark: *Presencia Nueva Research Study, 1988*
15. R. Cortina/A. Moncada: *Op. cit.*
16. Alberto Moncada: *Op. cit.*
17. Clara E. Rodríguez: *Puerto Ricans Born in the United States*
18. Carlos Ripoll: *Cubanos en los Estados Unidos*
19. R. Cortina/A. Moncada: *Op. cit.*
20. Carlos Castañeda: *Op. cit.*
21. Moisés Sandoval: *Op. cit.*
22. P.J. Kenedy & Sons: *The Official Catholic Directory, 1990*
23. *Ibid.*
24. U.S.C.C. Office of Publications: *National Pastoral Plan for Hispanic Ministry, 1987*
25. U.S. Bureau of Census: *The Hispanic Population in the United States, 1989*
26. Ford Foundation: *Hispanics, Challenges, and Opportunities, 1984*
27. U.S. Bureau of Census: *Op. cit.*
28. *Ibid.*
29. *Ibid.*
30. Alberto Moncada: *Op. cit.*
31. U.S. Bureau of Census: *Op. cit.*

32. R. Cortina/A. Moncada: *Op. cit.*
33. *Ibid.*
34. Roberto Gutiérrez: *Review of Hispanic Communications Media, 1990*
35. U.S.C.C. Office of Publications: *The Hispanic Presence — Challenge and Commitment, 1983*
36. Gallup Co.: *Study of Religious and Social Attitudes of Hispanic Americans, 1978*

Herbert E. Bolton: *History of the Americas*
Lawrence A. Cardoso: *Mexican Emigration to the United States*
L.H. Gann/P.J. Duignan: *The Hispanics in the United States: A History*
Hubert Herring: *History of Latin America*
J. H. Latané: *The United States and Latin America*
David Maciel y Patricia Bueno: *La Historia del Pueblo Chicano*
Joan Moore & Alfred Cuellar: *Mexican Americans*
Leonard M. Pitt: *The Decline of the Californias*
Silvio Selva: *The United States and Central America*
William R. Shepherd: *Hispanic Nations of a New World*
William R. Shepherd: *The Spanish Heritage in America*
Graham Stuart: *Latin America and the United States*
Curtis Wilgus: *The Development of Hispanic America*

B. Part Two: Select Bibliography

Acosta, José de: *De Procuranda Indorum Salute* (Consejo Sup. Inv. Cientifica, 1987)
Adams, Willi Paul: *Los Estados Unidos de America* (Ed. Siglo XXI, Mexico, 1990)
Alford, Harold J.: *The Proud Peoples* (McKay Co., 1972)
Alvear, Carlos: *Síntesis de Historia Mexicana* (Ed. Jus., Mexico 1974)
Amigo Vallejo, Carlos: *El Noventaidós* (Ed. J.R. Castillejo, Sevilla, 1990)
Andresco, Victor: *Juan de la Cosa, Gran Capitan* (Madrid, 1949)
Angle, Paul: *The American Reader* (Rand McNally, New York, 1958)
Arnade, Charles W.: *The Siege of St. Augustine in 1702* (U. of Florida Press, 1959)
Arnold, Anna E.: *A History of Kansas* (Topeka, 1914)
Arnoldson, Sverker: *La Leyenda Negra. Estudios sobre sus Orígenes* (Goteborg, 1960)
Asimov, Isaac: *El Nacimiento de los Estados Unidos* (Alianza Ed., Madrid, 1988); *La Formación de América del Norte* (Alianza Ed., Madrid, 1988)
Athearn, Frederick J.: *A Forgotten Kingdom* (Denver, Colo., 1989)
Bancroft, Hubert Howe: *Arizona and New Mexico, 1530-1888* (San Francisco 1888); *History of Nevada, Colorado, and Wyoming* (Vol.XXV; 1890); *History of North Mexican States and Texas* (Vol.XVII, 1884); *New Mexico and Texas* (Bancroft Publ., San Francisco)

Bannon, John F.: *Bolton and the Spanish Borderlands* (U. of Oklahoma Press, 1964); *The Spanish Borderland Frontier, 1513-1825* (U. of New Mexico Press, 1974)

Barcía Carballido, Andrés: *Ensayo Cronológico* (U. of Florida, Gainesville, 1951)

Barrera, Mario: *Race and Class in the Southwest* (U. of Notre Dame, 1979)

Barrientos, Bartolomé: *Pedro Menéndez de Avilés, Founder of Florida* (U. of Florida, 1965)

Bauman, J. N.: *The Names of the California Missions* (The Americas, XXI, 1965)

Bayle, Constantino: *La Expansión Misional de España* (Missionalia Hispanica, 1946); *Pedro Menéndez de Avilés* (Madrid, 1928)

Beck, Warren A.: *New Mexico* (U. of Oklahoma Press, 1962); *A History of Four Centuries* (U. of Oklahoma Press, 1963)

Benavides, Fr. Alonso de: *Memorial de 1630* (U. of New Mexico, Albuquerque Press, 1945)

Bernardino, Stephanie: *The Ethnic Almanac* (Doubleday, New York, 1981)

Bishop, Morris: *The Odyssey of Cabeza de Vaca* (New York-London, Century Co., 1933)

Bleiberg, Germán: *Diccionario de la Historia de España* (Madrid, 1953)

Bleznick, Donald W.: *Spanish and Spanish American Bibliographical Catalog* (Scarecrow Press, Metuchen, N.J., 1983)

Boid, Mark/Smith, Hale G.: *Here They Once Stood: Apalache* (Gainesville, Fla., 1988)

Bolton, Herbert Eugene: *Coronado, Knight of Pueblos and Plains* (Whittlesey House, New York, 1949); *Colonization of North America, 1492-1783* (Macmillan, New York, 1920); *Defensive Spanish Expansion* (U. of Colorado, 1929); *History of the Americas* (Ginn & Co., New York, 1928); *Texas in the Middle Eighteenth Century* (Berkeley, 1915) *The Padre on Horseback* (Loyola U. Press, 1963); *The Mission as a Frontier Institution* (American Historical Review, XXIII, 1917); *The Spanish Borderlands* (Yale U. Press, 1919); *Spanish Explorations in the Southwest* (Barnes & Noble, New York, 1963)

Bolton, Herbert E./Ross, Mary: *The Debatable Land* (Russell & Russell, New York, 1968)

Borges Morán, Pedro: *Conquista y Evangelización: Influencias Mutuas* (Conf.,1986)

Bourne, Edward G.: *Spain in America, 1550-1580* (Barnes & Noble, New York, 1962)

Boyd, E.: *Popular Arts of Colonial New Mexico* (Santa Fe Museum, 1959)

Boyd, Mark F.: *The Tragic End of the Apalache Missions* (U. of Florida, 1951)

Brinckerhoff, Sidney B.: *Lancers for the King* (Historical Society, Phoenix, Ariz., 1965)

Brooks, C. M.: *Texas Missions, Their Romance and Architecture* (Dallas, Tex., 1936)

Brune, Lester H.: *Chronological History of United States Foreign Relations* (Garland Pub., New York, 1985)

Burrus, Ernest J.: *Kino en Route to Sonora* (The Western Explorer III, 1964)

Cabeza de Vaca, Alvar Núñez: *Naufragios y Comentarios* (Espasa Calpe, 1932)

Callaway, James E.: *The Early Settlements of Georgia* (U. of Georgia Press, 1948)

Calle, Juan Diez: *Memorial de Noticias Sacras* (Hispanic Society Lib., 1646)

Campanario, El (Periodical Publication, Texas) "The Texas Old Missions and Forts Restoration Association"

Cardenas, Juan Francisco de: *Hispanic Culture and Language in the United States* (New York 1933)

Cardoso, Lawrence A.: *Mexican Emigration to the U.S., 1897-1931* (Arizona U. Press, 1980)

Carter, Hodding: *Doomed Road of Empire: the Spanish Trail of Conquest* (Mc-Graw-Hill, 1963)

Carter, Raymond: *Las 50 Américas* (Rialp., Madrid, 1963)

Caruso, John A.: *The Apalachian Frontier* (Bobbs/Merrill, Indianapolis, 1959); *The Southern Frontier* (Bobbs/Merrill, Indianapolis, 1963)

Casas, Augusto: *Fr. Junípero Serra, el Apostol de California* (Barcelona, 1949)

Castañeda, Carlos E.: *Our Catholic Heritage in Texas, 1519-1936* (Austin, 1936)

Castro, Américo: *The Structure of Spanish History* (Princeton U. Press, 1954)

Cate, Margaret Davis: *Early Days of Coastal Georgia* (Fort Frederica Assn., 1955)

Caughey, John W.: "Willing's Expedition Down the Mississippi" (Louisiana Historical Quarterly, XV, 1932); *Bernardo de Gálvez in Louisiana* (Berkeley U., 1934)

Chadwick, French E.: *The Relations of the United States and Spain* (New York 1968)

Chambers, Henry E.: *A History of Louisiana* (American Historical Society, Chicago 1925)

Cierva, Ricardo de la: *La Gran Historia de America* (Serie: Revista *Epoca*, Madrid)

Code, Joseph B.: *Dictionary of the American Hierarchy* (New York, 1939)

Congreso Franciscano, 1986: *Franciscanos Extremeños en el Nuevo Mundo* (Ed. Deimos, Madrid)

Congreso Internacional, 1985: *Los Franciscanos en el Nuevo Mundo* (Ed. Deimos, Madrid)

Congreso Internacional,1988: *Los Dominicos en el Nuevo Mundo* (Ed. Deimos, Madrid

Conly, Robert L.: "Saint Augustine, Nation's Oldest City" (*National Geographic*, 129)

Conrotte, Manuel: *Intervención de España en Independencia de Norteamérica* (Madrid, 1920)

Córdoba, Pedro de: *Doctrina Cristiana para Instrucción de Indios* (Salamanca 1987)

Cortina, Rodolfo y Moncada, Alberto: *Hispanos en Estados Unidos* (Ed. Cultura Hispanica, 1988)

Coulter, E. Merton: *Georgia, a Short History* (North Carolina U. Press, 1960)

Count of Galvez Historical Society: *Charles III: Florida and the Gulf* (Miami, Fla., 1990)

Cubeñas Peluzzo, José A.: *Presencia Española e Hispánica en la Florida* (Madrid, 1978)

Cumming, W.P., Skelton, R. A., Quinn, D. B.: "The Discovery of North America" (*American Heritage*, New York, 1972)

Cunningham, Graham R.: *Hernando de Soto* (Dial Press, New York, 1924)

Cutter, Donald C.: *Malaspina in California* (San Francisco, 1960)

D'Acosta, Helia: *Beato Junípero Serra* (Ed. Tradición, Mexico, 1990)

De La Cierva, Ricardo: *La Gran Historia de America* (Serie: Revista *Epoca,* Madrid)

Demarest, Donald: *First Californian: The Story of Fr.Junípero Serra* (Hawthorne, Dallas, 1963)

De Voto, Bernard: *The Course of Empire* (Houghton Mifflin Co., Boston 1960); *To the Totem Shore: Spanish Presence on the Northwest* (Boston, 1943)

Dickinson, Donald, et al., ed.: *Voices from the Southwest* (Northland Press, Flagstaff, Ariz., 1976)

Dobie, J. Frank: *Mustang and Cow Horses* (Austin, Tex., Folklore Society, SMU Press, 1940); *The Longhorns* (Austin, Tex., 1941)

Dodd, Dorothy: *Florida, the Land of Romance* (Peninsular Publ., Tallahassie, Fla., 1956)

Duell, Prent: *Mission Architecture, San Xavier del Bac* (Tucson, 1919)

Eckart, George B.: *Missions of Sonora* (Southwestern Mission Research, Tucson, Ariz., 1960)

Elliot, John H.: *Imperial Spain* (St. Martin's Press, New York, 1963)

Ellis, John Tracy: *American Catholic History* (Bruce Publ., Milwaukee 1956); *Catholics in Colonial America* (Helicon, Baltimore, 1965)

Englebert, Omer: *Father Junípero Serra* (Mexico, 1957)

Espinosa, Juan Manuel: *Journal of the Vargas Expedition into Colorado in 1694* (Mexico, 1939)

Fernández Flórez, Darío: *The Spanish Heritage in the U.S.* (Pub. Españolas, Madrid, 1965)

Fernández Shaw, Carlos M.: *Ayuda de España a la Independencia de Estados Unidos* (Rev. Int. Bibl., 1976); *Presencia Española en los Estados Unidos* (Cultura Hispanica, 1977); *Estados Independientes de Norteamérica* (Inst. Estudios Pol., 1977)

Fields, F.T.: *Texas Sketchbook* (Houston, Tex., 1962)

Figueroa Deck, Allan: *The Second Wave* (Paulist Press, Mahwah, N.J., 1989)

Fitzpatrick, Joseph, S.J.: *One Church, Many Cultures* (Sheed & Ward, Kansas City, 1987)

Forrest, Earle R.: *Missions and Pueblos in the Old Southwest* (Rio Grande Press, Glorieta, N.M., 1962)

Foster, George, M.: *Culture and Conquest: America's Spanish Heritage* (Quadrangle Books, Chicago, 1960)

Fraga Iribarne, Manuel: *Aportación de España al Nacimiento, Desarrollo e Independencia de los Estados Unidos* (Ed. Nacional, Madrid, 1965)

Galmés, Lorenzo: *Father Junípero Serra* (Ed. BAC, Madrid, 1988)

Gann, L.H.: *Hispanics in the United States: A History* (Westview Press, Boulder, Colo., 1986)

Gannon, Michael: *The Cross in the Sand* (U. of Florida, Gainesville, 1989)

García Mercadal, José: *Lo que España Llevó a América* (Taurus, Madrid, 1959)

García Villoslada, Ricardo: *Historia de la Iglesia en España* (BAC, Madrid, 1980)

Geiger, Maynard, O.F.M.: *The Franciscan Conquest of Florida* (Catholic Ed. Press, Washington, D.C., 1938); *Biographical Dictionary of the Franciscans in Spanish Florida and Cuba* (St. Anthony Guild Press, Paterson, N.J., 1940)

Gibson, Charles: *Spain in America* (Harper & Row, New York, 1966)

Giner Sorolla, Alfredo: *Contributions of Hispanic Scientists in the United States* (Carreta Press, Potomac, Md., 1980)

Gómez Gil, Alfredo: *Cerebros Españoles en Estados Unidos* (Ed. Esplugas de Llobregat, 1976)

González Dávila, Amado: *Diccionario Geográfico/Histórico de Sinaloa* (Mazatlan, Mexico, 1959)

González López, Emilio: "George Farragut" (*New York Times*, May 30, 1976)

González, Roberto, Lavelle, Michael: *The Hispanic Catholics in the U.S.* (NE Pastoral Center, 1985)

Gray, L.C.: *History of Agriculture in the Southern States* (Washington, D.C., 1933)

Griffin, Charles Carroll: *The U.S. and the Disruption of the Spanish Empire* (Columbia U. Press, New York, 1937)

Gutiérrez Escudero, Antonio: *America: Descubrimiento de un Nuevo Mundo* (Ed. Istmo, Madrid, 1990)

Hakluyt, Richard: *Voyages, Traffiques, and Discoveries of Foreign Voyagers* (London, 1928)

Halstead, Murat: *The Story of Cuba* (Werner Co., Akron, Ohio, 1896)

Hammond, George P.: *Don Juan de Oñate, Colonizer of New Mexico* (Albuquerque, N.M., 1953)

Hammond, George, Rey Agapito: *Narratives of the Coronado Expedition* (Albuquerque, N.M., 1949)

Hanke, Lewis: "The Conquest and the Cross" (*American Heritage* XIV, 1963); *The Spanish Struggle for Justice in the Conquest of America* (U. of Pennsylvania Press, 1949)

Hann, John H.: *Apalache: Land between the Rivers* (U. of Florida Press, 1988); *Summary Guide to Spanish Florida Missions* (Las Americas, 1990); *St. Augustine's Yamassee War* (Florida Hist. Soc., 1989)

Hanna, Kathryn A.: *Florida, Land of Change* (Bobbs-Merrill, Indianapolis, 1950)

Haring, Clarence H.: *The Spanish Empire in America* (Oxford U. Press, New York, 1947)

Hauberg, Clifford A.: *Puerto Rico and the Puerto Ricans* (Hippocrene Books, New York, 1974)

Hawthorne, Hildegarde: *California's Missions* (Appleton Century, New York, 1942)

Henderson, W. A.: *The Adventures of Hernando de Soto* (Nashville, Tenn., 1920)

Hennessey, James, S.J.: *American Catholics* (Oxford U. Press, New York, 1981)

Herring, Hubert: *History of Latin America* (Knopf, New York, 1961)

Hilton, Ronald: *Los Estudios Hispánicos en Estados Unidos* (Cultura Hispanica, 1957); *Handbook of Hispanic Source Materials and Research Organizations* (Stanford U. Press, 1956)

Hispanic Society of America: *The Handbook* (New York, 1938)

Hodge, Frederick W., and Lewis, Theodore H.: *Spanish Explorers in the Southern U.S.* (Barnes & Noble, 1959)

Hoffman, Paul E.: *A New Andalucia* (Louisiana State U. Press, 1990)

Holmes, Jack D.L.: *Gayoso* (Louisiana State U. Press, 1965)

Horgan, Paul: *Conquistadors in North American History* (Farrar, Straus New York, 1963), *Great River* (Holt/Rinehart/Winston, New York, 1954)

Houck, Louis: *The Spanish Regime in Missouri* (Donnelly & Sons, Chicago, 1909)

Howell, Clark: *History of Georgia* (S.J. Clark Publ., Chicago, 1926)

Hughes, Philip: *A Popular History of the Catholic Church* (Macmillan 1947)

Isern, José: *Obispos Cubanos de la Florida* (Ed. Universal, Miami)

Jahoda, Gloria: *River of the Golden Ibis* (Houghton Mifflin, Boston, Mass., 1973)

James, James A.: *Oliver Pollock: The Life & Times of an Unknown Patriot* (New York, 1937)

Jennings, John: *The Golden Eagle (Hernando de Soto)* (Dell Publ. Co., New York, 1958)

Jensen, Malcolm: *America in Time* (Houghton Mifflin, Boston, Mass.)

Johnson, Thomas: *The Oxford Companion to American History* (Oxford U. Press, 1966)

Jones, Charles Colcock: *History of Georgia* (Houghton, New York, 1883)

Juderías, Julián: *La Leyenda Negra* (Ed. Nacional, Madrid, 1954)

Keegan, P.G.H. and Sanz, L. Tormo: *Experiencia Misionera en la Florida: Siglos XV-XVII* (1957)

Kessell, John L.: *Remote Beyond Compare* (U. of New Mexico, 1989)

Kinder, Hermann: *Atlas Histórico Mundial* (Paris Library, 1958)

Kino, Eusebio F.: *Las Misiones de Sonora y Arizona* (Ed. Cultura, Mexico, 1913)

Landers, Jane: *Gracia Real de Santa Teresa de Mose* (U. of Florida, 1987)

Langley, Lester D.: *The United States and the Caribbean* (Georgia U. Press, 1980)

Lanning, John Tate: *The Spanish Missions of Georgia* (U. of North Carolina Press, 1935)

Lasaga, José I.: "Vidas Cubanas" (Revista *Ideal*, Miami, 1984)

Latané, John H.: *The United States and Latin America* (Doubleday, New York, 1920)

Lawson, Edward W.: *Discovery of Florida and Its First Discoverer, Ponce de León* (New York, 1946)

Lewis, Charles Lee: *David Glasgow Farragut, Admiral in the Making* (Annapolis, 1941)

Lewis, Clifford and Loomie, Albert J.: *The Spanish Missions in Virginia* (Chapel Hill, N.C., 1953)

Lewis, James A.: "Las Damas de La Habana y Yorktown" (*Americas*, 37, Julio 1980)

López, José Francisco: *Condición de las Misiones de Texas* (1785)

López de Lara, Guillermo: *Ideas Tempranas de la Política Social de Indias* (Mexico, 1977)

Louvier, Juan: *La Cruz en America* (U. de Puebla, México, 1990)

Lowery, Woodvery: *Spanish Settlements within the Limits of the U.S.* (Russell, N.Y., 1959)

Lucas, Isidro: *The Browning of America* (Fides/Claretian, Chicago, 1981)

Lummis, Charles F.: *Los Exploradores del Siglo XVI* (Espasa Calpe, 1960); *The Spanish Pioneers* (Chicago, 1893)

Lyon, Eugene: *The Enterprise of Florida* (U. of Florida Press, Gainesville, 1976)

McCarthy, Joseph: *Record of America* (Scribner)

Madariaga, Salvador de: *Auge y Ocaso del Imperio Español en América* (Espasa Calpe, 1979)

Maeztu, Ramiro de: *Norteamérica desde Dentro* (Ed. Nacional, Madrid, 1957)

Majó Framis, Ricardo: *Vida de los Navegantes, Conquistadores y Colonizadores Españoles de los Siglos XVI, XVII y XVIII* (Ed. Aguilar, Madrid, 1957)

Malagón, Javier: *A Hispanic Look at the Bicentennial* (Hisp. Culture Inst., Austin, Tex.)

Manucy, Albert C.: *Florida's Menéndez, Captain General of the Ocean Sea* (Florida, 1965); *The Building of the Castillo de San Marcos* (Washington D.C., 1959)

Marbán, Jorge: *La Florida: Cinco Siglos de Historia* (Hisp. Soc. Library, New York)

Marcus, Robert, ed.: *Encyclopedia of Florida* (Somerset Pub., New York, 1985)

Márquez Sterling, Carlos: *Historia de Cuba* (Las Americas Publ. Co., 1963)

Mártir, Pedro: *Décadas del Nuevo Mundo* (Buenos Aires, 1944)

Means, Philip A.: *The Spanish Main* (Scribner & Son, London, 1935)

Meltzer, Milton: *Hispanic Americans* (Thomas Y. Crowell, New York, 1982)

Mendieta, Jerónimo de: *Historia Eclesiástica Indiana, 1596* (BAC, vol. 260-261)

Menéndez Pidal, Ramón: *El P. Las Casas. Su Doble Personalidad* (Espasa Calpe, Madrid, 1963)

334

Milanich, Jerald, Milbrath, Susan: *First Encounters: Spanish Explorations in the Caribbean and the United States, 1492-1570* (U. of Florida Press, 1989)

Milanich, Jerald, Proctor, Samuel: *Tacachale: Essay on the Indians of Florida and Southeastern Georgia during the Historic Period* (U. of Florida Press, 1978)

Moncada, Alberto: *Americanización de los Hispanos* (Ed. Plaza/Janes, Barcelona, 1986)

Montiano, José A. de: "La Guerra de la Oreja de Jenkins" (*Encicl. Vasca*, 424-490)

Morales Carrión, Arturo: *Historia del Pueblo Puetorriqueño — Puerto Rico & the U.S.* (Ed. Academia, San Juan, 1990)

Morales Padrón, Francisco: *Conquistadores Españoles en E.E.U.U.* (Pub.Españolas, Madrid 1959); *Historia del Descubrimiento y Conquista de América* (Madrid, 1963); *Participación de España en Independencia de E.E.U.U.* (Madrid, 1963); *Teoria y Leyes de la Conquista* (Ed. Cultura Hispanica, 1979)

Morfi, José Agustín: *Memorias para la Historia de Texas* (Quivira Soc., Albuquerque, N.M., 1935)

Morison, Samuel Elliot: *European Discovery of America — Southern Voyages, 1492-1616* (New York, 1971); *The Great Explorers* (Oxford U. Press, New York, 1986)

Morris, Richard B.: *Encyclopedia of American History* (Harper & Row, New York, 1961)

Mouritz, A.: *The Spaniards in the Pacific* (Hawaii Printshop Co., 1939)

Mumey, Nolie: *History of the Early Settlements of Denver* (The Range Press, 1942)

Natella, Arthur A.: *The Spanish in America* (Ed. Oceana, 1980)

National Conference of Catholic Bishops: *Heritage and Hope* (USCC Press, 1990)

Navarrete, Martín Fernández: *Colección de Viajes y Descubrimientos* (Madrid, 1825)

Nussbaum, Arthur: *A History of the Dollar* (Columbia U. Press, New York, 1957)

O'Daniel, V.F.: *Dominicans in Early Florida* (New York, 1930)

Omaechevarría, Ignacio: *Mártires Franciscano de Georgia* (Missionalia Hisp., 1955)

Oré, Jerónimo de: *Relación Histórica de la Florida en el XVII* (1931)

Oviedo, Gonzalo H.: *Historia General y Natural de las Indias* (U. of North Carolina, 1969)

Patrick, Rembert W.: *Florida under Five Flags* (U. of Florida, Gainesville, 1945)

PAL, Equipo de Redacción: *Historia de España* (Ed. Mensajero, Bilbao, 1979)

Peñuelas, Marcelino C.: *Cultura Hispánica en Estados Unidos* (Ed.Cultura Hisp., Madrid, 1978); *Lo Español en el Suroeste de los Estados Unidos* (Madrid, 1964)

Pereña, Luciano: *La Protección del Indio* (U. de Salamanca, 1989);
Proceso a la Leyenda Negra (U. de Salamanca, 1989); *Catecismo Limense* (Consejo Sup. de Investigaciones, c.1986)

Perkings, Dexter: *The United States and Latin America* (Louisiana State U. Press, 1961)

Philips, Ulrich B.: *Life and Labor in the Old South* (Boston, 1929)

Pigafetta, Antonio: *Magellan Narrative* (Yale U. Press, 1969)

Portillo, Alvaro del: *Descubrimientos en California* (C.S.I.C., Madrid, 1947)

Powell, Philip W.: *The Tree of Hate* (Vallecito, Calif., 1985)

Priestly, Herbert I.: *The Coming of the White Man* (Macmillan, New York 1929); *Tristan de Luna, Conquistador of the Old South* (Glendale, CA 1936)

Prince, L. Bradfort: *History of New Mexico* (Rio Grande Press, 1983); *Spanish Mission Churches in New Mexico* (Rio Grande Press, 1915)

Quinn, David B.: *New American World: A Documentary History of North America to 1612* (Arno Press, 1979); *North American Discovery, 1000-1612* (U. of South C, 1971); *North America from Earliest Discovery* (Harper & Row, New York, 1977)

Raimo, John: *Biographical Directory of Governors of the United States* (Meckler Corp., Westport, Conn., 1985)

Ramsey, Davis: *History of South Carolina* (Spartanburg, S.C., 1959)

Reppelier, Agnes: *Junípero Serra* (All Saints Press, New York 1962)

Represa, Armando: *La España Ilustrada en el Lejano Oeste* (Junta Castilla/León, 1990)

Ribes Tovar, Federico: *Enciclopedia Puertorriqueña* (Plus Ultra Publ., San Juan, 1970)

Rich, Everett: *The Heritage of Kansas* (U. of Kansas Press, 1960)

Richman, Irving B.: *The Spanish Conquerors* (Yale U. Press, 1919)

Ripoll, Carlos: *Cubanos en Estados Unidos* (Las Americas Publ., New York, 1987)

Robles, Vito Alessio: *Coahuila y Texas en la Epoca Colonial* (Ed. Porrua, Mexico, 1978)

Rodriguez, Clara E.: *Puerto Ricans Born in the U.S.A.* (Unwin Hyman, Boston, 1989)

Rodríguez Lois, Nemesio: *Forjadores de México* (Ed. Tradicion, Mexico, 1983)

Rodríguez Valencia, Vicente: *Perfil Moral de Isabel la Catolica* (Valladolid, 1974)

Roller and Twyman: *Encyclopedia of Southern History* (Louisiana State U., 1979)

Rossi, Ernest and Plano, Jack: *The Latin American Political Dictionary* (Santa Barbara, Calif., 1980)

Ruidiaz, Eugenio: *La Florida: Su Conquista y Colonización* (Madrid, 1894)

Rush, N. Orwin: *Battle of Pensacola* (Florida Classics Ser., 1986)

Saavedra, Santiago: *To the Totem Shore: Spanish Presence* (Ed. El Viso, Madrid, 1986)

Salley, Alexander S.: *Narratives of Early Carolina* (New York, 1911)

Samora, Julián: *La Raza* (U. of Notre Dame Press, 1966)

Sánchez, George: *Forgotten People: A Study of New Mexicans* (U. of New Mexico, 1940)

Sandoval, Moisés: *On the Move* (Orbis Books, New York 1990)

Sauer, Carl O.: *XVI Century North America: Land and Peoples as seen by Europeans* (Berkeley, 1971)

Schlesinger, Arthur: *The Almanac of American History* (Putnam Publ., New York, 1984)

Secretariado para el V Centenario. Conf. Episcopal Española: *La Huella de España en America* (Serie de Conferencias, 1985-1987)

Senior, Clarence: *Our Citizens from the Caribbean* (McGraw-Hill, 1965)

Serrano y Sanz, Manuel: *Documentos Históricos de la Florida y Luisiana* (Madrid, 1912)

Sexton, R.: *Spanish Influence on American Architecture and Decoration* (New York, 1927)

Shea, John G.: *History of the Catholic Missions* (Excelsior Cath. Publ., New York, 1883); *The Catholic Church in Colonial Days* (McBride Co., NY 1888)

Shephard, William R.: "The Spanish Heritage in America" (*Modern Language Journal*)

Sigüenza y Góngora, Carlos: *Documentos Inéditos* (Hisp. Soc. Lib., Ed. Porrua, Mexico, 1960)

Silem, Sol: *Historia de los Vascos en el Oeste de los E.E.U.U.* (New York, 1917)

Sympson, Lesley Byrd, ed.: *San Saba Papers* (1959)

Solís de Merás, Gonzalo: *Memorial* (Trans. by J.T.H. Conner, DeLand, Fla., 1923)

Stevens-Arroyo, Antonio: *Prophets Denied Honor* (Orbis Books, New York, 1982)

Stimpson, George: *A Book about American History* (Fawcett Publ., New York, 1962)

Stuart, Graham H.: *Latin America and the United States* (Appleton-Century, New York, 1955)

Tailfer, Pat: *True Historical Narrative of the Colony of Georgia* (Athens, Ga., 1960)

Tebeau, Charlton: *A History of Florida* (U. of Miami Press, 1981)

Tepaske, John J.: *Governorship of Spanish Florida* (Duke U. Press, 1964)

Thompson, Buchanan P.: *La Ayuda Española en la Independencia Norteamericana* (Cultura Hispanica, 1966)

Ubieto Arteta, Antonio: *Historia de España* (Ed. Teide, Barcelona, 1963)

Urrutia, Francisco: *Los E.E.U.U. y las Repúblicas Hispanoamericanas* (Madrid, 1918)

Vaca de Osma, Jose A.: *Intervención de España en Independencia de E.E.U.U.* (Madrid, 1952)

Van Campens, J. T.: *St. Augustine, Capital of Florida* (St. Augustine Hist. Soc., 1959)

Van Every, Dale: *Ark of Empire: American Frontier, 1784-1803* (W. Morrow Co., New York, 1963)

Varona, Frank de: *Hispanics in U. S. History* (Globe Book Co., New Jersey, 1989)

Vega, Garcilaso de la: *La Florida del Inca* (Trans.by J.G. Varner, Austin, Tex., 1951)

Villagrá, Gaspar Pérez de: *Historia de la Nueva México, 1610* (Alcala 1610, Mexico, 1900)

Villaseñor y Sánchez, José Antonio: *Teatro Americano* (Univ. Aut. de Mexico, 1980)

Vitoria, Francisco de: *Doctrina sobre los Indios* (Ed. San Martín, Salamanca, 1989)

Wagner, H. R.: *Juan Rodríguez C., Discoverer of California* (San Francisco, 1941)

Warren, Nina de Otero: *Old Spain in Our Southwest* (Harcourt Brace Co., New York, 1937)

Weber, David J.: *New Spain's Far Northern Frontier in the West* (U. of New Mexico, 1979); *The Mexican Frontier* (U. of New Mexico Press, 1982)

Weber, Francis J.: "Catholicism in Colonial America" (*Homiletic and Pastoral Review*, 1965)

Weddle, Robert S.: *The San Saba Mission* (U. of Texas Press, Austin, 1964); *Spanish Sea: Gulf of Mexico* (Texas A & M U. Press, 1985); *San Juan Bautista* (U. of Texas Press, 1968)

Wellman, Paul I.: *Glory, God, and Gold* (Doubleday, New York, 1954)

Whitaker, Arthur P.: *The Spanish-American Frontier* (Boston, 1927); *Spanish Contribution to American Agriculture* (Vol III, Jan. 1929)

Wilgus, Alva Curtis: *The Development of Hispanic America* (Farrar Inc., New York, 1941)

Williams, Stanley T.: *Huella Española en Literatura Norteamericana* (Gredos, Madrid, 1957)

Wright, James L.: *Anglo-Spanish Rivalry in North America* (1971)

Wright, Ralph B.: *California's Missions* (Sterling Press, Los Angeles, 1962)

Ybarra y Bergé, Javier de: *De California a Alaska* (Madrid, 1945)

Yela Utrilla, Juan F.: *España ante la Independencia de E.E.U.U.* (Ed. Istmo, 1988)

Zubillaga, Felix, Lopetegui, León: *Historia de la Iglesia en la America Española* (BAC, 1965)

Zubillaga, Felix: *Monumenta Antiguae Floridae, 1566-1572* (Roma, 1946)

ALPHABETICAL NAME INDEX

339

341

342

343

Montero, Fr. Sebastian: 139, 140
Monterey (Calif.): 84, 95, 127, 156, 214, 215, 216, 217, 218, 219, 224, 235, 238, 250, 252, 255, 257, 261, 262, 263, 264, 269
Monterey (Mexico): 32, 46, 172
Montes, Fr. Blas: 150
Montesinos, Fr. Antonio de: 25, 57, 108, 114, 115
Montezuma, Emperor: 38
Montevideo (Uruguay): 236, 283
Montgomery (Ala.): 122
Montgomery, Col. Richard: 228
Montiano, Manuel de: 201, 202, 203
Montoya, Joseph: 95, 294, 299
Monzún, Martín: 75
Moore, James: 64, 184, 189, 190, 195
Moraga, Joaquin: 218, 222, 224,
Morell, Bishop Agustín: 211
Moreno, Fr. Antonio: 185
Moreno, Fr. José: 230
Moreno, Fr. Pedro: 172
Moreno, Rita: 289
Morris, Robert: 72, 73, 220, 223, 224
Morro, Castle of el: 146, 166, 241
Mosa Fort: 199
Moscoso, Fr. Luis: 125
Moscow (Russia): 31
Mosquito River: 215
Mota y Sarmiento, Iñigo de la: 165, 166
Mourelle, Francisco: 218
Moziño, José M.: 236
Munguia, Fr. José; 224
Muñoz, Fr. Pedro: 165
Muñoz Marín, Luis: 264, 283, 287, 301
Muñoz Rivera, Luis: 95, 264, 279

Nacogdoches (Tex.): 194, 217, 234, 247, 249, 252
NALEO, 298
Nanicapan, Santa Cruz de: 134
Nantucket Island: 114
Napoleon Bonaparte: 79, 245, 246
Napoleon III: 265

Narváez, Pánfilo de: 34, 92, 116
Natchez Fort: 74, 134, 213, 226, 239, 249, 264
Natchitoches (La.): 194-196, 200, 234
Nava, Manuel: 75, 225
Navidad Fort: 99, 100
NCCB, Hispanic Secretariat: 286
Nebraska, State of: 27, 31, 38, 48, 153, 155, 174, 194, 237, 245, 280
Neches River: 42, 183, 194, 196
Neraz, Bishop Claude: 269
Nevada, State of: 32, 79, 217, 253, 261, 264
Neve, Felipe de: 224, 230
Nevis Island: 163
New Brunswick (Canada): 114
New Hanover (Ga.): 208
New Hebrides Islands: 126
New Iberia (La.): 87, 225
New Jersey, State of: 83, 86, 114, 117, 280, 291, 301
New Mexico: 21, 22, 25, 30-32, 34, 38-40, 42-48, 52, 56, 57, 61-65, 79, 84, 87, 91-93, 95, 119-121, 123-127, 144, 194, 195, 196-200, 202-205, 207, 208, 210, 213-215, 221, 222, 226, 232-234, 237, 243-246, 250-253, 255-257, 261-264, 266, 267, 269, 270, 279, 280, 283, 284, 292, 294, 297-299, 308, 312
New Orleans: 32-34, 46, 72-75, 93, 94, 125, 212, 213, 215, 220, 222, 224, 228, 230, 231, 234, 236, 238, 239, 246, 255, 260, 264, 297, 302
New Spain (Mexico): 22, 37, 62, 87, 222
New York, State of: 72, 82, 86, 94, 95, 114, 159, 174, 203, 221, 231, 232, 235, 257, 258, 262, 264, 268, 269, 270, 275, 276, 278-280, 282-284, 286, 289-292, 295-298, 300, 301, 304
Newark (N.J.): 83, 280, 301
Newfoundland: 21, 30, 32, 73, 102, 114, 137
Newport, Captain: 158
Newport (R.I.): 172

Nicaragua: 83, 251, 263, 271, 278, 281-283, 299, 302, 303
Niña, Caravel: 43, 98, 99, 101, 304
Niño, Alonso: 101
Nixon, Richard: 296
Niza, Fr. Marcos de: 22, 30, 120, 121, 123
Noel, Csarret: 203
Nolan, Philip: 240
Nombre de Dios Mission: 144, 157, 161
Nootka (Alaska; see also Nutka): 217, 234-238
Noriega, Manuel A.: 303
Notre Dame, Sisters of: 278
Nova Scotia (Canada): 114
Novello, Antonia: 303
Nueces River: 171, 172, 180, 191, 204, 210, 256
Nueva Galicia (Mexico): 123, 125, 152
Nueva Granada (Colombia): 22, 37
Nueva Madrid (La.): 235
Nuevo León (Mexico): 37
Nutka (Nootka) Bay: 32, 94, 235

Oblate, Fathers: 151
Ocale (Fla.): 122
Ocampo, Andrés: 126
Ochoa, Severo: 291
Ocmulgee River: 122
Ocón, Fr. Juan: 177, 179
Oconee River: 171
Ocute (Ga.): 151
Odin, Bishop John: 255
Oglethorpe, James: 64, 200
Ohio River: 73, 228
Ojeda, Alonso de: 101
Oklahoma: 79, 124, 126, 153
Olivares, Fr. Antonio: 91, 194
Omaha (Neb.): 38, 239, 245, 280
Omaña, Antonio Gutiérrez: 151
Onachita River: 231
O'Neill, Arturo: 229
Onís, Federico de: 279
Onorato, Brother: 121
Oñate, Juan de: 21, 29, 39, 97, 152, 158
Oraibi (Ariz.): 164
Ordóñez, Fr. Isidro: 160
Ordoño, Fr. Diego de: 145
Ore, Fr. Luis Jeronimo de: 159, 160

350